CHINA
UNDER THE
EMPRESS
DOWAGER

THE HISTORY OF THE LIFE AND TIMES OF TZU HSI

J.O.P. Bland
Edmund Backhouse

EARNSHAW
BOOKS

China under the Empress Dowager

By J.O.P. Bland & Sir Edmund Backhouse

ISBN-13: 978-988-18667-4-5

Edition copyright © 2010 Earnshaw Books.

China Under the Empress Dowager was first published in 1910.
This edition with a new foreword is reprinted by
China Economic Review Publishing (HK) Limited for Earnshaw Books, Hong Kong

First printing March 2010
Second printing November 2010

FOREWORD

BY DEREK SANDHAUS

RARELY has a book on Chinese history captured the popular imagination like J.O.P Bland and Edmund Backhouse's *China under the Empress Dowager*. This unique look inside the scintillating and treacherous court life of China's last great despot, the Empress Dowager Cixi, appeared at just the right moment in history. In 1910, ten years after the Boxer Rebellion and two years after the death of Cixi, the Chinese Empire was on the verge of collapse and all eyes were on China. At a time when readers were hungry for news of the Middle Kingdom, this book gave them all that and more, providing a fresh perspective on China's previous fifty years with thrilling anecdotes from the court and newly translated first-hand accounts. Most amazing of all, the book featured the never-before-seen diary of a well-connected Manchu official, Ching Shan, providing an insider's perspective on the mysterious machinations of the court during the Boxer Rebellion.

But the story behind the book is equally captivating. John Otway Percy Bland, at the time of publication the more famous of the two authors, arrived in Shanghai in 1883. The Irish scholar had been recruited directly from Trinity College to work in the Imperial Maritime Customs Service under Sir Robert Hart, a position he held until 1896. During this time he rose to official rank in the Chinese government, gained fluency in the Chinese language and amassed a wealth of powerful connections. In 1897, now a member of Shanghai's Municipal Council, he accepted the position of Shanghai correspondent for *The Times* of London, and it was in this capacity that he came in contact with a rising star of Chinese scholarship, Edmund Trelawny Backhouse.

Backhouse was, by many accounts, a thoroughly strange yet endearing personality. He had arrived in Peking in 1898 as an Oxford dropout with a knack for languages. He chose to live outside of the foreign compound among the Chinese, shunning the company of other Europeans but allegedly amassing powerful Chinese and Manchu contacts. Within a year of arrival, he had become one of the most respected translators and informants in China, counting among his patrons the British Foreign Service, the Imperial Maritimes Customs Service and Dr. G.E. Morrison, the Peking correspondent of *The Times*. In 1899, Morrison introduced the two authors, sending a dog-bite wounded Backhouse to stay with Bland while seeking medical attention in Shanghai.

The two men hit it off right away. At first glance Bland, the outgoing sportsman, and Backhouse, the introverted scholar, were an odd pair, but they had much in common. Both shared a deeply rooted respect for their adopted country and its people, and sought to correct Western misconceptions of China. Morrison, meanwhile, spoke no Chinese and had an unflinchingly colonialist outlook which they both despised. Their mutual disdain for the Australian Anglophile provided another strand to their friendship.

In November 1908, Bland was covering all of China for *The Times* while Morrison was on vacation, and was consequently handed the biggest story of his career: the deaths of both the Empress and Emperor within a day of each other. At a bit of a loss, he turned to the well-informed Backhouse for assistance. Backhouse was able to provide all of the raw material and relevant cultural context for the obituary, while Bland was able to lend structure and a more polished style. The article was a great success, and shortly afterwards Bland suggested the pair compile a full-blown biography of Cixi along the same lines. Backhouse happily agreed and suggested including among other materials the diary of Ching Shan, which he claimed to have found while living in the deceased official's house following the aftermath of the Boxer Rebellion. Bland was understandably excited by the revelation and decided to make the diary a centerpiece of the work.

In 1910, China under the Empress Dowager was released to near universal acclaim. "Probably no such collection of Chinese documents has ever before been given to the world, or one that better reflects the realities of Chinese official life," wrote Sidney Coryn of *The New York Times*. To the delight and surprise of its publishers, the book went through nine years on the market. The Ching Shan diary was donated to the British Museum for posterity and, four years later, the two authors followed up with another highly-regarded work, Memoirs and Annals of the Court of Peking.

But *China Under the Empress Dowager* was not without its detractors. The most outspoken in the early years was Bland and Backhouse's colleague-turned-rival, G.E. Morrison, who charged that the Ching Shan diary was a fake. Two of the most prominent sinologists of the day, Sir Reginald Johnson and J.J.L. Duyvendak, studied and attested to the diary's authenticity, and Morrison was written off as a jealous instigator. About 25 years later, Shanghai-based journalist William Lewisohn again challenged the diary's veracity and submitted his findings to Duyvendak, who reexamined the diary and this time around concluded that it was indeed a forgery, though a masterful one in its complexity. "Why any one should have taken all this immense trouble," wrote Duyvendek, "is more than I can understand."

Though Backhouse, the linguist, was the obvious candidate for the forgery, most people during his lifetime chose to believe that he was the victim of an elaborate Chinese hoax. In the 1970s, Backhouse biographer Hugh Trevor-Roper reached a different conclusion. He traced a pattern of hucksterism throughout Backhouse's life, culminating in an outrageous autobiography in which Backhouse claimed to have been the Empress

Dowager's long-time lover. Backhouse having been branded as being pathologically compelled to deceive, China under the Empress Dowager's credibility as an historical document all but evaporated.

But it would be a grave error to overlook this most remarkable work on account of one suspect chapter. *China under the Empress Dowager* was, after all, one of the first books that attempted to portray the Chinese people and their leaders as something more than an amalgamation of clichés and stereotypes. At a time when, just like today, the outside world desperately wanted to know more about China and the Chinese, so much of the existing literature was founded in gross misunderstanding and racially-based fears of the 'Yellow Peril'. *China under the Empress Dowager* was one of the first books that sought to present a truly sympathetic portrayal of China. It might sound trite today, but the notion that the Chinese were people with similar wants and ambitions was groundbreaking in the days of 'spheres of influence' and 'White Man's burden'.

In this book, Backhouse and Bland succeeded in painting a nuanced picture of the Chinese as few had done before them because they truly knew the country and its people. Using this knowledge, they were able to breathe a degree of clarity and understanding into the complex processes that had mystified the aloof Peking diplomats and the world at large. They were masters at using even the most mundane details to illustrate the infinite complexities and competing interests of the Qing court. Chapter VII, A Question of Etiquette, for example, is a marvelous examination of the superficially simple question of whether foreigners should be exempt from kneeling when granted an official audience. Chinese attitudes of cultural superiority, the need to preserve long-standing tradition, and how to save face before a more powerful enemy all come to the surface in brilliant clarity.

The book's account of the Boxer Rebellion, embellished though it may be, is most compelling. The standard published narratives of this period focus on the triumph of noble Christians over the barbarous heathens, the bravery of the foreigners in the face of malicious unprovoked attacks. Backhouse and Bland, on the other hand, showed the crisis as the culmination of a decades-old debate playing out in a deeply fragmented court. In the book's narrative, the survival of most of the foreigners was not so much the result of their own grit and determination, but rather of the intervention of noble, self-sacrificing Manchu officials. The picture that emerges is thus one not of 'us versus them', but one with heroes and villains on both sides of the racial divide squaring off in a conflict with complex and tangled origins.

The portrait the book paints of its subject, Empress Dowager Cixi, the 'iron hand in the velvet glove', also remains one of the most memorable ever written. She is portrayed as a fickle and often rash ruler, but one entirely in her element at the helm of state. Through one of China's most turbulent periods, she is able to repeatedly outmaneuver her political opponents and come out of every palace intrigue with both feet on the ground. In such a way, she was able to prolong the life of a crumbling dynasty that had long since outlived its usefulness. She is worthy, Bland and Backhouse told us, of being compared with the most cunning rulers of all time.

By continually identifying with the Chinese and identifying the roots of misconceptions, *China under the Empress Dowager* forced its readers to grapple with a number of challenging notions: maybe the Chinese see us as the uncultured barbarians; maybe we are the ones being rude and presumptuous; maybe the root of conflict between our nations is misunderstanding rather than malevolence.

The strength of this book lies not only in its substance, but also in its style. The concepts it deals with are sometimes difficult and remarkably obtuse, yet Bland and Backhouse provide the necessary context, and just the right amount of humor and excitement, necessary to create an easily understandable and thoroughly entertaining read. Much more than merely a biography, it is a smart, clearly written epic by two authors with a highly sophisticated understanding of Chinese culture, customs and court practices. So it is with great pleasure that we present the unabridged original version of Backhouse and Bland's timeless masterpiece, *China under the Empress Dowager*.

Shanghai
November, 2009

CHINA UNDER THE EMPRESS

DOWAGER

大清國當今慈禧端佑康頤昭豫莊誠壽恭欽獻崇熙聖母皇太后

THE "HOLY MOTHER," HER MAJESTY TZU HSI.
(FROM A PHOTOGRAPH TAKEN IN 1903.)

CHINA UNDER THE EMPRESS DOWAGER

BEING THE HISTORY OF THE LIFE AND
TIMES OF TZŬ HSI

COMPILED FROM STATE PAPERS AND THE
PRIVATE DIARY OF THE COMPTROLLER OF
HER HOUSEHOLD

BY

J.O.P. BLAND AND E. BACKHOUSE

ILLUSTRATED

MCMX

NOTE

THE thanks of the Authors are hereby gratefully expressed
to Miss Katharine A. Carl, for permission to reproduce the
photograph of her portrait of the Empress Dowager; to Mr.
K. Ogawa, art publisher of Tokyo, for the use of his unique
pictures of the Palace at Peking; to Mr. Geo. Bronson Rea, of
the *Far Eastern Review*, for permission to reproduce illustrations
originally published in that journal; to Messrs. Betines, of
Peking, for the right to publish their views of the capital; and
to the Editor of *The Times*, for his courtesy in permitting the
inclusion in this volume of certain articles written for that
paper.

LONDON, *September 10th,* 1910.

CONTENTS

LIST OF ILLUSTRATIONS

INDEX TO NUMBERED
MAP OF PEKING

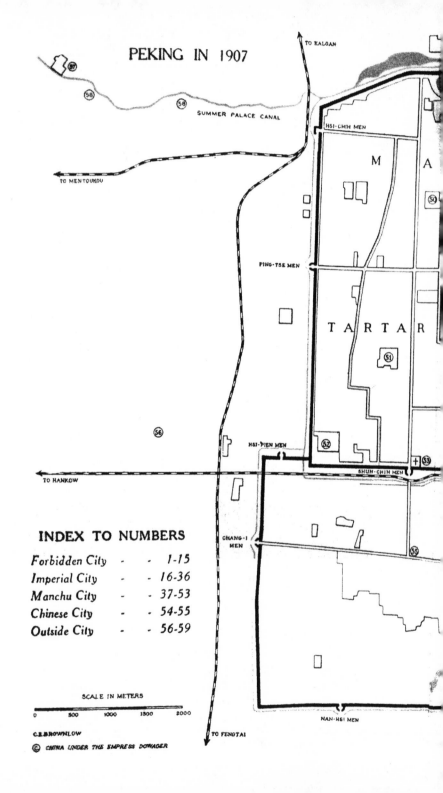

PEKING IN 1907

TO KALGAN

SUMMER PALACE CANAL

HSI-CHIH MEN

TO MENTOUKOU

PING-TSE MEN

M   A

TARTAR

HSI-PIEN MEN

TO HANKOW

SHUN-CHIH MEN

CHANG-I MEN

SCALE IN METERS

0   500   1000   1500   2000

C.E.BROWNLOW

© CHINA UNDER THE EMPRESS DOWAGER

NAN-HSI MEN

TO FENGTAI

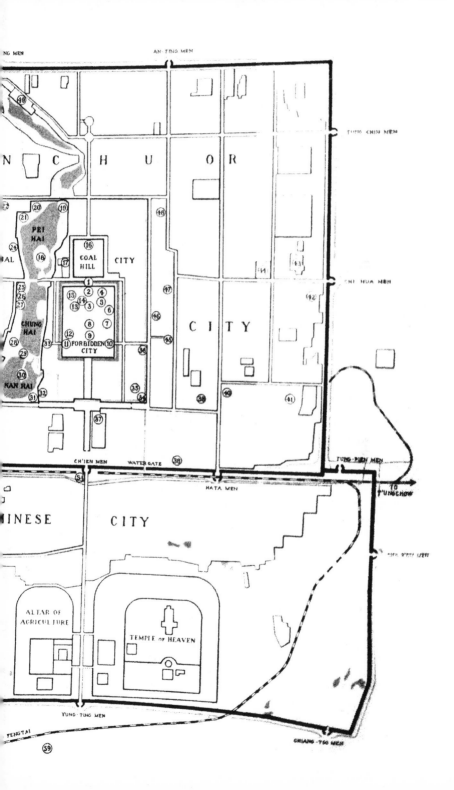

Glorious. This is the usual entrance to the Forbidden City for officials attending audience when the Court is there resident. (It was here that was suspended in a basket the head of the foreigner captured by the Boxers on 20th June.)

11. Hsi Hua Men, or West Gate Glorious. One of the main entrances to the Forbidden City.

12. The Nei Wu Fu, or Imperial Household Department Offices.

13. Chang Ch'un Kung, or Palace of Perpetual Spring, where Tzŭ Hsi resided during the reign of T'ung-Chih.

14. Yang Hsin Tien, or Throne Hall of Mental Growth. In this Palace the Emperor T'ung-Chih resided during the whole of his reign.

15. See 4.

16. Shou Huang Tien, or Throne Hall of Imperial Longevity. In this building the reigning sovereign unrolls on the day of the New Year the portraits of deceased Emperors, and pays sacrifice to them.

17. The Taoist Temple (Ta Kao Tien), where the Emperor prays for rain or snow.

18. The White Pagoda, built in the time of the Yüan dynasty (*circa* 1290 A.D.), when the artificial lake was also made.

19. The Altar of Silkworms, at which the Empress Consort must sacrifice once a year, and where the Old Buddha sacrificed on occasion.

20. Ta Hsi Tien. The Temple of the Great Western Heaven. A famous Buddhist shrine built in the reign of the Emperor Kang Hsi.

21. A Lama Temple where the Old Buddha frequently worshipped.

22. Residence of the Chief Eunuch, Li Lien-ying.

23. Residence of Yang Li-shan, the President of the Board of Revenue, executed by order of Prince Tuan.

24. The site of the Chan-Ta-ssu, a famous Lama Temple, destroyed by the French in 1900 for having been a Boxer drilling ground.

25. At this gate the Emperor was wont to await, humbly kneeling, the arrival of the Old Buddha on her way to or from the Summer Palace.

26. Tzu Kuang Ko: Throne Hall of Purple Effulgence. The building in which the Emperor is wont to receive, and entertain at a banquet, the Dalai and Panshen Lamas and certain feudatory chiefs. Before 1900, Foreign Envoys were also received here.

27. The Old Catholic Church built within the Palace precincts by permission of the Emperor Kang-Hsi. It was converted by the Empress Dowager into a Museum in which was kept the collection of stuffed birds made by the missionary Père David. Eye-witnesses of the siege of the French Cathedral in 1900 have stated that the Empress and several of the

ladies of the Court ascended to the roof of this building to watch the attack on the Christians; but it is not likely that they exposed themselves for any great length of time in what must have been a dangerous position.

28. Li Yüan Tien: Throne Hall of Ceremonial Phœnixes. Part of the Empress Dowager's new Palace, built for her in the early years of Kuang Hsü's reign. Here she received birthday congratulations when resident at the Lake Palace, and here she gave her valedictory audience, just before her death.

29. Ching Cheng Tien, or Throne Hall of Diligent Government. Used for the audiences of the Grand Council when the Court was in residence at the Lake Palace.

30. Ying Tai, or Ocean Terrace, where the Emperor Kuang Hsü was kept under close surveillance after the *coup d'état* in 1898, and which he never left (except on one occasion when he attempted to escape) between September 1898 and March 1900. By means of a drawbridge, this Ocean Terrace was made a secure place of confinement. After the return of the Court in 1902, His Majesty lived here again, but under less restraint, and it was here that he met his death.

31. At this point stood the high mound which Her Majesty is reported to have ascended on the night of 13th June, 1900, to watch the conflagrations in various parts of the city.

32. Residence of the actors engaged for Palace performances.

33. Hsi Yüan Men, Western Park Gate. It is through this that the Grand Council and other high officials pass to audience when the sovereign is in residence at the Lake Palace.

34. At this point was erected the scaffolding from which guns were trained on the Legations. The soldiers on duty here were quartered in the house of Ching Shan.

35. The residence of Wen Lien, Comptroller of the Household and friend of Ching Shan.

36. The residence of Ching Shan, where the Diary was written.

37. The Imperial Clan Court, in which is the "Empty Chamber," where the usurping Princes met their death.

38. Now the Belgian Legation premises, but formerly the residence of the Boxer protagonist, Hsü T'ung, that fierce old Imperial Tutor whose ambition it was to have his cart covered with the skins of foreign devils.

39. Residence of Yüan Ch'ang, where he was arrested for denouncing the Boxers.

40. The residence, in 1861 of Tsai Yüan, hereditary Prince Yi, who was put to death by Tzǔ Hsi for usurping the Regency.

41. Residence of the Grand Secretary, Wang Wen-shao.

42. Palace of Duke Kuei Hsiang,

elder brother of Tzǔ Hsi and father of the present Empress Dowager.

43. Residence of Duke Lan, the Boxer leader. At present occupied by Prince Pu Chün, the deposed Heir to the Throne and a most notorious reprobate.

44. Residence of the "Beileh" Tsai Ying, son of Prince Kung, cashiered for complicity in the Boxer rising.

45. Pewter Lane, where Yehonala was born.

46. Palace of Duke Chao, younger brother of Tzǔ Hsi.

47. Residence of Jung Lu.

48. Place of the Princess Imperial, the daughter of Prince Kung, whom the Empress Dowager adopted.

49. Birthplace of the present infant Emperor, Hsüan T'ung, son of Prince Ch'un and grandson of Jung Lu. In accordance with prescribed custom, it will be converted into a shrine.

50. Palace of Prince Chuang, the Boxer leader, mentioned by Ching Shan as the place where the Christians were tried.

51. Residence of Tuan Hua, the Co-Regent with Tsai Yüan, also allowed to commit suicide in 1861.

52. Birthplace of H.M. Kuang Hsü. Half of this building has been converted into a shrine in honour of His Majesty, and the other half into a memorial temple to the first Prince Ch'un, grandfather of the present infant Emperor.

53. At this point many Christians were massacred on the night of 13th June, 1900.

54. In the north-west corner of the *enceinte* of the Chien Men, a shrine at which the Empress Dowager and the Emperor sacrificed to the tutelary god of the dynasty (Kuan Yü), the patron saint of the Boxers.

55. The execution ground where were put to death the Reformers of 1898 and the Ministers who, in 1900, protested against the attack on the Legations.

56. The graves of the Empress Dow-ager's parents. They are adorned with two marble pillars, bearing laudatory inscriptions.

57. Wan Shou ssǔ, the Temple of Imperial Longevity. Here the Empress was accustomed to sacrifice on her journeys to and from the Summer Palace.

58. The Imperial Canal, by way of which the Old Buddha used to proceed in her State barge to the Summer Palace.

59. Here was erected the temporary railway station at which the Empress alighted on her return from exile.

I

THE PARENTAGE AND YOUTH OF
YEHONALA

THE family of Yehonala, one of the oldest of the Manchu clans,
traces its descent in direct line to Prince Yangkunu, whose daughter married (in 1588) Nurhachu, the real founder of Manchu rule
in China and the first direct ancestor of the Ta Ching Emperors.
Yangkunu was killed at Mukden in 1583, in one of his raids upon
the territories which still owed allegiance to the degenerate Chinese sovereign Wan Li. His clan lived and flourished in that region, near the Corean border, which is dominated by the Long
White Mountain, the true cradle of the Manchu stock. He and
his people seem to have acquired the arts of war, and much lust
of conquest, by constantly harassing the rich lands on their ever-
shifting borders, those rich lands which to-day seem to be about
to pass under the yoke of new invaders. Yangkunu's daughter
assumed the title of Empress by right of her husband's con-
quests, and her son it was who eventually wrested the whole of
Manchuria from the Ming Dynasty and reigned under the name
of Tien-Ts'ung.

   Into this clan, in November 1835, was born Yehonala, whose
life was destined to influence countless millions of human be-
ings, Yehonala, who was to be thrice Regent of China and its

autocratic ruler for over half a century. Her father, whose name was Hui Cheng, held hereditary rank as Captain in one of the Eight Banner Corps. Considering the advantages of his birth, he was generally accounted unsuccessful by his contemporaries; at the time of his death he had held no higher post than that of an Intendant of Circuit, or Taotai. Holding this rank in the province of Anhui, he died when his daughter was but three years of age. His widow and family were well cared for by a kinsman named Muyanga, father of her who subsequently became Empress Consort of Hsien-Feng and Co-Regent with Yehonala. From him the children received every advantage of education.

Many unfounded and ridiculous stories have been circulated in recent years attributing to the Empress Dowager humble, and sometimes disgraceful, antecedents. Many of these are nothing more than the fruit of Yellow Journalism, seeking sensational material of the kind which appeals to the iconoclastic instincts of its readers. Others, however, undoubtedly owe their origin to the envy, hatred and malice of Palace intrigues, to the initiative of the Iron-capped Princes and other high officials of the elder branch of the Imperial family, many of whom were addicted to besmirching the family and character of Tzǔ Hsi in order to inflict "loss of face" on the Yehonala clan. In this way, and because mud thrown from above usually sticks, their malicious stories were freely circulated, and often believed, in Peking and in the South: witness the writings of K'ang Yu-wei and his contemporaries.[1]

To cite an instance. One of these mythical stories used to be told, with every appearance of good faith, by Prince Tun, the fifth son of the Emperor Tao-Kuang. This Prince cherished a grudge against Tzǔ Hsi because of his disappointed ambitions: adopted himself out of the direct line of succession, he had nevertheless hoped, in 1875, that his son would have been chosen Emperor.

---

1. As an example of unbalanced vituperation, uttered in good faith and with the best intentions, *vide The Chinese Crisis from Within* by "Wen Ching," republished from the *Singapore Free Press* in 1901 (Grant Richards).

The story, as he used to tell it, was that when the Empress's mother had been left a widow with a large family (including the future ruler of China) they lived in the most abject poverty at the prefectural city of Ningkuo, where her husband had held office and died. Having no funds to pay for her return to Peking, she would have been reduced to beggary had it not been that, by a lucky accident, a sum of money intended for another traveller was delivered on board of her boat at a city on the way, and that the traveller, on learning of the mistake and being moved to pity at the sight of the family's destitution, insisted on her keeping the money. Twenty-five years later, when Tzŭ Hsi had become the all-powerful Regent, this official appeared for audience at Peking, when, remembering the benefits received at his hands, the Empress raised him from his knees and expressed her gratitude for his kindness. The story is prettier than many which emanate from the same source, and original, too, in the idea of a Manchu official dying at his provincial post in abject poverty, but unfortunately for the truth of the narrative, it has been established beyond shadow of doubt that neither the wife nor the family of Tzŭ Hsi's father were with him at the time of his death. They had gone on ahead to Peking, in anticipation of his early return thither to take up a new appointment in the White Banner Corps.

Before proceeding further, it may be well to refer briefly to the Yehonala clan and its position in relation to the elder branch of the Imperial family, a question of no small importance, past and future, in its effect on the history of modern China. Jealousy and friction there have always been between the Imperial house and this powerful patrician clan, since the first Yehonala became *de facto* ruler of the Empire after the collapse of the Tsai Yüan conspiracy, but their relations became more markedly strained after the *coup d'état* in 1898, and although the wholesome fear of the Empress Dowager's "divine wrath" prevented any definite cleavage, the possibilities of trouble were ever latent in the Forbidden City. Recent events at Peking, and especially the dismissal of the Chihli Viceroy, Tuan Fang, for alleged irreverence at the funeral ceremonies of the late Empress Dowager, have emphasised the divisions in the Manchu camp and the dangers that beset its Government, now bereft of the strong hand of Tzŭ Hsi. It is difficult for foreigners to form any clear idea of the actual conditions of life and of party divisions in the Palace, confused as they are by intricate questions of genealogy, of inter-marriage and adoptions by relatives, of ancient clan feuds. It should, however, be explained that the Imperial Clansmen (known in their own tongue as Aisin Gioros) divided into the Yellow and Red Girdles, are the descendants respectively of Nurhachu himself and of that ruler's ancestors, by virtue of which ancestry they consider themselves (and the Chinese would recognise the claim) to be the *sang pur* and highest nobility of the Manchu Dynasty. The Yehonala clan, although in no sense of Royal blood (as marriages between the sovereign and female members of a family do not entitle that family to claim more than noble rank) owes its great power not only to its numbers, but to the fact that it has given three Empresses Dowager to the Empire; but, above all, to the great prestige and personal popularity of Tzŭ Hsi. If recent events are to be interpreted in the light of history, and of her significant deathbed mandate, the present leaders of the Yehonala clan are determined that the present Empress Dowager, the widow of Kuang-Hsü, shall follow in the footsteps of her august aunt, and control the business of the State, at least during the Regency. And, thanks to Tzŭ Hsi's far-seeing statecraft, the young Emperor is a grandson of Jung Lu, and may be expected therefore to reverence the policy handed down by the Old Buddha.

One long-standing cause of suspicion and dissension between the parties in the Palace arises from the fear of the elder descendants of Tao-Kuang (of whom Prince P'u Lun and Prince Kung are the chief representatives) that the present boy-Emperor, or his father, the Regent, will hereafter elevate the founder of his branch, the first Prince Ch'un, to the posthumous rank of Emperor, a species of canonisation which Europeans might consider unimportant, but which, in the eyes of the Chinese, would

THE REGENT, PRINCE CH'UN, WITH HIS TWO SONS, THE PRESENT EMPEROR (STANDING) AND PRINCE P'U CHIEH.

constitute a sort of posthumous usurpation on the part of the junior branch of the Imperial clan, since the first Prince Ch'un would thus be placed on a footing of equality with Nurhachu, the founder of the Dynasty, and would practically become the founder of a new line. The first Prince Ch'un had himself foreseen the possibility of such an occurrence, and had realised that it could not fail to lead to serious trouble, for which reason, as will be seen hereafter, he had taken precautions to prevent it. It has not escaped the attention of those whose business it is to watch the straws that float down the stream of high Chinese policy that, since the accession of the present child-Emperor to the Throne, the ancestral sacrifices made at the mausoleum of the first Prince Ch'un have been greatly elaborated in pomp and circumstance, while in official documents his name has been given "double elevation," that is to say, in the eyes of the *literati* he is made to rank on the same level as a reigning Emperor. It is commonly believed by those Chinese who are in a position to speak with authority on the subject, that when the Emperor attains his majority, he will be led to confer further posthumous honours upon his grandfather, including that of "triple elevation," which would place him on a footing of equality with a deceased Emperor, and entitle him to worship at a special shrine in the Temple of the Ancestors of the Dynasty. From a Chinese constitutional point of view, the consequences of such a step would be extremely serious and difficult of adjustment.

The Old Buddha was a strong partisan, and during her lifetime her immediate kinsmen were practically above the law, basking in the sunshine of her protection or making hay thereby, so that there was always a strong undercurrent of friction between them and the Yellow and Red Girdles, friction of which echoes frequently reached the tea-houses and market places of the capital. Tzŭ Hsi delighted to snub the Aisin Gioros; in one Decree she forbade them to reside in the business quarter of the city, on the ground that she had heard it said that some of them were making money by disreputable trades. She was by no means beloved of the Iron-capped princes and other noble descendants of Nurha-chu, who, while they feared her, never ceased to complain that she curtailed their time-honoured privileges.

An interesting example of her masterful methods of dealing with these hereditary aristocrats occurred when one of the Imperial Dukes ventured to build himself a pretentious house in the immediate vicinity of the Imperial City, and overlooking a considerable portion of the palace enclosure. No sooner was the building completed than the Old Buddha confiscated it, reprimanding the owner for his lack of decorum in daring to overlook the Palace grounds, and forthwith she bestowed it upon her younger brother, the Duke Chao.

Another example of her clannishness, and of the difficulties which it created for the local authorities, occurred upon the establishment of the new Police Board at Peking, three years after the return of the Court from exile in 1902. The Grand Councillor, Hsü Shih-ch'ang, a Chinese by birth, and a favourite of Her Majesty, was placed at the head of this new Board, but he soon realised that the lot of his policemen, when dealing with the members of the ruling clan, was by no means a happy one. Her Majesty's third brother, the Duke Kuei Hsiang, was a particularly hardened offender, absolutely declining to recognise police regulations of any kind, and inciting his retainers to "gain face" by driving on the wrong side of the road and by committing other breaches of the regulations. On one occasion a zealous policeman went so far as to arrest one of the Duke's servants. Hsü Shih-ch'ang, hearing of the occurrence, promptly ordered the man's release, but the Duke, grievously insulted, insisted upon an abject apology from the head of the Board in person. Thrice did the unfortunate Hsü call at the Duke's palace without gaining admission, and it was only after he had performed a kowtow before the Duke in the open courtyard outside the palace that his apology was accepted. An idea of the importance of this incident in the eyes of the Pekinese, and of the power of the clansmen, may be inferred from the fact that Hsü subsequently became Viceroy of the Manchurian provinces, later President of the Ministry of Posts and Communications, and in August, 1910, was elevated to the Grand Council. On this occasion, however, the Old Buddha, learning of the incident, "excused" Hsü from further attendance at the Grand Council, and shortly afterwards he was transferred to Mukden.

Yehonala's mother, the lady Niuhulu, survived her husband for many years, residing in his house in "Pewter Lane" (Hsi-la-hu-t'ung), quite close to the Legation quarter. When her daughter became Empress Mother, she received the rank of Imperial Duchess. She appears to have been a lady of great ability and good sense, distinguished even amongst the members of a clan always noted for the intelligence of its women kind. After living to a ripe old age, she was buried beside her husband in the family graveyard which lies without the city to the west, in the vicinity of the Europeans' race-course, where her daughter's filial piety was displayed by the erection of an honorific arch and the customary marble tablets. When, in January 1902, the Empress Dowager returned from exile by railway from Cheng-ting fu, she gained great kudos from the orthodox by declining to enter the capital by the Hankow railway line, because that line ran close to her parents' graves, and it would have been a serious breach of respect to their memory to pass the spot without reverently alighting to make obeisance. She therefore changed her route, entering Peking from the south, to the great admiration of all her people.

Of Yehonala's childhood there is little to record except that among her youthful playmates was a kinsman, Jung Lu, who in after years was to play so prominent a part in many a crisis of her career. By common report she had been betrothed to him from birth. This report is not verifiable, but there is no doubt that the great influence which Jung Lu exercised over her, far greater than that of any of her family or highest officials, was founded in their early youth. K'ang Yu-wei and other Chinese officials opposed to the Manchu rule have not hesitated to assert that he was on terms of improper intimacy with her for years, dating from the flight to Jehol, and before the decease of her husband the Emperor.

Yehonala's education followed the usual classical course, but the exceptional alertness and activity of her mind, combined with her inordinate ambition and love of power, enabled her to rise superior to its usually petrifying influences and to turn her studies to practical account in the world of living men. She learned to paint skilfully and to take real pleasure in the art; she was an adept at the composition of verses, as classically wooden in form as anything produced by the most distinguished of English public schools. At the age of sixteen she had mastered the Five Classics in Chinese and Manchu, and had studied to good purpose the historical records of the twenty-four Dynasties. She had beyond doubt that love of knowledge which is the beginning of wisdom, and the secret of power, and she had, moreover, the chroniclers aver, a definite presentiment of the greatness of her destiny.

Upon the death of the Emperor Tao-Kuang in 1850, his eldest surviving son, aged nineteen, ascended the Throne under the reign-title of Hsien-Feng. After the expiry of the period of mourning (twenty-seven months) during which the new Emperor may not marry, a Decree was issued commanding that all beautiful Manchu maidens of eligible age should present themselves at the Imperial Household Office which would make from them a selection for the Emperor's harem. Prior to his accession, Hsien-Feng had married the eldest daughter of Muyanga, but she had died before his coming to the Throne. Among the maidens who obeyed the nuptial Edict were Muyanga's second daughter, Sakota, and the young Yehonala. On the 14th of June, 1852, about sixty of the beauty and fashion of the Manchu aristocracy appeared before the critical eye of the widow of Tao-Kuang, who selected twenty-eight from among them, and these she divided into the four classes of Imperial concubines, viz., "Fei," "P'in," "Kuei Jen," and "Chang Tsai." Sakota thus became a "P'in," and Yehonala a "Kuei Jen" or "honourable person." With rare exceptions, these Imperial concubines are much more the servants of their mother-in-law than the wives of their sovereign. In theory, their number is limited to seventy, but this number is seldom maintained; beside them, there are within the Palace precincts some two thousand female Manchus, employed as handmaidens and general servants under the direction of the eunuchs. In all domestic matters of the household, the widow of the Emperor last deceased exercises supreme authority, and although precedent allows the Emperor to inspect the ladies selected, he has no voice in their disposition or the determination of their rank.

Thus Yehonala left her home in Pewter Lane to become an inmate of the Forbidden City, cut off henceforth from all direct intercourse with her own people. An aged tiring woman who served her from the time of her first entry into the Palace until her death, is our authority for the following interesting description of the only visit which she ever paid to her family. It was in January 1857, nine months after the birth of her son, the heir to the Throne, that, by special permission of the Emperor, she was allowed to leave the Palace. Early in the morning, eunuchs were sent to announce to her mother that her daughter, the Concubine Yi, was coming to visit her at mid-day. There was much joyful excitement amongst the family and its friends at this rare honour. All the neighbours in Pewter Lane turned out to see the eunuchs and the yellow-draped chair. The mother and all the members of the household (including some of an elder generation) ranged themselves on either side of the entrance courtyard as the chair was borne within. At the head of the steps leading to the inner courtyard the eunuchs in attendance requested her to descend; she then entered the main room, where she took the seat of honour. Her family approached respectfully to salute her, all kneeling except her mother and the elder relatives. A banquet was then served at which, by special arrangement, the mother took a seat lower than that of the daughter, thus recognising her position as mother of the Heir Apparent. All present were most favourably impressed by Yehonala's unaffected and affectionate disposition; she seemed quite unspoiled by the formalities and splendours of Court life, talking with all the old vivacity as a daughter of the house, showing the keenest interest in the family's affairs, and particularly in the education of her sisters.

The banquet lasted till late in the afternoon, Yehonala asking and answering innumerable questions. As the short January day drew to its close, the eunuchs requested her to prepare to return to the Palace. She therefore took an affectionate farewell of her family, expressing sincere regret that her life must be cut off from theirs, but hoping that some day the Emperor might again permit her to visit them. Her mother, she said, would, in any case, be allowed to come and see her in the Palace. After distributing presents to all the members of her family, she entered her palanquin and was borne away. She never saw her home again, but in later years her mother used frequently to visit her in the Forbidden City.

Upon entering the Palace, Yehonala proceeded to establish herself firmly and speedily in the good graces of Tao-Kuang's widow; through her influence at first, and later by virtue of her own charm, she soon became first favourite with her weak and dissolute lord; and when, in April 1856, she crowned his long disappointed ambitions by presenting him with an heir to the Throne, her position was completely assured. At the time of her entering the Palace, the Taiping rebellion was causing great uneasiness at the capital. In March 1853, the rebels took Nanking, the southern capital. Yehonala, who had already made it her business to read, and advise on, all Memorials from the provinces, used her growing influence with the Son of Heaven to secure the appointment of Tseng Kuo-fan as Commander-in-Chief, and to provide him with funds for the raising of train-bands in Hunan, with which, and with the help of General Gordon, Tseng eventually suppressed the rebellion. Thus early she showed her superiority to environment and the fetters of tradition, displaying at a moment of national danger that breadth of mind and quick decision which distinguished her. By all official precedent, Tseng Kuo-fan was not available for service, being in mourning for his mother, but it was ever Yehonala's opinion that precedents were meant to be subordinate to the State and not the State to precedents, wherein lies the mark of the born ruler.

In August 1855 the widow of Tao-Kuang died and Yehonala, in recognition "of her dutiful ministrations," was raised to the rank of "P'in," her colleague Sakota having in the meanwhile become Empress Consort.

It was the common belief of Chinese writers at this time that the reign of Hsien-Feng would witness the end of the Dynasty, which was held to have "exhausted the mandate of Heaven." All over the Empire rebellion was rife; the sovereign himself was a weak debauchee, incapable of inspiring either loyalty or affection in his people. In the eyes of the *literati* he was a degenerate, having none of the scholarly tastes which had made his five predecessors famous in history, nor any disposition to follow their example in the compiling of monumental editions of the classics and dictionaries, which have endeared their memory to scholars. It was, moreover, considered ominous that no heir had yet been born to him, though he was now twenty-five, several of his predecessors having provided for the succession before they were fifteen. When, therefore, in April 1856, Yehonala gave birth to a son, and at the same time the rebels were driven from the provinces of Hunan and Kiangsi, it was felt that the tide of evil had turned and that Heaven's favour once more smiled upon the Throne.

At this period, the health of the Emperor, stricken with paralysis, had completely broken down and Yehonala, by virtue of her position as mother of the Heir Apparent, and even more by reason of her masterful character, became the real ruler of the Empire. Her colleague, the Empress Consort, took little or no active interest in the business of government. In actual rank, Yehonala had risen to the position of a concubine of the first grade "Fei" and was generally known in the metropolis as the "Kuei Fei, Yi," the last word being her honorific title, meaning "feminine virtue."

Her advice on foreign affairs at this period was generally of an aggressive character, and the fact is not matter for wonder when we bear in mind her youth, her pride of race and her complete ignorance of foreign countries and their resources. On the return of the special Envoy Ch'i Ying, who had been sent to endeavour to induce Lord Elgin to leave Taku and whose mission had ignominiously failed, it was to the haughty Yehonala that common report credited the Decree which ordered him to be presented with the "silken cord" of self-despatch, as a mark of "the Throne's benevolent leniency." To her also was ascribed the Emperor's refusal to permit the High Commissioner Yeh at Canton to negotiate with the British on trade questions, a decision which led directly to the capture of that city by the foreign barbarian in the following year. In the records left by chroniclers and diarists of that time it is generally noticeable that the Emperor's opinions and doings are ignored and that all the business of the Imperial City and the Empire had come to depend on the word of Yehonala, a fact in itself sufficiently remarkable in a country where no woman is supposed to rule, and particularly remarkable when we bear in mind that she was at this time only a concubine and twenty-two years of age.

To prevent confusion arising from the several names and titles of the Empress Dowager, it should be explained that her family or clan name of Yehonala was that by which she was known to the world of Peking before and at the time of her selection for the Imperial harem. In the Palace, until her accession to the rank of Empress Mother (Empress of the West), she was still Yehonala, but more usually described as the "Yi" concubine. As co-Regent and Empress Mother, her official designation, Imperially decreed, was Tzŭ Hsi, to which many other honorifics were added. To the mass of the people she was either the Empress Dowager (*Huang T'ai Hou*) or the Old Buddha, and towards the end of her reign this last affectionately respectful title was universally used in the North.

II

THE FLIGHT TO JEHOL

THE causes and history of the invasion of North China by the allied forces of England and France are too well known to need re-stating here, but the part played by Yehonala in the stirring days which preceded and followed the flight to Jehol are not familiar to European readers. Most interesting details are given on this subject by a certain Doctor of Letters and member of the Hanlin Academy, whose diary was printed privately in narrative form several years later, and from this document the following extracts are taken. It was originally entitled "A Record of Grief Incurable" and, as will be noted, it is primarily a monument of filial piety, into which the doings of the barbarians, and the already dominant personality of Yehonala, are artlessly interwoven, with a certain quality of sincerity that attracts. The narrative itself is full of human interest.

"In the 7th Moon of the 'Keng Shen' year (August 1860), five or six days after my mother fell sick, rumours began to circulate that the barbarians had already reached Taku. It was generally known that many Memorials had reached the Throne from the metropolitan and provincial officials, but as no mention of them had appeared in the Gazette, it was only natural that there should be a very widespread feeling of uneasiness and many alarming rumours. So far, however, there had been no fleeing from the city. His Majesty was seriously ill, and it was known that he wished to leave for the north, but the Imperial Concubine Yi and Prince Seng dissuaded him from this and assured him that the barbarians would never enter the city.

"At this time my mother was suffering from dysentery, but she ordered the servants to keep it from me. It was only one day, when I noticed a prescription lying on her table, that I realised that she was indeed seriously ill. Doctor Liu was in attendance, as usual, but I never had any confidence in him or his methods, which seemed to me far too drastic. Nevertheless he had advised and attended her for seven years, and my mother and all her household placed implicit confidence in him. Alas, the Ancients have rightly said that a good son should know something of the principles of medicine, and surely my ignorance has been the first cause of my mother's death. Though I should give up my life a hundred times, how can I ever atone for this?

"During the next few days, people began to leave Peking, for the report was spread that our troops had been defeated at Taku, and that a Brigadier General was among the slain; the garrison had fled from Pei T'ang and the forts were in the hands of the barbarians. Prince Seng had been ordered by Edict not to fight a pitched battle, so that our forces were idly confronting the enemy. Nothing definite was known as to the real cause of our defeat, and the people, being kept in ignorance, gradually got over their first alarm.

"On the 13th of the 7th Moon, I noticed a change for the worse in my mother's condition, and straightway applied for ten days' leave of absence from my official duties. I kept her ignorant of the political situation and urged her to abstain from worry of every kind. But every-day the news was worse, and people began to leave the city in thousands.

"On the following day, Magistrate Li Min-chai looked in to say good-bye, as he was leaving to join the troops in Anhui. He expressed strong disapproval of Dr. Liu's prescription and gave me one of his own. My mother was averse to taking his medicine, but I persuaded her to do so. In the night she was suddenly seized with shortness of breath, and hastily I sent for Mr. Li, who assured me that this was in no way due to his medicine. My mother, however, insisted upon returning to Dr. Liu's prescription, so all I could do was to urge him to compound it of drugs less strong and more suited to a patient of my mother's advanced years.

"My mother then bade me to prepare her coffin as she was certain that her death was near. Fortunately I had bought the wood eight years before at Mukden, and had stored it in a coffin shop in Peking, whence I now had it fetched. We set carpenters to work in our court-yard, and by the 20th, the coffin was finished. The wood was beautifully thick, and the whole appearance of the coffin most creditable. Never could I have expected that at such a time of haste and general disorder so perfect a piece of work could have been produced. The carpenters assured me that at the present time such a coffin would cost at least a thousand taels in Peking.[1] This comforted me not a little.

"Next morning the lacquer shop people sent over to put on the first coating of lacquer, in which at least two pounds were used. We then sent for the tailor and six assistants to make the grave clothes and purchased the materials for my mother's ceremonial 'going away dress.' I had a long sable robe made up, but next day, as my mother appeared to be slightly better, I decided to postpone having the long outer robes prepared. Rumours were now rife that the barbarians had already reached T'ungchou, and were going to bombard Peking on the 27th, so that everyone was escaping who could leave the city. On the 27th, we put on the second coating of lacquer.

"On that day, our troops captured the barbarian leader Pa Hsia-li (Parkes) together with eight others, who were imprisoned in the Board of Punishments. Thereupon the whole city was in

---

1. About £120

an uproar, and it became known that His Majesty was preparing to leave on a tour northwards. But the Concubine Yi persuaded some of the older officials to memorialise, urging him to remain, none of which Memorials have been published. All the Manchu and Chinese officials were now sending their families away and their valuables, but the large shops outside the main gate were doing business as usual. My mother's condition remained much the same, and I applied for another ten days' leave.

"On the 1st of the 8th Moon, we applied another coating of lacquer to the coffin. On the same day Dr. Liu changed my mother's medicine, but, the dysentery continued unabated.

"On the 4th my mother called me to her bedside and said: 'I cannot possibly recover. See that all is prepared for the burial. I shall take no food to-day.' I felt as if a knife had been thrust into my vitals, and sent straightway for the tailor to hurry on with the ceremonial robes. My friend, P'an Yu-shih, called and recommended a purgative, but my mother was very angry, and refused point-blank to take it. In the night she had a violent attack of vomiting, which seemed to relieve her so much so, that I told the tailor not to be in too great a hurry. Next morning the robes were finished, but my mother thought the coverlet too heavy, and I substituted therefor a lighter material, silk. To this she objected as being too luxurious and more expensive than she had any right to expect; she observed that her parents-in-law had not had grave-wrappings of such valuable stuff. Meanwhile the confusion in Peking was hourly increasing, and huge crowds were hurrying from the city. Most of the city gates were closed for fear of the barbarians, but the 'Chang-yi' gate in the southern city was still open.

"On the 7th, our troops engaged the barbarians outside the Ch'i Hua gate. The van was composed of untrained Mongol cavalry, who had never been in action. No sooner had the barbarians opened fire than they turned as one man, broke their ranks and stampeded upon the infantry in their rear. Many were trampled to death, and a general rout followed, our men fleeing in every direction and the barbarians pressing on to the city walls.

"Certain Princes and Ministers besought the Concubine Yi to induce the Emperor to leave on a tour. His Majesty was only too anxious to start at once, but the Concubine Yi persuaded two of the Grand Secretaries to memorialise against his doing so, and in response to this a Decree was issued stating that under no circumstances would the Emperor leave his capital. Another Decree was put out by the Concubine Yi offering large rewards to any who should slay the barbarians. It was generally thought that the Emperor would now forgo his intended departure.

"Early next morning we heard the news of another engagement outside the Ch'i Hua gate, upon which news His Sacred Majesty, attended by all his concubines, the Princes, Ministers and Dukes, and all the officers of the Household, left the city in a desperate rout and disorder unspeakable, affording a spectacle that gave the impression that hordes of barbarians were already in close pursuit. As a matter of fact, the foreigners were still at a considerable distance, and at the Summer Palace, where the Court lay, there was nothing whatsoever to cause the slightest apprehension. I cannot understand why His Majesty was allowed to leave; up to the very last the Yi Concubine begged him to remain in his Palace, as his presence there could not fail to awe the barbarians, and thus to exercise a protecting influence for the good of the city and people. How, said she, could the barbarians be expected to spare the city if the Sacred Chariot had fled, leaving unprotected the tutelary shrines and the altars of the gods? She begged him to bear in mind that episode in the Chou Dynasty, when the Son of Heaven fled his capital, 'his head covered with dust,' and was forced to take refuge with one of his feudatory Princes. The Chinese people have always regarded this as a humiliating event in the history of their country, but the present flight of the Court appears more humiliating still.

"Meantime my mother's condition was becoming critical, and I had scant leisure for considering the political situation. Every official of any standing had either left the capital by this time

THE IMPERIAL DAIS IN THE CHIAO-TAI HALL

or was leaving, and all the merchants who could afford it were sending their families away. The cost of transport was prohibitive for many; the price of a cart with one mule to go to Chochou was twenty taels, and to Pao-ting fu (60 miles) they charged thirty taels. In my case there could be no question of removing my mother, and there was nothing for it therefore but to sit still and face the situation.

"As the dysentery grew more acute every day, with Dr. Liu's permission I tried Dr. Yang's prescription. It was, however, too late, and nothing could help her now. On the morning of the 12th she was *in extremis*, and had lost the power of swallowing; so we sent for Li, the tailor, to put a few finishing touches on the burial robes, and to prepare the 'cockcrow pillow' and coverlets. At 11 P.M. she passed away, abandoning her most undutiful son. Alas, there is no doubt that her death lies at my door, because of my ignorance of medicine. Smiting my body against the ground, I invoke Heaven, but ten thousand separate deaths could not atone for my sins.

"We arrayed her, then, in her robes. First her handmaiden put on the inner garments, a chemise of white silk, then a jacket of grey silk, and outside that a wadded robe of blue satin. Then were put on the robe and mantle of State, with the badge of her official rank, the jade girdle and necklace of amber. After the gold hair ornaments had been placed in position, the Phœnix hat was set upon her head; red mattresses were laid upon the couch, and we placed her in a comfortable position, with her head reclining on the 'cockcrow' pillow of red satin. Not a friend came near us, and every door in the neighbourhood was closed. Next morning I lined the coffin with red satin, and then padded it with straw to prevent it shaking, and at 3 P.M. I invited my mother to ascend into her 'long home.'

"The city was in a terrible tumult, and a friend came in to advise me to bury my mother temporarily in a temple outside the city. It would not be safe, he said, to inter her in the courtyard of this house, for the barbarian is suspicious by nature, and will assuredly search every house in Peking as soon as the city is taken. It was impossible for me to consider calmly what might happen if they were to find and to desecrate my mother's coffin. I remembered what has been told of their doings in Canton under similar circumstances.

"On the 14th, the 'Chang-yi' gate was opened, and I found a temple, suitably situated, which the priest was willing to allow me to rent. I prepared therefore to watch over my mother's remains, sending my family in the meanwhile to live with an old pupil of mine at Pa-chou. Only the two western gates of the Chinese city were still open, and as the Hata Men and the Ch'ien Men had been closed for four days, the stream of traffic through the Shun-chih Men caused perpetual blocks in that gateway. All the small pedlars, hawkers and barbers were fleeing the city, but still the large business houses remained open.

"On the 19th I conveyed my mother's remains to the temple; I found all quiet there, but my progress through the city gate was very slow because of the crowd. On the 23rd there were but few people abroad, and these clustering together in small groups and speaking in low voices. Suddenly, a little after mid-day, an immense blaze was seen to the north-west, and speedily it was reported that the barbarians had seized Hai-tien and the Summer Palace. Our army is said to number half a million men, and yet it seems that not one of them dare oppose the barbarians' advance. They have about a thousand of cavalry, yet they move about at will in our midst as if in an uninhabited wilderness! 'Tis passing strange! The troops of Prince Seng and General Sheng have retreated to the Te-sheng gate.

"On the 24th all the shops were closed, and the higher the price of vehicles, the greater the number of people to wish to engage them. The poorer class were using wheelbarrows, on which they packed their most valuable moveables for flight.

"Prince Kung sent an Envoy to the barbarians' camp with a despatch asking for an armistice. On arriving in the vicinity of the camp, however, the messenger saw the barbarians pointing

H.I.H. P'u Ju, Cousin of the Present Emperor, Son of the Boxer Prince Tsai-Ying, and Grandson of Prince Kung.

rifles at him, so that he turned and fled.

"On the afternoon of the 24th, vast columns of smoke were seen rising to the north-west, and it was ascertained that the barbarians had entered the Summer Palace, and after plundering the three main halls, leaving them absolutely bare, they had set fire to the buildings. Their excuse for this abominable behaviour is that their troops got out of hand, and had committed the incendiarism. After this they issued notices, placarded everywhere, in very bad Chinese, stating that unless terms of peace had been arranged before mid-day on the 29th, they would then bombard Peking, in which case all inhabitants who did not wish to share the fate of the city had better remove themselves to a safe distance.

"On this day it was reported that The Sacred Chariot had reached Jehol in safety, but His Majesty had been greatly alarmed, and had issued a Decree expressing regret for his failure to commit suicide on the approach of the invaders. The Emperor is reported to be ill, and it is said that the Princes Tsai Yüan and Tuan Hua are trying to get themselves appointed to the Grand Council. Should the Emperor die (*lit.* 'when ten thousand years have passed') the Yi concubine will be made Empress Dowager, but at present she is reported to be at variance with the Princes, who are endeavouring to prejudice the Emperor against her.

"I learnt that all was quiet at the temple where my mother's coffin rests. Troops were passing there daily, but, so far, none had occupied it. On the 29th, my servant-boy, Yung 'Erh, came to tell me that troops from Tientsin in the pay of the barbarians had occupied the temple, but on proceeding thither I found them to be General Sheng's men. Prince Seng's troops were also near at hand, so that, if a bombardment had taken place, what could have prevented the destruction of the temple, and what would then have become of my mother's remains? I therefore decided to engage wheelbarrows and handcarts, at six taels apiece, to take my family to Pao-ting fu, and I arranged with the undertakers to hire bearers for the coffin.

"At 11 A.M. of the same day the barbarians entered the city by the Anting gate, occupying its tower and the wall adjoining. One large cannon and four small ones were placed in position on the wall, and a five-coloured flag hoisted there. With the exception of the officials entrusted with the duty of negotiating, not one remained in the city. Two days ago the prisoner Parkes, and his companions, were sent back to the enemy with every mark of courtesy. Scarcely had they reached their camp when a special Decree, post-haste from Jehol, ordered Prince Kung to decapitate them all forthwith as a warning to the bandits who had dared to invade the sacred precincts of the Palace. As the Yi concubine had urged their execution from the very first, it would seem as if her influence were again in the ascendant.

"On the 1st of the 9th Moon, the 'Chang-yi' gate was closed, but I managed to leave the city by the Hsi-pien Men, where I was nearly crushed to death in the enormous crowd. Upon my arrival at the temple, I had a nice wadded cover made to put over the coffin, and then hurried back to the city to arrange for the *cortège* leaving next morning. The President of the Board of Finance, Liang Hai-lou, was hiding in the temple precincts with his family and chief concubine, all wearing common clothes and unshaven. This is a good example of the condition to which the very highest had been reduced.

"Next morning, on reaching the temple, I found the coffin-bearers and transport coolies on the spot. But, unfortunately, in my hurry, I failed to notice that the undertakers had supplied the frame, on which the coffin is carried, of a size smaller than had been agreed upon, so that instead of sixteen bearers there were but eight. We started, however, and the procession's appearance of panic-stricken fugitives was most distressing to contemplate. But what could I do? The first and only object in my mind was to protect my mother's coffin. I have omitted to state that my small servant-boy, Yung 'Erh, had started to accompany the coffin on foot. But, after they had started, it occurred to me that the lad could never stand so long a journey, and that should my mother

be aware of it, she would be extremely anxious about him. Therefore, I quickly engaged another wheelbarrow for Yung 'Erh, and
bade the coolies hurry after the procession.

"On returning home I felt uneasy about the jolting which my
mother's coffin must have experienced on the undersized frame.
I went, therefore, to the undertakers and expostulated with them
for having cheated me. After much altercation they agreed to
change the frame, but I was to pay two taels more for the larger
size. I subsequently learned that they failed to keep their promise, but there was no good to be got by suing them for breach of
faith. They are sordid tricksters. Yung 'Erh wrote, however, to
assure me that the party had reached Pao-ting fu in safety, and
that the coffin had not been jolted in the least. On removing the
wrappings the lacquer was found to be undamaged.

"The barbarians were now in full possession of the city, and
rumours were rife on all sides. Everyone in Peking—there were
still a good many people—was terrified, and the Manchus were
sending their families from the Tartar to the southern (Chinese)
city to save their women from being outraged by the barbarian
bandits. The condition of the people was indeed deplorable in
the extreme. One of the Censors had sent a Memorial to Jehol,
reproaching the Emperor for the pass to which he had brought
his people, and for the neglect of ancestral worship caused by
his absence. He blamed His Majesty for listening to evil advisers,
and besought him to return to his capital.

"The minds of the people were becoming more than ever disturbed, because it was now reported that the negotiations for
peace had so far failed, either because Prince Kung would not
entertain the barbarians' conditions, or because the latter were
too utterly preposterous.

"On the 6th, a despatch arrived from the British barbarians,
accusing China of having violated all civilised usage in tortur-
ing to death their fellow-countrymen. For this they demanded
an indemnity of 500,000 taels. At the same time came a despatch from the Russian barbarians, saying that they had heard

that England was demanding this indemnity, but they (the Russians) were prepared to use their influence and good offices to persuade the British to abate their claims. Prince Kung was of opinion that, even if they should be successful in this proposed mediation, China would only save some 100,000 taels, and for this she would place herself under heavy obligations to Russia. So he replied, declining the offer on the ground that the British claim had already been accepted by China, and that further discussion of the matter was therefore impossible. Thereupon the Russians wrote again, saying that if China had definitely accepted the British terms there was, of course, nothing more to be said, but they asked Prince Kung to note that they had induced England to forgo half of the indemnity of two million taels originally asked, as a set-off to China for the destruction of the Summer Palace. On the 9th, Prince Kung forwarded the 500,000 taels to the British barbarians.

"The whole sixteen articles of the barbarians' demands have finally been accepted without modification. The only thing that our negotiators asked was the immediate withdrawal of the invading army, and to obtain this they were prepared to yield everything. Therefore, the barbarians openly flout China for her lack of men. Woe is me; a pitiful tale, and one hard to tell! When the Yi concubine heard of Prince Kung's complete surrender to the barbarians she reproached the Emperor for allowing his brother to negotiate, and she implored him to re-open hostilities. But His Majesty was dangerously ill, and refused to leave Jehol, so that our revenge must be postponed for the time being."

Bearing in mind the frequent allusions made by the Hanlin diarist to the Emperor's indecision of purpose at the time of the advance of the British and French armies on Peking, it is reasonable to assume that Yehonala prompted, if she did not write, the following vigorous Edict, which appeared on the 3rd day of the 8th Moon in the 10th year of Hsien-Feng (6th September 1860): —

"Swaying the wide world, we are nevertheless animated by one and the same instinct of benevolence to all. We have never forbidden England and France to trade with China, and for long years there has been peace between them and us. But three years ago the English, for no good cause, invaded our city of Canton, and carried off our officials into captivity. We refrained at that time from taking any retaliatory measures, because we were compelled to recognise that the obstinacy of the Viceroy Yeh had been in some measure a cause of the hostilities. Two years ago the barbarian Commander Elgin came north, and we then commanded the Viceroy of Chihli, T'an Ting-hsiang, to look into matters preparatory to negotiations. But the barbarian took advantage of our unreadiness, attacking the Taku forts and pressing on to Tientsin. Being anxious to spare our people the horrors of war, we again refrained from retaliation and ordered Kuei Liang to discuss terms of peace. Notwithstanding the outrageous nature of the barbarians' demands, we subsequently ordered Kuei Liang to proceed to Shanghai in connection with the proposed Treaty of Commerce, and even permitted its ratification as earnest of our good faith.

"In spite of all this the barbarian leader Bruce again displayed intractability of the most unreasonable kind and once more appeared off Taku with a squadron of warships in the 8th Moon. Seng Ko Lin Ch'in thereupon attacked him fiercely and compelled him to make a hasty retreat. From all these facts it is clear that China has committed no breach of faith and that the barbarians have been in the wrong. During the present year the barbarian leaders Elgin and Gros have again appeared off our coasts, but China, unwilling to resort to extreme measures, agreed to their landing and permitted them to come to Peking for the ratification of the Treaty.

"Who could have believed that all this time these barbarians have been darkly plotting and that they had brought with them an army of soldiers and artillery, with which they attacked the Taku forts from the rear, and, having driven out our forces, advanced upon Tientsin! Once more we ordered Kuei Liang to go to Tientsin and endeavour to reason with them, in the hope that they might not be lost to all sense of propriety, and with the full intention that their demands, if not utterly unreasonable, should be conceded. To our utter astonishment, Elgin and his colleague had the audacity to demand an indemnity from China; they asked, too, that more Treaty ports should be opened, and that they should be allowed to occupy our capital with their army. To such lengths did their brutality and cunning lead them! But we then commanded Prince Yi and Mu Yin, the President of the Board of War, to endeavour to induce in them a more reasonable spirit and to come to some satisfactory arrangement. But these treacherous barbarians dared to advance their savage soldiery towards Tungchow and to announce their intention of compelling us to receive them in audience.

"Any further forbearance on our part would be a dereliction of our duty to the Empire, so that we have now commanded our armies to attack them with all possible energy and we have directed the local gentry to organise train-bands, and with them either to join in the attack or to block the barbarians' advance. Hereby we make offer of the following rewards:—For the head of a black barbarian, 50 taels, and for the head of a white barbarian, 100 taels. For the capture of a barbarian leader, alive or dead, 500 taels, and for the seizure or destruction of a barbarian vessel, 5,000 taels. The inhabitants of Tientsin are reputed brave. Let them now come forward and rid us of these pestilential savages, either by open attack or by artifice. We are no lovers of war, but all our people must admit that this has been forced upon us.

"As to the barbarians' seizure of portions of our territory in Kuangtung and Fukhien, all our subjects are alike our children and we will issue large rewards to any of them in the south who shall present us with the head of a barbarian chief.

"These barbarians live in the remote parts of the earth, whence they come to China for purposes of trade. Their outrageous proceedings have, we understand, been encouraged by abominable traitors among our own subjects. We now command that all the Treaty ports be closed and all trade with England and France stopped. Subjects of other submissive States are not to be molested, and whensoever the British and French repent them of their evil ways and return to their allegiance, we shall be pleased to permit them to trade again, as of old, so that our clemency may be made manifest. But should they persist in their wicked violation of every right principle, our armies must mightily smite them, and pledge themselves solemnly to destroy utterly these evil-doers. May they repent while yet there is time!"

Three days later Yehonala was present at the morning audience, when the Emperor made the following statement: —

"We learn that the barbarians continue to press upon our capital. Their demands were all complied with, yet they insist upon presenting to us in person their barbarous documents of credentials, and demand that Prince Seng shall withdraw his troops from Chang-Chia wan. Such insolence as this makes further parley impossible. Prince Seng has gained one great victory already, and now his forces are holding the enemy in check at Palich'iao."

Orders were issued that the landing of troops from the warships which had appeared off Kinchou should be stoutly resisted.

On the 7th of the Moon His Majesty sacrificed at the Temple of Confucius, but on the next morning he was afraid to come into the city from the Summer Palace, although he wished to sacrifice to the tutelary deities and inform them of his intended departure. Early on the following day Prince Kung was appointed Plenipotentiary in the place of Prince Yi (Tsai Yüan) and the Emperor, despite the brave wording of his Decree, fled from the capital, after making obeisance to the God of War in a small temple of the Palace grounds. In the Decree announcing his departure, the flight was described as an "autumn tour of inspection."[1]

The Court started in utter confusion, but proceeded only some eighteen miles on the road northwards from Peking, stopping for the first night in a small temple. Here a Decree was issued calling upon all the Manchurian troops to hasten to Jehol for the protection of the Court. On the evening of the following

---

1. The same euphemism was employed to describe the Court's flight in August 1900.

day a Memorial was received from Prince Kung, reporting on the latest doings of the barbarians, but His Majesty ordered him, in reply, to take whatever steps he might think fit to deal with the situation. It was out of the question, said the Rescript, for the Emperor to decide on any course of action at a distance: in other words, the Throne divested itself of further responsibility.

On the 11th, the Court lay at the Imperial hunting lodge north of Mi-Yun hsien. The Chinese chronicler records that the Emperor was too sick to receive the Grand Council, and delegated his duties to Yehonala, who thereupon issued the following Decree:—

"We are informed that the pestilent barbarians are pressing upon our capital, and our Ministers have asked us to summon reinforcements from the provinces. Now the highest form of military art is to effect sudden surprises, carefully pre-arranged. The barbarians' superiority lies in their firearms, but if we can only bring them to a hand-to-hand engagement they will be unable to bring their artillery to bear, and thus shall our victory be assured. The Mongol and Manchu horsemen are quite useless for this kind of warfare, but the men of Hupei and Ssŭ-ch'uan are as agile as monkeys and adepts at the use of cover in secret approaches. Let them but surprise these bandits once, and their rout is inevitable. Therefore let Tseng Kuo-fan, the Viceroy of Hukuang, send up at least three thousand of his best troops to Peking, and let as many be despatched from Ssŭ-ch'uan. Prince Seng's troops have been defeated again and again, and the capital is in great danger. At such a crisis as this, there must be no delay; it is our earnest hope that a sufficient force will speedily be collected, so that we may be rid of this poisonous fever-cloud. For bravery and good service, there will be great rewards. A most important Decree."

At the Court's halting place at Pa-Ko shih, close to the Great Wall, a Memorial came in from Prince Seng Ko Lin Ch'in, stating that small scouting parties of the barbarian troops had been seen in the neighbourhood of Peking, but that as yet there had been no general bombardment. A Rescript was issued as follows:—

"Inasmuch as it would appear that the pertinacity of these barbarians will only increase with opposition, it seems desirable to come to terms with them as soon as possible. With reference to the French barbarian Gros's petition to be permitted to discuss matters with Prince Kung in person, at Peking, we command the Prince to receive him. But should the bandits attempt to approach the city in force, Prince Seng should take them in the rear and cut off their retreat. If by any chance, however, Peking should be already taken, let the Mongol regiments be sent up to the Great Wall for the protection of our person."

After a leisurely journey, the Court reached Jehol on the 18th. On the 20th, the opinion of the advisers of the Emperor seemed to be in favour of continuing the war at all costs. A Decree was issued, referring to the fact that the foreign troops had dared to encamp near the Summer Palace, and forbidding Prince Kung to spare the lives of any captured barbarians upon any pretext whatsoever. To this Prince Kung replied stating that the prisoners had already been released and that the Anting gate had been surrendered to the foreigners. Prince Kung, in fact, was statesman enough to realise that the only chance for China lay in submission; he therefore ignored the Imperial Decrees. Before long the Emperor was persuaded to allow negotiations to be resumed, and on the 15th of the 9th Moon he confirmed the Treaty, which had been signed in Peking, in the following Edict:—

"Prince Kung, duly appointed by us to be Plenipotentiary, concluded, on the 11th and 12th days of this Moon, Treaties of Peace with the British and the French. Hereafter amity is to exist between our nations in perpetuity, and the various conditions of the Treaty are to be strictly observed by all."

III

THE TSAI YÜAN CONSPIRACY

IT was originally intended that the Emperor Hsien-Feng should return from Jehol to Peking in the spring of 1861, and a Decree was issued to that effect. In January, however, his illness had become so serious that travelling was out of the question, and this Decree was rescinded.

At Jehol, removed from the direct influence of his brothers, and enfeebled by sickness, the Emperor had gradually fallen under the domination of the Prince Yi (Tsai Yüan) with whom were associated, as Grand Councillors, the Prince Tuan Hua and the Imperial Clansman Su Shun. These three, recognising that the Emperor's end was near and that a Regency would be necessary, determined on securing the power for themselves. Prince Yi was nominally the leader of this conspiracy, but its instigator and leading spirit was Su Shun. Tuan Hua, whose family title was Prince Cheng, was the head of one of the eight princely Manchu families, descended in the direct line from Nurhachu's brother. Su Shun was foster-brother to this Prince. In his youth he was a conspicuous figure in the capital, famous for his Mohawk tendencies, a wild blade, addicted to hawking and riotous living. He had originally been recommended to the notice of the Emperor by the two Princes and soon won his way into the dissolute monarch's confidence and goodwill. From a junior post in the Board of Revenue, he rose rapidly, becoming eventually an Assistant Grand Secretary, in which capacity he attained an unenviable reputation for avarice and cruelty. He had made himself hated and feared by persuading the Emperor to order the decapitation of his chief, the Grand Secretary Po Chun,[1] on the pretext that he had shown favouritism as Chief Examiner for the Metropolitan Degree, — the real reason being that he had offended the two Princes by his uncompromising honesty and blunt speech. It was at this period that he first came into conflict with the young Yehonala, who, dreading the man's growing influence with the Emperor, endeavoured to counteract it, and at the same time to save the life of the Grand Secretary; she failed in the attempt, and Su Shun's position became the stronger for her failure. All those who opposed him were speedily banished or degraded. The Court was terrified, especially when it was realised that Yehonala was out of favour, and Su Shun took care to give them real and frequent cause for alarm. At his instance, all the Secretaries of the Board of Revenue were cashiered on a charge of making illicit profits by cornering the cash market. The charge was possibly well-founded, since such proceedings are part of a Metropolitan official's recognised means of subsistence, but coming from the notoriously corrupt Su Shun, it was purely vindictive, as was shown by his subsequent action; for upon this charge he obtained the arrest of over a hundred notables and rich merchants whom he kept in custody of no gentle kind until they had ransomed themselves with enormous sums. Thus was founded the great fortune which enabled him to conspire with the Princes Yi and Cheng[2] for the supreme power, and which led him eventually to his ruin. To this day, many of his millions lie in the Palace vaults, to which they were carried after his impeachment and death — millions carefully hoarded by Tzŭ Hsi and buried during the Court's flight and exile in 1900.

---

1. Grandfather of Na T'ung, the present head of the Waiwupu.
2. Yi "and Cheng" are honorific names, meaning respectively "harmonious" and "sedate."

It was chiefly because of the advice of Su Shun that the Emperor fled his capital at the approach of the Allies, in spite of the urgent appeals of Yehonala and the Grand Council. By his advice also most of the high officials and Metropolitan Ministers were prevented from accompanying the Court, by which means the conspirators were able to exercise steadily increasing influence over the Emperor, and to prevent other advice reaching him. It was only the supreme courage and intelligent grasp of the situation shown by Yehonala, that frustrated the conspiracy at its most critical moment. Immediately after the death of the Emperor, and while the plotters were still undecided as to their final plans, she sent an urgent message secretly to Prince Kung which brought him with all speed to Jehol, where, by the help of Jung Lu and other loyal servants, she put into execution the bold plan which defeated the conspiracy and placed her at the head of China's government. On the day when, the game hopelessly lost, the usurping Regents found themselves in Yehonala's hands and heard her order their summary trial by the Court of the Imperial Clan, Su Shun turned to his colleagues and bitterly reproached them. "Had you but taken my advice and slain this woman," he said, "we should not have been in this plight to-day."

To return, however, to the beginning of the conspiracy. At the outset, the object of Prince Yi was to alienate the Emperor from the influence of his favourite concubine, Yehonala. With this object they informed him of the intrigue which, by common report, she was carrying on with the young Officer of the Guards, Jung Lu, then a handsome athletic man of about twenty-five. The Empress Consort they regarded as a negligible factor, whose good-natured and colourless personality took little interest in the politics of the day; but if their plot was to succeed, Yehonala must either be dismissed from the Court for good and all, or, at the very least, she must be temporarily relegated to the "Cold Palace," as is called the place where insubordinate or disgraced concubines are isolated. They knew that, however successful their plans at Jehol, there must always be danger in the event of the Emperor returning to Peking, where access to his person is not possible at all times for officials (even those nearest to the Throne), whereas Yehonala would be in a position, with the help of her eunuchs, to recover his favour and her power. Emphasising, therefore, the alleged misconduct of the young concubine, they quoted the precedent of a certain Empress Consort of Ch'ien-Lung who, for less grievous disrespect (shown to the Emperor's mother), was imprisoned for life. Thus, by inventions and suggestions, they so worked on the sick man's mind that he finally consented to have Yehonala's infant son, the Heir Apparent, removed from her care, and authorised the child's being handed over to the wife of Prince Yi, who was summoned to the hunting-lodge Palace for that purpose. At the same time, the conspirators thought it well to denounce Prince Kung to the Emperor, his brother, accusing him of treachery, of conniving with the foreigners against the Throne, and of abusing his powers as Plenipotentiary. Prince Yi had been for years Prince Kung's sworn enemy.

The further intentions of the conspirators, instigated by Su Shun, were to massacre all Europeans in the capital and to put to death, or at least imprison for life, the Emperor's brothers. Accordingly they drafted in advance the Decrees necessary to justify and explain these measures, intending to publish them immediately after the Emperor's death, which was now imminent. But here an unforeseen obstacle presented itself, the first of many created for them by the far-seeing intelligence of Yehonala; for they found that she had somehow managed to possess herself of the special seal, which inviolable custom requires to be affixed to the first Edict of a new reign, in proof of validity of succession, — a seal, in the personal custody of the Emperor, which bears the characters meaning "lawfully transmitted authority." Without this seal, any Decrees which the usurpers might issue would lack something of legal finality and, according to Chinese ideas, their subsequent cancellation would be justifiable. But Prince Yi did not feel himself strong enough to risk a crisis by accusing her or taking overt steps to gain possession of it.

Angry with his favourite concubine by reason of the reports of her intimacy with Jung Lu, and his sickness ever increasing, the Emperor lingered on in Jehol all the summer of that year, his duty in the ancestral sacrifices at Peking being taken by Prince Kung. On the 4th of the 6th Moon, the day before his thirtieth birthday, he issued the following Decree in reply to a Memorial by the Court of Astronomers, which had announced an auspicious conjunction of the stars for the occasion: —

"Last month the Astronomers announced the appearance of a comet in the north-west, which intimation we received as a solemn warning of the impending wrath of Heaven. Now they memorialise saying that the stars are in favourable conjunction, which is doubtless a true statement, in no way inspired by their desire to please us. But since we came to the Throne, we have steadily refused to pay any attention to auspicious omens, and this with good reason, in view of the ever-increasing rebellions in the south and the generally pitiable condition of our people. May the present auspicious conjunction of the stars portend the dawning of a happier day, and may heaven permit a speedy end to the rebellion. In token of our sincerity, we desire that the Astronomical Court shall refrain from reporting to the Chronicler's Office the present favourable omen for inclusion in the annals of our reign, so that there may be ascribed to us the merit of a devout and sober mind."

On the following morning the Emperor received the congratulations of his Court in a pavilion of the Palace grounds, but Yehonala was excluded from this ceremony. This was His Majesty's last appearance in public; from this date his illness became rapidly worse.

On the 7th of the 7th Moon Yehonala contrived to despatch a secret courier to Prince Kung at Peking, informing him of the critical condition of his brother and urging him to send with all haste a detachment of the Banner Corps to which the Yehonala clan belonged. Events now moved swiftly. On the 16th, the Grand Councillors and Ministers of the Presence, all adherents of Tsai Yüan's faction, entered the Emperor's bedroom and, after excluding the Empress Consort and the concubines, persuaded the Emperor to sign Decrees appointing Tsai Yüan, Tuan Hua and Su Shun to be Co-Regents upon his decease, with full powers. Yehonala was to be expressly forbidden from exercising any form of control over the Heir Apparent. As the necessary seal of State had been taken by Yehonala and could not be found, these proceedings were irregular. At dawn on the following day the Emperor died, and forthwith appeared the usual valedictory Decree, prepared in advance by the conspirators, whereby Tsai Yüan was appointed to be Chief Regent, Prince Kung and the Empress Consort being entirely ignored.

In the name of the new Emperor, then a child of five, a Decree was issued, announcing his succession, but it was observed to violate all constitutional precedent in that it omitted the proper laudatory references to the Imperial Consort. On the following day, however, the Regents, fearing to precipitate matters, rectified the omission in an Edict which conferred the rank of Empress Dowager both on the Empress Consort and on Yehonala. The chroniclers aver that the reason for this step lay in the Regents' recognition of Yehonala's undoubted popularity with the troops (all Manchus) at Jehol, an argument that weighed more heavily with them than her rights as mother of the Heir Apparent. They hoped to rid themselves of this condition of affairs after the Court's return to Peking, but dared not risk internal dissensions by having her removed until their positions had been made secure at the capital.

That they intended to remove her was subsequently proved; it was evident that their position would never be secure so long as her ambitious and magnetic personality remained a factor of the situation: but it was necessary, in the first instance, to ascertain the effect of the Regency at Peking and in the provinces.

Tsai Yüan's next move was to publish Decrees, in the names of the Joint Regents, by virtue of which they assumed charge of the Heir Apparent and by which the title of "Chien Kuo"

慈禧端佑康頤昭豫莊誠壽恭欽獻崇熙皇太后之像 大清國當今聖母皇太后

HER MAJESTY TZU HSI IN THE YEAR 1903

(practically equivalent to Dictator) was conferred on the Chief Regent, a title heretofore reserved exclusively for brothers or uncles of the Emperor.

When the news reached Peking, a flood of Memorials burst from the Censorate and high officials. The child Emperor was implored to confer the Regency upon the two Empresses, or, as the Chinese text has it, to "administer the Government with suspended curtain."[1] Prince Kung and the Emperor's other brothers were at this time in secret correspondence with Yehonala, whom they, like the Censorate, had already recognised as the mastermind of the Forbidden City. They urged her to do all in her power to expedite the departure of the funeral *cortège* for the capital. To secure this end, it was necessary to proceed with the greatest caution and diplomacy, for several of the late Emperor's wives had been won over to the side of the usurpers, who could also count on a certain number of the Manchu bodyguard, their own clansmen. The influence of Su Shun's great fortune was also no inconsiderable factor in the situation. The man was personally unpopular with the people of Peking, because of his abuse of power and too frequent connection with speculations in banknote issues and cash, which cost the citizens dear, but his vaults were known to be full to over-flowing, and there is no city in the world where money buys more political supporters than in Peking. Su Shun's career has had its counterpart, in everything except its sanguinary dénouement, in the capital to-day.

At the moment the position of the Emperor's family was prejudiced, and the aims of the conspirators assisted, by the political situation. With the capital occupied by foreign troops, and many of the provinces in the throes of a great rebellion, the people might be expected to welcome a change of rulers, and the ripe experience of the usurping Regents in all matters of State was undeniable. But the virile and untiring energies of Yehonala, ably

---

1. The expression has reference to the fact that the Empresses Regent are supposed to be concealed from the sight of Ministers at audience by a curtain suspended in front of the Throne.

supported by Jung Lu and other faithful followers, soon put a
new complexion on affairs, and the situation was further modified in her favour by the success of her nominee, the Commander-in-Chief, Tseng Kuo-fan, in capturing the city of An-ch'ing (in
Anhui) from the rebels, a victory that was regarded as of good
augury to her cause. Thereafter her courage and diplomacy enabled her to play off one opponent against another, gaining time
and friends until the conspirators' chance was gone. Her own
aims and ambitions, which had been voiced by her friends in the
Censorate, were, however, to some extent impeded by the fact
that a House-law of the Dynasty forbids the administration of
the Government by an Empress Dowager, while there were quite
recent precedents for a Regency by a Board, in the cases of the
Emperors Shun-Chih and K'ang-Hsi. In neither of these instances had the Empress Tai-Tsung had any voice in the Government.
The precedent for Boards of official Regents had, however, come
to be recognised as inauspicious, because the several Regents of
K'ang-Hsi's minority had either been banished or compelled to
commit suicide. It is probable, too, that Prince Kung, in instigating and supporting the claims of the Empresses, failed to appreciate Yehonala's strength of character, and believed that a women's
Regency would leave the supreme power in his own hands.

A Manchu, who accompanied the flight to Jehol, describing
his experiences, lays stress upon Yehonala's unfailing courage
and personal charm of manner, to which was due her popularity
with the Imperial Guards and her eventual triumph. At the most
critical period of the conspiracy she was careful to avoid pre-
cipitating a conflict or arousing the suspicions of the usurpers by
openly conferring with Jung Lu, and she employed as her confidential intermediary the eunuch An Te-hai (of whom more will
be heard later). By means of this man daily reports were safely
despatched to Prince Kung at Peking, and, in the meanwhile, Yehonala affected an attitude of calm indifference, treating Prince
Yi with a studied deference which lulled his suspicions.

On the 11th of the 8th Moon, the Board of Regents, after

meeting to discuss the situation, issued a Decree condemning in strong terms a proposal put forward in a Memorial by the Censor, Tung Yüan-ch'un, that the two Empresses should be appointed Co-Regents, and referring to the death-bed Decree of the late Emperor as their own warrant of authority. At the same time they announced, in the name of the young Emperor, that the funeral *cortège* would start on its journey to the capital on the second day of the next Moon. This was the step for which Yehonala had been working and waiting. As Ministers of the Presence, the Regents were perforce obliged to accompany the coffin throughout the entire journey (some 150 miles) to the capital, and the great weight of the catafalque, borne by one hundred and twenty men, would necessarily render the rate of progress very slow through the stony defiles of the hills. Resting places would have to be provided at stages of about fifteen miles along the route to shelter the Imperial remains and the attendant officials by night, so that the Regents might count on a journey of ten days at least, and longer in the event of bad weather. To the Empresses, the slow progress of the *cortège* was a matter of vital advantage, inasmuch as they were not to take part in the procession, and, travelling ahead of it, could reach the capital in five days with swift chair-bearers. Dynastic custom and Court etiquette prescribe that upon the departure of the funeral procession, the new Emperor and the consorts of the deceased sovereign should offer prayers and libations, and should then press on so as to be ready to perform similar acts of reverence on meeting the *cortège* at its destination. Yehonala thus found herself in a position of great strategic advantage, being enabled to reach the capital well in advance of her enemies, and she speedily laid her plans with Prince Kung to give them a warm reception.

Tsai Yüan and his colleagues were well aware that they were placed at grave disadvantage in having to remain behind the young Empress, with every prospect of serious trouble ahead; they, therefore, decided to have Yehonala and the Empress Consort assassinated on the road, and to that end gave orders that

they should be escorted by the Chief Regent's personal bodyguard. Had it not been for Jung Lu, who got wind of the plot,
the Dowagers would assuredly never have reached the capital
alive. Acting with the promptitude which Yehonala inspired, he
deserted the funeral *cortège* by night with a considerable following of his own men, and hastened on to the protection of the
Empresses, overtaking them before they reached Ku-pei K'ou, at
the end of the pass from the plains into Mongolia, which was the
spot where the assassination was to have taken place.

Heavy rains had fallen just after the departure of the procession from Jehol. The roads became impassable, and the Empresses were compelled to seek shelter in the Long Mountain gorge,
where no sort of accommodation had been provided. The *cortège*
was then ten miles in their rear. Yehonala, mindful ever of the
proprieties, sent back several men of her escort with a dutiful
enquiry, in the name of her colleague and herself, as to the safety
of the Imperial coffin. The reply, in the form of an Edict by Prince
Yi and his Co-Regents, reported that the catafalque had reached
the first resting place in safety; whereupon Yehonala, asserting
as of right the prerogatives of supreme authority, donated to the
bearers a thousand taels from her Privy Purse in recognition of
their arduous services. Prince Yi, knowing full well that his own
danger was increasing every hour, and would continue so long
as the Empresses remained free to work against him, nevertheless played bravely the part prescribed for him, conforming in
the grand manner to the traditions of his position. He forwarded
a Memorial to the Empresses, humbly thanking them for their
solicitude for the Emperor's remains. Yehonala, in reply, praised
him for his faithful devotion to duty. Thus, on the road to Death,
they played at Etiquette. Both these documents are filed in the
Dynastic records and afford remarkable evidence of the supreme
importance which Chinese and Manchus alike attach to forms
and the written word even at the most critical moments. Similar
instances could be cited at the height of the Boxer chaos.

The rains having ceased, the Empresses were able to proceed

on their journey, and having come safely through the hill passes under Jung Lu's protection, they were free from further danger of ambush. They reached Peking on the 29th of the 9th Moon, three full days' journey ahead of the procession. Immediately upon their arrival a secret Council was held, at which were present the Emperor's brothers, together with the Ministers and Imperial clansmen known to be loyal to their cause. Long and anxiously did they confer. Although the Empress Mother was in possession of the seal of legitimate succession, there was no known precedent for so drastic a step as the summary, and possibly violent, arrest of high officers of State convoying the Imperial coffin. Such a course, it was felt, would be regarded as disrespectful to the late Emperor and an inauspicious opening to the new reign. The consensus of opinion was, therefore, on the side of slow and cautious measures, and it was decided thus to proceed, conforming to all the outward observances of dynastic tradition. The coffin once arrived, the first step would be to deprive the Regents of their usurped authority; the rest would follow.

The *cortège* was due to arrive at the north-west gate of the city on the morning of the 2nd of the 10th Moon, and on the previous evening Prince Kung posted a large force of troops at this point to prevent any attempt at a *coup de main* by Tsai Yüan's followers. The boy Emperor, accompanied by the Empresses Dowager, came out to meet the coffin as it approached the city, and with him were the late Emperor's brothers and a great following of officials. As the catafalque passed through the gate, the Imperial party knelt and performed the prescribed acts of reverence. Before the coffin came the Imperial insignia, and behind it a large body of Manchu cavalry. Prince Yi and his Co-Regents, having performed their duty in bringing the coffin safely to the city, next proceeded, as required by custom, to make formal report in person to the young Emperor, upon fulfilment of their charge. For this purpose they were received in a large marquee erected just inside the city gate. Both Empresses were present, together with the late Emperor's brothers and the Grand Secretaries Kuei Liang and Chou Tsu-p'ei.

Yehonala, calmly assuming, as was her wont, the principal *rôle* and all attributes of authority, opened the proceedings by informing Prince Yi that the Empress Consort and she herself were grateful to him and to his colleagues for the services which they had rendered as Regents and Grand Councillors, of which duties they were now relieved. Prince Yi, putting a bold face on it, replied that he himself was Chief Regent, legally appointed, that the Empresses had no power to divest him of authority properly conferred by the late Emperor, and that, during the minority of the new Emperor, neither she herself nor any other person was entitled to attend audience without his express permission.

"We shall see about that," said Yehonala, and forthwith gave orders to the attendant guards to place the three Regents under arrest. The Imperial party then hastened to the Palace to be ready to meet the coffin upon its arrival at the main entrance to the Forbidden City, for, however acute the crisis, the dead take precedence of the living in China. The deposed Regents quietly followed. All hope of escape or resistance was out of the question, for the streets were lined with troops faithful to Yehonala's cause. Her triumph was complete, essentially a triumph of mind over matter. It was her first taste of the pomp and circumstance of supreme power.

Forthwith the Empresses proceeded to regularise their position by issuing the following Decree, which bore the Great Seal of "Lawfully transmitted authority":—

"Last year the coasts of our Empire were disturbed and our capital was in danger, misfortunes entirely due to the mismanagement of affairs by the Princes and Ministers to whom they had been entrusted. Prince Yi (Tsai Yüan) in particular and his colleagues failed to deal satisfactorily with the peace negotiations, and sought to lessen their responsibility by their treacherous arrest of the British emissaries, thus involving China in charges of bad faith. In consequence of these their acts, the Summer Palace was eventually sacked by the British and French troops and the

Emperor was forced, greatly against his will, to seek refuge in Jehol.

"Later, the Ministers of the newly established Tsungli Yamên were able to arrange matters satisfactorily, and peace was restored to the capital. Thereupon His late Majesty repeatedly summoned the Grand Council to decide upon a date for his return to Peking, but Tsai Yüan, Su Shun and Tuan Hua conspired together, and, by making him believe that England and France were not sincere in regard to peace, were able to prevent his return and thus to oppose the will of the people.

"Subsequently His Majesty's health suffered severely from the cold climate of Jehol and from his arduous labours and anxiety, so that he died on the 17th of the 7th Moon. Our sorrow was even as a burning fire, and when we consider how wickedly deceitful has been the conduct of Tsai Yüan and his colleagues, we feel that the whole Empire must unite in their condemnation. On ascending the Throne, it was our intention to punish them, but we kept in mind the fact that to them the Emperor had given his valedictory instructions, and we therefore forbore, whilst observing carefully their behaviour. Who could possibly have foretold their misdeeds?

"On the 11th of the 8th Moon, a Memorial was presented to us by the Censor Tung Yüan-ch'un, at an audience of the eight Grand Councillors, in which it was asked that the Empresses Dowager should for the time being, and during our minority, administer the Government, that one or two of the Princes should advise them and that a high official should be appointed as tutor to ourselves. These suggestions met with our entire approval. It is true that there exists no precedent in the history of our Dynasty for an Empress Dowager to act as Regent, but the interests of the State are our first concern, and it is surely wiser to act in accordance with the exigencies of the time than to insist upon a scrupulous observance of precedent.[1]

"We therefore authorised Tsai Yüan to issue a Decree concurring in the Censor's proposals; but he and his colleagues adopted an insolent tone towards us and forgot the reverence due to our person. While pretending to comply with our wishes, they issued a Decree quite different

---

1. The age of the Emperor was less than six, but the solemn farce of his alleged acts and opinions is solemnly accepted by the Chinese as part of the eternal order of things.

from that which we had ordered, and promulgated it in our name. What was their object? They professed to have no idea of usurping our authority, but what else was their action but usurpation?

"Undoubtedly they took advantage of our extreme youth and of the Empresses' lack of experience in statecraft, their object being to hoodwink us. But how could they hope to hoodwink the entire nation? Their behaviour displays monstrous ingratitude for His late Majesty's favours, and any further leniency on our part would be a just cause of offence to the memory of the departed sovereign, and an insult to the intelligence of the Chinese people. Tsai Yüan, Su Shun and Tuan Hua are hereby removed from their posts. Ching Shou, Mu Yin, Kuang Tu-han and Chiao Yu-ying are removed from the Grand Council. Let Prince Kung, in consultation with the Grand Secretaries, the six Boards and the nine Ministries consider, and report to us as to the proper punishment to be inflicted upon them, in proportion to their respective offences. As regards the manner in which the Empresses shall administer the Government as Regents, let this also be discussed and a Memorial submitted in reference to future procedure."

The Empresses duly performed the proper obeisances to the Imperial coffin at the eastern gate of the Palace, escorting it thence to its temporary resting place in the central Throne Hall.

In the security of Peking, and confident of the devotion of the troops, Yehonala now proceeded to act more boldly. She issued a second Decree in her own name and that of the Empress Consort, ordering that the three principal conspirators be handed over to the Imperial Clansmen's Court for the determination of a severe penalty. Pending the investigation, which was to be carried out under the Presidency of Prince Kung, they were to be stripped of all their titles and rank. The vindictive autocrat of the years to come speaks for the first time in this Edict.

"Their audacity in questioning our right to give audience to Prince Kung this morning shows a degree of wickedness inconceivable, and convicts them of the darkest designs. The punishment so far meted out to them is totally inadequate to the depth of their guilt."

Against Su Shun, in particular, the Empress's wrath burned fiercely. His wife had insulted her in the days of her disgrace at Jehol, and Yehonala had ever a good memory for insults. Next morning she issued the following Decree for his especial benefit: —

"Because of Su Shun's high treason, his wanton usurpation of authority, his acceptance of bribes and generally unspeakable wickedness, we commanded that he be degraded and arrested by the Imperial Clansmen's Court. But on receipt of the Decree, Su Shun dared to make use of blasphemous language in regard to ourselves, forgetful of the inviolable relation between Sovereign and subject. Our hair stands on end with horror at such abominable treason. Moreover he has dared to allow his wife and family to accompany him, when on duty accompanying the Imperial coffin from Jehol, which is a most disgraceful violation of all precedent.[1] The whole of his property, both at Peking and at Jehol, is therefore confiscated, and no mercy shall be shown him."

As Su Shun's property was worth several millions sterling at the lowest estimate, the Empress Dowager thus acquired at one stroke the sinews of war and a substantial nucleus for that treasure hoard which henceforward was to be one of the main objects of her ambition, and a chief source of her power. During the present Dynasty there is a record of one official wealthier than Su Shun, namely Ho Sh'en, a Grand Secretary under Ch'ien Lung, whose property was similarly confiscated by that Emperor's successor.

But Yehonala's lust of vengeance was not yet appeased. Her next Decree, issued on the following day, gives evidence of that acquisitive faculty, that tendency to accumulate property and to safeguard it with housewifely thrift, which distinguished her to

---

1. To allow women privily to accompany the Imperial *cortège* is a crime punishable by law with the penalty of the lingering death.

the end: —

"Su Shun was erecting for himself a Palace at Jehol, which is not yet completed. Doubtless he has vast stores of treasure there. Doubtless also he has buried large sums of gold and silver somewhere in the vicinity of his Jehol residence, in anticipation of the possible discovery of his crimes. Let all his property in Jehol be carefully inventoried, when a Decree will be issued as to its disposal. Let all his property be carefully searched for treasure, to be handed over when found. Any attempt at concealment by the Jehol authorities will entail upon them the same punishment as that which is to be inflicted upon Su Shun."

On the 6th of the 10th Moon, Prince Kung and the Imperial Commission sent in their report on the quite perfunctory enquiry into the charges against Tsai Yüan and the other conspirators. In the following Decree the offenders were finally disposed of: —

"The Memorial of our Imperial Commission recommends that, in accordance with the law applying to cases of high treason, the punishment of dismemberment and the lingering death be inflicted upon Tsai Yüan, Tuan Hua and Su Shun. Our Decrees have already been issued describing their abominable plot and their usurpation of the Regency.

"On the day of His late Majesty's death, these three traitors claimed to have been appointed a Council of Regency, but, as a matter of fact, His late Majesty, just before his death, had commanded them to appoint us his successor, without giving them any orders whatsoever as to their being Regents. This title they proceeded to arrogate to themselves, even daring to issue orders in that capacity and without the formality of our Decree. Moreover they disobeyed the personal and express orders given them by the Empresses Dowager. When the Censor Tung Yuan-ch'un petitioned that the Empresses should assume the government, they not only dared to alter the Decree which we issued in reply, but they openly asserted at audience their claim to be our Regents and their refusal to obey the Empresses. If, said they, they chose to permit the Empresses to see Memorials, this was more than their duty required. In fact, their insubordination and violent rudeness found expression in a hundred ways. In forbidding us to give audience to our uncles and to the Grand Secretaries, they evidently meant to set us at variance with our kindred. The above remarks apply equally to all three traitors.

"As to Su Shun, he insolently dared to seat himself upon the Imperial Throne. He would enter the Palace precincts unbidden, and whether on duty or not. He went so far as to use the Imperial porcelain and furniture for his own purposes, even refusing to hand over certain articles that we required for ourselves. He actually demanded an audience with the Empresses separately, and his words, when addressing them, indicated a cunning desire to set one Empress against the other, and to sow seeds of discord. These remarks apply to the individual guilt of Su Shun.

"Her Majesty the Empress Dowager, and Her Sacred Majesty the Empress Dowager, our mother, duly informed the Commission of Enquiry of these facts, and they have to-day given audience to all the Princes and Ministers to enquire of them whether the guilt of these three traitors admits of any extenuating circumstances. It is unanimously determined that the law allows of no leniency being shown to such flagrant treason and wickedness as theirs. When we reflect that three members of our Imperial kindred have thus rendered themselves liable to a common felon's death in the public square, our eyes are filled with tears. But all these their misdeeds, in usurping the Regency, have involved our tutelary deities in the direst peril, and it is not only to ourselves but to our illustrious ancestors that they must answer for their damnable treason. No doubt they thought that, come what may, they were sure of pardon, because of their having received the mandate of His late Majesty, but they forgot that the mandate which they have claimed was never legally issued, and if we were now to pardon them we should render the law of no effect for all time and prove unfaithful to the trust reposed in us by our late father. The punishment of dismemberment and the lingering death, which the Commission recommends, is indeed the proper punishment for their crimes, but the House-law of our Dynasty permits of leniency being shown, to a certain extent, to members of the Imperial Family. Therefore, although, strictly speaking, their crimes allow of no indulgence, we decide that they shall not suffer the penalty of public disgrace. In token of our leniency, Tsai Yüan and Tuan Hua are hereby permitted to commit suicide, and Prince Su and Mien Sen are ordered to proceed forthwith to the 'Empty Chamber,'[1] and command the immediate fulfilment of this order. It is not from any feeling of friendliness towards these traitors that we allow this, but simply to preserve the dignity of our Imperial family.

"As to Su Shun, his treasonable guilt far exceeds that of his accomplices, and he fully deserves the punishment of dismemberment and the slicing process, if only that the law may be vindicated and public indignation satisfied. But we cannot make up our mind to impose this extreme penalty and therefore, in our clemency, we sentence him to immediate decapitation, commanding Prince Jui and Tsai Liang to superintend his execution, as a warning to all traitors and rebels."

NOTE. — The hereditary Princedoms of Yi and Cheng which were forfeited by the conspiring Princes after the death of Hsien-Feng, in 1861, were restored by the Empresses Regent to commemorate their thanksgiving at the suppression of the Taiping rebellion and the recapture of Nanking (1864). In an Edict on the subject, Tzǔ Hsi recalled the fact that the original patent of the Princedom of Yi was given to a son of the Emperor K'ang-Hsi in 1723 and was to endure, according to the word of that Monarch, until "the T'ai Mountain dwindles to the size of a grindstone, and the Yellow River shrinks to the width of a girdle." After referring to the main features of the Tsai Yüan conspiracy and the guilt of the traitors, Tzǔ Hsi proceeded "We permitted these Princes to commit suicide because they were ungrateful to ourselves, and had brought disrepute on the good name of their ancestors. If these are now conscious of their descendants' misdeeds, while they wander beside the Nine Springs,[2] how great must be the anguish of their souls! At the time we were advised by our Princes

---

1. The Prison of the Imperial Clan Court.
2. Poetical term for Purgatory.

and Ministers of State, to put an end for ever to these Princely titles, and we did so in order to appease widespread indignation. Since then, however, we have often thought sorrowfully of the achievements of these Princely families during the early reigns of our Dynasty, and now the triumph of our arms at Nanking provides us with a fitting occasion and excuse to rehabilitate these Princedoms, so that the good name of their founders may remain unblemished. We therefore hereby restore both titles as Princes of the blood with all the estates and dependencies appertaining thereto, and we command that the genealogical trees of these two Houses be once more placed upon our Dynastic records in their due order, it being always understood that the usurping Princes Tuan Hua and Tsai Yüan, together with their descendants in the direct line for two generations, are expressly excluded from participation in these restored privileges. Original patents of the Princes of Yi and Cheng are hereby restored, together with their titles, to the Dukes Cheng Chih and Tsai Tun. And take heed now both of you Princes, lest you fall away from the ancient virtue of your Houses! See to it that you long continue to enjoy our favour by adding fresh lustre to your ancestral good name!"

The intention was undoubtedly well meant, but the Houses of Yi and Cheng continued to incur the displeasure of the gods. The next Prince Yi but one, was permitted to commit suicide in 1900, for alleged complicity in the Boxer rising, but it is significant that his name was not on any Black List drawn up by the foreign Powers, and that his death was due to his having incurred the displeasure of the Old Buddha at a time when her nerves were not particularly good, and when she was therefore liable to hasty decisions. As to the House of Cheng, the holder of the title in 1900 committed suicide on the day when the Allies entered the city, a disappointed patriot of the best Manchu model.

Tzŭ Hsi's wrath against Su Shun found further vent three years after his death in a Decree which debarred his sons and descendants from ever holding public office, this punishment being inflicted on the ground that he had allowed personal spite to influence him, when consulted by the Emperor Hsien-Feng regarding the penalty to be inflicted on an offending rival.

IV

THE FIRST REGENCY

ALTHOUGH the collapse of the Tsai Yüan conspiracy, and the stern justice administered to its leaders, rendered Yehonala's position secure and made her *de facto* ruler of the Empire (for her colleague was, politically speaking, a negligible quantity, or nearly so), she was extremely careful, during the first years of the Regency, to avoid all conspicuous assumption of power and to keep herself and her ambitions in the background, while she omitted no opportunity of improving her knowledge of the art of government and of gaining the support of China's leading officials. For this reason all the Decrees of this period are issued in the name of the Emperor, and Tzǔ Hsi's assumption of authority was even less conspicuous than during her period of retirement at the Summer Palace after the conclusion of Kuang-Hsü's minority. The first Regency (1861-1873) may be described as Tzǔ Hsi's tentative period of rule, in which she tasted the sweets, while avoiding the appearance, of power. During the second Regency (1875-1889), while her name appeared only occasionally as the author of Imperial Decrees, she was careful to keep in her hands all official appointments, the granting of rewards and punishments and other matters of internal politics calculated to increase her personal popularity and prestige with the mandarinate. The "curtain was not suspended" during Kuang-Hsü's minority, as he was the nominee of the Empresses, whereas the Emperor T'ung-Chih held his mandate direct from the late Emperor, his father. It was not until the final Regency (1898-1908), which was not a Regency at all in the strict sense of the word but an usurpation of the Imperial prerogative during the lifetime of the sovereign, that, assured of the strength of her position, she gave full rein to her love of power and, with something of the contempt which springs from long familiarity, took unto herself all the outward and visible signs of Imperial authority, holding audience daily in the Great Hall of the Palace, seated on the Dragon Throne, with the puppet Emperor relegated to a position of inferiority, recognised and acclaimed as the Old Buddha, the sole and undisputed ruler of the Empire.

At the outset of her career, she appears to have realised that the idea of female rulers had never been popular with the Chinese people; that even the Empress Wu of the eighth century, the greatest woman in Chinese history, was regarded as a usurper. She was aware that the Empress Lü (whose character, as described by historians, was not unlike her own), to whom was due the consolidation of power that marked the rise of the Han Dynasty, enjoys but scant respect from posterity. On the other hand, she knew — for the study of history was her pastime — that the Empresses Dowagers of the past had often wielded supreme power in the State, principles and precedents notwithstanding, and their example she determined to follow. Upon the taking off of the three chief conspirators, the Censors and Ministers urged her to deal in similar drastic fashion with their aiders and abettors, and Prince Kung was anxious, if not for revenge, at least for precautions being taken against those who had had the ear of the late Emperor during the last months of his reign. But Yehonala showed statesmanlike forbearance: early in life she realised that a few victims are better than many, and that lives spared often mean whole families of friends. After cashiering Prince Yi's remaining colleagues of the Grand Council, she dealt leniently with other offenders. When, for instance, Ch'en Tu-en, President of the Board of Civil Appointments, was impeached on the ground that it was he who had first persuaded the Emperor to flee to Jehol against her advice, and that, after the Emperor's death, he alone of all the high officials at the capital had been summoned to Jehol by the usurping Regents, she contented herself with removing him from office, though his guilt was clearly proved. Another official, a Minister of the Household, who had endeavoured to further the aims of the conspirators, by dissuading Hsien-Feng from returning to Peking in the spring of 1861, on the plea that an insurrection was impending, was also cashiered. But there was nothing in the nature of a general proscription, in spite of the pecuniary and other advantages which usually commend retaliation to the party in power at Peking. In an able Decree, Tzŭ Hsi let it be understood that she wished to punish a few only, and those chiefly *pour encourager les autres*. It was always a characteristic of hers that, when her ends were safely secured, she adopted a policy of watchful leniency: *moderata durant*. In this instance she was fully aware of the fact that Tsai Yüan and his colleagues would never have had the opportunities, nor the courage, to conspire for the Regency had they not been assured of the sympathy and support of many of the higher officials, but she preferred to let the iron hand rest in its velvet glove unless openly thwarted. She would have no proscriptions, no wreaking of private grudges and revenges. It was this characteristic of hers that, as will be seen in another place, obtained for her, amongst the people of Peking in particular, a reputation for almost quixotic gentleness, a reputation which we find expressed in frequent references to the "Benign Countenance," or "Benevolent Mother," and which undoubtedly represented certain genuine impulses in her complex nature. So, having crushed the conspiracy, she contented herself with exhorting all concerned to "attend henceforth strictly to their duty, avoiding those sycophantic and evil tendencies which had brought Chen Tu-en and Huang Tsung-han to their disgrace." In another Decree she emphasised the principle that sins of omission are not much less grave than overt acts, roundly censuring the Princes and Ministers of her Government for having failed to denounce the conspirators at once, and charging them with cowardice. It was fear and nothing else, she said, that had prevented them from revealing the truth; and then, with one of those *naïve* touches which makes Chinese Edicts a perpetual feast, she added that, should there be any further plots of usurpers, she would expect to be informed of their proceedings without delay. Above all, she bade the Imperial Clan take warning by the fate of the three conspirators, and intimated that any further attempts of this kind would be far more severely dealt with.

One of the first steps of the Regency was to determine the title of the new reign. The usurping Princes had selected the characters "Chi-Hsiang," meaning "well-omened happiness," but to Yehonala's scholarly taste and fine sense of fitness, the title seemed ill-chosen and redundant, and as she wished to obliterate all memory of the usurpers' *régime*, she chose in its place the characters "T'ung-Chih," meaning "all-pervading tranquillity," probably with one eye on the suppression of the rebellion and the other on the chances of peace in the Forbidden City. As far as all good augury for the Emperor himself was concerned, one title was, as events proved, no more likely to be effective than the other.

On the same day as the proclamation of the new reign was made by Edict, the Empresses Dowager issued a Decree explaining, and ostensibly deprecating, the high honour thrust upon them.

"Our assumption of the Regency was utterly contrary to our wishes, but we have complied with the urgent request of our Princes and Ministers, because we realise that it is essential that there should be a higher authority to whom they may refer. So soon as ever the Emperor shall have completed his education, we shall take no further part in the Government, which will then naturally revert to the system prescribed by all dynastic tradition. Our sincere reluctance in assuming the direction of

EXTERIOR OF THE CH'IEN CH'ING PALACE.

affairs must be manifest to all. Our officials are expected loyally to assist us in the arduous task which we have undertaken."

Following upon this, a Decree was issued in the name of the Emperor, which represented the boy as thanking their Majesties the Regents and promising that, so soon as he came of age, he would endeavour, by dutiful ministrations, to prove his gratitude.

For the procedure of Government it was then arranged that the Empresses should daily hold joint audiences in the side Hall of the main Palace. At these, and at all except the great Court ceremonies, the Emperor's great-uncle and four brothers were excused from performing the "kotow," the Emperor's respect for the senior generation being thus indirectly exhibited.

Upon their acceptance of the Regency, honorific titles were conferred upon both Empresses. Each character in these titles represents a grant from the public funds of 100,000 taels per annum (say, at that time, £20,000). Thus the Empress Consort became known by the title of Tzŭ An (Motherly and Restful) while Yehonala became Tzŭ Hsi (Motherly and Auspicious), one being the Empress of the Eastern, and the other of the Western Palace. At various subsequent periods, further honorific characters, in pairs, were added unto them, so that, on her seventieth birthday, Tzŭ Hsi was the proud possessor of sixteen. On that occasion she modestly and virtuously refused the four additional characters with which the Emperor Kuang-Hsü (not unprompted) desired to honour her. Tzŭ An lived to receive ten in all; both ladies received two on their thirtieth birthdays, two on the Emperor Tung-Chih's accession, two just before his death in recognition of their "ministrations" during his attack of small-pox, and two on their fortieth birthdays. Tzŭ Hsi received two more on her fiftieth birthday, two on Kuang-Hsü's marriage, and two on her sixtieth birthday. Tzŭ Hsi's complete official designation at the end of her life was not easy to remember. It ran, "Tzŭ-Hsi-Tuan-yu-K'ang-yi-Chao-yu-Chuang-ch'eng-Shou-kung-Ch'in-hsien-Ch'ung-hsi

Huang Tai-hou," which, being translated, means "The Empress Dowager, motherly, auspicious, orthodox, heaven-blessed, prosperous, all-nourishing, brightly manifest, calm, sedate, perfect, long-lived, respectful, reverend, worshipful, illustrious and exalted."

At the beginning of the Regency it suited Yehonala to conciliate and humour Prince Kung. In conjunction with her colleague, she therefore bestowed upon him the titles of "I-Cheng Wang," or Prince Adviser to the Government, and by special Decree she made the title of "Ch'in Wang," or Prince of the Blood (which had been bestowed upon him by the late Emperor), hereditary in his family for ever.[1] Prince Kung begged to be excused from accepting the former honour, whereupon ensued a solemn parade of refusal on the part of the Empresses, one of whom, as events proved, certainly wanted no adviser. Eventually, after much deprecation, Their Majesties gave way as regards the hereditary title, but on the understanding that the offer would be renewed at a more fitting season. Yehonala who, in her better moments of grateful memory, could scarcely forget the brave part which Prince Kung had played for her at Jehol, made amends by adopting his daughter as a Princess Imperial, granting her the use of the Yellow palanquin. The influence of this Princess over Tzŭ Hsi, especially towards the end, was great, and it was strikingly displayed in 1900 on behalf of Prince Tuan and the Boxer leaders.

Ignorant at the outset of many things in the procedure of Government routine, feeling her way through the labyrinth of party politics and foreign affairs, afraid of her own youth and inexperience, it was but natural that Tzŭ Hsi should have recourse to the ripe wisdom of the late Emperor's brother and be guided by his opinion. But as time went on, as her knowledge of affairs broadened and deepened, her autocratic instincts gradually asserted themselves in an increasing impatience of advice and restraint. As, by the study of history and the light of her own intelligence,

---

1. Hereditary titles in China usually descend in a diminishing scale.

she gained confidence in the handling of State business and men, the guidance which had previously been welcome became distasteful, and eventually assumed the character of interference. Despotic by nature, Tzŭ Hsi was not the woman to tolerate interference in any matter where her own mind was made up, and Prince Kung, on his side, was of a disposition little less proud and independent than her own. When the young Yehonala began to evince a disposition to dispense with his advice, he was therefore not inclined to conceal his displeasure, and relations speedily became strained. As Tzŭ Hsi was at no pains to hide her resentment, he gradually came to adopt a policy of instigating her colleague, the Empress of the East, to a more independent attitude, a line of action which could not fail to produce ill-feeling and friction in the Palace. In the appointment of officials, also, which is the chief object and privilege of power in China, he was in the habit of promoting and protecting his own nominees without reference to Yehonala, by direct communications to the provinces. Eye-witnesses of the events of the period have recorded their impression that his attitude towards both Empresses at the commencement of the Regency was somewhat overbearing; that he was inclined to presume upon the importance of his own position and services, and that on one occasion at audience, he even presumed to inform the Empresses that they owed their position to himself, a remark which Tzŭ Hsi was not likely to forget or forgive.

At the audiences of the Grand Council, it was the custom for the two Empresses to sit on a raised dais, each on her separate Throne, immediately in front of which was suspended a yellow silk curtain; they were therefore invisible to the Councillors, who were received separately and in the order of their seniority, Prince Kung coming first in his capacity as "adviser to the Government." Beside their Majesties on the dais stood their attendant eunuchs; they were in the habit of peeping through the folds of the curtain, keeping a careful eye upon the demeanour of the officials in audience, with a view to noting any signs of disrespect or breach of etiquette. Strictly speaking, no official, however high his rank, might enter the Throne room unless summoned by the chief eunuch in attendance, but Prince Kung considered himself superior to such rules, and would enter unannounced. Other breaches of etiquette he committed which, as Her Majesty's knowledge of affairs increased, were carefully noted against him; for instance, he would raise his voice when replying to their Majesties' instructions (which were always given by Tzŭ Hsi), and on one occasion, he even ventured to ask that Tzŭ Hsi should repeat something she had just said, and which he pretended not to have understood. His attitude, in short (say the chroniclers), implied an assumption of equality which the proud spirit of the young Empress would not brook. Living outside the Palace as he did, having free intercourse with Chinese and foreign officials on all sides, he was naturally in a position to intrigue against her, did he so desire. Tzŭ Hsi, on the other hand, was likely to imagine and exaggerate intrigues, since nearly all her information came from the eunuchs and would therefore naturally assume alarming proportions. There is little doubt that she gradually came to believe in the possibility of Prince Kung working against her authority, and she therefore set herself to prove to him that his position and prerogatives depended entirely upon her good will.

She continued watching her opportunity and patiently biding her time until the occasion presented itself in the fourth year of the Regency (April, 1865). In a moment of absent-mindedness or bravado, Prince Kung ventured to rise from his knees during an audience, thus violating a fundamental rule of etiquette originally instituted to guard the Sovereign against any sudden attack. The eunuchs promptly informed their Majesties, whereupon Tzŭ Hsi called loudly for help, exclaiming that the Prince was plotting some evil treachery against the persons of the Regents. The Guards rushed in, and Prince Kung was ordered to leave the presence at once. His departure was speedily followed by the issue of an Imperial Decree, stating that he had endeavoured to usurp the authority of the Throne and persistently overrated his own importance to the State. He was accordingly dismissed from his position as adviser to the Government, relieved of his duties on the Grand Council and other high offices in the Palace; even his appointment as head of the Foreign Office, or Tsungli Yamên, was cancelled. "He had shown himself unworthy of their Majesties' confidence," said the Edict, "and had displayed gross nepotism in the appointment of high officials: his rebellious and usurping tendencies must be sternly checked."

A month later, however, Tzŭ Hsi, realising that her own position was not unassailable, and that her treatment of this powerful Prince had created much unfavourable comment at Court and in the provinces, saved her face and the situation simultaneously, by issuing a Decree in the name of herself and her colleague, which she described as a Decree of explanation. In this document she took no small credit to herself for strength of character and virtue in dealing severely with her near kinsmen in the interests of the State, and pointed to the fact that any undue encouragement of the Imperial clansmen, when inclined to take a line of their own, was liable, as history had repeatedly proved, to involve the country in destructive dissension. Her real object in inflicting punishment on the Prince for treating the Throne with disrespect was to save him from himself and from the imminent peril of his own folly. But now that several Memorials had been sent in by Censors and others, requesting that his errors be pardoned, the Throne could have no possible objection to showing clemency and, the position having been made clear, Prince Kung was restored to the position of Chamberlain, and to the direction of the Foreign Office. The Prince, in fact, needed a lesson in politeness and, having got it, Her Majesty was prepared to let bygones be bygones, it being clearly understood that, for the future, he should display increased energy and loyalty as a mark of his sincere gratitude to their Majesties.

A week later, Tzŭ Hsi, in order to drive the lesson home, issued the following Decree in the name of the Empresses Regent.

"We granted an audience this morning to Prince Kung in order to permit him to return thanks for his re-appointment. He prostrated himself humbly and wept bitterly, in token of his boundless self-abasement. We naturally took occasion to address to him some further words of warning and advice, and the Prince seemed genuinely grieved at his errors and full of remorse for misconduct which he freely acknowledged. Sincere feeling of this kind could not fail to elicit our compassion.

"It is now some years since we first assumed the burden of the Regency and appointed Prince Kung to be our chief adviser in the Government; in this position his responsibility has been as great as the favour which we have bestowed upon him. The position which he has occupied in special relation to the Throne, is unparalleled; therefore we expected much from him and, when he erred, the punishment which we were compelled to inflict upon him was necessarily severe. He has now repented him of the evil and acknowledged his sins. For our part we had no prejudice in this matter, and were animated only by strict impartiality; it was inconceivable that we should desire to treat harshly a Councillor of such tried ability, or to deprive ourselves of the valuable assistance of the Prince. We therefore now restore him to the Grand Council, but in order that his authority may be reduced, we do not propose to reinstate him in his position as 'adviser to the Government.' Prince Kung, see to it now that you forget not the shame and remorse which have overtaken you! Strive to requite our kindness and display greater self-control in the performance of your duties! Justify our high confidence in you by ridding your mind of all unjust suspicions and fears."

In the autumn of this year, 1865, took place the burial of the late Emperor, Hsien-Feng, the preparation of whose tomb had been proceeding for just four years. With him was buried his consort Sakota, who had died in 1850, a month before her husband's accession to the Throne; her remains had been awaiting burial at a village temple, seven miles west of the capital, for fifteen years. As usual, the funeral ceremonies and preparation of the tombs involved vast expenditure, and there had been considerable difficulty in finding the necessary funds, for the southern provinces, which, under ordinary circumstances would have made the largest contributions, were still suffering severely from the ravages of the Taiping rebellion. The Emperor's mausoleum had cost nominally ten million taels, of which amount, of course, a very large proportion had been diverted for the benefit of the officials of the Household and others.

The young Emperor, and the Empresses Regent proceeded, as in duty bound, to the Eastern Tombs to take their part in the solemn burial ceremonies. Prince Kung was in attendance; to him had fallen the chief part in the preparation of the tomb and in the provision of the funds, and Her Majesty had no cause to complain of any scamping of his duties. The body of the Emperor, in an Imperial coffin of catalpa wood, richly lacquered and inscribed with Buddhist sutras, was borne within the huge domed grave chamber, and there deposited in the presence of their Majesties upon its "jewelled bedstead," the pedestal of precious metals prepared to receive it. In the place of the concubines and eunuchs, who in prehistoric days used to be buried alive with the deceased monarch, wooden and paper figures of life size were placed beside the coffin, reverently kneeling to serve their lord in the halls of Hades. The huge candles were lighted, prayers were recited, and a great wealth of valuable ornaments arranged within the grave chamber; gold and jade sceptres, and a necklace of pearls were placed in the coffin. And when all was duly done, the great door of the chamber was slowly lowered and sealed in its place.

Next day the Empresses Dowager issued a Decree in which Prince Kung's meritorious acts are graciously recognised, and their Majesties' thanks accorded to him for the satisfactory fulfilment of the funeral ceremonies.

"Prince Kung has for the last five years been preparing the funeral arrangements for his late Majesty and has shown a due sense of decorum and diligence. To-day, both the late Emperor and his senior consort have been conveyed to their last resting place, and the great burden of our grief has been to some extent mitigated by our satisfaction in contemplating the grandeur of their tombs, and the solemn ceremonies of their burial. No doubt but that the spirit of His Majesty in Heaven has also been comforted thereby. We now feel bound to act in accordance with the fraternal affection which always animated the deceased Emperor towards Prince Kung, and to bestow upon him high honours. But the Prince has repeatedly declined to accept any further dignities, lest perchance he should again be tempted to arrogance. His modesty meets with our approval, and we therefore merely refer his name to the Imperial Clan Court, for the selection of a reward. But we place on record the fact that as Grand Councillor he has been of great service to us, and has of late displayed notable circumspection and self-restraint in all matters.

"The Decree which we issued last Spring was caused by the Prince's want of attention to small details of etiquette, and if we were obliged to punish him severely, our motives have been clearly explained. No doubt everyone in the Empire is well aware of the facts, but as posterity may possibly fail to realise all the circumstances, and as unjust blame might fall upon the memory of Prince Kung, if that Decree were allowed to remain inscribed amongst the Imperial Archives, thus suggesting a flaw in the white jade of his good name, we now command that the Decree in which we announced Prince Kung's dismissal from office be expunged from the annals of our reign. Thus is our affection displayed towards a deserving servant, and his good name preserved untarnished to all time."

The Empress Dowager was essentially a woman of moods, and these Imperial Decrees simply reflect the fact, at the beginning of her autocratic rule, as they did until its close. Four years later Prince Kung was to incur her deep and permanent dislike by conspiring with her colleague to deprive her of her favourite, the chief eunuch An Te-hai.

V

TSENG KUO-FAN AND THE
TAIPING REBELLION (1864)

THE first years of Yehonala's Co-Regency, during which she was steadily acquiring the arts and crafts of Government, and gradually relegating her easy-going colleague to the background, were joyfully associated in the minds of her subjects with the decline and final collapse of the great rebellion which had devastated the best part of the Empire since 1850. Chinese historians (a body of writers who depend largely on each others' writings for material) agree in attributing the final deliverance from this scourge to the ability and courage of the famous Viceroy Tseng Kuo-fan,[1] and for once their praises are well-deserved, for this military scholar like his fellow provincial and colleague, Tso Tsung-t'ang,[2] was a man of the heroic breed of philosophers which, with all its faults, the Confucian system has always produced, and continues to produce, to the great benefit of the Chinese people, a man whose name ranks high among China's worthies, a household word for

---

1. He was the father of that Marquis Tseng who, as Minister to England (1878), lived to be credited by the British press with literary abilities which he did not possess and liberal opinions which he did not share. His grandsons, educated partly in England, have lately been distinguished for that quality of patriotic Conservatism which prides itself on having no intercourse with foreigners.
2. A short biographical note on Tso Tsung-t'ang, the hero of the Mahomedan rebellion who gained distinction under Tseng against the Taipings, is given in the appendix.

honesty and intelligent patriotism.

It was one of the secrets of Tzŭ Hsi's success as a ruler that she recognised and appreciated merit whenever she found it, and especially the merit of a military commander: it was only when she allowed her superstitious tendencies to outweigh her judgment that she failed. For the character and talents of Tseng Kuo-fan she had the highest respect, due, no doubt, in the first instance to the effect of his military despatches, stirring tales of camp and siege, on her imaginative mind, but later to personal acquaintance with his sterling qualities. With the single exception of Jung Lu, probably no high official ever stood so high in her affectionate esteem, and Jung Lu was a Manchu kinsman, while Tseng came from one of the proverbially independent gentry families of Hunan. From a Chinese narrative of the Taiping rebellion, we are able to obtain a very clear impression, not only of Tseng's character and of his conception of patriotism but also of the remarkable and undisputed position of autocratic power already at that time enjoyed by the youthful Empress Tzŭ Hsi. Before turning to this narrative, however, certain points in connection with the final defeat of the Taipings deserve to be noted, events with which Englishmen were prominently identified, but which, as recorded by British eye-witnesses, confirm our doubts as to the historical value of Imperial Edicts and Chinese official despatches.

The Emperor Hsien-Feng had died in exile and defeat at Jehol in August 1861. The Summer Palace had been destroyed by the British and French forces, peace had been restored, and the Co-Regency of the Empresses Dowager had commenced. One of the first acts of Prince Kung, in his capacity as "Adviser to the Government" after the conclusion of the Peace Convention of October 1860, was to invoke the aid of his country's conquering invaders against the Chinese rebels, whose strong position on the Yangtsze was causing the Court ever increasing anxiety. It is an illuminating example of Chinese methods of government, not without parallels and value to-day, that even while the British

and French forces were concentrating at Shanghai for their invasion of north China, high Chinese officials in the Yangtsze provinces had not hesitated to invoke their aid against the rebels, and
had been chagrined at a refusal which appeared to them unwise
since it ignored the interests of British trade at its most important centre. The history of the "Ever-Victorious Army" need not
be referred to here. It kept the rebels in check in the province
of Kiangsu throughout the year 1862, and in February 1863 the
British Government sanctioned the lending of "Chinese Gordon"
to take command of that force, which was speedily to turn the
tide of war in favour of the Imperialists and effectively to pave
the way for Tseng Kuo-fan's final restoration of law and order.
Soochow, the provincial capital, was regained in December 1863,
and in the following July the fall of the rebel capital (Nanking)
and the death of the rebel "King" practically ended the insurrection. A considerable number of Europeans, including a French
Admiral, had given their lives to win back China for the Manchu
Dynasty, although at the outset public opinion was in favour of
strict neutrality and there were many, even then, who thought
China would be well rid of her degenerate rulers: nevertheless,
the triumphant Edict in which is recorded Tseng Kuo-fan's capture of Nanking contains no word of reference to Gordon and
the invaluable help which he rendered, and, as will be seen,
Tseng's only reference to the British Commander is to accuse him
of having recommended the inhuman treatment of a defenceless
prisoner. In accordance with the invariable classical tradition, he
ascribes his success to "the consummate virtue and wisdom" of
the late Emperor Hsien-Feng; the tradition represents, in conventional phraseology, the Oriental conception of the divine right of
kings, and their infallibility (a conception which we find reproduced almost verbatim in the modern Japanese Generals' modest reports of their greatest victories), and it is incompatible in
China with any reference to the existence, much less the services,
of foreign barbarians. The fact is worth noting, for Tseng was an
exceptionally intelligent and courageous man who could, sooner

than most men, have ventured on a new departure; and he knew full well that this same Gordon, who had steadily driven the rebels before him, cane in hand for over a year, had come hot-foot to the task from the sacking of the Manchu sovereigns' Summer Palace!

But Yehonala's joy at the fall of Nanking was unfeignedly great, and the Decree in which, in the name of the boy Emperor, she records the event and rewards the victors, is a brilliant example of her literary style. We take the following extracts from this document, as of permanent interest and throwing light on the character of Tzŭ Hsi.

Decree on the Fall of Nanking.

"An express courier from Tseng Kuo-fan, travelling two hundred miles a day, has just arrived, bearing the red banner of decisive victory and a Memorial describing the capture of Nanking, the suicide by burning of the rebel Prince, the complete destruction of the Taiping host and the capture of two of their leading commanders. Perusal of this Memorial fills us with the deepest joy and gratitude, which all our people will share. The leader of the long haired rebels[1] Hung Hsiu-ch'uan first raised his standard of revolt in the thirtieth year of Tao-Kuang (1850); from Kuangsi the movement spread gradually through Hunan, Hupei and the Yangtsze provinces to Chihli itself and Shantung, until scarcely a spot in the whole Empire but bore the footprints of the rebel armies. In the third year of Hsien-Feng (1853) they took Nanking and there established the seat of their Government. Uncounted thousands of our subjects have fallen victims to their savage crimes. The cup of their guilt has indeed overflowed. Gods and men alike hold them in abhorrence.

"Our Imperial father, in the majesty of his wrath, and in all

---

1. So called because they declined to plait the queue, as a sign that they rejected Manchu rule.

reverence to Heaven, began a punitive campaign against them and named Kuan Wen, the Viceroy of Wu-Ch'ang, to be his Imperial Commissioner for the war. This officer successfully cleared the Hupei region of rebels and then marched eastwards towards Kiangsu in order to extirpate them there also. Later, Tseng Kuo-fan was made Viceroy of Nanking and Imperial Commissioner for the campaign in Kiangsu and Anhui, and he achieved great results, proportionate to his high responsibility.

"On the death of our late father (1861), half the cities of Kiangsu and Chekiang had been retaken by our forces, and it was a source of grief to His Majesty, recorded in his valedictory Decree, that he could not have lived to see the end of the rebellion. Upon our succeeding to the goodly heritage of the Throne, obeying our late father's commands and listening to the sage counsel of the Empresses Regent, we promoted Tseng Kuo-fan to be an Assistant Grand Secretary and gave him full powers as Commander-in-Chief over the four provinces of Kiangsu, Kiangsi, Anhui and Chekiang, so as to secure an undivided plan of campaign.

"Ever since his appointment he has adopted a policy of masterful strategy in combination with the forces of P'eng Yu-lin and Tseng Kuo-ch'uan,[1] attacking the rebels both by land and by water. Over a hundred cities have been recaptured and over a hundred thousand rebels, who were advancing to the relief of Nanking, have been slain and 'their left ears cut off.'[2] Nanking was thus completely invested and its relief became impossible. Early this month the outer defences of the city were taken and some thirty thousand rebels put to the sword, but their so-called King and his desperate followers were still at bay in the inner city, fighting fiercely to the end.

"Tseng Kuo-fan now reports that after the capture by our troops of the outer city ramparts, the rebels greatly strengthened the inner defences. Our men succeeded in taking the 'Dragon's Elbow' hill and a general bombardment followed. Mining and

---

1. His younger brother, subsequently made an earl and Viceroy of Nanking for many years.
2. This is merely figurative, referring to an ancient and obsolete custom.

counter-mining went on furiously in the vicinity of the chief forts amidst desperate encounters. At dawn on the 16th all our forces were collected, and by springing a mine under the wall of the city a breach was made some sixty yards in width. Our men rushed the gap, burst into the city and were advancing on all sides when the rebels from the wall exploded a magazine, and many of our men were slain. A panic was only averted by our leaders cutting down a number of those who were attempting to fly.

[*Here follows a detailed description of the fighting, which we omit.*]

"By 1 A.M. flames were bursting from the Palace of the 'Heavenly King' and the residences of other rebel leaders. One of them rushed from the main Palace Hall with one thousand followers and sought refuge in some houses near the south gate of the city. After some seven hundred of his men had been slain, he was captured, and on his person were found two Imperial seals of jade and one official seal of gold. At 3 A.M. about a thousand of the rebels, disguised in our uniforms, escaped through the tunnel at the Gate of Heavenly Peace but our cavalry pursued them and captured or destroyed the whole force at Hu-Shu chen, where their leader, the 'Glorious Prince,' was taken alive. On being examined, this leader whose name was Li Wan-ts'ai, admitted that seven of the so-called Princes of the Taipings had been slain by our forces, while seeking to escape under cover of darkness, on the night of our entrance into the city.

"According to the evidence of other rebels, the arch-leader Hung Hsiu-ch'uan, had committed suicide by taking poison a month before. He had been buried in the courtyard of his Palace, and his son, the so-called Boy-Prince, had succeeded to the usurped title. He also had committed suicide by burning when the city fell. Another of their chiefs, one Li Hsiu-cheng, had been wounded and was in hiding at a spot near by, where our men found him together with the elder brother of the 'Heavenly King.' During these three days, over a hundred thousand rebels were killed, of whom some three thousand were their so-called Princes, generals, and high officers.

"This glorious victory is entirely due to the bountiful protection of Heaven, to the ever-present help of our Ancestors, and to the foresight and wisdom of the Empresses Regent, who, by employing and promoting efficient leaders for their armies, have thus secured co-operation of all our forces and the accomplishment of this great achievement, whereby the soul of our late father in Heaven must be comforted, and the desire of all people fulfilled. For ourselves we feel utterly unworthy of this crowning triumph, and we are truly distressed at the thought that our late father could not live to witness this consummation of his unfinished plans. This rebellion has now lasted fifteen years, during twelve of which Nanking has been held by the rebels. They have devastated about a dozen provinces, and have captured some hundreds of cities. Their final defeat we owe to our Generals, 'who have been combed by the wind and bathed in the rain,' and who have undergone every conceivable hardship in bringing about the destruction of these unspeakable traitors. We are therefore bound to recognise their exceptional services by the bestowal of exceptional rewards. Tseng Kuo-fan first contributed to this glorious end by raising a force of militia in Hunan and a fleet of war-vessels with which he won great victories, saving his province from complete ruin. He re-captured Wu-Ch'ang, cleared the whole province of Kiangsi, and, advancing eastwards, recovered city after city. That glorious success has finally crowned our efforts is due chiefly to his masterly strategy and courage, to his employment of able subordinates and to his remarkable powers of organisation. We now confer upon him the title of Senior Guardian of the Throne, a marquisate of the first rank, hereditary in perpetuity, and the decoration of the double-eyed peacock's feather.

[Here follows a long list of officers rewarded, beginning with Tseng Kuo-fan's brother, above mentioned, who was given an earldom.]

"As soon as the troops have found the body of the usurper known as the 'Heavenly King,' Hung Hsiu-ch'uan, let it be dismembered forthwith and let the head be sent for exhibition in every province that has been ravaged by his rebellion, in order that the public indignation may be appeased. As to the two captured leaders, let them be sent in cages to Peking, in order that they may be examined and then punished with death by the lingering process."

A further Decree announced that the Emperor would go in person to offer thanksgiving and sacrifice at all Imperial Temples and shrines, and make sacrifice to deities of the chief mountains and rivers of the Empire.

A Chinese diarist of the rebellion, referring to the manner in which the 'Heavenly King' met his death, says:—

"From the moment that the Imperialists captured Ch'u-yung, the rebels, pent up in Nanking like wild beasts in a cage, were in a hopeless plight. From the commencement of the 4th Moon, the city was completely invested, and without hope of relief. They were living on reduced rations of one meagre meal a day. The 'Heavenly King' caused roots and leaves to be kneaded and rolled into pellets which he had served out to his immediate followers, the rebel chiefs, saying, 'This is manna from Heaven; for a long time we in the Palace have eaten nothing else.' He gave orders that every household should collect ten loads of this stuff for storage in the Palace granaries; some of the more ignorant people obeyed the order, but most of the rebels ignored it.

"The rebel Li Hsiu-ch'eng, known as the 'Patriotic Prince,' escaped from Ch'u-yung and made his way to Nanking. Upon entering the city, he had drums beaten and bells rung as a signal for the 'Heavenly King' and his followers to ascend to the Throne Chamber for the discussion of the perilous situation. Hung Hsiu-ch'uan came, and boastfully ascending the Throne, spake as follows 'The Most High has issued to me his sacred Decree. God the Father, and my Divine elder brother (Christ) have commanded me to descend unto this world of flesh and to become the one true lord of all nations and kindreds upon earth. What cause have I then for fear? Remain with me, or leave me, as you choose: my inheritance of this Empire, which is even as an iron girdle of defence, will be protected by others if you decline to protect it. I have at my command an angelic host of a million strong: how then could a hundred thousand or so of these unholy Imperialists enter the city'? When Li Hsiu-ch'eng heard this non-sensical boasting, he burst into tears and left the hall.

"But before the middle of the 5th Moon, Hung Hsiu-ch'uan had come to realise that the city was doomed, and on the 27th day, having abandoned all hope, he procured a deadly poison which he mixed with his wine. Then raising the cup on high, he cried, 'It is not that God the Father has deceived me, but it is I who have disobeyed God the Father.' After repeating this several times he drank the poison. By midnight the measure of his iniquity was full, and, writhing in agony, he died. Even his last words showed no true repentance, although they amounted to an admission of guilt. When his followers learned what had happened, they wrapped his body in a coverlet of yellow silk, embroidered with dragons and then, following the rule of their religion, buried it, uncoffined, in a corner of the Palace ground. They then placed on the Throne the rebel's son, the so-called Boy-Emperor, but they tried to keep secret the news of the 'Heavenly King's' death. It eventually leaked out, however, and the courage of the besieged dropped to the last depths of despair."

In his Memorial to the Throne, Tseng Kuo-fan described the exhumation of the rebel Emperor's body.

"Even the feet of the corpse were wrapped in dragon embroideries," he says; "he had a bald head and a beard streaked with grey. After examining the body I beheaded it and then burnt it on a large bonfire. One of the concubines in the usurper's palace, a woman named Huang, who had herself prepared the body for burial, told me that the 'Heavenly King' seldom showed himself to his Court, so that they were able to keep his death a secret for sixteen days. I am sending his bogus seals to Peking that they may be deposited in the Imperial Archives Department."

The Memorial then proceeds: —

"The prisoners Li Hsiu-ch'eng, known as the 'Patriotic Prince,' was minutely cross-examined by myself, and his statement, which he wrote out with his own hand, extends to some thirty thousand words. He narrated in detail the first causes of the rebellion and described the present position of the rebels still at large in Shensi and elsewhere. He strongly advised that we should not be too hard on the defeated rebels from Kuangtung and Kuangsi, on the ground that severity would only lead to an increase of the anti-dynastic feeling in those provinces. It seems to me that there is much sense in his advice.

"All my staff were most anxious that Li Hsiu-ch'eng should be sent to Peking in a cage, and even the foreigner Gordon, when he called to congratulate me, strongly urged this course. But it seems to me that the high prestige of our Sacred Dynasty needs no such sending of petty rebels to Peking as trophies or prisoners of war. The 'Heavenly King's' head is now being sent round those provinces which were laid waste by the rebellion, and this should suffice. Besides, I feel that there would be some risk of Li starving himself to death on the journey, or that a rescue might even be attempted, for this Li was extraordinarily popular with the common people. After the fall of the city, some peasants gave him shelter, and when he was finally captured the people of the village where he was taken decoyed and slew one of our men in revenge. After he had been put in his cage here, another rebel leader, the so-called 'Pine Prince,' was brought into camp. As soon as he caught sight of Li, he went down on his knees and saluted him most respectfully, I therefore decided to behead him and the sentence was duly carried out on the 6th instant.

"The two elder brothers of the 'Heavenly King' were men of a cruel and savage nature, who committed many foul and impious crimes. Li detested them both heartily. When captured, they were in a dazed state, and could only mumble 'God the Father, God the Father.' As I could get no information from them, and as they were sick unto death, I had them both beheaded, two days before the execution of Li Hsiu-ch'eng. I am now in receipt of your Majesties' Decree, approving my action and ordering me to forward the heads of the three rebel chiefs to the various provinces in order that public indignation may be appeased. I have duly suspended the heads from long poles, and the sight of them has given great and general satisfaction.

"And now, victory being ours, I am led to the reflection that this our Dynasty surpasses all its predecessors in martial glory and has suppressed several rebellions by achievements which shed lustre on our history. The Ssǔ-ch'uan and Hupei rebellion of half a century ago was, however, limited to four provinces, and only some twenty cities were held by the rebels. The insurrection of Wu San-kuei, in the reign of K'ang-Hsi, overran twelve provinces, and the rebels captured some three hundred cities and towns. But this Taiping rebellion has been on a scale vaster than any before, and has produced some great leaders in its armies. Here in Nanking not a single rebel surrendered. Many burned themselves alive rather than be taken. Such things are unparalleled in history, and we feel that the final happy issue is due to the consummate virtue and wisdom of his late Majesty, which alone made victory possible. By dint of careful economy in the Palace, he was able to set aside large sums for the equipment of adequate forces. Most careful in his choice of leaders, he was lavish of rewards; all wise himself, yet was he ever ready to listen to the advice of his generals. Your Majesties the Empresses and the Emperor have faithfully carried out and even amplified these principles, and thus you have succeeded in wiping out these usurpers and have shed great glory on your reign. We, who so unworthily hold your high command, grieve greatly that His Majesty did not live to see his work crowned with triumph."

For four years after the collapse of the rebellion, Tseng Kuo-fan remained at Nanking as Viceroy. (The Hunanese still regard that post as belonging by prescriptive right to a Hunanese official.) His only absence was during a brief expedition against the Mahomedan rebels in Shantung. In September 1868 he was appointed Viceroy of Chihli, and left for Peking at the end of the year, receiving a remarkable ovation from the people of Nanking. In Peking he was received with great honours, and in his capacity of Grand Secretary had a meeting with the Council on the morning after his arrival, followed immediately by an Audience, to which he was summoned and conducted by one of the Princes. The young Emperor was sitting on a Throne facing west, and the Empresses Regent were behind him, screened from view by the yellow curtain, Tzŭ An to the left and Tzŭ Hsi to the right of the Throne. In the Chinese narrative of the rebellion to which we have already referred, the writer professes to report this audience, and several that followed, practically verbatim, and as it affords interesting information as to the manner and methods of Tzŭ Hsi on these occasions, the following extracts are worthy of reproduction. It is to be observed that the writer, like all his contemporaries, assumes *ab initio* that the Empress Tzŭ An, though senior, is a negligible quantity and that the whole interest of the occasion lies between Tzŭ Hsi and the official in audience.

Upon entering the Throne room, Tseng fell upon his knees, as in duty bound, and in that position advanced a few feet, saying "Your servant Tseng Kuo-fan respectfully enquires after Your Majesties' health." Then removing his hat and performing the kowtow, he humbly returned thanks for Imperial favours bestowed upon him. These preliminaries completed, he rose and advanced a few steps to kneel on the cushion prepared for him below the dais. The following dialogue then took place: —

Her Majesty Tzŭ Hsi. When you left Nanking, was all your official work completed?

Tseng. Yes, quite completed.

Tzŭ Hsi. Have the irregular troops and braves all been disbanded?

Tseng. Yes, all.

Tzŭ Hsi. How many in all?

Tseng. I have disbanded over twenty thousand irregulars and
have enrolled thirty thousand regulars.

Tzŭ Hsi. From which province do the majority of these men
hail?

Tseng. A few of the troops come from Hunan, but the great majority are Anhui men.

Tzŭ Hsi. Was the disbandment effected quite quietly?

Tseng. Yes, quite quietly.

Then follow numerous questions regarding Tseng's previous
career, his family, &c. As soon as the questions cease, after waiting
a few minutes, the audience is at an end, and Tseng kowtows and
retires. On each occasion, and they were many, the Empress had
evidently worked up her questions carefully from study of reports and despatches, and invariably put them in the short sharp
form indicated; always peremptory, *de haut en bas* and Cæsarian,
this woman "behind the screen," addressing the veteran who had
saved China for her rule.

After describing Tseng's important position at the Court
banquet given to high officials, Manchu and Chinese, on the the
16th day of the 1st Moon (at which six plays were performed
and the dishes "passed all reckoning"), the narrative gives an
account of his farewell audience, at which Her Majesty closely
cross-examined him as to his plans for the reorganisation of the
naval and military forces of Chihli. He held the post of Chihli
Viceroy for a little over a year. The viceregal residence in those
days was at Pao-ting fu, so that when the Tientsin massacre
occurred (1870) he was not directly to blame, though officially
responsible. In June of that year the Nanking Viceroy was assassinated, and Tseng was ordered to resume duty at that post,

his place in Chihli being taken by Li Hung-chang, who held it for twenty-four years. Tseng, whose health was failing, endeavoured to have his appointment to Nanking cancelled, but Tzŭ Hsi would take no excuses. She issued a Decree in which she laid stress on the arduous nature of the work to be done at the southern capital and Tseng's special fitness for the post which he had so ably administered in the past. "Even if his eyesight troubles him," she said, "he can still exercise a general supervision."

Before leaving for the south, Tseng celebrated his sixtieth birthday, receiving many marks of Imperial favour and rich gifts. The Empress sent him a poem of congratulation in her own handwriting, and a tablet bearing the inscription "My lofty pillar and rock of defence," together with an image of Buddha, a sandal wood sceptre inlaid with jade, a dragon robe, ten rolls of "auspicious" silk, and ten of crape. At his farewell audience the following interesting conversation took place:—

Tzŭ Hsi. When did you leave Tientsin?

Tseng. On the 23rd.

Tzŭ Hsi. Have the ringleaders in the massacre of foreigners been executed yet?

Tseng. Not yet. The Consul told me that the Russian Minister was coming to Tientsin and that the French Minister was sending a deputy to witness the executions, so that the decapitations could not be summarily carried out.

Tzŭ Hsi. What date has Li Hung-chang fixed for the executions?

Tseng. On the day of my departure, he sent me word that he expected to dispose of them yesterday.

Tzŭ Hsi. Have the Tientsin populace calmed down?

Tseng. Yes, things are now quite settled and orderly.

Tzŭ Hsi. What made the Prefect and Magistrate run away to Shun-Te after the massacre?

Tseng. When first removed from their posts, they knew not what sentence would be decreed against them, so they boldly and shamelessly ran away from the city.

Tzŭ Hsi. Have you quite lost the sight of your right eye?

Tseng. Yes, it is quite blind; but I can still see with the left.

Tzŭ Hsi. Have you entirely recovered from your other maladies?

Tseng. Yes, I think I can say that I have.

Tzŭ Hsi. You appear to kneel, and to rise from that posture quite briskly and freely, as if your physique were still pretty good?

Tseng. No; it is not what it used to be.

Tzŭ Hsi. That was a strange thing, the assassination of Ma Hsin-yi (the late Viceroy of Nanking), was it not?

Tseng. Extraordinary.

Tzŭ Hsi He was a first-rate administrator.

Tseng. Yes, he took great pains, and was honest and impartial.

Tzŭ Hsi. How many regular troops have you raised in Chihli?

Tseng. Three thousand. The former Viceroy had four thousand men trained under the old system. I had intended to raise three thousand more, making a total force of ten thousand. I have arranged with Li Hung-chang to carry out this programme.

Tzŭ Hsi. It is of vital importance that we should have a force of properly trained troops in the south. You must see to this.

Tseng. Yes. At present peace prevails, but we must be prepared for all possible emergencies. I propose to build forts at several places on the Yangtsze.

Tzŭ Hsi. It would be a fine thing if we could secure ourselves properly against invasion. These missionary complications are perpetually creating trouble for us.

Tseng. That is true. Of late the missionaries have created trouble everywhere. The native converts are given to oppressing those who will not embrace Christianity (literally "*eat the religion*") and the missionaries always screen the converts, while the Consuls protect the missionaries. Next year, when the time comes for revising the French Treaty, we must take particular pains to reconsider carefully the whole question of religious propaganda.

In November Tseng had his farewell audience, and Tzŭ Hsi never saw him again. A month later he took over the seals of office at his old post, one of his first acts being to try the assassin of his predecessor, who was condemned to death by the slicing process. In the following summer he went for a cruise of inspection and visited various places of interest, noting with satisfaction the complete restoration of law and order in the districts which had been for so long the scene of the Taipings' devastations. On one occasion, seeing the gaily decked "flower-boats" and listening to the sounds of their revelries, he joyfully exclaimed: "I am glad to have lived to see my province as it was before the rebellion." In December he moved into the Viceregal residence which he had known as the Palace of the Taiping "Heavenly King." But he was not long to administer that high office, for in the early part of 1872 he had a first stroke of paralysis. A few days later, going in his chair to meet a high official arriving from Peking, and reciting, as was his wont, favourite passages from the classics, he suddenly made a sign to his attendants, but speech failed him and he could only mumble. In his diary that same evening, he wrote:— "This illness of mine prevents me from attending to my work. In the 26th and 27th years of Tao-Kuang (1846-7) I found that efforts at poetical composition brought on attacks of eczema and insomnia. Now it is different. I feel all dazed and confused. Spots float before my eyes and my liver is disordered. Alas, that I can neither obtain a speedy release, like the morning dew which swiftly passes away, nor hope for the restoration of energies to enable me to perform my duty. What sadder fate than thus to linger on, useless, in the world!" On the next day he wrote:— "My strength is rapidly failing, and I must leave behind me many unsettled questions and business half completed. The dead leaves of disappointed hopes fill all the landscape, and I see no prospect of settling my affairs. Thirty years have passed since I took my degree, and I have attained to the highest rank; yet have I learned nothing, and my character still lacks true solidity. What shame should be mine at having reached thus uselessly old age!" Next day, while reading a despatch, he had another stroke. Rallying, he told his eldest son, Tseng Chi-tsê, to see to it that his funeral ceremonies were conducted after the old usages, and that neither Buddhist nor Taoist priests be permitted to chant their liturgies over his corpse. On the following morning, though very weak, he insisted on perusing one of the essays which had been success-ful at the provincial examination. In the evening he was taken out into his garden and was returning thence with his son when the last seizure occurred. They carried him into the great Hall of audience, where he sat upright, as if presiding at a meeting of Council, and thus passed away, well stricken in age, though only sixty-two by the calendar. "Every man in Nanking," says the writer of this narrative, "felt as if he had lost a parent; it was rumoured that a shooting star had fallen in the city at the very moment of his death. The news was received by the Throne with profound grief. All Court functions were suspended for three days."

The Empress Dowager issued a Decree praising her faithful servant in unmeasured terms of gratitude and esteem, describing him as the "very backbone of the Throne," reciting his glorious achievements and ordering the erection of Temples in his hon-our in all the provinces that had been the scene of his campaign against the Taipings, in order "to prove our sincere affection for this good and loyal man."

VI

TZǓ HSI AND THE EUNUCHS

ONE of the facts upon which modern Chinese historians, Censors, Imperial Tutors and Guardians of the Heir Apparent have repeatedly laid stress, is that the Ming Dynasty became effeminate, then degenerate, and was eventually lost, because of the demoralising influence of the eunuch system on the Court and its official entourage. Upon this text, moral exhortations in the best classical manner have been addressed to the Throne for centuries, regardless of the consideration that most of the writers owed their positions, and hoped to owe further advancement, to the eunuchs, who had the sovereign's ear. These Memorials were usually only a part of the hoary fabric of pious platitudes and shadowy shibboleths which loom so large in the stock in trade of China's bureaucracy (in which matter China stands not alone), and the Empress Dowager, under whose rule the evil grew and assumed monstrous proportions, was ever wont to play her part in this elaborate farce, by solemnly approving the views of the bold critics and by professing the greatest indignation at the misdeeds of her eunuch myrmidons and retainers.

There have been, of course, sincere and eloquent critics of this pernicious system and its attendant evils; in fact, scarcely a reformer worthy of the name during the past fifty years has failed to place the abolition of eunuchs in the front rank of the measures necessary to bring China into line with the civilised Powers. There is no doubt that one of the first causes of the *coup d'état* in 1898 arose from the hatred of the Chief Eunuch, Li Lien-ying, for the Emperor Kuang-Hsü (who years before had ventured to have him beaten), and his not unnatural apprehension that the Emperor intended to follow up his reforms of the Peking Administration by devoting his attention to the Palace and to the abolition of eunuchs. As to the Boxer rising, it has been clearly proved that this notorious and powerful Chamberlain used all the weight of his great influence with his Imperial mistress on behalf of the anti-foreign movement, and that, if justice had been done (that is to say had he not been protected by the Russian Legation), his should have been one of the very first names on the Peace Protocol "Black List." The part which Li Lien-ying played in these two national crises of recent years is mentioned here chiefly to emphasise the fact that the platitudinous utterances of the orthodox express, as usual, a very real and widespread grievance, and that the falsetto notes of the Censorate are answered by a deep undertone of dissatisfaction and disgust throughout the provinces. It is for this reason that, especially during the past five years, progressive and patriotic Chinese officials (*e.g.* men like the Viceroy Yüan Shih-k'ai and T'ang Shao-yi, who realise how greatly the persistence of this barbarous medievalism lowers China in the eyes of the world), as well as the unanimous voice of the vernacular Press, have urged that the Court should now dispense with eunuchs, a measure which the Regent is said to favour, but which — such is the power wielded by these "fawning sycophants" — would undoubtedly be difficult and possibly dangerous. As early as 1906, *The Times* correspondent at Peking was discussing the possibility of their early removal as one of the many reforms which then shone so brightly on the horizon. In the Chinese conservative's opinion, however, which still weighs heavily in China, there are centuries of precedents and arguments to be adduced in favour of a system which has obtained continuously since long before the beginning of the

Christian era, which coincides with the Chinese accepted ideas of polygamy, and recognises the vital importance of legitimacy of succession in relation to the national religion of ancestor worship. On the other hand, it is true that in the golden days of the Sage Emperors at the beginning of the Chou Dynasty, eunuchs had no place in the body politic. Later, during the period of that Dynasty's decay and the era of the feudal States, Confucius refers with disapproval to their baneful influence, so that the Sage's authority may be adduced against them and their proceedings.

With the establishment of the present Dynasty at Peking (1644), the Manchus took over, as conquerors, all the existing machinery and *personnel* of the Chinese Court, eunuchs included, but they lost no time in restricting the latter's activities and opportunities. At the first audience held by the young Emperor Shun-Chih, the high officials, Manchu and Chinese, united to protest against the recent high-handed proceedings of the Court menials, declaring them to be "fit only to sweep floors, and in no wise entitled to have access to the Monarch." Regulations were promptly introduced, which remain in force (on paper) to this day, forbidding any eunuch to occupy any official position, or to hold any honorific rank or title higher than a Button of the fourth class. More important still, in view of the far-reaching conspiracy of the Chief Eunuch, Wei Chung (whom the last of the Mings had beheaded), was the law then introduced, which forbade any eunuch to leave the capital on any pretext whatsoever. For the next two hundred years, thanks to the wise rule and excellent traditions handed down by the two famous Emperors K'ang-Hsi and Ch'ien-Lung, the Palace eunuchs were kept generally under very strict discipline; but with the present century, when degeneration had set in strongly under the dissolute monarch Hsien-Feng, and even before the appearance of Yehonala on the scene, their evil influence had again become paramount in the Forbidden City. With Tzǔ Hsi's accession to power, all the corruption, intrigues and barbarous proceedings, that had characterised the last Mings, were gradually re-established and became permanent features of her Court.

Of the power which the eunuchs exercised throughout the whole of Tzǔ Hsi's reign, there is no possible doubt: the abuses which they practised under her protection, abuses flagrant and unconcealed, increased with the passing years and her own growing indifference to criticism, until, after 1898, her favourite and chief body-servant, Li Lien-ying did not scruple to boast that he could make or mar the highest officials at his pleasure and defy the Son of Heaven on his Throne. Of the countless legends of debauchery in the Palace, of orgies devised for Tzǔ Hsi by the Court eunuchs and actors, there is naturally nothing approaching to direct evidence: the frequent denunciations by Censors and the scurrilous writings of Cantonese and other lampooners, afford at best but circumstantial proof. The writings of K'ang Yu-wei and his associates, in particular, are clearly inspired by blind and unscrupulous hatred, and so inaccurate in matters of common knowledge and history, that one must perforce discount the value of their statements wherever the Empress Dowager or Jung Lu are concerned. But common report in China, as elsewhere, is usually based on some foundation of truth, and in Peking, where the mass of the population has always been conspicuously loyal to Tzǔ Hsi, there have never been two opinions as to the extravagance and general profligacy of her Court and of the evils of the eunuch *régime*. Nor is there room for doubt as to the deplorable effect exercised by these vicious underlings on weak and undisciplined Emperors, rulers of decadent instincts often encouraged in vicious practices to their speedy undoing. That this was the fate of Tzǔ Hsi's own son, the Emperor T'ung-Chih, is well-known, nor is there any doubt that the deaths of both Hsien-Feng and Kuang-Hsü were hastened, if not caused, by the temptations to which they were exposed by their vicious environment. The inner history of the Celestial Empire and the Manchu Dynasty during the last seventy years is inextricably bound up with that of the Palace eunuchs and their far-reaching intrigues. During the half century of Tzǔ Hsi's rule, the power behind the Throne (literally a power of darkness in high places) was that of her favourite Chamberlains. Of these the last, who has survived her, Li Lien-ying, is known by his nickname of "Cobbler's Wax Li" (P'i Hsiao Li)[1] from one end of the Empire to the other as the chief "squeezer" and arch villain of many a Palace tragedy. His influence over his Imperial mistress was indeed remarkable; on all occasions, except State audiences, she was wont to treat him with an affectionate familiarity, and to allow him a *sans-géne*, to which no courtier, nor any member of her own family (save perhaps Jung Lu) dared ever aspire.

During the Court's residence, and the Emperor's illness, at Jehol in 1861, the young Yehonala had occasion to notice and to appreciate the intelligence and willing service rendered by one of the eunuchs in immediate attendance upon her; this servant, by name An Te-hai, became her faithful henchman throughout the crisis of the Tsai Yüan conspiracy, and her intermediary and confidant in her dealings with the young guardsman, Jung Lu. Upon her accession to the Co-Regency, he became her favourite attendant and emissary, and later her *âme damnée*, sharing in all her ambitious hopes and plans, with no small advantage to himself, while at the same time employing his undeniable talents to the diversion of the young widow's mind by the provision of the elaborate Court pageants and theatrical entertainments which her soul loved. An Te-hai was himself an actor of no mean ability and exceedingly handsome of his person.

It was at this time, before the Regency was firmly established and while yet the reverberating echoes of the Tsai Yüan conspiracy lingered in Chihli, that the leading Censors began to send in Memorials against the self-evident extravagance and the rumoured profligacy of Tzŭ Hsi's Palace. The young Yehonala, headstrong and already impatient of criticism and restraint, confident also in the strength and loyalty of her immediate following, never

---

1. So named because, before becoming a eunuch at the age of sixteen, he was apprenticed to a cobbler at his native place, Ho-Chien fu, in Chihli, from which district most of the eunuchs come.

allowed these remonstrances to affect her conduct in the slightest degree; nevertheless, a stickler always for etiquette and appearances, and an adept at "face-saving" arts, she had no objection to expressing the heartiest approval of, and agreement with, her professional moralists. On more than one occasion, in those first years, we find her proclaiming in most suitably worded Edicts, pious intentions which were never intended to be taken seriously by anyone, and never were. The following Decree, issued in the third year of the Regency, (1864) is a case in point, and particularly interesting in that it refers to the wholesale pilfering by eunuchs in the Palace, which has continued without interruption to this day.

A Decree in the name of the two Empresses Regent, in the third year of the Emperor T'ung-Chih:—

"The Censor Chia To memorialises, saying that it has come to his knowledge that certain of the eunuchs who perform theatricals in the Imperial Household, have had their costumes made of tribute silks and satins taken from the Imperial storehouses. He asserts that they perform daily before the Throne and regularly receive *largesse* to the amount of thousands of taels. He asks that these practices be forbidden and discontinued forthwith, in order that all tendency towards vicious courses may be checked.

"With reference to this Memorial, it should be stated that last year, although the twenty-seven months of Imperial mourning for the late monarch were drawing to their close, we issued a Decree forbidding all festivities, for the reason that His late Majesty's remains had not yet been removed to their final place of sepulture; at the same time we gave orders that the seasonal tribute in kind, and provincial offerings, should be forwarded, as usual, in order to provide eventually for the costuming of the Palace theatricals, with reference to which matter we intended to issue another Decree in due course, upon the conclusion of the funeral ceremonies. We seized the opportunity, in this same Edict, to abolish once and for all the custom of bringing actors to the Palace to be made eunuchs, holding it to be wise, while His Majesty is still a minor, that everything that might tend in any way to lead him into paths of extravagance and dissipation should be firmly nipped in the bud. The Censor's present Memorial has therefore filled us with real amazement. At a time like this, when rebellions are still raging, and our people are in sore distress, when our treasuries are empty and our revenues insufficient for the needs of Government, our hearts are heavy with sorrowful thoughts, and must be so, especially as long as His late Majesty's remains have not yet been borne to their final resting place. How then could we possibly permit such a state of things as the Censor describes?[1] Furthermore, it is the duty of the Comptroller of our Household to keep a complete inventory of all bullion and silken stuffs in the Palace, none of which can be touched without our express permission. Surely this is sufficient to prove that all these rumours are utterly devoid of foundation.

"Nevertheless, in our remote seclusion of the Palace, it is inevitable that we should be kept in ignorance of much that goes on, so that it is just possible there may be some ground for these reports. It may be that certain evil-disposed eunuchs have been committing irregularities beyond the Palace precincts, and, if so, such conduct must be stopped at all costs. We hereby command that drastic measures be taken to deal with the offenders at once.

"It is imperatively necessary that the Emperor, in the intervals of his studies, should have about his person only honest and steady retainers, with whom he may converse on the arts and practice of government. If his attendants are evil men and make it their business to flatter his ears and divert his eyes with luxurious and effeminate pastimes, the result might well be to produce in His Majesty most undesirable tendencies; and any fault in the Emperor, however trifling, is liable to involve the State in far-reaching misfortunes. We therefore hereby authorise the Ministers of our Household to see to it that the Chief Eunuch enforces strict discipline upon all his subordinates, and should any of them hereafter venture to commit presumptuous acts, or to display their overweening arrogance, they must at once be arrested by the police and severely punished. And should such a case occur the Chief Eunuch will also be

---

1. This form of argument, under similar conditions, obtains all over the Empire. "How could I possibly squeeze my master?" says the servant.

dismissed for neglect of his duty of supervision, and the Comptrollers of the Household will incur our severe displeasure, with penalties. Let this Decree be copied and preserved in the archives of the Household and the Ante-Chambers."

As everyone in the capital was well aware of Yehonala's passion for the theatre, this Decree was naturally regarded as so much "fine writing on waste paper," and it is noticeable that from this time until her favourite and chief eunuch An Te-hai, came to his dramatic end, the Censors continued to impeach her and to denounce the ever increasing extravagance, which was already seriously disorganising the Metropolitan Government's finances and entailing fresh *corvées* in the provinces.

In 1866, two courageous Censors memorialised on this subject, having particularly in their minds the abuses caused by the unlawful proceedings of An Te-hai.

"More care," said they, "should be shown in the selection of the Emperor's body-servants. All the disasters that have overtaken previous Dynasties have been directly due to the machinations and evil influence of eunuchs. These creatures worm their way into the confidence and even into the affection of the Throne by their protestations of loyalty and faithful service; they are past-masters in every art of adroit flattery. Having once secured the Imperial favour and protection, they proceed to attach to themselves troops of followers, and gradually make for themselves a place of power that in time becomes unassailable. We, your Memorialists, therefore beg that this danger be now averted by the selection of well-bred and trustworthy attendants to wait upon His Majesty. There should not be about the Throne any young eunuchs of attractive appearance, creatures who make it their aim to establish influence over the Emperor and who would certainly turn it to their own ends so soon as he assumes the control of affairs."

In the Decree commenting on this Memorial, the Empresses Regent, in the name of the Emperor, observe: —

"This Memorial is very much to the point. History is full of instances where disaster has been brought about by eunuchs, and the example afforded us by those rulers who have been corrupted and undone by these 'rats and foxes,' should serve as timely warning to ourselves. By the divine wisdom of our predecessors on the Throne, not only have eunuchs been forbidden to meddle in all business of State, but they have never been permitted to gain the ear of the sovereign, or to influence him in any way, so that, for the past two hundred years, eunuch influence has been a thing of the past, and these fawning sycophants have enjoyed no opportunity of practising their evil arts of intrigue. Ever since their Majesties, the present Empresses Dowager, assumed the Regency, they also have conformed strictly to this House-law of our Dynasty, and have refused to allow these artful minions undue access to their Presence. As we peruse the present Memorial, we must admit that it evinces a very clear perception of those dangers which may overtake the State because of the undue influence of eunuchs. Our feelings, while reading it, are like those of the man who 'treading upon the hoar-frost, realises that winter is at hand.'[1] We therefore now command that if any of these noisome flatterers are attempting to pervert the intelligence of the Throne, the matter must be dealt with promptly, and we must be informed, so that their fitting punishment may be secured. We desire that all our attendants shall be of indisputable integrity and good morals, so that the door may be firmly shut on all evil and degrading tendencies."

Thus, Tzŭ Hsi, in her best manner, "for the gallery." But, "in the deep seclusion of our Palace," life went on as before, the merry round of an Oriental Trianon, while the Chief Eunuch's influence over the young Empress became greater every day. It was common knowledge, and the gossip of the tea-houses, that his lightest whim was law in the Forbidden City; that Yehonala and he, dressed in fancy costumes from historical plays, would make frequent excursions on the Palace lake; that he frequently wore the Dragon robes sacred to the use of the sovereign, and that the Empress had publicly presented him with the jade "ju-yi," symbol

---

1. Quotation from the Book of Changes, implying a sense of impending danger.

of royal power. Under these circumstances it was only natural, if not inevitable, that unfounded rumours should be rife in exaggeration of the real facts, and so we find it reported that An Te-hai was no eunuch, and again, that Yehonala had been delivered of a son[1] of which he was the father; many fantastic and moving tales were current of the licentious festivities of the Court, of students masquerading as eunuchs and then being put out of the way in the subterranean galleries of the Palace. Rumours and tales of orgies; inventions no doubt, for the most part, yet inevitable in the face of the notorious and undeniable corruption that had characterised the Court and the seraglio under the dissolute Hsien-Feng, and justified, if not confirmed, as time went on, by an irresistible consensus of opinion in the capital, and by fully substantiated events in the Empress Dowager's career.

Of these events, one, which had far-reaching results, was her violation of the dynastic house-law which forbade eunuchs to leave the capital. In 1869, being short of funds, and desiring to replenish her Privy Purse without consulting Prince Kung or her colleague the Co-Regent, she despatched her favourite An Te-hai on a special mission to Shantung, where he was to collect tribute in her name.[2] By this time the Chief Eunuch had incurred the bitter enmity of several of the Princes of the Imperial Clan, and especially of Prince Kung, not only because of his growing influence over Tzŭ Hsi, but because of his insolent bearing to all at Court. On one occasion the Empress had curtly sent word to Prince Kung that she could not grant him audience because she was busy talking to the eunuch, an insult which the Prince never forgot and which cost the favourite his life, besides leading to the disgrace of the Prince and other consequences serious to the Empire.

1. Chinese pamphleteers in Canton record the event with much detail, and state that this son is alive to-day under the name of Chiu Min.
2. A fantastic account of this mission is contained in an imaginative work recently published (*La Vie Secrete de la Cour de Chine*, Paris, 1910), where the Chief Eunuch's name is given as "*Siao*." This curious blunder is due to the fact that the Eunuch's nickname, on account of his stature, was "Hsiao An'rh" (little An), just as Li Lien-Ying's is "P'i Hsiao" Li all over China.

H.M. Tzu Hsi with the Consort (Lung Yu) and Principal Concubine (Jen Fei) of H.M. Kuang-Hsu, accompanied by Court Ladies and Eunuchs.

The Chief Eunuch's illegal mission to Shantung, and his out-rageous behaviour in that province, provided Prince Kung with a long-sought opportunity not only of wreaking vengeance on him but of creating rivalry and enmity between the Empresses Regent. The Governor of Shantung, an able and courageous offi-cial named Ting Pao-chen, who had distinguished himself in the Taiping rebellion, was highly incensed at the arrogant eunuch's assumption of Imperial authority, and being quite *au courant* with the position of affairs in the Palace, he reported direct to Prince Kung and asked for instructions. The Governor's despatch reached the Prince while Tzŭ Hsi was amusing herself with the-atricals; without a moment's delay he sought audience of Tzŭ An, the Co-Regent Empress, and, playing upon her vanity and weak disposition, induced her to sign a Decree, which he drafted in her presence, ordering the eunuch's summary decapitation, the customary formality of a trial in Peking being dispensed with. Tzŭ An, hard pressed as she was, gave her consent reluctantly and with a clear presentiment of evil to come from the wrath of her masterful colleague. "The Western Empress will assuredly kill me for this," she is reported to have said to the Prince, as she handed him the sealed Decree, which Kung sent off post-haste by special courier.

The following is the text of this interesting document:—

"Ting Pao-chen reports that a eunuch has been creating disturbances in the province of Shantung. According to the Department Magistrate of Te Chou, a eunuch named An and his followers passed through that place by way of the Imperial Canal, in two dragon barges, with much display of pomp and pageantry. He announced that he had come on an Imperial mission to procure Dragon robes. His barges flew a black banner, bearing in its centre the triple Imperial emblems of the Sun, and there were also Dragon and Phœnix flags flying on both sides of his vessels.[1] A goodly company of both sexes were in attendance on this person; there were female musicians, skilled in the use of string and

---

1. The Phœnix flag signified that he was sent by the Empresses Regent.

wind instruments. The banks of the Canal were lined with crowds of spectators, who witnessed with amazement and admiration his progress. The 21st day of last month happened to be this eunuch's birthday, so he arrayed himself in Dragon robes, and stood on the foredeck of his barge, to receive the homage of his suite. The local Magistrate was just about to order his arrest when the barges set sail and proceeded southwards. The Governor adds that he has already given orders for his immediate arrest.

"We are dumfoundered at this report. How can we hope ever to purify the standard of morals in the Palace and frighten evil-doers, unless we make an example of this insolent eunuch, who has dared to leave Peking without our permission and to commit these lawless deeds? The Governors of the three provinces of Shantung, Honan and Kiangsu are ordered to seek out and arrest the eunuch An, whom we had formerly honoured with rank of the sixth grade and the decoration of the crow's feather. Upon his being duly identified by his companions, let him be forthwith beheaded, without further formalities, no attention is to be paid to any crafty explanations which he may attempt to make. The Governors concerned will be held responsible in the event of failure to effect his arrest."

Tzǔ Hsi remained for some time in blissful ignorance of her favourite's danger, and even of his death. No doubt the Chief Eunuch's great unpopularity enabled Prince Kung and the Empress Tzǔ An to keep the matter secret until the offender was past helping. Ten days later, Tzǔ An issued a second Decree, extracted from her like the first by Prince Kung, in which the eunuch's execution is recorded, as follows:—

"Ting Pao-chen now reports that the eunuch An was arrested in the T'ai An prefecture and has been summarily beheaded. Our dynasty's house-law is most strict in regard to the proper discipline of eunuchs, and provides severe punishment for any offences which they may commit. They have always been sternly forbidden to make expeditions to the provinces, or to create trouble. Nevertheless, An Te-hai actually had the brazen effrontery to violate this law, and for his crimes his execution is only a fitting reward. In future, let all eunuchs take warning by his example; should we have further cause to complain, the chief eunuchs of the several departments of the Household, will be punished as well as the actual offender. Any eunuch who may hereafter pretend that he has been sent on Imperial business to the provinces shall be cast into chains at once, and sent to Peking for punishment."

This Decree has a half-hearted ring, as if some of the conspirators' fear of the coming wrath of Yehonala had crept into it. Very different in wording are the Edicts in which Tzŭ Hsi condemns an offender to death. We miss her trenchant style, that "strength of the pen" which was the secret of much of her power.

Simultaneously with the death of An, in Shantung, several eunuchs of his following were put to death by strangling; six others escaped from the police, of whom five were re-captured and executed. The Chief Eunuch's family were sent as slaves to the frontier guards in the north-west. Several days after the execution of Tzŭ Hsi's favourite, the eunuch who had escaped made his way back to Peking, and sent word to the Empress through Li Lien-ying, another of her confidential attendants. At first she could scarcely believe that her timorous and self-effacing colleague could have dared to sign these Decrees on her own responsibility and in secret, no matter what amount of pressure might have been brought to bear upon her. When she realised what had occurred, the Palace witnessed one of those outbursts of torrential rage with which it was to become familiar in years to come. Swiftly making her way to the "Palace of Benevolent Peace," the residence of her Co-Regent, she wrathfully demanded an explanation. Tzŭ An, terrified, endeavoured to put the whole blame upon Prince Kung; but the plea did not serve her, and Tzŭ Hsi, after a fierce quarrel, left, vowing vengeance on them both. This event marked a turning point in the career of Yehonala, who, until then, had maintained amicable relations with her less strong-minded colleague, and all the appearances of equality in the Co-Regency. Henceforward she devoted more time and closer attention to affairs of State, consolidating her position and power with a clear determination to prevent any further interference with her supreme authority. From this time forward she definitely assumes the first place as ruler of China, relegating her colleague completely to the background.

When, on the morning after the storm, Prince Kung appeared in the Audience Hall, Tzǔ sternly rebuked him, threatening him with dismissal and the forfeiture of his titles. For the time being, however, she allowed him to go unpunished, but she never forgave the offence, and she took her revenge in due season: he suffered the effects of her resentment as long as he lived. Her first act was to pass over his son, the rightful heir to the Throne, upon the death of T'ung-Chih. It is true that in after years she permitted him to hold high office, but this was, firstly, because she could not afford to dispense with his services, and, secondly, because of her genuine affection for his daughter, whom she had adopted as her own child.

An Te-hai was succeeded in the post of Chief Eunuch and confidential attendant on her Majesty by Li Lien-ying, of whom mention has already been made. For the next forty years this Palace servant was destined to play a leading part in the government of China, to hold in his supple hands the lives and deaths of thousands, to make and unmake the highest officials of the Empire, and to levy rich tribute on the eighteen provinces. As a youth of sixteen, when he "left the family" (as the Chinese euphemistically describe the making of a eunuch),[1] Li was remarkable for his handsome appearance and good manners, advantages which never failed to carry weight with Tzǔ Hsi. It is recorded on trustworthy authority that at an early stage in his career he had so ingratiated himself with Her Majesty that he was permitted unusual liberties, remaining seated in her presence, aye, even on the Throne itself. In the privacy of her apartments he was allowed to discuss whatever subjects he chose, without being

---

1. The same expression is used of a novice taking the vows of Buddhist priesthood.

spoken to, and as years passed and his familiarity with the Old Buddha increased, he became her regular and authoritative adviser on all important State business. In later years, when speaking of Her Majesty to outsiders, even to high officials, he would use the familiar pronoun *"Tsa-men"* meaning "we two," which is usually reserved for blood relations or persons on a footing of familiar equality, and he was currently known among his followers by the almost sacrilegious title of "Lord of nine thousand years," the Emperor being Lord of ten thousand. Only on solemn State occasions did he observe the etiquette prescribed for his class and a modest demeanour.

Corrupt, avaricious, vindictive, and fiercely cruel to his enemies and rivals, it must be said in Li's favour that he was, at least, wholly devoted and faithful to his Imperial mistress, and that at times of peril he never failed to exert himself to the utmost for her comfort and protection. He possessed moreover, other good qualities which appealed not only to Tzŭ Hsi but to many of the high Manchu officials, who did not consider it beneath their pride to throng for admission at his private residence. He was cheerful, fond of a joke, an excellent actor[1] and *raconteur*, and a generous host: above all, he was passing rich. At the Empress Dowager's funeral, in November 1909, this aged retainer presented a pathetic and almost venerable spectacle, enough to make one forget for a moment the accumulated horrors of his seventy years of wickedness. Smitten with age and sickness, he could scarcely totter the short distance which the *cortège* had to make on foot; but of all that vast throng of officials and Palace servants, he alone showed unmistakable signs of deep and genuine grief. Watching the intelligent features of this maker of secret history, one could not but wonder what thoughts were passing through that subtle brain, as he shuffled past the Pavilion of the Diplomatic Body, escorting for the last time his great mistress, — the close confidant,

---

1. Tzŭ Hsi was fond of masquerading with her favourite, till well advanced in years. One photograph of her is on sale in Peking, wherein she is posing as the Goddess of Mercy (Kuanyin) with Li in attendance as one of the Boddhisatvas.

not to say comrade, of all those long and eventful years. For half
a century he had served her with unremitting zeal and fidelity,
no small thing in a country when the allegiance of servants is so
commonly bought and sold. In his youth it was he who walked
and ran beside her chair as body servant; through what scenes
of splendour and squalor had they both passed since then, and
now he was left alone, surrounded by new faces and confronted
by imminent peril of change. Yet in spite of his long life and the
enervating influences of his profession, the old man's powerful
physique was by no means exhausted.

Too wise to follow in the footsteps of his unfortunate predecessor, Li never made raids on his own account into the provinces, nor did he ever attempt to gain or claim high official rank,
remaining prudently content with the fourth class button, which
is the highest grade to which eunuchs may legally aspire. But,
under the protection and with the full knowledge of the Empress
Dowager, he organised a regular system of *corvées*, squeezes and
douceurs, levied on every high official in the Empire, the proceeds
of which he frequently shared with the Old Buddha herself. As
shown in another place, the Empress and her Chief Eunuch practically made common cause and a common purse in collecting
"tribute" and squeezes during the wanderings of the Court in
exile after 1900. At that time the Chief Eunuch, less fortunate
than his mistress, had lost the whole of his buried treasure in
the capital. It had been "*cached*" in a safe place, known only to
his intimate subordinates, but one of these sold the secret to the
French troops, who raided the hoard, a rich booty. One of Li's
first steps after the Court's return was to obtain the Old Buddha's permission to have the traitor beheaded, which was done
without undue formalities. The Chief Eunuch's fortune is estimated by Peking bankers to-day at about two millions sterling,
invested chiefly in pawn-shops and money-changing establish-
ments at the capital; this sum represents roughly his share of the
provincial tribute and squeezes on official appointments for the
last eight years, and the total is not surprising when we bear in

mind that the price of one official post has been known to bring him in as much as three hundred and twenty thousand taels, or say forty thousand pounds.

One of the secrets of his wealth was that he never despised the day of small things. The following is the text of a letter in our possession (of which we reproduce a facsimile), written by him to one of the regular contractors of the Palace, with whom he must have had many similar transactions. The paper on which it is written is of the commonest, and the visiting card which, as usual, accompanies it, is that of an unpretentious business man; the style of the writer is terse and to the point: —

"To my worthy friend, Mr. Wang, the Seventh (of his family): —

"Since I last had the pleasure of seeing you, you have been constantly in my thoughts. I wish you, with all respect, long life and prosperity: thus will your days fulfil my best hopes of you. And now I beg politely to tell you that I, your younger brother,[1] am quite ashamed of the emptiness of my purse and I therefore beg that you, good Sir, will be so good as to lend me notes to the amount of fifteen hundred taels, which sum kindly hand to the bearer of this letter. I look forward to a day for our further conversation,

"Your younger brother,

"Li Lien-ying."

As to the amount, Li knew exactly how much the contractors and furnishers of the Palace should pay on every occasion, and that there was no need to question the possibility of the "loan" not being forthcoming.

That he encouraged lavish expenditure at the Court is certain, and scarcely a matter for wonder, but his control of finance extended far beyond the Privy Purse, and wrought great harm to the Empire on more than one historic occasion. For instance, China's humiliating defeat at the hands of Japan in 1894 was

---

1. A term of humility.

very largely due to his diversion of vast sums of money from the Navy to the reconstruction and decoration of the Summer Palace, a work from which he and his underlings profited to no small extent. In 1885, Prince Ch'un had been appointed head of the Admiralty Board, assisted by Prince Ch'ing, Li Hung-chang and the Marquis Tseng. After the death of the Marquis, however (who had been a moving spirit in the organisation of the Board), Naval affairs passed into the control of a clique of young and inexperienced Princes, and when, in 1889, the Emperor assumed the direction of the Government, one of his first acts was to order the re-building of the Summer Palace, which Imperial residence had remained in ruins since its destruction by the Allies in 1861. There being no funds available, Li advised that the Naval appropriations should be devoted to this purpose, so that the Old Buddha might be suitably provided with a residence; this was accordingly done, and the Naval Department became a branch of the Imperial Household (Nei Wu Fu) for all purposes of Government finance. When the war with Japan broke out, the Empress Dowager issued orders that the Naval Department should be abolished. This order evoked very general criticism, but, as the Department and the Summer Palace rebuilding fund had come to be treated as one and the same account, her Decree simply meant that as the Palace restoration was now complete, and as the funds were quite exhausted, the account in question might be considered closed. There was obviously nothing to be gained by useless enquiries for money to be transferred from the Palace to the Navy.

In 1889 the Chief Eunuch accompanied Prince Ch'un on his first tour of inspection to the northern Naval ports, including the Naval bases of Port Arthur and Weihaiwei. It was a matter of very general comment at the time that the honours paid to the eunuch were noticeably greater than those shown to the Prince. Every officer in the Peiyang squadron, from Admiral Ting downwards, did his best to ingratiate himself with this powerful Chamberlain, and to become enrolled on the list of his *protégés*, so that he

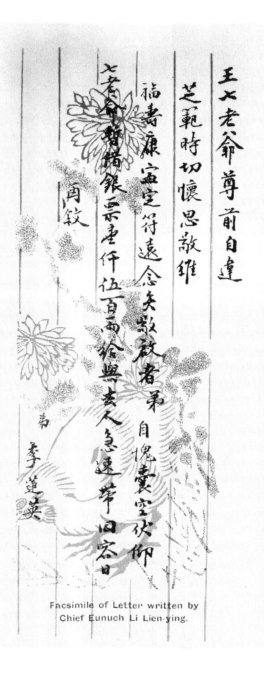

王七老爺尊前自達

芝範時切懷思敬維

福壽康寧定符遠念矣敷啓者弟自愧囊空欲仰

七老爺質墊銀票壹仟伍百兩給興素人急速帶回容日

面欽

李蓮英

Facsimile of Letter written by
Chief Eunuch Li Lien-ying.

was *entouré* with all manner of bribery and adulation. Many critics, foreign and Chinese, have cast on Li Hung-chang the blame for the disasters of the Japanese war, but they surely overlook the fact, to which even the great Viceroy dared not openly refer, that nine-tenths of the funds which should have gone to the up-keep and provisioning of the Navy and the maintenance of the Coast Defences, had been diverted by the Chief Eunuch to the Palace (and much of them to his own pocket), so that the ships' crews were disaffected, and their ordnance defective, in the hour of need. Readers of Pepys will remember a very similar state of affairs obtaining in the British Navy, happily without affecting the *moral* of its officers and men, at a similarly critical period of British history.

Li Lien-ying's hatred of the Emperor Kuang-Hsü was beyond doubt a most important factor in the *coup d'état*, and in the subsequent estrangement and hostility between Tzŭ Hsi and the nominal ruler of the Empire; there are not lacking those who say that it had much to do with the Emperor's death, which certainly created no surprise in the capital. The eunuch hated and feared the Emperor's reforming zeal, as well as the Cantonese advisers who in 1898 came swarming to Peking as the apostles of a new dispensation, and it was therefore only natural that he should become the foremost adviser and partisan of the reactionaries and their emissary in urging the Empress to resume control of affairs. It is quite safe to assert that had his great influence with Tzŭ Hsi been exercised against, instead of for, the Boxers, had he abstained from encouraging her superstitious belief in their magic arts, the anti-foreign movement would never have gone further than the borders of Shantung, and the Chinese people would have been spared the heavy burden of the indemnities. How interesting a study of Asiatic politics and Court life presents itself in the spectacle of this cobbler's apprentice and his influence on the destinies of so great a race! Seeing him as he was on the day of his mistress's burial, how bitter must have been the innermost thoughts of the man, left alone on the brink of the grave with the ill-gotten wealth that his country has paid for so heavily!

At the height of the Boxer crisis when the power wielded by Li Lien-ying was enormous, it was the custom of Prince Tuan, when explaining his views to the Empress Dowager and the Grand Council, to emphasise the fact that no step had been taken except with the advice and approval of the Chief Eunuch. "Such and such a Decree," he would say, "is issued with the chief Chamberlain Li's approval." His object in so doing was to head off opposition, for he well knew that few would dare to oppose any measures that the Chief Eunuch approved. When Her Majesty granted rewards to the Boxers and offered head-money to the troops for the killing of Europeans, it was at Li's urgent request that she consented to defray these unusual charges from her Privy Purse.

When the relieving forces drew near to Peking and it became clear, even to the most obstinate, that the Boxer bolt was shot, the Chief Eunuch passed through a period of deep depression and mortification, not only because of the failure of his prophecies, but because it was clear to all at Court that his Imperial mistress, seeking, as was her wont, a scapegoat, was disposed to vent her wrath upon him. Herself deeply stirred by fear and wrath, it was only natural that she should turn on him, who had been foremost in advising her to follow the path of destruction. On the day when the relief of the Legations took place, Duke Lan rushed headlong into the Palace, loudly announcing that the foreign devils were already within the city walls. Tzǔ Hsi turned on him and asked how he could reconcile such a statement with his previous boasts. "I presume that the devils have flown here," said she, "for you were telling me only two days ago of our glorious victories near Tientsin; and yet all the time you knew well, as I knew, that the Viceroy and the Li Ping-heng were both dead." Li Lien-ying, who was standing close by, hearing this, went out and informed the trembling crowd of eunuchs, adding, "The Old Buddha is in an unspeakable rage. There is nothing for it; we must make our escape and retire into Shensi. There we will await the arrival of our reinforcements which will easily drive all these devils back into the sea." But the hardships and dangers of the flight told even more severely on the chief eunuch than on the Old Buddha herself, and it was not until the Court's safe establishment at Hsi-an that he recovered his self-possession.

Certain information conveyed by an official of the Household in exile to a fellow provincial at Peking, throws considerable light on the manner in which the Court lived during those troublous days, and the part played in affairs of State by the chief eunuch and Tzŭ Hsi's other favourites of the Household. We take the following disconnected notes from this correspondence.

When Ts'en Ch'un-hsüan (Governor of Shensi) came to meet the Court on the Shansi frontier, the Old Buddha, raising the curtain of her sedan-chair, looked out and said to him, "Have you any idea of what we have suffered in Peking?" "I do not know all," he replied. Pointing angrily at Li, she said, "It was all his doing; he has brought ruin upon me." The chief eunuch hung his head, and for once had nothing to say. Later on, when the fearless Ts'en saw the eunuchs under Li's orders mercilessly harassing the countryside in their search for plunder, he promptly reported matters to the Empress and obtained her somewhat reluctant permission to execute three of the offenders on the spot. He was sorely tempted to include the chief eunuch in the number of his victims, but realising how greatly Her Majesty depended upon her favourite attendant, he feared to run the risk of inconveniencing and offending her. Nevertheless, Li had a narrow escape. Later on, when Li had recovered his equanimity, and the Court had settled down to its usual routine, the eunuch revenged himself on the Governor, with the help of Jung Lu, by having him transferred to the Governorship of Shansi. He did this, not only because the post in Shansi was considered a dangerous one, owing to the fear of pursuit by the Allies, but because Ts'en had gradually made himself most useful to Her Majesty by superintending the expenditure of her Household. The Governor was justly famous throughout the Empire for his incorruptible honesty, so that, when placed in

charge of the Palace accounts, these speedily showed a very considerable reduction in expenditure. The first result of this *régime*
was to put a stop to all the "squeeze" of the eunuchs, and to place
their salaries upon a definite and moderate basis. Ts'en rapidly
attained an intimate and confidential position with Her Majesty,
to the great and increasing wrath of the chief eunuch, who left
no stone unturned to injure him, and eventually succeeded, with
the help of Jung Lu, in inducing Her Majesty to dispense with his
personal services. For over a month, however, the Old Buddha
spent hours daily discussing public and private affairs with this
fearless and upright official, and it would have been well for her
had she retained him and others of his quality about her to counteract the corrupt tendencies of her Manchu clansmen and the
eunuchs. After Ts'en's transfer to Shansi, the chief eunuch did not
scruple to suppress and destroy many of the memorials which as
Governor he addressed to the Old Buddha, and which Li did not
desire his mistress to see. Gradually he re-established himself as
completely as before in the confidence and favour of his mistress,
and before the Court's return to Peking he had become if anything more familiarly arrogant than at any previous stage in his
career. At audiences given to the highest officials he would even
go so far as to refuse to transmit Her Majesty's orders, bluntly
informing her that he was tired and that there had been enough
public business for that day!

The vast quantities of tribute levied by the Court from the
Southern Provinces at this time were handled in the first instance
by Li Lien-ying, whose apartments were stacked with heaps of
dragon robes, tribute silk and other valuables. Of all the tribute
paid in bullion, the Empress Dowager's share was one-half, while
the eunuchs divided one-fifth, and the balance was handed over
to Jung Lu for military purposes and his own emolument. So
profitable was the eunuchs' business at Hsi-an and Kai-feng, that
Li Lien-ying did his utmost to dissuade the Old Buddha from
returning to Peking, endeavouring to frighten her by alarming
prognostications of the vengeance of the foreign Powers. Li's

motives were not entirely mercenary, however, for there is no doubt that for a long time he fully expected to find his own name on the "black list" of the Legations, and that it fully deserved to figure there. He directed the second eunuch, named Ts'ui, to communicate to him daily the latest news from Peking, and it was only when reassured by reports from Prince Ch'ing, that his courage returned, and his opposition to the Court's return ceased. The conciliatory attitude, which he eventually adopted towards the Empress Dowager's reform policy, was largely induced by the good advice which he received from Jung Lu, who strongly urged him to control his reactionary opinions and violent temper.

The amount of tribute paid in silver to the Court at Hsi-an was over five million taels, the quota from each Province being kept separate. The chief eunuch was assisted in the supervision of the tribute accounts by another favourite of the Old Buddha, a eunuch named Sun, whose covetousness and bullying methods of "squeeze" were almost equal to those of his chief. On one occasion the deputy in charge of the tribute from Hupei was paying in bullion to the Imperial Household, and Sun was tallying the amounts with a steelyard. He said there was a shortage. "That cannot be so," said the deputy, "for every shoe of Hupei silver weighs fifty taels exactly, so that there can be no mistake." The eunuch looked at him insolently, and said, "How many times have you brought tribute, and what do you know about the customs of the Court?" The frightened deputy persisted that all was in order. Sun then said angrily: "I suppose, then, you mean that the Old Buddha's scales are false?" He was just proceeding to assault the unfortunate deputy, when the Old Buddha herself, overhearing the argument (the court-yards of her residence being very small) came out and directed the eunuch to bring the silver into her own apartments, where she would weigh it herself. "I believe there has been a great deal of leakage lately," she said; "it is the business of my eunuchs to see that I am not cheated." The deputy took his departure, looking extremely crestfallen, but on his way out he was met by Chi Lu, the Controller of the Household, who said to him, "We all know you have been having a bad time of it, but you must not mind. These eunuchs have been making very little money of late, for the Old Buddha has been keeping a very sharp watch on them; you must therefore excuse them. And they have lost a great deal in Peking."

Tribute of twenty-four kinds was received from Canton, but the eunuchs on their own initiative, and in order to compel *largesse*, rejected nine different kinds of articles, so that the official in charge was greatly alarmed, fearing that the Old Buddha would accuse him of having stolen the things which the eunuchs refused to receive. This was one of their commonest methods of levying tribute on their own account; another was to make large purchases in the name of the Empress, and refuse to pay for them. Much hardship was inflicted on the people of Hsi-an, and indeed of the entire province, from their depredations, especially because at the time Shensi was already suffering from the beginnings of famine, caused by the prolonged drought. It is recorded in the accounts of the Governor Ts'en, that flour cost 96 cash a pound, eggs 34 cash apiece, and pork 400 cash a pound, while fish was almost unobtainable; these prices being about six times as high as those ruling in southern China.

Many of the eunuchs appeared to take pleasure in humiliating the Emperor, and subjecting him to petty annoyances, which often roused him to petulant outbursts of temper. In one letter from the Court at Hsi-an it was reported that His Majesty appeared to be a little wrong in the head, for he would spend his time playing foolish games, such as hide-and-seek, with the younger eunuchs, until interrupted by the Empress Dowager, when he would immediately get into a corner and assume a sullen demeanour. At other times, when irritated, he would give way to violent fits of rage and throw the household crockery at the heads of his attendants. These reports must be received with caution, as they were frequently spread abroad by the chief eunuch and members of the reactionary party in order to damage His Majesty in the eyes of the outside world.

As above stated, after the return of the Court from its journeying in the wilderness (1902) Li's influence with the Empress Dowager was, if anything, greater than before, all the internal affairs of the Palace being under his supreme control. Following Her Majesty's example, however, he professed his complete conversion to the necessity of reform, and even gave his approval, after certain amendments had been made by the Grand Council and by himself, to her programme for the granting of a Constitution. Jesting with Her Majesty in his usual familiar manner, he was heard on more than one occasion to predict her conversion to Christianity. "We are only sham devils now, Old Buddha," he said.

Nevertheless, and in spite of advancing years and infirmity, he has clung, and still clings, tenaciously to the perquisites and privileges of his stewardship, fiercely defending the eunuch system and his own post by all the means (and they are many) in his power. When, in 1901, T'ao Mo, late Viceroy of Canton, sent in his famous Memorial urging that, in view of the greatly reduced number of the Imperial concubines, the eunuchs should be replaced by female attendants, Li successfully intrigued to prevent this document reaching Her Majesty until he had taken effective steps to prevent her being advised in favour of the suggestion. T'ao Mo's Memorial was as follows:—

"The prosperity of the State depends absolutely upon the virtue of the ruler. Where the sovereign surrounds himself with wise and just men, the country must benefit; where he chooses time-servers to advise him, rebellion and chaos will be the inevitable result. If one human being be called upon to attend to the multifarious duties of the State, in addition to managing the internal affairs of the Palace, his position may be glorious indeed, but the responsibilities thereof are too great for any man to bear. Even a sovereign, surrounded by men of the sternest integrity, might well pause and falter at the dread chances of failure. But how can a nation possibly escape dire misfortune when, between sovereign and subjects is set up a barrier composed of men of the most contemptible and degraded kind? These creatures are not necessarily all traitors or notorious scoundrels; it is sufficient, for the undoing of a sovereign, that he be surrounded at all hours by illiterate persons, lacking in moral perception, who pander to his moods and minister to his caprices. Even the worst Minister of State has not the same opportunity of influencing his Emperor for evil: but these eunuchs are for ever about and around him. Intimacy with eunuchs necessarily brings about a sapping of the moral fibre; any ruler exposed to their influences cannot possibly keep in touch with his people.

"But if we wish to root out these influences, we must proceed as if we were weeding out tares in a field. If we leave the roots in the ground, they will sooner or later spring up again to fresh life. Complete eradication is the only cure. His Majesty is come of age and his character is daily developing; how deeply he must deplore the fact that he is compelled to associate with this class of men at a time when he is doing his best to introduce a policy of reform! If previous Dynasties employed eunuchs it was because of the large number of concubines in the Palace, but his present Majesty's harem is small, and he might therefore preferably employ female attendants to minister to his personal wants, while the official duties of the Household might be discharged by men of good birth and education. Why should it be necessary to employ eunuchs for such posts?

"At the present time, the Court at Hsi-an employs an enormous number of eunuchs; a favourable opportunity therefore presents itself for reducing their number, retaining only some twenty or thirty of the more respectable among them. Orders should be given, after the Court's return, that for the future no more eunuchs shall be engaged, and the Palace administration should be thoroughly reorganised. By this means, long-standing abuses will be removed, and the glory of your Majesty's reign will be enhanced for all time.

"At this moment, many reforms are being projected, in regard to which Your Majesties have received numerous suggestions from many high officials. But in my opinion, this question of the employment of eunuchs, though apparently of minor importance, transcends all others, and the possibility of reform depends largely on their removal. The system has been abolished in all foreign countries and persists only in China. It exposes us to much adverse criticism and contumely, and by abolishing it we should gain the respect of civilised nations. As an official holding a provincial post, I am prohibited by law from criticising the administration of the Palace; nevertheless, I hold it to be my duty at this juncture to offer my suggestions, however humble and worthless, in token of my gratitude to Your Majesties for your generous favours."

Since that day, there have been repeated denunciations of the eunuch system, and rumours of their impending removal, but their influence shows little sign of diminution, and officials of the courage and integrity of T'ao Mo are a small minority in the Mandarinate. Reform measures on paper are numerous enough, measures forecasting self-denial and zeal for the common good at some future and undetermined date, but it is significant of the existing condition of affairs and the strong hold of the powers of reaction, that the native Press has lately passed from its former robust independence under complete official control, and that the voice of Young China, which formerly denounced the eunuchs and other causes of national degeneration, is but faintly heard in the land.

VII

A QUESTION OF ETIQUETTE

THE following secret Memorial, submitted by the Censor Wu K'o-tu, in 1873, casts no direct light on the life and character of the Empress Dowager; it is of permanent interest nevertheless, and valuable, in that it enables us to realise something of the unbounded arrogance of the Chinese official class and the childish ignorance of that Court in which Tzŭ Hsi lived and moved and had her being. Documents like these — their number is legion for those who look for them — throw into strong relief the futility of western diplomacy confronted by a national sentiment of contempt for the barbarian so deep-rooted and far-reaching; and they make one wonder at the persistence of those comfortable delusions, those facile lines of least resistance, which the foreign Powers and their Legations have cherished to this day in spite of many humiliating experiences. And if, from the general, one returns to particular study of the remarkable woman whose personality dominated the destinies of men and the foreign relations of her country for half a century, the state of affairs revealed by documents like these must compel unstinted admiration for a mind so obviously superior to its environment. Finally, there lurks in this Memorial a certain quality of (possibly unconscious) humour which may justify its inclusion, in the nature of an *entremets*, at this stage of our narrative: —

"A Secret Memorial urging the Throne to put a stop to official wrangling and to excuse the Ministers of foreign nations from kneeling at audiences, in order that our magnanimity may be proved and our prestige exalted. A prayer based, moreover, on the fact that our demands in this matter cannot be successfully pressed and that protracted discussion has so far resulted in a hopeless deadlock.

"From the day when first the foreign Ministers asked to be permitted to present their credentials, nearly six months ago, our statesmen have discussed the question, without arriving at any solution of its difficulties. First, they debated whether the Ministers should be granted audience at all, and having agreed upon this, they proceeded to discuss whether they should be compelled to kneel.

"In discussing this matter with certain minor officials, it has occurred to me to wonder wherein really lies the gravity of the question sufficient to justify all this bother and excitement? As Mencius remarks, 'Why should the Superior Man engage in altercation with birds and beasts?'

"I have heard, and believe, that the rulers of foreign nations are deposed by their subjects for all the world like pawns on a chess board. I have seen with my own eyes the foreigners who live in Peking walking abroad, preceded by the females of their household either on foot or in sedan chairs; the men folk following meekly in their rear, like servants — all unashamed. They have made some score of treaties with China, containing at least ten thousand written characters. Is there a word in any one of them concerning reverence for parents, or the cultivation of virtue and respect for the nine canons of rightful conduct? No! Is there one word in any one of them as to the observance of ceremony, as to duty, integrity and a proper sense of shame, the four cardinal principles of our nation? Again, no! All that they speak of is material profit. 'Such and such a clause implies benefits or profits for China.' They think only of profit, and with the meretricious hope of profit they beguile the Chinese people. These men know not even the meaning of duty and ceremony, wisdom and good faith, yet we profess, forsooth, to expect them to act as if they were endowed with the five cardinal virtues! They know not the meaning of the Heaven-ordained relationship between Sovereign and Minister, between father and son, husband and wife, elder and younger brother, friend and friend — yet we propose to require them to conform to the five principles of duty! It seems to me that one might as well bring together dogs and horses, goats and pigs, in a public hall and compel these creatures to perform the evolutions of the dance!

"If we insist upon their reverently kneeling, in what manner will it increase the lustre of the Throne's prestige? If we excuse them from kneeling, how can this possibly affect the Sovereign's majesty?

"But our statesmen hold that long and careful deliberation before assenting to the foreigners' wishes in this matter will cause the latter to say: 'If so great pressure be required to extract even this trifling concession from China, how small must be our hopes of future success in dealing with great matters.' In this way, it is thought, we may cause their everlasting demands on China to cease, and we should thus gain, while they lose, prestige. But, in my humble opinion, our nation's prestige depends not on any foreigners' estimate of us, nor is their humiliation to be brought about in this way. If once they perceive that we attach a real importance to their kneeling at audience, and that we are loth to exempt them from this ceremony, while at the same time they are fully aware that we dare not go to war with them, they will simply insist the more firmly on their demands and threaten us with war if we fail to comply. Our weakness once exposed, they will stick at nothing.

"I have heard that, in their despatches and treaties, the puny hobgoblin or petty monsters whom they have the audacity to call 'Emperors' are placed on a level of equality with His Sacred Majesty! If our statesmen can brook an outrage like this and feel no shame, why should they trouble themselves about the foreign Envoys' refusal to kneel? Two years ago, when the

Russian barbarians were pressing in upon China from Ili and all the North-west, when they were seizing vast stretches of our territory, and carrying out their policy of aggression on a scale unparalleled in all the history of our relations with barbarians; when their crafty and deep-laid plans threatened the Empire with the gravest dangers — our statesmen showed no sense of shame. But now, we are to believe that there is humiliation to China in the Ministers' unwillingness to kneel! Our statesmen appear to imagine that if foreign nations decline to comply with the formalities of Chinese etiquette, China will thereby be disgraced, but in my humble opinion, compliance on their part would jeopardise our country. From ancient times immemorial the policy of the Government has been guided by two main factors, viz., the exigencies of the moment and the amount of force available to carry out a given line of action. At the present moment China's position does not justify her in contending for this point and our national forces are quite inadequate to impose our will upon any other nation. China should therefore seek to develop efficiency and in the meantime resort to compromises.

"A disciple of Confucius once asked the Sage in what lay the art of government. The Master replied that the three first requisites were, a sufficiency of food, a sufficiency of troops and the confidence of the people. The disciple then asked which of these three could be dispensed with, in case of urgent necessity? Confucius replied, 'Dispense first with the troops and next with the food supply.' From this we may learn that the Sage, aiming at perfection in the art of government, would approve of no rash or ill-considered action in deciding a matter of this kind. A clear course of action should be definitely pre-arranged by careful thought; there should be no question of any hasty or immature decision, calculated only to involve the country in difficulties. Our statesmen ought, in the first instance, to have examined this Audience question in all its bearings, weighing carefully the issues involved, and should have considered whether, in view of the relative strength of China and foreign nations, resistance was advisable. If China were not well aware of her own weakness, she would insist upon her rights, and without weighing the relative importance in each case; but as, in the present instance, she does not feel strong enough to insist, the Ministers should have been told at once that the Throne would waive the question of their kneeling at audience, and that His Majesty would dispense in their case with the formalities and ceremonies required by the etiquette of the Chinese Court. By so doing we should have avoided the outward and visible manifestations of weakness, and foreigners would have been led to perceive how small is the importance we attach to them as individuals. Would not this be an example of enlightenment and statesmanship to impress Chinese and barbarians alike?

"But no; we must needs begin by raising objections to receiving the foreign Envoys, and then, having been compelled to yield this point, we proceeded to require them to kneel at audience. The only possible result of this will be that we shall finally have to yield to their protest; but our acquiescence will perforce be performed with bad grace and with every appearance of an act performed under compulsion. It was precisely in this way that we blundered when we made the Treaty of Tientsin. I am convinced that the Throne's position will be an unenviable one if the views of these statesmen be adopted, and would suggest as a solution of the difficulty, that His Majesty should decide for himself, and inform his Councillors that the question is really one of minor importance. The foreign Ministers are not Chinese subjects; why, then, should they conform to a Chinese ceremony? If they were to do so, and if the ceremonial were slovenly or awkwardly performed, might it not become a burlesque? And if the foreign Ministers were thus made to look ridiculous, would not China be violating the principle which lays down that we must 'treat strangers from afar with courtesy and consideration'? If it should happen—as well might be—that the spectators should be unable to control their mirth at so ridiculous a spectacle, might not the humiliation felt by the foreigners at their discomfiture, and their consequent rage, lead them to declare war against China? It seems, therefore, advisable that the Throne should issue a Decree excusing the Envoys from performing the ceremonies of our Court, and, in the event of their ignorantly offending against any of the rules of etiquette, that we should exercise a wise forbearance. Our statesmen should refrain from querulous arguments; they should bear in mind that to dispute with these foreigners is unworthy of us. In this they will display the perfection of magnanimity. At the same time it should be carefully explained that this Decree is an act of clemency, of the Emperor's own initiative, and contrary to the advice of his Ministers. It must not serve as a precedent by reason of which foreigners may be led to demand other concessions from China, or to coerce her in other directions. By these means we shall preserve our self-respect, and at the same time prevent all possibility of our people attempting reprisals against foreigners, to avenge what they might regard as an insult to China. And for the rest, let us proceed to develop our strength, biding our time.

"One word only would I add, of warning. It is possible that the audacious and treacherous foreigners may endeavour to address His Majesty at audience. Our statesmen should be prepared in advance with the proper reply to make in such a case, so that they may avoid being put to sudden confusion.

"I, the writer of this worthless Memorial, am but an ignorant inhabitant of a wild and remote district, and know nothing of affairs of State. Greatly daring and of rash utterance, I present this my Memorial, knowing the while that in so doing I risk the penalty of death."

To this Memorial the following Rescript was issued by the Empresses Dowager:—

"We have perused this Memorial and find it not lacking in point. The foreign Ministers are hereby permitted to appear at Audience and to act thereat in accordance with their own national Court ceremonies. Thus the Throne will display its benevolent indulgence to the strangers from afar and make a proper distinction between Chinese and barbarians."

It is worthy of note that the author of the Memorial was the same upright and fearless Censor, Wu K'o-tu, whose name became a household word upon his committing suicide at the grave of T'ung-Chih, as an act of protest against the illegality of the succession ordained by Tzǔ Hsi. If such were (and are) the views held by China's bravest and best, can we wonder at the absurdities that have led the ignorant masses to sudden uprisings and deeds of violence against the foreigners? Wu K'o-tu's trenchant scorn of the sordid commercialism that marks the foreigners' Treaties, is typical of the attitude of the orthodox Chinese scholar.

VIII

MAJORITY AND DEATH OF THE EMPEROR TUNG-CHIH

IN the eleventh year of T'ung-Chih (November 1872) the Empresses Dowager, as Co-Regents, issued a Decree, recounting the circumstances which had led to the Regency (which they once more described as having been thrust upon them), and announced the fact that His Majesty's education having been completed, they now proposed to hand over to him the reigns of government; they therefore directed that the Court of Astronomers should select an auspicious day upon which His Majesty should assume control. The astrologers and soothsayers having announced that the 26th day of the 1st Moon was of fortunate omen (wherein, as far as the Emperor was concerned, they lied), the Co-Regents issued on that day the last Decree of their first Regency, which is worth reproducing: —

"His Majesty assumes to-day the control of the Government, and our joy at this auspicious event is in some degree blended with feelings of anxiety as to the possible results of this change; but we bear in mind the fact that his sacred Ancestors have all feared the Almighty, and endeavoured to follow in the sacred traditions of their predecessors. At the moment, peace has not been completely restored throughout the Empire, for rebellion is still rife in Yunnan, Shensi and the North-West region. It behoves the Emperor to bear steadily in mind the greatness of the task which God and his ancestors have laid upon him alone, and carefully to obey the House laws of the Dynasty in all things. When not actually engaged on business of State, he should employ his time in studying the classics and the precedents of history, carefully enquiring into the causes which have produced good or bad government, from the earliest times down to the present day. He should be thrifty and diligent, endeavouring to make perfect his government. This has been our one constant endeavour since we took upon ourselves the Regency, the one ideal that has been steadily before our eyes."

The Decree concludes with the usual exhortation to the Grand Council and the high officers of the Provincial administration, to serve the Throne with zeal and loyalty.

As far as the Emperor was concerned, these admirable sentiments appeared to have little or no effect, for his conduct from the outset was undutiful, not to say disrespectful, to his mother. Nor was this to be wondered at, when we remember that since his early boyhood he had shown a marked preference for the Empress Dowager of the East (Tzŭ An) and that he was well aware of the many dissensions and intrigues rife in the Palace generally, and particularly between the Co-Regents. He had now attained his seventeenth year, and, with it, something of the autocratic and imperious nature of his august parent. He was encouraged in his independent attitude by the wife whom Tzŭ Hsi had chosen for him, the virtuous A-lu-te. This lady was of patrician origin, being a daughter of the assistant Imperial tutor, Ch'ung Ch'i. In the first flush of supreme authority, the boy Emperor and his young wife would appear to have completely ignored the danger of their position, but they were speedily to learn by bitter experience that Tzŭ Hsi was not to be opposed, and that to live peacefully with her in the Palace was an end that could only be attained by complete submission to her will. The first trouble arose from the Emperor's refusal to submit State documents for his mother's inspection, but there were soon other and more serious causes of friction. But above and behind all lay the ominous fact that, in the event of an heir being born to the Emperor, A-lu-te would from that day become Empress mother, and in the event of the Emperor's subsequent decease, to her would belong by right the title of Empress Dowager, so that, come what might, Tzŭ Hsi would be relegated to a position of obscurity and insignificant authority. It is impossible to overlook this fact in forming our opinion of subsequent events, and especially of the motives which actuated the Empress Dowager when, after the death of T'ung-Chih, she insisted on the election of another infant Emperor at all costs and in violation of the sacred laws of Dynastic succession. Apart from her inability to brook any form of opposition and her absolutely unscrupulous methods for ridding herself of anything or anyone who stood in the path of her ambition, no impartial estimate of her action at this period can deny the fact that it was entirely to her interest that the Emperor T'ung-Chih should not have an heir, and that his Consort should follow him speedily, in the event of his "mounting the Dragon chariot, and proceeding on the long journey." All commentators agree that Tzŭ Hsi encouraged the youthful Emperor's tendencies to dissipated habits, and that, when these had resulted in a serious illness, she allowed it to wreck havoc with his delicate constitution, without providing him with such medical assistance as might have been available. One of the members of the Imperial Household, by name Kuei Ching,[1] deploring the Emperor's licentious habits and foreseeing his early death, took occasion to urge that the deplorable influence exercised over him by disreputable eunuchs should be removed, and that greater care should be taken of his manners, morals and health. He even went so far, in his zeal, as to decapitate several of the offending eunuchs, but in so doing he incurred not only the displeasure of the Empress Dowager, but of the Emperor himself, who desired neither criticism nor

---

1. This Kuei Ching was an uncle of Tuan Fang, recently Viceroy of Chihli, and a man generally respected.

assistance from anyone around him. The unfortunate Kuei Ching was therefore compelled to resign his post, and to leave the Emperor to his fate. His colleagues, the Ministers of the Household, Wen Hsi and Kuei Pao, men of a very different stamp, and open partisans of the Empress Dowager, not only did nothing to restrain the Emperor from his vicious courses, but actually encouraged him, so that it became a matter of common knowledge and notorious in the capital that they and the Emperor together were wont to consort with all the evil characters in the worst localities of the Southern City. It became cause for scandal in the Palace itself that His Majesty would return from his orgies long after the hour fixed for the morning audience with his high officers of State. He was mixed up in many a drunken brawl and consorted with the lowest dregs of the Chinese city, so that it was no matter for surprise when he contracted the germs of disease which speedily led to his death. Already in 1873 it was apparent that the Dragon Throne would soon be vacant. In December 1874, he contracted smallpox and during his illness the Empresses Dowager were called upon to assume control of the Government. Towards the end of the month, he issued the following Decree.

"We have had the good fortune[1] this month to contract smallpox, and their Majesties, the Empresses Dowager, have shown the greatest possible tenderness in the care for our person. They have also consented to peruse all Memorials and State papers on our behalf, and to carry on the business of the State, for which we are deeply grateful. We feel bound to confer upon their Majesties additional titles of honour, so as to make some return, however small, for their infinite goodness."

The Emperor's enfeebled constitution was unable to resist the ravages of his combined diseases, and his physical condition became in the highest degree deplorable; at 8 P.M. on the 13th January 1875, in the presence of the Empresses Dowager and some

---

1. This disease is regarded amongst the Chinese as one of good omen, especially if the symptoms develop satisfactorily.

twenty Princes and Ministers of the Household, he "ascended the Dragon" and was wafted on high. Amongst those present at his death-bed were the Princes Kung and Ch'un, as well as Tzŭ Hsi's devoted henchman and admirer Jung Lu. After the Emperor's death, a Censor, bolder than his fellows, impeached the two Ministers of the Household who had openly encouraged the Emperor in his dissipated courses, and Tzŭ Hsi, having no further use for their services, dismissed them from office. As further proof of her virtuous admiration for faithful service and disinterested conduct, she invited Kuei Ching to resume his appointment, praising his loyalty; but he declined the invitation, having by this time formed his own opinion of the value of virtue in Her Majesty's service.

The Emperor having died without issue, all would have been plain and meritorious sailing for Tzŭ Hsi and her retention of supreme power, had it not been for the unpleasant fact, known to all the Court, that the Emperor's consort, A-lu-te, was *enceinte* and therefore might confer an heir on the deceased sovereign. In the event of a son being born, it was clear that both A-lu-te and Tzŭ An would *ipso facto* acquire authority theoretically higher than her own, since her title of Empress Mother had lapsed by the death of T'ung-Chih, and her original position was only that of a secondary consort. As the mother of the Emperor, she had by right occupied a predominant position during his minority, but this was now ended. It was to her motherhood that she had owed the first claims to power; now she had nothing but her own boundless ambition, courage and intelligence to take the place of lawful claims and natural ties. With the death of her son the Emperor, and the near prospect of A-lu-te's confinement, it was clear that her own position would require desperate remedies, if her power was to remain undiminished.

Among the senior members of the Imperial Clan, many of whom were jealous of the influence of the Yehonala branch, there was a strong movement in favour of placing on the Throne a grandson of the eldest son of the venerated Emperor Tao-Kuang, namely, the infant Prince P'u Lun, whose claims were excellent, in so far as he was of a generation lower than the deceased T'ung-Chih, but complicated by the fact that his father had been adopted into the direct line from another branch. The Princes and nobles who favoured this choice pointed out that the infant P'u Lun was almost the only nominee who would satisfy the laws of succession and allow of the proper sacrifices being performed to the spirit of the deceased T'ung-Chih.[1]

Tzŭ Hsi, however, was too determined to retain her position and power to allow any weight to attach to sentimental, religious, or other considerations. If, in order to secure her objects, a violation of the ancestral and House-laws were necessary, she was not the woman to hesitate, and she trusted to her own intelligence and the servility of her tools in the Censorate to put matters right, or, at least, to overcome all opposition. At this period she was on bad terms with her colleague and Co-Regent, whom she had never forgiven for her share in the decapitation of her Chief Eunuch, An Te-hai; she hated and mistrusted Prince Kung, and there is hardly a doubt that she had resolved to get rid of the young Empress A-lu-te before the birth of her child. The only member of the Imperial family with whom she was at this time on intimate terms was her brother-in-law, Prince Ch'un, the seventh son of the Emperor Tao-Kuang. This Prince, an able man, though dissolute in his habits, had married her favourite sister, the younger Yehonala, and it will, therefore, be readily understood that the reasons which actuated her in deciding to place this Prince's infant son upon the Throne were of the very strongest. During his minority she would continue to rule the Empire, and, should he live to come of age, her sister, the Emperor's mother, might be expected to exert her influence to keep him in the path of dutiful obedience. Tzŭ Hsi's objection to the son of Prince Kung was partly due to the fact that she had never

---

1. The annual and seasonal sacrifices at the ancestral Temple and at the Imperial tombs involve "kowtowing" before each tablet of the sacred ancestors, and this cannot be done in the presence of one of the same generation as the last deceased, much less by him.

forgiven his father for his share in the death of the eunuch, An Te-hai, and other offences, and partly because the young Prince was now in his seventeenth year, and would, therefore, almost immediately have assumed the Government in his own person. Tzŭ Hsi was aware that, in that event, it would be in accordance with tradition and the methods adopted by the stronger party in the Forbidden City for ridding itself of inconvenient rivals and conflicting authorities, that either she should be relegated to complete obscurity here below, or forcibly assisted on the road to Heaven. It was thus absolutely necessary for her to put a stop to this appointment, and, as usual, she acted with prompt thoroughness, which speedily triumphed over the disorganised efforts of her opponents. By adroit intrigues, exercised chiefly through her favourite eunuch, she headed off any attempt at co-operation between the supporters of Prince P'u Lun and those of Prince Kung, while, with the aid of Jung Lu and the appearance on the scene of a considerable force of Li Hung-chang's Anhui troops, she prepared the way for the success of her own plans; her preparations made, she summoned a Council of the Clans-men and high officials, to elect and appoint the new Emperor.

This solemn conclave took place in the Palace of "Mind Nur-ture," on the western side of the Forbidden City, about a quarter of a mile distant from the palace in which the Emperor Tung-Chih had expired. In addition to the Empresses Regent, those present numbered twenty-five in all, including several Princes and Imperial Clansmen, the members of the Grand Council, and several of the highest metropolitan officials; but of all these, only five were Chinese. Prince Tsai Chih, the father of Prince P'u Lun, was there, as well as Prince Kung, both representing the proposed legitimate claims to the Throne. The approaches to the Palace were thronged with eunuchs, and Tzŭ Hsi had taken care, with the assistance of Jung Lu, that all the strategical points in the Forbidden City should be held by troops on whose loy-alty she could completely depend. Amongst them were many of Jung Lu's own Banner Corps, as well as detachments chiefly composed of members and adherents of the Yehonala clan. By Tzŭ Hsi's express orders, the newly-widowed Empress A-lu-te was excluded from the Council meeting, and remained dutifully weeping by the bedside of her departed lord, who had already been arrayed in the ceremonial Dragon robes.

In the Council Chamber Tzŭ Hsi and her colleague sat opposite to each other on Thrones; all the officials present were on their knees. Taking precedence as usual, and assuming as of right the *rôle* of chief speaker, Tzŭ Hsi began by remarking that no time must be lost in selecting the new Emperor; it was not fitting that the Throne should remain vacant on the assumption that an heir would be born to His late Majesty. Prince Kung ventured to disagree with this opinion, expressing the view that, as A-lu-te's child would shortly be born, there should be no difficulty in keeping back the news of the Emperor's death for a little while; the child, if a boy, could then rightly and fittingly be placed on the Throne, while in the event of the posthumous child being a daughter, there would still be time enough to make selection of the Emperor's successor. The Princes and Clansmen appeared to side with this view, but Tzŭ Hsi brushed it aside, observing that there were still rebellions unsuppressed in the south, and that if it were known that the Throne was empty, the Dynasty might very well be overthrown. "When the nest is destroyed, how many eggs will remain unbroken?" she asked. The Grand Councillors and several senior statesmen, including the three Chinese representatives from the south, expressed agreement with this view, for they realised that, given conditions of unrest, the recently active Taiping rebels might very easily renew the anti-Dynastic movement.

The Empress Dowager of the East then gave it as her opinion that Prince Kung's son should be chosen heir to the Throne; Prince Kung, in accordance with the customary etiquette, kowtowed and professed unwillingness that such honour should fall to his family, and suggested that the youthful Prince P'u Lun should be elected. P'u Lun's father in turn pleaded the unworthiness of his

INTERIOR OF THE YANG HSIN TIEN. (Palace of "Mind Nurture".)
The Emperor T'ung-Chih used this Palace as his residence during the whole of his reign.

offspring, not because he really felt any qualms on the subject, but because custom necessitated this self-denying attitude. "That has nothing to do with the case," said Tzǔ Hsi to the last speaker, "but as you are only the adopted son of Yi Wei" (the eldest son of the Emperor Tao-Kuang) "what precedent can any of you show for placing on the Throne the heir of an adopted son?" Prince Kung, called upon to reply, hesitated, and suggested as a suitable precedent the case of a Ming Emperor of the fifteenth century canonised as Ying-Tsung. "That is a bad precedent," replied the Empress, who had every precedent of history at her finger ends. "The Emperor Ying-Tsung was not really the son of his predecessor, but was palmed off on the Emperor by one of the Imperial concubines. His reign was a period of disaster; he was for a time in captivity under the Mongols and afterwards lived in retirement at Peking for eight years while the Throne was occupied by his brother." Turning next to her colleague she said, "As for me, I propose as heir to the Throne, Tsai Tien, the son of Yi Huan (Prince Ch'un), and advise you all that we lose no time." On hearing these words Prince Kung turned to his brother and angrily remarked: "Is the right of primogeniture[1] to be completely ignored?" "Let the matter then be decided by taking a vote," said Tzǔ Hsi, and her colleague offered no objections. The result of the vote was that seven of the Princes, led by Prince Ch'un, voted for Prince P'u Lun, and three for the son of Prince Kung; the remainder of the Council voted solidly for Tzǔ Hsi's nominee. The voting was done openly and the result was entirely due to the strong will and dominating personality of the woman whom all had for years recognised as the real ruler of China. When the voting was concluded, Tzǔ An, who was always more anxious for an amicable settlement than for prolonged discussion, intimated her willingness to leave all further arrangements in the hands of her colleague. It was now past nine o'clock, a furious dust-storm was raging and the night was bitterly cold, but Tzǔ Hsi, who never wasted time at moments of crisis, ordered a strong detachment

---

1. Prince Kung was the sixth, Prince Ch'un the seventh, in order of seniority.

of Household troops to be sent to the residence of Prince Ch'un in the Western City, and with it the Imperial yellow sedan chair with eight bearers, to bring the boy Emperor to the Palace. At the same time, to keep Prince Kung busy and out of harm's way, she gave him charge of the body of the dead Emperor, while she had the Palace surrounded and strongly guarded by Jung Lu's troops. It was in her careful attention to details of this kind that lay her marked superiority to the vacillating and unbusinesslike methods of those who opposed her, and it is this Napoleonic characteristic of the woman which explains much of the success that her own people frequently attributed to luck. Before midnight the little Emperor had been duly installed in the Palace, weeping bitterly upon his ill-omened coming to the Forbidden City. With him came his mother (Tzŭ Hsi's sister) and several nurses. The first event of his reign, imposed upon him, like much future misery, by dynastic precedent, was to be taken at once to the Hall where his deceased predecessor was lying in State, and there to kowtow, as well as his tender years permitted, before the departed ruler. A Decree was thereupon issued in the names of the Empresses Dowager, who thus became once more Regents, announcing, "that they were absolutely compelled to select Tsai Tien for the Throne, and that he should become heir by adoption to his uncle Hsien-Feng, but that, so soon as he should have begotten a son, the Emperor T'ung-Chih would at once be provided with an heir."

By this means the widowed Empress A-lu-te was completely passed over, and the claims of her posthumous son ignored in advance. Once more Tzŭ Hsi had gained an easy and complete victory. It was clear to those who left the Council Chamber after the issue of this Decree, that neither the young widowed Empress nor the unborn child of T'ung-Chih were likely to give much more trouble.

For form's sake, and in accordance with dynastic precedents, a Memorial was submitted by all the Ministers and Princes of the Household, begging their Majesties the Empresses to resume

the Regency, who, on their part, went through the farce of ac-
ceding graciously to this request, on the time-honoured ground
that during the Emperor's minority there must be some central
authority to whom the officials of the Empire might look for the
necessary guidance. It was only fitting and proper, however,
that reluctance should be displayed, and Tzŭ Hsi's reply to the
Memorial therefore observed that "the perusal of this Memorial
has greatly increased our grief and sorrowful recognition of the
exigencies of the times, for we had hoped that the Regency was
merely a temporary measure of unusual expediency. Be it known
that so soon as the Emperor shall have completed his education,
we shall immediately hand over to him the affairs of the Government."

The infant Emperor was understood to express "dutiful
thanks to their Majesties for this virtuous act" and all the formalities of the tragic comedy were thus completed. The Empress
Dowager gave orders that the repairs which had been begun at
the Lake and Summer Palaces should now be stopped, the reason given being that the Empresses Regent would have no time
nor desire for gaiety in the years to come; the real reason being,
however, that the death of the Emperor removed all necessity for
their Majesties leaving the Forbidden City.

Tzŭ Hsi's success in forcing her wishes upon the Grand Council and having her sister's infant son appointed to the Imperial
succession, in opposition to the wishes of a powerful party and
in violation of the dynastic law, was entirely due to her energy
and influence. The charm of her personality, and the convincing directness of her methods were more effective than all the
forces of tradition. This fact, and her triumph, become the more
remarkable when we bear in mind that she had been advised,
and the Grand Council was aware, that the infant Emperor suffered from physical weaknesses which, even at that date, rendered it extremely unlikely that he would ever provide an heir
to the Throne. Those who criticised her selection, knowing this,
would have been therefore in a strong position had they not been

lacking in courage and decision, since it was clear, if the fact were admitted, that Her Majesty's only possible motive was personal ambition.

From that time until the death of the Emperor and her own, on the 14th and 15th November 1908, the belief was widespread, and not infrequently expressed, that the Emperor, whose reign began thus inauspiciously, would not survive her, and there were many who predicted that his death would occur before the time came for him to assume supreme control of the Government. All foretold that Tzŭ Hsi would survive him, for the simple reason that only thus could she hope to regulate once more the succession and continue the Regency. The prophets of evil were wrong, as we know, inasmuch as Kuang-Hsü was allowed his years of grace in control of affairs, but we know also that after the *coup d'état* it was only the fear of an insurrection in the south that saved his life and prevented the accession of a new boy Emperor.

The designation of the new reign was then ordered to be "Kuang-Hsü," meaning "glorious succession"; it was chosen to emphasise the fact that the new Emperor was a direct lineal descendant of the last great Manchu Emperor, Tao-Kuang, and to suggest the hope that the evil days of Hsien-Feng and T'ung-Chih had come to an end. The next act of the Empresses Regent was to confer an honorific title upon the late Emperor's widow; but the honour was not sufficient to prevent her from committing suicide on the 27th of March as an act of protest at the grievous wrong done to her, to the memory of her husband and to the claims of his posthumous heir. This was the unofficial explanation current, but opinions have always differed, and must continue to differ, as to the truth of the suicide, there being many who, not unnaturally, accused Tzŭ Hsi of putting an end to the unfortunate woman. Against this the Empress's advocates observe that, having succeeded in obtaining the appointment of Kuang-Hsü to the Throne, and the matter being irrevocably settled, there existed no further necessity for any act of violence: but few, if any, suggest that had circumstances necessitated violent measures they would not have been taken. The balance of evidence is undoubtedly in the direction of foul play. But, however administered, it is certain that the death of the Empress A-lu-te influenced public opinion more profoundly than she could ever have done by living; as a result, thousands of Memorials poured in from the Censorate and the provinces, strongly protesting against the selection of the infant son of Prince Ch'un for the Throne, as a violation of all ancestral custom and the time-honoured laws of succession. It is significant that all these protests were clearly directed against Tzŭ Hsi, her colleague's nonentity being practically and generally recognised. For a time Tzŭ Hsi's popularity (and therefore the position of the Yehonala clan) was seriously affected, and when, four years later, the Censor, Wu K'o-tu, committed suicide near T'ung-Chih's grave to emphasise the seriousness of the crime and to focus public attention on the matter, the Empress was compelled to bow to the storm and to give a second and more solemn pledge that the deceased Emperor should not permanently be left without heirs to perform for him the sacrifices of ancestral worship. It will be seen hereafter how she kept that pledge.

Prince Ch'un, in the capacity of father to the new Emperor, submitted a Memorial asking leave to be permitted to resign his various offices, because, as an official, he would be bound to kowtow to the Emperor, and as a father he could not kowtow to his own son. In the course of this Memorial, which reminds the reader unpleasantly of Mr. Pecksniff, the Prince observes that when first informed of his son's selection as heir to the Dragon Throne, "he almost fainted and knew not what to do. When borne to his home, his body was trembling and his heart palpitating severely; like a madman, or one who walks in dreams, was he, so that he incurred a serious recurrence of his liver trouble and the state of his health became really a matter for anxiety. He would prefer that the silent tomb should close forthwith over his remains rather than to continue to draw the breath of life as the useless son of the Emperor Tao-Kuang."

The Empress Dowager, in reply, directed her faithful Ministers to devise a careful compromise "based on the special requirements of the case," the result of which was that Prince Ch'un was permitted to resign his offices and excused from attendance at all Court ceremonies involving obeisance to the Emperor, but was retained in a sort of general capacity as "adviser to the Empresses Regent" to serve when called upon. On the birthdays of the Empresses Regent, he would be permitted to prostrate himself before them in private, and not as a member of the Court in attendance on the Emperor. His first class Princedom was made hereditary for ever, and he was commanded to give the benefit of his experience and sage counsel to his successor, Prince Tun, as officer commanding the Manchu Field Force — an order which he must have obeyed, for the Force in question became more and more notorious for its tatterdemalion uselessness and the corruption of its commanders.

Remembering the institution of the first Regency, it will be noted how faithfully history can be made to repeat itself in the Celestial Empire.

IX

THE PROTEST AND SUICIDE OF WU K'O-TU

IMMEDIATELY after the death of T'ung-Chih's young widow, the validity of the Imperial succession and the violation of all traditions which Tzŭ Hsi had committed, became a matter of grave concern to the conservative and more conscientious supporters of the Dynasty. The first evidence of dissatisfaction was contained in a Memorial submitted by a Manchu sub-Chancellor of the Grand Secretariat who, while accepting the situation as it stood in regard to the boy Emperor, Kuang-Hsü, stipulated that safeguards or guarantees should be given by the Throne for the eventual regulation of the succession and for the provision of heirs to His orbate Majesty, T'ung-Chih. The Memorial was as follows: —

"The selection of an heir to the Throne is a matter resting entirely with the Sovereign and beyond scope of interference or criticism by any subject. But in cases where the arrangements made necessitate modification in order to render them perfect, a loyal subject is justified, if not compelled, to speak his mind freely.

"The whole Empire looked forward to seeing our late Emperor enjoy a long and prosperous reign, but he has passed away without leaving any posterity. The selection of a successor which your Majesties the Empresses Dowager have, in your wisdom, decided upon is admirable no doubt, particularly since you have promised that an heir shall eventually be provided for His Majesty, T'ung-Chih. This proves that in regulating the dynastic succession, you are proceeding precisely as if it were a case of adoption from one family into another: you have therefore wisely decided that not only shall a son be adopted to the late Emperor, but that in due course his succession will be carried on by a grandson in the direct line of generation, so that His Majesty's posterity may be established without a break, and perpetuated without intermission for all time.

"The proposal in itself is excellent, but study of the Sung Dynasty's history has led me to view the matter with no small apprehension. The founder of that Dynasty, the Emperor Chao Kuang-yin (tenth century), following the directions of his mother the Empress Dowager, made his brother heir to the Throne instead of his son, it being understood that upon his brother's death the succession should revert to his son.[1] Subsequently however, the brother, having come to the Throne, and having listened to the evil suggestions of his Privy Councillors, ignored the claims of his nephew, and placed his own son upon the Throne. In that instance, obedience to the wishes of his mother has brought down upon the Emperor Chao Kuang-yin the undying censure of posterity. If the Empress, on that occasion, had done her duty, and had caused unbreakable bonds to be given assuring the reversion of the succession to the direct line, no irregularities could possibly have occurred: the Decrees would have been as immovable as the Sacred Mountain, and as self-evident as the nine tripods of the Emperor Yü. It would have been impossible for any misguided Councillors of State to justify their unlawful interference

---

1. On the occasion to which the Memorialist refers, the lawful heir to the Throne committed suicide. The allusion would be readily understood (if not appreciated) by the Empress Dowager, whose irregular choice of Kuang-Hsü and violation of the dynastic laws had certainly led to the death of A-lu-te. Looked at from the Chinese scholar's point of view, the innuendo was in the nature of a direct accusation.

with the rightful course of succession.

"From all this we learn that the succession, although decided in a moment, affects all posterity. Was it not, moreover, by self-sacrifice and strong family affections[1] that our Dynasty acquired the Empire: have we not for example the records of each succeeding virtuous Emperor? We cannot therefore entertain any doubt but that the present Emperor, when he comes to have an heir, will forthwith make him son by adoption to the late Emperor, so that the succession may proceed along the direct line. No doubt this is the intention, but, as history shows, there exists a danger that, with the lapse of time, suggestions may be put forward similar to those of the Privy Council nine centuries ago, which would utterly frustrate the wise policy animating your Majesties the Empresses Dowager, and leave no fixed principles for posterity to follow. With your approval, therefore, we would ask that the Princes and Ministers be now required to draw up and record an unbreakable and unchangeable pledge as to the succession to the Throne, which should be proclaimed for the information of all your Majesties' subjects."

Tzŭ Hsi was becoming decidedly irritable on this subject of the succession, and there can be little doubt that her own conscience and the views of patriotic Memorialists came to much the same conclusion. The Rescript which she issued on the present occasion was short, sharp, and suggestive of temper:—

"We have already issued an absolutely clear Decree on this subject," she said, "providing for an heir to the late Emperor, and the Decree has been published all over the Empire. The Memorialist's present request gives evidence of unspeakable audacity and an inveterate habit of fault-finding, which has greatly enraged us, so that we hereby convey to him a stern rebuke."

---

1. The writer refers to the united action of the Manchu Princes and nobles who assisted in the establishment of law and order, and the expulsion of the Chinese rebels and Pretenders, during the troublous time of the first Regency (1644) and the minority of the infant Emperor, Shun-Chih.

The Memorials and remonstrances of many high officials emphasised the seriousness of this question of the legitimacy of the
Imperial succession to the nation at large, and its profound effect
on the fundamental principles of ancestor worship. Nevertheless, having delivered their souls, the Mandarinate, led by the
Peking Boards, were disposed to acquiesce in the *fait accompli*;
in any case, there was no sign of organised opinion in opposition to the will of the Empress Dowager. The irregularity was
evidently serious, and Heaven would doubtless visit the sins of
the Throne, as usual, on the unoffending "stupid people"; but the
individualism and mutual suspicion that peculiarly distinguish
the Chinese official world, precluded all idea of concerted action
or remedial measures.

One official, however, had the full courage of his convictions, and, by the time-honoured expedient of self-destruction,
focussed the attention of the nation on the gravity of the question, as no amount of fine writing could have done. Resort to
suicide by indignant patriots, as a proof of their sincere distress,
is a practice praised and justified alike by historians in China and
Japan, and there is no denying that, as an argument against all
forms of despotism, it has the crowning merit of finality. It has,
moreover, certain qualities of deliberate courage and cultured
philosophy that bring irresistibly to mind the Roman patrician at
his best, and which fully account for the distinction which such
a death confers amongst a people that loves its orthodoxies, as it
loves peace, undisturbed.

The name which will go down in Chinese history, as the de-
fender of the national and true faith in connection with the illegal
succession of the infant Emperor Kuang-Hsü, is that of the Censor, Wu K'o-tu, an upright and fearless scholar of the best type.
For the reasons stated in his farewell Memorial, he waited four
years after the death of the Emperor T'ung-Chih, hoping against
hope that the widespread dissatisfaction of the *literati* and officials would take definite form, and lead the Empress Dowager
to regulate the future succession, and to placate the disinherited

ghost of T'ung-Chih, by the issue of a new Decree. Disappointed in this hope, he seized the classically correct occasion of the late Emperor's funeral (1879) to commit suicide near his grave, taking care to leave behind him a swan-song which, as he knew, will live long in the memory of scholars and officials throughout the Empire. His death had the immediate effect of convincing Tz ŭ Hsi of error. Realising the strength of public opinion underlying the Censor's protest, she endeavoured at once to placate his accusing spirit by giving the pledges for which he had pleaded, in regard to provision in the future of a successor to T'ung-Chih. Nor was it on this occasion only that the death of Wu K'o-tu influenced her actions and disturbed her superstitious mind. In after years, and especially at the time of the flight to Hsi-an, she recognised his influence, and the punishment of her misdeed, in the disasters which had overtaken the Throne.

As an example of the principles of action, and the calm frame of mind which are the fine flower of the Confucian system of philosophy, and, therefore, worthy of our close and sympathetic study, we give the full story of the death of this patriotic protestant, as well as a translation of his Memorial.

His suicide took place in a small temple at Ma-shen ch'iao, close to the mausoleum of T'ung-Chih. His minutely detailed instructions for the disposal of his remains, with the least possible trouble to his family and friends, bespeak the gentleman and the scholar. To the priest in charge of the shrine, a "bad man," he addressed the following characteristic letter:—

"Priest Chou, be not afraid. I have no desire to bring evil upon you. I was compelled to borrow the use of your plot of hallowed ground, as a spot appropriate for the death of an honest man. Inform now the Magistrate at once, and see that the Memorial enclosed in my despatch box is forwarded without delay. Buy for me a cheap coffin and have it painted black inside. My clothes are all in order, only the leather soles of my boots require to be cut off before you lay me in your coffin. I have cut my finger slightly, which accounts for the blood stains that you may notice. Twenty taels will be ample for my coffin. I should not think that the Magistrate will need to hold an inquest. Please have a coating of lacquer put on the coffin, to fill up any cracks in the joints, and have it nailed down, pending the Empresses' decision as to my remains. Then, buy a few feet of ground adjoining the late Emperor's tomb, and have me buried quickly.[1] There is no need for me to be buried in my ancestral cemetery; any spot is a good enough resting place for a loyal and honest man.

"You will find forty-five taels in my box, of which you may keep the balance after paying for my coffin and burial expenses. As to my watch, and the other articles on my person, it is known at my home exactly what I brought here with me. You must see to it that no one is permitted to insult my corpse, and my son will be deeply grateful to you for performing these last offices for me, in his place. You need not fear that the Magistrate's underlings will make trouble for you, but be careful not to tamper with the box containing my Memorial to the Empresses.

"You can cut my body down to-morrow morning, and then have it placed in some cool and shady spot. Fearing that possibly you might come in by accident and find me hanging, I have taken a dose of opium, so as to make certain of death. If you should dare to meddle with my private affairs, as you have been trying to do these past few days, it will only lead to your being mixed up in the case, which might bring you to grief.

"All I ask of you is that you notify the Magistrate at once, and that you do not allow women and children to come in and gaze upon my remains. There is nothing strange or abnormal here; death had become an unavoidable duty. Those who understand me, will pity; that is all. The last earnest instructions of Wu K'o-tu."

Next, to his son, he expressed his dying wishes in a letter

---

1. The burial place was close to, but necessarily outside, the large enclosed park which contains the Imperial mausolea.

which embodies many of the Confucian scholar's most cherished ideals and beliefs, a document pathetic in its simple dignity, its pride of ancient lineage and duty well done according to his lights.

"Chih-huan, my son, be not alarmed when you hear the news of my death, and on no account allow your grief to disturb the family. Your mother is old, your wife is young, and my poor little grandchildren are but babies. Tell them that I am dead, but bid them not to grieve over my suicide. Our family tree goes back over five hundred years; for two centuries there have been members of our clan among the Imperial concubines, and for three hundred years we have devoted ourselves to husbandry and scholarship. For eighteen generations our family has borne a good name; I, who am now seventy years of age, can claim an unsullied record, although as a lad I was somewhat given to dissipation. No man can truthfully accuse me of having failed to observe the main principles of duty, and it is for this reason that my friends and former pupils have always sought my services as a teacher of the Confucian doctrine. Quite recently I declined the pressing invitation of the Grand Secretary, the Marquis Tso Tsung-t'ang, who wished me to become tutor to his family, because the date was at hand for His late Majesty's burial, and I desired quietly to await to-day's event.

"Ever since, at the age of twenty-four, I took my M.A. degree, I have been of prudent conduct, and have observed the proprieties in official life. In the study of history I have ever been deeply touched by examples of patriotism and loyalty to the Sovereign, and the splendid lives of the ancients have moved me, now to tears and again to exuberance of joy.

"Upon the death of the late Emperor, I had determined to memorialise the Empresses Dowager, through the Censorate, and had fully made up my mind to accept my fate for so doing; but an old friend, to whom I showed the draft, begged me not to forward it, not only because I had already been punished for similar rashness on a former occasion, but because he said some of its allusions to current events were not absolutely accurate. Therefore I waited until to-day, but now I can wait no longer. It is my wish to die, in order that the purpose of my life may be fittingly accomplished and a lifetime of loyalty consummated. My death is in no way due to the slanders which have been circulated about me.

"When you receive this letter, come straightway to the Temple of the Threefold Duties at the bridge of the God of Horses, twelve miles to the east of Chi Chou and quite close to the Imperial mausolea. There seek out the Taoist priest, Chou; he knows my burial place, and I have asked him to buy me a coffin and to have it painted black inside. My burial clothes are all in order, but I have asked him to cut off the leather soles from my boots.[1] He is to buy a certain small piece of ground, close to the Imperial tomb, which is to be my grave. This will be far better than having my remains taken to the ancestral burial ground, and there is really no need for me to rest there, as my younger brother already lies beside your grandparents. He, you remember, committed suicide twenty years ago at his house in Peking, because of private troubles, and now I follow his example, because of disorder in the State. People will say, no doubt, that our family burial ground is become a place of evil omen, but pay no heed to them. No doubt you will desire to take home my remains, but do not so. Take instead my photograph, the one I had taken just before I left Peking, and have an enlargement of it hung up in our family hall. Thus shall you observe the old custom which preserves relics of the departed. Why go to the expense and trouble of transporting a coffin over a thousand miles?

"Even though it should happen that the Empresses should cause dire penalties to be inflicted upon my corpse because of my effrontery of language, you may be sure that in this enlightened age, there is no possibility of my offences being visited

---

1. Burial clothes should all be new and clean by cutting away the soles, his boots would look less shabby.

upon my wife and family. All you need do is to borrow from our friends money enough to take you from Peking, and after that, you must make the best of your way to our family home, begging if necessary. On no account must you remain in Peking, for by so doing you will only attract attention and further endanger your father.[1]

"What I chiefly deprecate in you, my son, is your quick tongue; you must really try to amend your ways in this respect and endeavour to be less hasty. If people tell you that your father was loyal, do not contradict them; if they say he was an honest man, you should agree. Read carefully the advice of Ma Yuan, the great General, to his nephew, and Wang Hou's admonitions to his sons.

"When your mother married me she had good prospects, as the daughter of an old military family. Since her marriage she has dutifully served my parents, and her reputation for filial devotion is excellent. I regret that I was not destined to bring her happiness and good fortune: she is old now, and you alone are left to her. It is your duty to take her to our home and minister to her old age.

"As regards the few poor acres of land left me by my father, I feel that I cannot reasonably expect you to follow the example of the ancient worthies and to surrender it all to your brothers, but at least I ask that you should allow them to live amicably with you. Your wife is a sensible woman — tell her from me that the happiness of every household depends on the temper of its womenfolk. I knew one woman who feigned death in order to induce her husband to treat his brothers more kindly, but this was a heroic act, far above the moral capacity of your wife.

"As to the forty taels[2] which you will find on my person, you will hand over to the Taoist priest, Chou, any balance there may remain after he has paid for my coffin and burial expenses. On arriving at Chi Chou, go at once and see the Magistrate, to whom

---

1. *i.e.* by causing the Empresses to have his corpse mutilated.
2. About £10.

I have written; thence proceed to the temple, where you must give them some extra money to compensate them for all the trouble they have had. Thereafter return to Peking, and there await the Empresses' decision in regard to my case.

"See to it that my small debts are all paid, that my life may end in fitting and harmonious dignity. At a moment like this, I am naturally agitated in mind. It is hard to foretell what the decision of the Empresses may be, but at least my conscience is clear, and what does anything else matter? For your own personal safety, I do not think you need have any fear.

"Present my compliments to Chang Chih-tung: I only wish I could have had more of the old time talks with him. Go also to the Marquis Tso Tsung-t'ang. He has not treated me well of late, but slanders poisoned his sympathy, at which I do not wonder. The memory of his former kindnesses is precious to me, and I know that he will never let you starve.

"Your wife, in giving birth to my grandchildren, has conferred blessings upon me; you must never think of allowing her parents to provide for you. Leave therefore at once for our family home. There must be no delay about this. As to the Taoist priest, it irks me to make use of people in this way. He is a bad man; yet must we bear with him. Tell him that I regret having put his temple to this purpose; he need only spend ten taels on my coffin and a few taels more for the little plot of ground to bury me in. I am a worthless official and deserve nothing better than this.

"Why have I delayed so long? Because I did not wish to disturb the Empresses with the news of my death at this critical time. All the Decrees which have appeared since the Emperor Kuang-Hsü came to the Throne have moved me greatly, and much have I deplored my inability to serve Their Majesties better. In days of old, loyal servants of the State were wont to commit suicide as an act of remonstrance against the degeneracy of their Sovereigns. Not for a moment are the Empresses to be compared to monarchs like Ming Huang of the T'ang Dynasty, who deserted his capital before the invader, or Li Tsung, of the Sungs, whose foolishness led to the Mongol wars. Nevertheless my death is due to the same principles as those which actuated those faithful Councillors.

"Go home now, and teach your children to study. Do not open my Memorial to the Empresses. It is sealed, and I have asked the local Magistrate to forward it for presentation."

His Memorial to the Throne was, in fact (as the letter to his son plainly indicates), an indictment of the degeneracy of the ruler of the Empire; incidentally, it throws much light on the orthodox point of view in regard to the question of the Imperial succession. Its preamble sets forth the object with which it was written, and in the hope of which the writer died, namely, to induce the Empress Dowager to determine the future succession, providing an heir to the Emperor Tung-Chih, in accordance with precedent and the laws of the Dynasty. The text of this remarkable document is as follows: —

"I, your worthless servant, have heard that the fact of a nation being well governed does not necessarily preclude all possibility of anarchy, nor does a nation at peace dismiss altogether from mind the chances of violent disturbance; should anarchy and rebellion be regarded as possibilities too remote to merit a thought, it were idle and superfluous to advise the Sovereign of so perfect a State. To ask the Imperial wisdom to see danger where no real peril exists would be simply inviting evil omens.

"On a former occasion I, your guilty servant, wittingly incurred danger of death or imprisonment, because, in the heat of indignation, I dared to remonstrate with the Throne. At that time the Princes and Ministers about your Throne asked permission to subject me to a criminal enquiry, but His late Majesty T'ung-Chih was pleased to spare me, so that I neither suffered death by the headsman's sword nor imprisonment, nor did I run the risk of further exciting the Imperial wrath by my evidence before a criminal court. Thrice have I deserved, without receiving, the penalty of death. Without desiring my forfeit life, it was granted me, so that my last few years have been, as it were, a boon at the hands of His late Majesty.

"But on the 5th day of the 12th Moon of the 13th year of T'ung-Chih the earth was rent and heaven itself was shaken by the great catastrophe, and on that day their Majesties the Empresses Dowager issued the following Decree: 'The departed Emperor has mounted the Dragon and is become a guest on high, leaving no heir to the Throne. We are compelled to appoint Tsai T'ien, son of Prince Ch'un, to be heir to His Majesty Hsien-Feng, to enter on the great inheritance as the new Emperor. When to him an heir shall be born, he shall become son by adoption to the late Emperor T'ung-Chih.'

"I, your unworthy servant, wept bitterly as, reverently kneeling, I read this Decree. I cannot but feel, after most careful consideration, that the Empresses Dowager have doubly erred in appointing an heir to the Emperor Hsien-Feng and not to His late Majesty. For thus the new Emperor, being heir to His Majesty Hsien-Feng, enters upon the great heritage not, as he should, by mandate of His late Majesty T'ung-Chih, but by mandate of the Empresses. Hence the future succession must, as a matter of course, revert to the heir of the new Emperor, even though there should be no explicit instructions to that effect. But, as this Decree expressly ordains that this shall be so, it follows that a precedent will be established, whereby the great inheritance may pass by adoption.

"I, your unworthy servant, realise that it is no light matter for a loyal subject to refer to the future death of a Sovereign while that Sovereign is still alive, entitled to all his reverence and devotion. But, for more than two centuries, the ancestral tradition of our House-law has been observed that the Throne shall pass from father to son, and this law should be steadfastly maintained for ten thousand generations amongst those of us who recognise a common descent. Moreover, Prince Ch'un is a loyal statesman, justly revered by all as a virtuous Prince. His Memorial has inspired every one of us with fresh feelings of enthusiastic loyalty.

His words are but the mirror of his mind; how could any false-
ness find therein a place? When I perused his Memorial, tears of
joy irrepressible fell from my eyes. If ever the Prince should learn
of this my humble Memorial, he may perchance be wroth at my
perversity or pity my folly; at all events he will never blame me
for endeavouring to stir up vain strife by my words.

"The new Emperor is of gentle disposition; from the Empress
Dowager he had received the 'precious inheritance' and until his
dying day he will naturally be of one mind with the Empresses
in this matter. But in the Palace there are sycophants as well as
honest men, and many conflicting opinions. To take examples
from history: at the beginning of the Sung Dynasty, even that
great and good man the Grand Secretary Chao P'u, led the way
in obeying the orders of the Empress Dowager Tu. Again, under
the Ming Dynasty, a venerable servant of the State, the Grand
Secretary Wang Chih, was ashamed that it should be left to a barbarian like Huang Kung (native of an aboriginal tribe in Kuangsi)
to memorialise urging the lawful Heir Apparent's succession to
the Emperor Ching-T'ai, when no Chinese official dared to do so.
If even virtuous men could act thus, what need to enquire about
disloyal subjects? If such be the conduct of old servants, how
shall we blame upstarts? To set aside settled ordinances may be
bad, but how much worse is our case where no ordinances exist?
We should therefore seek if perchance we may find some way
out of this double error, whereby we may return to the right way.
I therefore beg that the Empresses may be pleased to issue a second Decree explicitly stating that the great inheritance shall hereafter revert to the adopted son of His late Majesty T'ung-Chih,
and that no Minister shall be allowed to upset this Decree, even
though the new Emperor be blessed with a hundred sons. If, in
this way, the succession be rectified and the situation defined,
so that further confusion be hereafter impossible, the House-law
of the present Dynasty will be observed, which requires that the
Throne be handed down from father to son. Thus, to the late Emperor, now childless, an heir will be provided and the Empresses

Dowager will no longer be without a grandson. And, for all time, the orderly maintenance of the succession will be ascribed to the Empresses, whose fame will be changeless and unending. This is what I, your guilty servant, mean, when I say that the double error which has been committed may yet serve to bring us back to the right way.

"I, your most unworthy slave, had intended to memorialise on this matter when His Majesty died, and to present the Memorial through the Censorate. But it occurred to me that, since I had lost my post, I was debarred from addressing the Throne. Besides, how grave a matter is this! If advice in such a matter be given by a Prince or a Minister, it is called the sage and far-reaching counsel of a statesman; but if it comes from a small and insignificant official it is called the idle utterance of a wanton babbler. Never could I have believed that the many wise and loyal statesmen of your Court could one and all regard this as a matter of no immediate urgency, dismissing it as a question unprofitable for discussion. I waited, therefore, and the precious moments passed, but none of them have moved in the matter.

"Afterwards, having received renewed marks of the Imperial favour, and being again summoned to audience, I was granted the position of a Board Secretary, and placed on the Board of Appointments. This was more than four years ago; yet all this time apparently not one of all the Ministers of your Court has even given this grave matter a moment's consideration. The day for His late Majesty's entombment has now arrived, and I fear that what has happened will gradually pass from the minds of men. The time, therefore, is short, and the reasons which led me to delay hold good no longer. Looking upward, as the divine soul of His Majesty soars heavenward on the Dragon, wistfully I turn my eyes upon the Palace enclosure. Beholding the bows and arrows left behind on the Bridge Mountain,[1] my thoughts turn to the cherished mementoes of my Sovereign. Humbly I offer up

---

1. The point whence, according to legend, the Yellow Emperor ascended to heaven and where his clothes were buried.

these years of life that have been added unto me by His Majesty's clemency; humbly I lay them down in propitiation of the Empresses Dowager, to implore from them a brief Decree on behalf of the late Emperor.

"But, on the point of leaving this world, I feel that my mind is confused. The text of this, my Memorial, lacks clearness; there are manifold omissions in it. It has ever been my custom to revise a draft twice before handing in a Memorial, but on this occasion I have not been able to make such careful revision. I, your unworthy servant, am no scholar like to the men of old; how, then, could I be calm and collected as they were wont to be? Once there went a man to his death, and he could not walk erect. A bystander said to him 'Are you afraid, sir?' He replied, 'I am.' 'If you are afraid, why not turn back?' He replied, 'My fear is a private weakness; my death is a public duty.' This is the condition in which I find myself to-day. 'When a bird is dying its song is sad. When a man is dying his words are good.'[1] How could I, your worthless servant, dare to compare myself with the sage Tseng Tzu? Though I am about to die, yet may my words not be good; but I trust that the Empresses and the Emperor will pity my last sad utterance, regarding it neither as an evil omen nor the idle plaint of one who has no real cause for grief. Thus shall I die without regret. A statesman of the Sung Dynasty has remarked: 'To discuss an event before it occurs is foolhardy. But if one waits until it has occurred, speech is then too late, and, therefore, superfluous.' Foolhardiness notwithstanding, it is well that the Throne should be warned before events occur; no Minister should ever have to reproach himself with having spoken too late. Heartily do I wish that my words may prove untrue, so that posterity may laugh at my folly. I do not desire that my words may be verified, for posterity to acclaim my wisdom. May it be my fate to resemble Tu Mu,[2] even though to imitate him be a transgression of duty. May

---

1. A quotation from Tseng Tzu, one of the most noted disciples of Confucius.
2. A sort of Chinese Mr. Malaprop, known to history as one who invariably spoke at the wrong time.

I be likened, rather, to Shih Ch'iu, the sight of whose dead body proved, as he had hoped, an effective rebuke to his erring Prince. Thus may my foolish but loyal words be justified in the end.

"I pray the Empresses and Emperor to remember the example of Their Majesties Shun-Chih and K'ang-Hsi, in tempering justice with mercy: that they may promote peace and prosperity, by appointing only worthy men to public offices; that they may refrain from striving for those objects which foreigners hold dear, for by such striving they will surely jeopardise the future of our Middle Kingdom; that they may never initiate any of the innovations disdained by their ancestors, which would assuredly leave to posterity a heritage of woe. These are my last words, my last prayer, the end and crown of my life.

POSTSCRIPT.

"Having been a Censor, I venture thus to memorialise the Throne. But as my present official position does not permit of my forwarding this direct, I request the high officials of my Board to present it for me. As my name did not figure originally in the list of officials to represent my Board at the ceremonies preparatory to His late Majesty's burial, I begged the Grand Secretary Pao Yün to allow me to be included in the list. Pao Yün could not have foretold my suicide, so that no blame can attach to him for being my sponsor. Under our enlightened Dynasty, how could anyone imagine a return to the ancient and happily obsolete practice of being buried alive with one's Sovereign? But my grief is too great and cannot be restrained; for to-day my Sovereign returns, dragon-borne, to Heaven, and all the world weeps with me in woe unutterable.

"I have respectfully but fully explained my feelings in this question of the lawful succession to the Throne, and now, under the title of your guilty servant, I present this my Memorial."

X

TZǓ HSI BECOMES SOLE REGENT

THE days of mourning for T'ung-Chih being done, his remains
disposed of as auspiciously as the Court of Astronomers could
desire, and his ghost placated, thanks to Wu K'o-tu, by solemn
promises on the part of his mother to provide him with a suitable and legitimate heir in due season, life in the Forbidden City
settled down once more into the old grooves under the joint Regency of the Empresses of the Eastern and Western Palaces.

But before long the new Emperor, a nervous and delicate boy,
became, all unconsciously, a thorn in the side of the woman who
put him on the Throne. As he passed from infancy to boyhood,
it was a matter of common knowledge and report in the Palace
that he showed a marked preference for the Empress Tzǔ An,
who, by her kind and sympathetic treatment, had won the child's
heart. In the innocence of his lonely youth he frequented therefore the Eastern Palace, while Tzǔ Hsi, whose pride could brook
no rivals, even in the heart of a child, was compelled to look on,
and to realise that the forming of the future ruler's mind was in
the hands of another woman. There were not lacking those who
told her that her colleague, secretly and with ulterior motives,
encouraged the boy to oppose and displease her. Under these
conditions, it was inevitable that the young Emperor should

gradually become a cause of increasing jealousy and friction between the two women.

Tzŭ Hsi undoubtedly resented the boy's predilection as much as her colleague's action in encouraging it. At Court, where everyone and everything is a potential instrument for intrigue and party faction, the young Emperor's attitude could not fail to cause her grave concern. She was well aware that Tzŭ An could never become, of herself, a formidable rival, but should she hereafter enjoy the Emperor's confidence and support, and instigate him to become the centre of a faction against her (which he did), there might be danger in the situation for herself. As the Emperor's minority approached its end, it therefore became the more necessary for her to take all possible precautions. She had no intention of sharing the fate of that Empress Consort of Ch'ien Lung who was banished to the "Cold Palace" and whose honours and titles were taken from her on charges of "wild extravagance, love of the theatre and insubordination to the Emperor's mother."

A further cause of friction occurred between the two Empresses Regent on the occasion of the Imperial progress to the Eastern tombs, in 1880, when the boy Emperor was nine years old. On this occasion, Tzŭ An, evidently prompted by Prince Kung to assert herself and her rights, insisted on taking precedence in all the ceremonies of the ancestral sacrifices at the Imperial Mausolea and at the prostrations which custom decrees shall be made before each of the "Jewelled Cities," as the mounds are called which cover the Imperial grave chambers. When their Majesties arrived at the grave of Hsien-Feng, there was serious friction. Tzŭ An, as the senior Consort of the deceased monarch, claimed as her right the central position, at the same time relegating her colleague to the place on her right, leaving the place of honour on the left unoccupied. Not content with this, Tzŭ An went on to remind her Co-Regent that, where sacrifices to Hsien-Feng were in question, Tzŭ Hsi was entitled only to claim precedence as a senior concubine, her elevation to the position of Empress Mother having taken place after his decease. As a concubine, etiquette required her, during the sacrifice, to take a position on one side and slightly in the rear, while the vacant place of honour to Tzŭ An's left belonged to the shade of Hsien-Feng's first consort, who had died before his accession, but had been posthumously raised to the rank of senior Empress. Tzŭ Hsi, realising that this indignity was put upon her at the instigation of Prince Kung and the Princes of the Imperial family, had no intention of submitting, and peremptorily insisted upon taking the position to which her actual rank and authority entitled her. The quarrel was sharp but short. Tzŭ Hsi, as might have been expected, carried the day, but she felt that such a scene before the ancestral tombs, witnessed by a large entourage, was semi-sacrilegious and from every point of view unseemly. She had been made to lose face by the incident — clearly premeditated — and the fact had immediate effect upon her subsequent actions and her relations with her colleague.[1]

At the time of this progress to the tombs, Jung Lu was in command of the Metropolitan Gendarmerie, entrusted with the duty of escorting their Majesties. Shortly after their return to Peking, however, he incurred her sharp displeasure by reason of conduct which Tzŭ Hsi was not likely to overlook, even in her chief favourite. Ever since the Jehol days of the Tsai Yüan conspiracy, and particularly during the crisis that followed the death of T'ung-Chih, this powerful Manchu had enjoyed her favour and confidence in an unusual degree, and as Comptroller of her Household, he had the right of *entrée* to the Forbidden City at all times. But in 1880, suffering no doubt from *ennui* induced by the inactivity of Court life, he committed the indiscretion of an intrigue with one of the ladies of the late Emperor's seraglio. Information of the scandal was laid before Her Majesty by

---

1. It is curious to note how frequently the Imperial tombs have been the scene of such unseemly wrangles, wherein grievances and passions, long pent up within the Palace precincts, find utterance. A case of this kind occurred in 1909, on the occasion of the burial of Tzŭ Hsi, when the surviving consorts of T'ung-Chih and Kuang-Hsü, having quarrelled with the new Empress Dowager (Lung Yü) on a similar question of precedence, refused to return to the City and remained in dudgeon at the tombs until a special mission, under an Imperial Duke, was sent humbly to beg them to come back, to the no small scandal of the orthodox.

INTERIOR OF THE I KUN KUNG

Tzŭ Hsi lived in these Apartments for some time after the death of Tung-Chih

the Imperial tutor Weng T'ung-ho, between whom and Jung Lu there was never love lost. It was commonly rumoured at Court, after the event, that Tzŭ Hsi, leaving nothing to chance, had herself discovered the culprit in the women's quarters of the Palace, a heinous offence. Be this as it may, Jung Lu was summarily, though quietly, deprived of all his posts, and for the next seven years he lived in retirement. In this case Tzŭ Hsi vindicated her pride at the expense of her own comfort and sense of security, and it was not long before she had reason to regret the absence of her most loyal and trusty adviser. Amongst her courtiers she found none to replace him; she missed his wise counsel, courage and fidelity. But having once committed herself to the step of dismissing him, she was unwilling to lose face with him and with her Court by changing her mind. His removal, however, undoubtedly led to increased friction between herself and Tzŭ An, whom she suspected of being a party to Jung Lu's *liaison*.

Finally, in March 1881, a serious quarrel took place between the two Empresses, on the subject of the influence which the Chief Eunuch Li Lien-ying had come to exercise, and the arrogance of his manner. Tzŭ An complained that this favourite and confidential servant of her colleague ignored her, setting her authority at nought, so that she was mocked even by her own subordinates. She deplored and denounced the existing state of affairs, commenting unpleasantly on the notorious fact that the eunuch was openly known by the title of "Lord of nine thousand years," a title which implied that he was but one degree lower than the Emperor ('Lord of ten thousand years') and entitled to something approximating to Imperial honours.[1]

The quarrel on this occasion was exceedingly bitter, nor was any reconciliation subsequently effected between the Empresses. It is very generally believed, and was freely stated at the time, that, incensed beyond measure and impatient of any further

1. This title was originally given to an infamous eunuch of the Court of the Ming Emperor Chu Yü-hsiao, who, because of his influence over his dissolute master, was canonised by the latter after his death. The same title was claimed and used by the Eunuch An Te-hai, *vide supra*, p.92.

interference with her authority, Tzŭ Hsi brought about the death of her colleague, which was commonly attributed to poison. In the atmosphere of an Oriental Court such charges are as inevitable as they are incapable of proof or disproof, and were it not for the unfortunate fact that those who stood in the way of Tzŭ Hsi's ambitions, or who incurred her displeasure, frequently failed to survive it, we should be justified in refusing to attach importance to the imputations of foul play raised on this and other occasions. But these occasions are too numerous to be entirely overlooked or regarded as simple coincidences. In the present instance, the Empress Tzŭ An fell ill of a sudden and mysterious sickness, and, in the words of the Imperial Decree, she "ascended the fairy chariot for her distant journey" on the evening of the 10th day of the 3rd Moon. In accordance with prescribed custom, she drafted just before her decease a valedictory Decree which, as will be observed, touches hardly at all on the political questions of the day. These, even at the moment of her death, she appeared to leave, as by established right, to her strong-minded colleague. After referring to her position as Senior Consort of the Emperor Hsien-Feng, and recording the fact that during his minority the young Emperor had done justice to his education (in which she had always been much interested), the Edict proceeds as follows: —

"In spite of the arduous duties of the State, which have fully occupied my time, I was naturally of robust constitution and had therefore fully expected to attain to a good old age and to enjoy the Emperor's dutiful ministrations. Yesterday, however, I was suddenly stricken with a slight illness and His Majesty thereupon commanded his physician to attend me; later His Majesty came in person to enquire as to my health. And now, most unexpectedly, I have had a most dangerous relapse. At 7 P.M. this evening I became completely confused in mind and now all hope of my recovery appears to be vain. I am forty-five years of age and for close on twenty years have held the high position of a Regent of the Empire. Many honorific titles and ceremonies of congratulation have been bestowed upon me: what cause have I therefore for regret?"

At her request, and with that modesty which custom prescribes, the period of Imperial mourning was reduced from twenty-seven months to twenty-seven days. There is a human touch in the conclusion of this Decree which seems to preclude the conclusion that Tzŭ Hsi had any hand in its drafting, for it describes Tzŭ An as having been careful to "set a good example of thrift and sobriety in the Palace and to have steadily discountenanced all pomp and vain display in her share of the Court ceremonies." As most of the charges levelled for many years against Tzŭ Hsi by Censors and other high officials referred to her notorious extravagance, this, and Tzŭ An's last request for a modest funeral as the fitting conclusion to a modest life, were a palpable hit.

Tzŭ An was dead. The playmate of her youth, the girl who had faced with her the solemn mysteries of the Forbidden City, the woman who later, because of her failure to provide an heir to the Throne, had effaced herself in favour of the Empress Mother, her poor-spirited rival of many years—Tzŭ An would trouble her no more. Henceforth, without usurpation of authority, Tzŭ Hsi was free to direct the ship of State alone, sole Regent of the Empire.

And with the death of her colleague came the desire to be free from the restraints of advice given by prescriptive right of long-standing authority, the ambition to be the only and undisputed controller of the nation's destinies, and acknowledged Head of the State. For many years—in fact, since the decapitation of her favourite eunuch, An Te-hai, by Prince Kung and her Co-Regent—she had been on bad terms with that Prince, and jealous of his influence and well-earned reputation for statesmanship. The manner in which, years before, she had taken from him his title of Adviser to the Government has already been described. Unable to dispense with his services, desirous of profiting by his ripe experience, especially in foreign affairs, she had borne with her Prime Minister grudgingly and of necessity. In 1884, however, she felt strong enough to stand alone, and the war with France (caused by the dispute as to China's claims to suzerainty over Tongking) gave her an opportunity and an excuse for getting rid at one stroke of Prince Kung and his colleagues of the Grand Council.

The immediate pretext for their dismissal was the destruction of the Chinese fleet of junks by the French in the Min River, but Her Majesty's real reason was that she believed that the Prince was intriguing against her with the young Emperor, and that he was to some extent responsible for a recent Memorial, in which several Censors had roundly denounced her for depraved morals and boundless extravagance.

The Decree in which she dismissed this able adviser of the Throne is in her best manner, displaying many of the qualities which explain this remarkable woman's long and successful rule. The facts to which she refers have a direct and interesting connection with much subsequent history: —

"Our country has not yet returned to its wonted stability, and its affairs are still in a critical state. There is chaos in the Government and a feeling of insecurity amongst the people. It is, therefore, of the utmost importance that there should be competent statesmen at the head of affairs, and that our Grand Council should be an efficient pivot and centre of administration.

"Prince Kung, at the outset of his career, was wont to render us most zealous assistance; but this attitude became modified, as time went by, to one of self-confident and callous contentment with the sweets of office, and of late he has become unduly inflated with his pride of place, displaying nepotism and slothful inefficiency. On occasions when we have urged the Grand Council to display zeal and single-hearted devotion to the State, he and his colleagues have ruthlessly stuck to their preconceived ideas, and have failed to carry out our orders, for which reason they have more than once been impeached, either on grounds of obstructiveness or general uselessness. It has even been said of them that their private lives are disreputable, and that they have dared to recommend persons for high office from improper and corrupt motives.

"The House-laws of our Dynasty are most severe, and if there were any truth in the accusations of treason that have been made against Prince Kung, we should not hesitate for a single moment to inflict upon him the extreme penalty of the law. We do not believe, however, that he can have dared to act in the manner suggested. We set these aside, therefore, and will deal only with the other charges to which we have referred, and for which there would appear to be good foundation. They are in themselves more than sufficient to cause the gravest injury to the State, and if we continue to treat the Prince with leniency, how shall we justify ourselves hereafter in the eyes of our glorious ancestors? We shall incur no small blame in the eyes of posterity, and when the day comes for the Emperor to take over charge of the Government there can be no doubt that he would be likely to fail, under such conditions, to shed lustre, by his reign, on the Dynasty.

"If we were to make public even one or two of the accusing Memorials that have reached us, it would be impossible for us, on grounds of privilege, to extenuate the Prince's faults, and we should be forced to cashier several of our senior advisers. In the magnanimity of our heart we shrink, however, from any such drastic steps, being moved to deep compassion at the thought that Prince Kung and his colleague, the Grand Secretary, Pao Yün, should have served us so long and now have come to deserve our stern censure and severe punishment. We are prompted to leniency by remembrance of the fact that Prince Kung suffers from a complication of diseases, while Pao Yün has reached an advanced old age. In recognition of their past merits we have, therefore, decided that their good fame may be left to them, and remain unsullied for the rest of their days. As a mark of our Imperial clemency we have decided to permit Prince Kung to retain his hereditary Princedom, together with all the emoluments thereof, but he is hereby deprived of all his offices, and the double salary which he has hitherto enjoyed is withdrawn. He is permitted to retire into private life and attend to the care of his health.

"As regards the Grand Secretary, Pao Yün, he also is allowed to retire from public life, retaining his present rank and titles. As for Li Hung-tsao,[1] who has been a member of the Council for many years, his

---

1. Tzŭ Hsi had no love for this official, for it was he who drafted Hsien-Feng's valedictory Decree, at the dictation of Su Shun, in 1861.

narrow views and lack of practical experience have caused him to fail completely in his duties. Finally, Ching Lien, the President of the Board of War, seems to think that his duties are satisfactorily performed by adherence to a routine of procrastination, the man being devoid of the first elements of knowledge. Both these officials are hereby relieved of their posts, to be employed in lower positions hereafter. Weng T'ung-ho, the President of the Board of Works, has only recently been appointed a member of the Council, at a time of serious complications, and has, so far, taken no active part in its proceedings. He therefore escapes censure or penalty. As a mark of our consideration we hereby remove him from his post on the Grand Council, but permit him to retain his position on the Board of Works, and he will continue his services as Tutor to the Emperor.

"For a long time past we have been quietly observing the behaviour and general tendencies of Prince Kung and his colleagues, and we are quite convinced in our mind that it is useless to look to them for any activity or awakening of their petrified energies. If they were retained in office, we firmly believe that they would end by incurring severe punishment by causing some really serious disaster to the State. For this reason we now content ourselves with mild censure from a sense of pity, as a measure of precaution. It is not because of any trivial misdemeanour, or because of the impeachment by Censors that we thus dismiss from office a Prince of the Blood and these high Ministers of our Government, nor is our action taken on any sudden impulse and without full consideration."

As the result of this Decree, Prince Kung retired from the scene, to remain in unemployed obscurity until 1894, when, after the first disasters of the war with Japan, Tzŭ Hsi, older and wiser, turned to him once more for assistance. He never completely regained the influence with the Empress which he had enjoyed in the earlier days of the first Regency, but after his return to office until his death in 1898, his prestige, especially among foreigners, was great. Tzŭ Hsi, though she loved him not, was forced to admit that he had accepted and borne his degradation with dignity.

After the issue of the above Decree, Prince Kung was succeeded in office by Prince Li, the head of the eight Princely families and a descendant of a younger son of Nurhachu. With him
were associated on the Grand Council, amongst others, the elder
brother of Chang Chih-tung and Sun Yu-wen.[1] The latter was a
bitter enemy of the Imperial Tutor, Weng T'ung-ho. In appointing him to the Council, Tzŭ Hsi followed her favourite tactics
of creating dissension among her advisers and maintaining the
equilibrium of her own authority as the resultant of their conflicting forces.

Her Majesty's next step aroused a storm of opposition and
criticism. She decreed that in all matters of urgency, the Grand
Council, before advising the Throne, should confer with the Emperor's father, Prince Ch'un, but added that upon the Emperor's
attaining his majority, she would issue further instructions on
this subject. This was not only an entirely new and irregular departure, since it made the Emperor's father *de facto* head of the
executive, but it implied the possibility of violation of the solemn
pledges given to the nation in 1875, as to the provision of an heir
to the Emperor T'ung-Chih. Fears were once more aroused in an
acute form that Prince Ch'un might hereafter persuade his son to
ignore the ancestral claims of the late Emperor, and thus constitute the house of Ch'un founders of a new line. The Prince would
have great inducement to adopt this policy, as it would confer
upon him and upon his wife (Tzŭ Hsi's sister) Imperial rank during their lives and Imperial honours after their death. The reign
of T'ung-Chih would in that case be practically expunged, going
down to posterity dishonoured as the ignominious end of the
senior branch of the Ta Ching Dynasty, and the Yehonala clan
would become of paramount influence. A wide field would thus
be left for future dissensions, treasons, stratagems and Court

---

1. Sun remained in high favour until December 1894, when the Emperor was induced by
   Weng T'ung-ho to dismiss him. At that time the Empress was taking little active part in
   the direction of affairs, occupying her time with theatricals and other diversions at the
   Summer Palace, and playing a watching game in politics, so that for a while Sun's life
   was in real danger.

intrigues. In fact the position thus created would be somewhat similar to that which arose from the rivalry of the Houses of York and Lancaster in English history.

An Imperial Clansman, named Sheng Yü, and other scholars, memorialised in the most urgent terms praying the Empress to cancel this appointment and suggesting that if Prince Ch'un's advice were really needed, it should be given to herself direct and not to the Grand Council. The writers advanced numerous arguments, all calculated to save the face of Prince Ch'un while preventing him from accepting the position. They doubted whether his health would stand the strain, and whether the duties of the post were consistent with his high calling; at the same time they foresaw that a post which practically conferred the powers of a Dictator must undoubtedly make him unpopular, a result which Her Majesty herself would be the first to deplore.

Besides, had not the Emperor Chia-Ch'ing declared (in 1799) that Princes of the Blood were not eligible for service on the Grand Council, except in cases of urgent and exceptional emergency?

"The truth is," they concluded, "that a Prince of the Blood, by virtue of his position, cannot be liable to the same punishments as ordinary subjects, and for this reason he should not hold a Government office. Prince Kung has held this high post, it is true, but this was merely temporary, and in any case, the power conferred upon him was much less than that which it is now proposed to confer upon Prince Ch'un. We therefore respectfully invite Your Majesty reverently to conform to the laws of the Dynasty, and to cancel the Decree conferring these functions upon Prince Ch'un."

As final objections, the Memorialists observed that the Prince could not be expected to attend every morning at the Palace, nor could he usurp the Imperial prerogative by expecting the Grand Council to meet at his residence; and it would be irregular for the Censors to denounce any errors committed by a Prince of the

Blood as head of the Council.

The Censor Chao Erh-hsün (an upright official who has since held office as Viceroy in Manchuria and in Ssŭ-Ch'uan) memorialised in the same sense, observing that the Grand Council would be superfluous if everything had to be referred to Prince Ch'un, whose position as father of the Emperor made him impossible for this post. "Why," said he, "could not Her Majesty command the Prince to attend before her, whenever she needed his advice, and let him expound his views to her in person? There could be no objections to this course."

To these remonstrances Tzŭ Hsi replied:

"There is no doubt that the sage decisions of former Emperors deserve to be treated with every consideration and respect, but it is to be observed that, ever since I assumed the Regency, I have been by circumstances compelled to confer regularly on confidential business with a Prince of the Blood. You must all be aware that this situation has been forced upon me owing to the exigencies of the times, and was none of my seeking. The Decree in which, some days ago, I appointed Prince Ch'un to be Adviser to the Council, had no reference to ordinary routine business, with which he has no concern, but only to urgent matters of State. I had not, and have not, any intention of giving him a definite appointment, and he himself was most reluctant to accept at my hands even this advisory position; it was because of his repeated entreaties that I promised to issue further instructions in the matter upon the Emperor's reaching his majority. The present arrangement is of a purely temporary nature. You cannot possibly realise how great and numerous are the problems with which I have to deal single-handed. As to the Grand Council, let them beware of making Prince Ch'un's position an excuse for shirking their responsibilities. In conclusion, I wish that my Ministers would for the future pay more respect to the motives with actuate their Sovereign's actions, and abstain from troubling me with their querulous criticisms. The Memorialists' requests are hereby refused."

Rescripts of this kind are curiously suggestive of Queen

Elizabeth, and her manner of dealing with similar petitions from her loyal and dutiful subjects.

XI

TZǓ HSI "EN RETRAITE"

IN 1887 Kuang-Hsü completed his seventeenth year, and Tzǔ Hsi saw herself confronted by the necessity of surrendering to him the outward and visible signs of sovereignty. The change was naturally viewed with apprehension by those of her courtiers and kinsmen who for the last ten years had basked in the sunshine of her unfettered authority and patronage, whose places and privileges might well be endangered by a new *régime*. When, therefore, as in duty bound, she expressed a desire to retire from public life, it was not surprising that urgent petitions and remonstrances poured in, begging her to continue yet a little while in control of affairs, nor that she should finally allow herself to be persuaded. It was not until February 1889 that she definitely handed over the reins of government to the Emperor, on the occasion of his marriage to the daughter of her brother, Duke Kuei Hsiang.

Tzǔ Hsi was now fifty-five years of age. For nearly thirty years she had been *de facto* ruler of the Celestial Empire. She had tasted the sweets of autocracy, had satisfied all her instincts of dominion, and it seemed as if she were not unwilling to enjoy the fruit of her labours and to exchange the formal routine of the Forbidden City for the pleasures and comparative freedom

of life at the Summer Palace, which was now in course of reconstruction. Always avid of movement and change, weary of the
increasing toil of audiences and Rescripts, apprehensive, too, of
the steadily increasing pressure of the earth-hungry Powers on
China's frontiers, she could not fail to be attracted by the prospect
of a life of gilded leisure and recreation. Nor could she have remained on the Throne, Kuang-Hsü being alive, without an overt
and flagrant act of usurpation for which, until he had been tried
and found wanting, there was no possible justification. Certain
writers, foreign and Chinese, have imputed to her at this period
a policy of *reculer pour mieux sauter*, suggesting that her hand,
though hidden, was never really withdrawn from the affairs of
the Forbidden City. To some extent the suggestion is justifiable;
but Tzŭ Hsi's retirement in the I-Ho Yüan lasted, roughly speaking, for ten years, during a considerable portion of which period
she undoubtedly ceased to concern herself with affairs of State,
other than those which directly affected the replenishing of her
privy purse.

But while divesting herself of the outward and visible signs
of rulership, Tzŭ Hsi had no intention of becoming a negligible
quantity, or of losing touch with current events. From her luxurious retreat at the foot of the hills which shelter Peking, she could
keep close watch on the doings of the Emperor, and protect the
interests of her personal adherents in the capital and the provinces. Her power of appointing and dismissing officials, which
drew much of its inspiration from the Chief Eunuch, was never
surrendered.

In marrying the Emperor to her favourite niece, Tzŭ Hsi intended to avoid a repetition of the mistake which she had committed in the case of her son, the Emperor T'ung-Chih, whose
marriage with the virtuous and courageous A-lu-te had resulted
in dangerous intrigues against herself, until death had removed
the offenders. Warned by this experience, she made her selection
in the present instance less with a view to the Emperor's felicity
than to the furtherance of her own purposes, which necessitated

the presence by his side of someone who would watch over, and report on, his proceedings and proclivities. This part her niece played to perfection. In appearance she was unattractive, and in disposition and temper unsympathetic, but she possessed a considerable share of the Yehonala intelligence and strength of will. From the very first she was on bad terms with the Emperor. It was no secret at Court that they indulged in fierce and protracted quarrels, in which the young Empress generally came off victorious. As a natural result, Kuang-Hsü developed and showed a marked preference for the society of his two senior concubines, known respectively as the "Pearl" and "Lustrous" consorts.

Upon the Emperor's assumption of rulership, there was shown a strong feeling amongst the senior members of the Yehonala clan that the opportunity should be taken to consolidate its position and power by conferring on the Emperor's father rank in the hierarchy higher than that which he had hitherto held, with a view to his ultimate canonisation as Emperor. The manner in which this proposal was put forward, and Tzŭ Hsi's refusal to act upon it — while giving all possible "face" to Prince Ch'un — throw light upon one of the undercurrents of China's dynastic affairs which are so difficult for Europeans to follow.

The views of Prince Ch'un's adherents were voiced in a Memorial addressed to the Empress Dowager by Wu Ta-ch'eng, formerly Vice-President of the Censorate, who at that time held the post of Director of the Yellow River Conservancy. This Memorial, after referring to the services rendered by Prince Ch'un as head of the Admiralty, and praising his patriotism, zeal and extreme modesty, proceeded to observe that he was, after all, the Emperor's own father, and, as such, entitled to higher respect in a Dynasty which "won the Empire by virtue of its respect for filial piety." The Memorialist further recommended that the Son of Heaven should be authorised to grant special recognition and honour to his parent, on the principle laid down by Mencius that "the main principle underlying all ceremonies is that satisfaction should be felt by those concerned." As usual, the Memorialist strengthened his request with reference to historical precedents, and quoted a case, referred to by the Emperor Ch'ien Lung in his edition of Chu Hsi's famous historical work, where two parties in the State under the Sung Dynasty disagreed as to the title to be accorded to the father of the Emperor (A.D. 1050). In that instance the opinion of His Majesty Ch'ien-Lung (as a commentator) was opposed to that of the historians, for he supported the contention that the Emperor's father, as a simple matter of filial piety, is entitled to special honour. He quoted a case where, under the Ming Dynasty (1525), the Emperor desired to have his father raised to the rank of Emperor, although he also had been born only to princely rank; in other words, the Emperor Ch'ien Lung, who is justly regarded as the highest authority on precedents produced by the present Dynasty, placed the blood-tie between father and son above all the theories and conventions that might be raised by courtiers as to their official relationship. The Memorialist concluded by recommending that the title of "Imperial father" be given to Prince Ch'un, and that the Empress Dowager should announce this as the last act of her rule, so that His Majesty's filial piety might be fittingly displayed.

There is every reason to believe that the above Memorial was inspired in the high quarters immediately concerned, so as to afford Her Majesty an opportunity for putting on record her own views, while bestowing great honour on the house of Ch'un. After praising the Prince and his unswerving loyalty, she continues: —

"Whenever I have wished to bestow any special honour upon him, he has refused it with tears in his eyes. On one occasion I granted him permission to ride in a sedan chair with curtains of apricot yellow[1] silk, but not once has he ventured to avail himself of this honour. He has thus displayed his loyalty and unselfish modesty, already well known to my people as well as to myself.

"Years ago, in the first month of the present reign, the Prince put in a secret Memorial, in which, after reciting numerous precedents, he

---

1. Apricot yellow is a colour reserved, strictly speaking, for the use of the Throne.

expressed a fear that the very example which has now been cited by the present Memoralist (Wu Ta-ch'eng) might be used by sycophants and other evil persons to advance improper proposals on his behalf. For this reason he handed in his secret Memorial in advance, with a request that, when the Emperor should attain his majority, no change whatsoever should be made in his own rank and titles. Never was there a more brilliant example of devoted service by a Minister of the Crown, and, while heartily praising him, I yielded reluctantly to his request. Now that I am about to hand over the reins of Government, the very thing that Prince Ch'un feared has come to pass, and I therefore feel bound to take this occasion to publish to the world his original Memorial, so that none may hope to work mischief by any further proposals of a similar kind, and that this worthy Prince's sincerity, thus manifested, may become an example for all to follow."

Prince Ch'un's original Memorial, dated 1875, is of no particular interest except in that it reveals, even at that date, a sense of the dangers arising from the confusion of the Imperial succession and considerable anxiety as to the future adjustment of the situation. His own object in declining further honours was clearly stated to be that he wished to prevent sycophants and persons of doubtful loyalty from establishing claims upon him or forming a party in the Forbidden City, which (it may be observed) has actually come to pass. He deplored the possibility that when His Majesty the Emperor begins to rule in person, "officials of obscure origin may be led to think that, by artful and treasonable suggestions, they may delude His Majesty and thus rise to high office by creating opportunities of dissension."

The rank of the Emperor's father therefore remained that of an hereditary Prince, but there is no doubt that the matter is by no means disposed of, and may possibly be revived upon the conclusion of the present Regent's term of office.[1]

---

1. In that event it would not be the Yehonala clan alone which would benefit, as the present Emperor's grandmother (who was one of Prince Ch'un's concubines) is still alive and would necessarily share in any honours posthumously conferred on her husband, whilst Kuang-Hsü's mother would be excluded.

Shortly after Tzŭ Hsi's retirement from public affairs the Emperor's father, Prince Ch'un fell ill of a sickness which increased until, on 1st January 1891, he died. In 1890, the Censorate, deeply concerned for a strict observance of the laws and ceremonial etiquette of filial piety, took occasion, in a Memorial of remonstrance, to draw Her Majesty's attention to her duty, and that of the Emperor, of visiting the invalid. Tzŭ Hsi's reply took the form of a rebuke to the Censors, whom she bluntly directed to mind their own business, in a manner which forcibly brings to mind Queen Elizabeth's methods of dealing with similar remonstrances. Nevertheless she took the hint and thenceforward, throughout the summer of 1890, she paid repeated visits to Prince Ch'un's bedside.

This Prince had always been a favourite with Tzŭ Hsi, who greatly preferred him to his elder brothers; she regretted his death and felt the loss of his wise and fearless counsel, which had often guided her policy. He was a staunch Manchu, jealous of the power and privileges of the Clans, and will long be remembered in Chinese history for the remark which he made at a meeting of the Council after the campaign in Tongking. "It were better." said he, "to hand over the Empire to the foreign devils, than to surrender it at the dictation of these Chinese rebels," a remark which was prompted by the growing discontent of the province of Canton against the Manchus and their rule.

In her Decree recording the Prince's death and praising his eminent services as Chamberlain of the Palace, Head of the Navy[1] and Commander of the Manchu Field Force, Tzŭ Hsi gave detailed instructions for the mourning and funeral ceremonies, donating in her own name a Tibetan prayer coverlet for the body. She conferred upon him the somewhat obvious (but according to Chinese ideas, highly honourable) title of "deceased father of the Emperor" and ordered that the funeral should be upon a scale

---

1. The results of the Prince's eminent services in naval and military reorganisation were demonstrated three years later, not entirely to the nation's satisfaction, in the war with Japan.

"which shall simultaneously display His Majesty's favour and his sense of filial piety," due care being taken at the same time not to outrage the deceased's conspicuous modesty. By these means, which were in accordance with her guiding principle of the "happy mean," she hoped to set at rest all question of "usurping tendencies" and to reassure the Aisin Gioros as to their fears of the undue ambition of the house of Ch'un. Finally, in accordance with the precedent established by the Emperor Ch'ien-Lung, she decreed that the late Prince's residence should be divided into two portions, one to be set aside as his own ancestral Hall and the other as a shrine (it being the birthplace) of his Majesty Kuang-Hsü.

In 1894 the Empress Dowager reached her sixtieth year, which, according to Chinese ideas, is an event calling for special thanksgiving and honour. Secure in her great and increasing popularity, safely entrenched in her prestige and influence, the Old Buddha had expected to devote her leisure at the Summer Palace to preparations for celebrating this anniversary on a scale of unparalleled magnificence. The I-Ho Yüan, as the Summer Palace is called,[1] had been entirely rebuilt, by the Emperor's orders, with funds taken from the Navy Department and other Government Boards since 1889, and had just been completed. Most of the high provincial authorities had been summoned to the capital to take part in these festivities (and, incidentally, to help to pay for them), and amongst them the faithful Jung Lu returned once more to his mistress's side, in high favour, as General in command of the Forces at Peking. (For the last three years he had been at Hsi-an, holding the sinecure post of Tartar General.) Every high official in the Empire had been "invited" to contribute twenty-five per cent. of his salary as a birthday gift to Her Majesty, and the total amount of these offerings must have amounted to several millions of taels. Everything pointed to festivities of great splendour; orders had already been given for the

---

1. From a sentence in the Book of Rites, which means "to give rest and peace to Heaven-sent old age."

INTERIOR OF THE TAI HO TIEN.
This palace is used only for occasions of high ceremony, such as
Imperial birthday celebrations.

erection of triumphal arches in her honour throughout the whole five miles of the Imperial highway between Peking and the Summer Palace, when the continued disasters which overtook China's forces, immediately after the outbreak of the war with Japan, caused Her Majesty to reconsider the situation, and eventually to cancel all arrangements for the celebration. In the Emperor's name she issued the following somewhat pathetic Decree:—

"The auspicious occasion of my sixtieth birthday, occurring in the 10th Moon of this year, was to have been a joyful event, in which the whole nation would unite in paying to me loyal and dutiful homage. It had been intended that His Majesty the Emperor, accompanied by the whole Court, should proceed to offer congratulations to me, and make obeisance at the Summer Palace, and my officials and people have subscribed funds wherewith to raise triumphal arches, and to decorate the Imperial highway throughout its entire length from Peking to the I-Ho Yüan; high altars have been erected where Buddhist Sutras were to have been recited in my honour. I was not disposed to be unduly obstinate and to insist on refusing these honours, because, at the time that the celebration was planned, my people were enjoying peace and prosperity; moreover, there is precedent for such displays of pageantry and rejoicing in the occasions on which the Emperors K'ang-Hsi and Ch'ien-Lung celebrated their sixtieth birthdays. I, therefore, consented to His Majesty's filial request, and decided to receive birthday congratulations at the Summer Palace. Who would ever have anticipated that the Japanese (literally, 'dwarf men') would have dared to force us into hostilities, and that since the beginning of the summer they have invaded our tributary State (Corea) and destroyed our fleet? We had no alternative but to draw the sword and to commence a punitive campaign; at this moment our armies are pressing to the front. The people of both nations (China and Corea) are now involved in all the horrors of war, and I am continually haunted by the thought of their distress; therefore, I have issued a grant of three million taels from my privy purse for the maintenance and relief of our troops at the front.

"Although the date of my birthday is drawing close, how could I have the heart, at such a time, to delight my senses with revelries, or to receive from my subjects congratulations which could only be sincere if we had won a glorious victory? I therefore decree that the ceremonies to be observed on my birthday shall be performed at the Palace in Peking, and all preparations at the Summer Palace shall be abandoned forthwith. The words of the Empress."

To which the Emperor adds the filial remark on his own account: "That Her Majesty had acted in accordance with the admirable virtue which always distinguished her, and that, in spite of his own wishes, he was bound reverently to obey her orders in the matter."

China's complete and ignominious defeat by the Japanese forces undoubtedly inflicted no small loss of prestige on the Manchu Dynasty, and was a direct cause of the violent agitation of the Southern Provinces for reform, which led in turn to the *coup d'état* and to the Boxer rising. It is doubtful whether war could have been avoided without even greater sacrifices and humiliation, and the Empress Dowager showed her usual sagacity therefore in refraining from expressing any opinion or taking any share of responsibility in the decision taken by the Emperor. She knew, moreover, that, by the action and advice of her Chief Eunuch, the Navy had for years been starved in order to provide her with funds to rebuild and decorate the Summer Palace, a fact of which some of China's most distinguished advisers were at that time unaware.

As Viceroy of the Metropolitan Province, Li Hung-chang was generally blamed for advising the Court to maintain China's suzerainty over Corea by force of arms, but, speaking from personal knowledge of this subject, we may state that, like many other Ministers similarly situated, he hesitated until the very last moment before taking risks which he knew to be enormous in both directions. The documents upon which history might have been written with full knowledge of the facts were unfortunately destroyed in the Viceroy's Yamên at Tientsin and in the Inspector-General of

Customs' quarters at Peking, in 1900, so that the immediate causes of that disastrous war will probably never be established with complete accuracy. Li Hung-chang was aware that twice already Japan had been bought off from a war of aggression against China, the first time (in 1874) by payment of an indemnity, and again (in 1885) by admitting her to a share in the control of Corea, a concession which had led directly to the present crisis. He realised that even had he been willing to surrender China's rights over Corea (which were of no real advantage to the Chinese Government) the concession might have purchased peace for the time being, but it would certainly have led before long to the loss of the Manchurian Provinces; just as certainly, in fact, as the doom of those provinces was sealed in 1905, on the day that China acquiesced in the terms of the Portsmouth Treaty. Japan's attack on China's positions was diplomatically as unjustifiable as the methods which she adopted in commencing hostilities. Li Hung-chang was fully aware of the preparations that Japan had been making for years, and equally aware of the disorganised state of his own naval and military resources, but he was surrounded by officials who, like the Manchus in 1900, were convinced of China's immense superiority, and he was assured by the Chinese Resident in Corea (Yüan Shih-k'ai) that help would be forthcoming from England in the event of Japan's commencing hostilities. There was no doubt of the British Government's sympathy, which was clearly reflected in the attitude and actions of the Consul-General at Seoul.[1]

Chinese historians have openly accused Li Hung-chang of instigating the Court and the Emperor to a war of aggression, and the accusation has been generally credited abroad. The truth is, that while Li was originally all in favour of sending a Chinese force to suppress the Corean insurrection, he became opposed to taking any steps that might lead to war with Japan, as soon as he realised that war was Japan's object; nevertheless, it

---

1. Sir Walter Hillier, appointed by Yüan Shih-k'ai to be foreign adviser to the Grand Council in 1908. When Yüan was compelled to flee from Seoul before the advance of the Japanese, he was escorted to Chemulpo by a guard of blue-jackets.

is certain that, in the last instance, he was persuaded against his better judgment by the military enthusiasm of his German advisers, and that the sending of the ill-fated "Kow-hsing" and her doomed crew to Corea was a step which he authorised only after consultation with Peking and in full knowledge of the fact that it meant war. No sooner had the "Kow-hsing" been sunk, and the first military disasters of the campaign reported, than he naturally endeavoured to minimise his own share of responsibility in the matter.

Foreigners blamed him for making war on Japan, while his own countrymen attacked him for betraying China to the Japanese, as they subsequently attacked him for selling Manchuria to Russia. Tzŭ Hsi had no great love for the Viceroy, although she admired his remarkable intelligence and adroit methods: but when, after the war, he was fiercely attacked by several of the Censors, and when she found her own name associated with the blame imputed to him, she loyally defended him, as was her wont. In 1895, a Censor named An Wei-chün boldly blamed Her Majesty and the Viceroy for the disasters which had overtaken China. He said: —

"Li Hung-chang has invariably advanced himself because of his relations with foreigners, and thus been led to conceive an inflated opinion of his own merits. The 'dwarf bandits'[1] having rebelled, he seems to have been afraid that the large sums of money, saved from numerous peculations, which he had deposited in Japan might be lost; hence his objections to the war. When the Decree declaring war reached him, his disappointment was great, and he showed his resentment and treachery by supplying the 'dwarf bandits' with supplies and munitions of war. His only hope was that the 'dwarfs' would prove victorious and his prophecy would thus be justified; to this end be curtailed the supplies for our troops at the front, diverting the funds for the same to his own pockets. He would strongly oppose all those who urged a vigorous prosecution of the campaign, rejoicing at our defeats and deploring our

1. *i.e.* the Japanese (literal translation).

successes. All the military commanders of the forces under his orders humbly complied with his wishes, and invariably ran away at the first sight of the enemy. The Censorate has been full of Memorials denouncing the treacherous and unpatriotic action of Li Hung-chang, so that there is no need for me to say anything further on this subject.

"But I would like to add that Generals Yeh and Wei, who have been cashiered and whose arrest has been decreed, are at this very moment in hiding at Tientsin; they have made the Viceroy's Yamên itself a place of refuge for absconding criminals. This is a matter of common knowledge and undoubtedly true. Then again we have the case of Ting Ju-chang, who was ordered to be arrested, but who persuaded Li Hung-chang to intercede for him, on the plea that he was indispensable to China, being in possession of a mysterious secret, an American invention which he alone could manipulate, whereby all surrounding objects can be rendered invisible. Li Hung-chang actually had the audacity to make mention of this ridiculous invention in addressing your Majesty, and it seems to me that if he is to be permitted to refer to fables and unclean magic of this kind, he is treating the Throne with shameless disrespect. Nevertheless, none of your Majesty's Councillors have ever dared to oppose him, possibly because they themselves are too far gone in senile decay to be able to bear any further burden of distress. Their thoughts are far away, wool-gathering, or it may be that they too have been smitten with fear at the thought of this marvellous invention of Li Hung-chang's whereby the landscape may be completely befogged. If so, the fact would account for the nebulous tendencies of their policy, and for their remaining in ignorance of Li Hung-chang's remarkable mendacity.

"The Imperial Decree whereby Shao Yu-lien and Chang Yin-huan have been appointed Plenipotentiaries to discuss terms of peace, has not yet been made public, because the Grand Council are actually afraid openly to mention the word peace, notwithstanding that they failed utterly in prosecuting the war and in dignified insistence on our lawful rights. Their action appears to me like that of a thief who having stolen a bell, shuts his ears while carrying it away, blissfully forgetting that everybody else can hear its tinkling. They do not seem to be aware, these Councillors, that throughout the whole Empire everybody is already aware of the fact that we are suing for peace. Japan having objected to Shao on personal grounds, the Grand Council has now actually gone so far as to suggest that in his place Li Hung-chang's son, Li Ching-fang[1] should be appointed. This is simply an outrage. Li Ching-fang is nothing more than the son-in-law of a Japanese traitor who calls himself Chang Pang-chang, a man whom I have already impeached. If such unspeakable traitors are permitted to go to Japan, nothing will suit the Japanese better, and the negotiations must inevitably result in our being badly cheated by these pernicious robbers. Japan's strength is purely superficial; as a matter of fact, she is rotten to the core; if now we are debarred from compelling Japan to fight a decisive battle, if we meekly accept terms dictated by these low-born dwarfs, we are simply in the position of a tributary State, and cannot be described as equals in any treaty that may be made. In other words, our glorious Empire is not only being ruined by muddlers, but sold by traitors. There is not a single subject of the Throne who does not gnash his teeth with rage, and long to sink them in the flesh of Li Hung-chang.

"There are not lacking people who declare that this humiliating policy of peace has been prompted by the Empress Dowager's Chief Eunuch, Li Lien-ying. For myself, I do not care to attach undue importance to tea-house gossip, but as the Empress Dowager has now handed over the reins of Government to your Majesty, how can you possibly justify your position before your ancestors and to your subjects, if you permit her still to dictate to you, or to interfere in the business of the State? What sort of a person is this Li Lien-ying who dares to interfere in Government matters? If there be any truth whatsoever in the rumour, it is assuredly incumbent upon your Majesty to inflict severe punishment on this creature, if only because of that House-law of your Dynasty which forbids eunuchs to concern themselves in State affairs.

"The truth is that the Throne has been intimidated by Li Hung-chang, and has taken his statements for granted, while the Grand Council, chiefly composed of Li's humble and obedient servants, shields him from detection and punishment, fearing that, if thwarted, he may raise the standard of rebellion. They accordingly do their best to justify him

---

1. At present Chinese Minister in London.

in the eyes of your Majesty, failing to realise that he has always been a traitor at heart. His is the will, if not the power, to rebel. His army is composed of corrupt and useless creatures quite devoid of any military knowledge or instincts, while his troops are ever on the verge of mutiny, because they are always defrauded of their pay. They are quite deficient in *esprit de corps*, and the small foreign forces lately organised at Tientsin would more than suffice to overcome Li Hung-chang and all his host. The truth of these statements can easily be verified. Long ago, if he had had the power, he would surely have rebelled; but as he cannot do so, he contents himself with bullying your Majesty and disregarding your Imperial Decrees. He totally ignores the existence of the Empress Dowager and of your Majesty, a fact which may be inferred from his daring to insult your intelligence with his mysterious powers of conferring invisibility.

"I am covered with shame and amazement. My only hope is that your Majesty will now display the majesty of your wrath, and, after disclosing Li Hung-chang's treason to all men, will put this traitor to death. By this means our troops would at once be inspired to valour, and the 'dwarf bandits' would be completely annihilated. At the same time, I would ask you to be so good as to behead me also, as a fitting punishment for this plain speaking. Your Majesty's Imperial ancestors are present in the spirit, and they bear me witness. I am quite easy in my mind as to the issue, and I therefore lay bare the innermost thoughts of my heart and lay them before your Majesty, anxiously begging for your Imperial decision."

In reply to this outspoken document, the Emperor issued the following Decree, which bears unmistakable signs of Tzǔ Hsi's hand. The attack upon her favourite, Li Lien-ying, was in itself sufficient to bring her to the front, and there is no doubt that at the time she was keeping very close watch on the Emperor's proceedings, and regularly perusing all State papers.

"Owing to the seriousness of recent events, we have been particularly anxious of late to receive and attend to the unprejudiced suggestions of our Censors, and we have abstained from punishing any of them, even when they have made use of improper expressions in addressing

us. With the gracious consent of Her Majesty the Empress Dowager, we
have given particular attention to all projects whereby the welfare of our
people may be advanced, and all our people must by this time be aware
of our sincere desire to promote good Government. In spite of this the
Censor, An Wei-chün, has to-day submitted a Memorial based entirely
upon rumours, and containing the following sentence:—'How can you
possibly justify your position before your ancestors and to your subjects
if you permit the Empress Dowager still to dictate to you, or to interfere
in the business of the State?'

"Language of this kind reveals depths of audacity unspeakable, the
unbridled licence of a madman's tongue. Were we to fail in inflicting
stern punishment in a case of this kind, the result might well be to produce estrangement between Her Majesty the Empress and ourselves.
The Censor is, therefore, dismissed from office and sentenced to banishment at the post-roads, on the western frontier where he shall expiate
his guilt and serve as a wholesome warning to others. His Memorial is
handed back to him with the contempt it deserves."

Tzŭ Hsi felt deeply the humiliation of her country's defeat by
the Japanese, a race which, as Chinese historians never fail to remind themselves, took its first lessons in civilisation and culture
from Chinese scholars and artists. Anxious at all costs to avoid
another invasion of Chihli by the conquerors, she approved the
Treaty of Peace, especially when assured by Li Hung-chang that
Russia and her Continental allies would not allow Japan to an-
nex any portion of the Manchurian Provinces. As above stated,
she declined to permit Li to be made a scapegoat either by her
chagrined Manchu kinsmen or by his fierce critics in the south,
for she recognised the difficulty of his position, and the fact that
he was not directly responsible for the deplorable condition of
China's defences. But, woman-like, she had to blame someone
for the disasters that had deprived her and her capital of festivities whose splendour should have gone down, making her name
glorious, to all posterity; and it was not surprising, therefore, if
she heaped reproaches on the Emperor for entering upon so

disastrous a war without her full knowledge and consent. It was at this time that began the estrangement which thenceforward gradually grew into the open hostility and secret plottings of 1898, the long bitterness between Tzŭ Hsi and her nephew which was to divide the Palace into camps of strife, and to cease only with their death. From this time also, as they aver who were in close touch with the life of the Court, the Emperor's Consort,[1] Tzŭ Hsi's niece, became openly alienated from him, and their relations grew more severely strained as his reform tendencies developed and took shape. From 1894 to 1896 there was no noticeable change in the attitude of the Emperor to his august aunt, nor any diminution of his respectful attentions, but the man in the street knew well, as he always knows in China, of the rift in the lute, and when, in 1896, the Emperor's mother (Tzŭ's sister) died, it was realised that the last bond of amity and possible reconciliation between Kuang-Hsü and the Empress Dowager had been severed.

---

1. Now known as the Empress Dowager Lung Yü.

XII

THE REFORM MOVEMENT OF 1898

AT the beginning of 1898 the Grand Council was composed of the following officials: Prince Kung, the Emperor's uncle, Prince Li, whose son was married to Jung Lu's daughter, Kang Yi,[1] Liao Shou-heng and Weng T'ung-ho, the Grand Secretary and ex-tutor to the Emperor. The Empress Dowager was still leading her life of dignified leisure at the Summer Palace, generally in company with her two confidential friends, the wife of Jung Lu and her adopted daughter, the Princess Imperial. By all accounts she was amusing herself with picnics on the K'un Ming lake, elaborate theatrical performances and excursions to the neighbouring temples and hill shrines, devoting her leisure from these pursuits to verse-making and painting, but keeping herself fully informed, through Kang Yi and Prince Li, of all that took place in the Forbidden City. Although leaving the conduct of State affairs to the Emperor, she occasionally visited the city for a day or two, while the Emperor, on his side, punctiliously repaired to the Summer Palace five or six times a month to pay his respects to the Old

1. Kang Yi was a bigoted reactionary and the arch instigator of the Boxer movement at the capital. Young China has carefully preserved one of his sayings of that time: "The establishment of schools and colleges has only encouraged Chinese ambitions and developed Chinese talent to the danger of the Manchu Dynasty: these students should therefore be exterminated without delay."

Buddha. Their relations at this period were outwardly friendly. Kuang-Hsü never failed to consult Her Majesty before the issue of any important Decree, and Tzŭ Hsi was usually most cordial in her manner towards him. She had, it is true, occasion to reprove him more than once on account of reports which reached her, through the eunuchs, of his violent temper and alleged bad treatment of his attendants, reports which were probably instigated and exaggerated by Li Lien-ying for his own purposes. But Kuang-Hsü, as events subsequently proved, was fully aware of the iron hand in the velvet glove. Whenever the Empress came to Peking, he obeyed strictly the etiquette which required him reverently to kneel at the Palace gates to welcome her. When visiting her at the Summer Palace, he was not permitted to announce his arrival in person, but was obliged to kneel at the inner gate and there await the summons of admission from the Chief Eunuch. Li, who hated him, delighted in keeping him waiting, sometimes as much as half an hour, before informing the Old Buddha of his presence. At each of these visits he was compelled, like any of the Palace officials, to pay his way by large fees to the eunuchs in attendance on Her Majesty, and as a matter of fact, these myrmidons treated him with considerably less respect than they showed to many high Manchu dignitaries. Within the Palace precincts, the Son of Heaven was indeed regarded as of little account, so that the initiative and determination which he displayed during the hundred days of reform in the summer of 1898 came as a disturbing surprise to many at Court and showed that, given an opportunity, he was not wholly unworthy of the Yehonala blood of his mother, Tzŭ Hsi's sister.

The official who had hitherto exercised most influence over the Emperor was Weng T'ung-ho, the Imperial tutor. He had only rejoined the Grand Council in November 1894, at the critical time when the disastrous opening of the war with Japan had brought about the dismissal of the former Council; but as Imperial tutor he had had the *entrée* of the Palace ever since the Emperor was five years old. He was the leader of the southern party in the capital. A native of Kiangsu (the birthplace of all the greatest scholars of China during the present Dynasty, and the centre of national culture), he hated the narrow conservatism of the Manchus, and included in his dislike the Chinese of the Metropolitan Provinces, whose politics and point of view are very similar to those of the Manchus. The strife between north and south really dated from the beginning of Kuang-Hsü's reign. The two protagonists on the northern side were Hsü T'ung, a well-educated Chinese Bannerman (for all practical purposes, a Manchu at heart) who had been tutor to the Emperor T'ung-Chih; and Li Hung-tsao, a native of Chihli, who had joined the Grand Council at the same time as Weng T'ung-ho. The southern party was led by Weng T'ung-ho and P'an Tsu-yin, the latter a native of Soochow and a most brilliant scholar and essayist. It is necessary to dwell on this party strife and its development, because it was the first cause of the reform movement of 1898, of the subsequent resumption of the Regency by Tzǔ Hsi, and, eventually, of the Boxer rising.

For more than twenty years these four high officials had been colleagues in Peking, meeting one another constantly in social as well as official circles. Their literary arguments, in which the quick-witted southerners generally scored, were the talk of the capital. All four men bore good reputations for integrity, so that literary graduates entering official life were glad to become their *protégés*; but the adherents of the southern party were the more numerous. This fact aroused the jealousy of Li and Hsü, which grew until it found vent publicly at the metropolitan examination for the "Chin Shih," or Doctor's, degree in 1899, on which occasion Li was Grand Examiner and P'an Tsu-yin his chief Associate. P'an, whose duty it was to select the best essays, recommended a native of Kiangsu for the high honour of *optimus*, but Li declined to endorse his decision, and gave the award to a Chihli man. P'an thereupon openly accused Li of prejudice and unfairness towards the southerner, and twitted him besides on his second-rate scholarship.

At the time of Russia's seizure of Ili, in 1880, Hsü T'ung and Weng T'ung-ho were respectively Presidents of the Boards of Ceremonies and Works. At a conference of the highest officials, held in the Palace, Weng declared himself in favour of war with Russia, but Hsü, after promising to support him, left him in the lurch at the last moment, causing him discomfiture and loss of face. Hence, bitter enmity between them, which increased in intensity when they became the leaders of the rival factions. Weng was also on bad terms with Jung Lu, who had never forgiven him for the part he played in 1880, when Weng denounced his impious *liaison* to the Empress Dowager and brought about his dismissal. Jung Lu, as a loyal Manchu, naturally favoured the northern faction and his personal feelings prompted him in the same direction.

The enmity between the rival parties increased steadily in the early nineties, and when Li and Weng were appointed to the Grand Council, in 1894, the Court itself became involved in their strife, the Empress siding with the north and the Emperor with the south. At that time people were wont to speak of the Li faction and the Weng faction, but later they came to be known as the Empress Dowager's party, irreverently nicknamed the "Old Mother set," and the Emperor's party, or "Small Lad's set." Both P'an and Li died in 1897. It was after the latter's death that Hsü T'ung began to instigate secret and sinister designs against the Emperor, whom he called a Chinese traitor. Hsü T'ung, having been tutor to T'ung-Chih, naturally enjoyed considerable influence with the Empress, but Kuang-Hsü flatly refused to have him on the Grand Council. So great was his dislike for the old man that he only received him once in audience between 1887 and 1898. Hsü had a valuable ally in Kang Yi, who hated all Chinese, southerners and northerners alike, and whose influence was used effectively to sow dissension between Tzǔ Hsi and the Emperor. In 1897, Kang Yi urged the Emperor to give orders that the Manchu troops should be efficiently trained and equipped. Kuang-Hsü replied: "You persist, it seems, in the exploded idea that the Manchu soldiery are good fighting men. I tell you that they are absolutely useless." Kang Yi, highly incensed, promptly informed the Old Buddha and the Iron-capped Princes that the Emperor was the enemy of all Manchus, and was plotting to appoint Chinese to all high offices, a statement which naturally created a strong feeling against His Majesty at Court.

Even the foreign policy of the Empire felt the effects of this rivalry of the opposing parties in the capital. The Empress, the Manchus, and the Chinese Bannermen were in favour of coming to an understanding with Russia, while the Emperor, Weng, and the southern Chinese, inclined to a *rapprochement* with Japan, with a view to imitation of that country's successful reforms. Li Hung-chang counted for little at the time, the fact being that, owing to his alleged responsibility for the war with Japan, his opinions were at a discount; but such influence as he had was used against the Emperor's party. Prince Kung, the doyen of the Imperial family, to whose ripe judgment the Empress herself would yield at times, was the only high Manchu to maintain friendly relations with the Chinese party. A fine scholar himself, he had always admired Weng T'ung-ho's literary gifts; the war with Japan had been none of his seeking, and he had been recalled to the Grand Council, at the same time as Weng, after a retirement of fourteen years.

The fact is not generally known that Weng T'ung-ho was most anxious at this time to be sent as Special Envoy to the coronation of the Czar, for the reason that, realising the Empress Dowager's growing hostility towards himself, he wished to be out of harm's way in the crisis which he felt to be impending. By a Decree of 1895, Weng had been "excused from further attendance to instruct His Majesty at the Palace of Happy Education," so that he could no longer influence His Majesty, as heretofore, at all times and seasons, and his rivals were thus enabled successfully to misrepresent him.

Prince Kung, the head of the Grand Council, went on sick furlough at the beginning of 1898, afflicted with incurable lung and heart complaints. The Emperor accompanied the Empress Dowager on three occasions to visit him at his residence, and ordered the Imperial physicians to attend him. On the 10th day of the 4th Moon he died, and the following Decree was issued by Tzǔ Hsi:—

"Prince Kung (Yi Hsin) was my near kinsman; for many years he has assisted in my Privy Councils. When, with my colleague, the deceased Empress Tzǔ An, I assumed the Regency at the beginning of the late Emperor's reign, the coast provinces were in rebellion and the Empire in danger, Prince Kung ably assisted me in restoring order; and I then bestowed upon him high honours commensurate with his services. For over thirty years he has supported me with unswerving loyalty, although for part of that time he took no part in the business of the State. Again I recalled him to the Council, where he has ever done yeoman service, despite many and great difficulties. Of late his old sickness came upon him again, and I therefore went repeatedly with the Emperor to visit him, hoping for his fortunate recovery. Of a sudden, yesterday, he passed away, and thus, at this time of need, a trusty adviser is lost to me. How describe my grief? To-day I have visited his residence, there to make oblations. In the remembrance of bygone days I am completely overcome. I now bestow on him the posthumous title of 'Loyal,' I command that seasonal sacrifices be offered to his spirit in the Temple of the Virtuous and Good, and I ordain that the care of his grave shall be a charge on the public funds. Thus I manifest my sincere regard for my worthy kinsman and deep sorrow at the loss of my trusted Councillor."

The above Decree clearly reflected the immediate effect on the Empress of party factions and intrigues in the Palace, and showed that, though nominally retired from control of the Government, she was still, whenever she chose, the autocratic ruler of the Empire and ready to assert herself in that capacity. The Emperor on this occasion issued a Decree on his own account, entirely subordinate to Tzǔ Hsi's, and this in turn was followed by another, which called upon the Ministers of State to imitate

Prince Kung's devoted loyalty. It concluded with the significant announcement that the Prince's valedictory Memorial had advised the Emperor to follow the Empress Dowager's advice in all things, to organise an efficient army and to purify the administration.

Prince Kung's death was a serious matter. On the one hand the Manchu party lost in him its senior representative, an elder whose wise counsel had guided them, and a statesman whose influence had been steadily exercised against their tendencies towards an anti-Chinese and anti-foreign policy. As the last survivor of the sons of Tao-Kuang, he held, *vis-à-vis* the Empress Dowager, a position very different from that of the other princes, his contemporaries. It is probable that, had he survived, there would have been no Boxer rising. On the other hand, the Emperor had always deferred to Prince Kung's advice, and it was not until after his death that he embarked headlong on the reform schemes of K'ang Yu-wei and his associates, many of which the Prince, though no bigoted Conservative, would certainly have condemned. To Weng T'ung-ho also the loss was serious, as well he knew, for Prince Kung had been his best friend.

It was shortly after the Prince's death that Weng recommended K'ang Yu-wei to the Emperor's notice, informing His Majesty that K'ang's abilities were far superior to his own. Weng undoubtedly hoped that K'ang would gain the Sovereign's favour and use it to assist the southern party against the Manchus, and especially against his arch enemies, Kang Yi and Hsü T'ung; but he certainly never anticipated that K'ang would go so far as to advise the Emperor to defy the Old Buddha herself, and to plot against her sacred person. His idea was simply to gain kudos and to strengthen his own position and that of his party. The Emperor accepted his recommendation of K'ang, and summoned the latter to audience on the 28th of the 4th Moon (14th June, 1898).

Weng told his friend and colleague, Liao Shou-heng, that he would await the result of this audience before coming to a decision as to his own future movements. If K'ang Yu-wei made a good impression, he would remain in office; if not, he would resign. He added that if the usual gifts of the Dragon Festival were sent him by the Emperor, he would feel that there was no immediate danger in his position. All he asked was that he might escape the open hostility of the Empress Dowager, such as had fallen upon the Cantonese Vice-President, Chang Yin-huan, whose dismissal was expected at any moment. As it happened, however, K'ang Yu-wei and his friends persuaded the Emperor to insist on retaining Chang Yin-huan in office, and for the next hundred days he became Kuang-Hsü's right-hand man, playing his part, foredoomed, while in the "deep seclusion of her Palace" the Old Buddha bided her time.

On the 20th of the 4th Moon, Weng T'ung-ho applied for a week's sick leave, a face-saving device which showed that he was aware of the impending storm. On the 23rd, His Majesty issued the first of his Reform Decrees. He had duly conferred on the subject with the Empress at the Summer Palace, and had accorded a special audience to Jung Lu. Tzŭ Hsi assured him that she would raise no obstacles to his proposed policy, provided that the ancient privileges of the Manchus were not infringed; at the same time, she insisted on his getting rid of Weng T'ung-ho without delay, as he was instigating an anti-Manchu movement which, if it gained headway, might involve the Dynasty in ruin. Jung Lu strongly recommended to His Majesty a notable progressive, the son of Ch'en Pao-chen, Governor of Hupei. The fact is of interest because of the idea prevalent among Europeans, that Jung Lu was ever opposed to reform. Subsequent events compelled him to turn against the very man whom he now recommended, but this was not so much on account of a change in his views, as because the policy of the reformers had developed on unexpected and dangerous lines. The first Reform Decree was as follows:—

"Of late years many of our Ministers have advocated a policy of reform, and we have accordingly issued Decrees which provide for the institution of special examinations in political economy, for the abolition of useless troops and the old form of examination for military degrees, as well as for founding Colleges. No decision has been taken in these matters without the fullest care, but the country still lacks enlightenment, and views differ as to the course which reform should follow. Those who claim to be Conservative patriots consider that all the old customs should be upheld and new ideas repudiated without compromise. Such querulous opinions are worthless. Consider the needs of the times and the weakness of our Empire! If we continue to drift with our army untrained, our revenues disorganised, our scholars ignorant, and our artisans without technical training, how can we possibly hope to hold our own among the nations, or to cross the gulf which divides the weak from the strong? It is our belief that a condition of unrest creates disrespect for authority and produces friction, which in turn leads to the formation of factions in the State, hostile to each other as fire and water. Under such conditions, our Government would find itself confronted by the abuses and errors of the Sung and Ming Dynasties, to its imminent peril. The virtuous rulers of remote antiquity did not cling obstinately to existing needs, but were ready to accept change, even as one wears grass-cloth garments in summer, and furs in winter.

"We now issue this special Decree so that all our subjects, from the Imperial family downwards, may hereafter exert themselves in the cause of reform. The basis of education will continue to rest on the canons of the Sages, but at the same time there must be careful investigation of every branch of European learning appropriate to existing needs, so that there may be an end to empty fallacies and that by zeal efficiency may be attained. Parrot-like plagiarisms of shallow theories are to be avoided, and catchwords eschewed. What we desire to attain is the elimination of useless things and the advancement of learning which, while based on ancient principles, shall yet move in harmony with the times. The Peking University is to be made a model for the Empire, and all officials of the rank of Board Secretaries, officers of the bodyguard, expectant Magistrates, sons of high officials and Manchus of hereditary rank, are to be entitled to enter upon a college course in order that their talents may be trained to meet the needs of these critical times. No procrastination or favouritism will be tolerated, nor any disregard of these, the Throne's admonitions."

On the following day was proclaimed the result of what the Emperor fully intended to be the last examination under the old classical-essay system. The candidate originally selected for the high honour of Optimus was again a Kiangsu man, but the Empress herself altered the list and conferred the coveted distinction upon a native of Kueichou province, to mark her displeasure against the province which had given birth to Weng T'ung-ho. At the same time a Decree advised members of the Imperial Clan to seek education in Europe; even Princes of the Blood were to be encouraged to go abroad and to investigate political conditions. Among the Manchus, the sensation created by these Decrees was very great; they felt that, for the first time in history, fundamental things were being challenged, the ancient bulwarks of the Dynastic privileges in danger. Had not Mencius himself said: "We have heard of Chinese ideas being employed to convert barbarians, but have never heard of China being converted by barbarians."

On the morning after the issue of the second Decree, Weng T'ung-ho, on return from his week's leave, proceeded as usual at 4 A.M. to the Summer Palace to attend the audience of the Grand Council. He was met by one of the Secretaries to the Council who, handing him an Imperial Decree, informed him of his dismissal. It was Tzŭ Hsi's first open move on behalf of the Manchu party, and a clear admission of tutelage on the part of the Emperor. This was the Decree:

"A Vermilion Rescript. — We have recently had occasion more than once to observe that the Grand Secretary Weng T'ung-ho has failed in the proper performance of his duties, and that he is the object of very general criticism. He has frequently been impeached, and when questioned by ourselves at audience, he has allowed his manner to betray his feelings, even daring to express approval or displeasure in our presence. His conduct has gradually revealed a wild ambition and a tendency to usurp our authority: it is no longer possible to retain him on the Grand Council. Strictly speaking, his conduct merits close scrutiny and punishment, but bearing in mind that for years he has served us as our tutor, we are averse to inflicting any severe penalty. Weng T'ung-ho is ordered forthwith to vacate his post on the Council, and to return to his native place. Thus is our clemency made manifest."

Another Decree proved even more plainly that the Emperor was completely under Tzŭ Hsi's orders; it directed that all officials above the second rank should thenceforward return thanks to Her Majesty in person upon receiving appointments. This was a new departure, for, since the war with Japan, she had ceased to hold daily audiences, receiving officials only on her birthday and other State occasions. Another Decree of the same day transferred Jung Lu to Tientsin as Viceroy of Chihli. He and K'ang Yu-wei were received in audience next morning. To Jung Lu the Emperor gave orders to reorganise the forces in Chihli, adding that he looked to him for loyal co-operation in the reform movement. The audience to K'ang Yu-wei, first of many similar interviews (but the only one recorded in the official Gazette), lasted several hours. K'ang deeply disliked and feared Tzŭ Hsi, and from the outset he did his best to prejudice the Emperor against her. He reiterated his opinion that her sympathy for reform was merely a feint, and he roundly denounced her wanton extravagance and dissipated life at the Summer Palace. He described the unpopularity of the Manchu rule in the south as chiefly due to the people's contempt for Her Majesty, and compared her private life to that of the notorious Empress Wu of the T'ang Dynasty. He advised Kuang-Hsü to relegate her permanently to retirement, she being the chief obstacle to reform. The Emperor fell speedily and completely under K'ang's influence, and none of his subsequent Edicts was issued without K'ang's assistance. In the light of later knowledge, and of almost universal Chinese opinion on this subject, it is difficult to acquit K'ang Yu-wei of personal and interested motives, of a desire to wield power in the State as the result of his influence over the Emperor, whose emotional pliability he made to serve his own ends. Looked at in this light, his denunciations of the Empress Dowager and Jung Lu were evidently less the outcome of patriotic indignation than of his recognition of the fact that, so long as Tzŭ Hsi remained in power, his ambitions could never be achieved, nor his own position secured.

XIII

THE HUNDRED DAYS OF REFORM

IMMEDIATELY following upon K'ang Yu-wei's first audience, reform Decrees followed one another in rapid succession. The old examination system which had been in force, with one brief intermission (in K'ang-Hsi's reign), since the days of the Sung Dynasty, was definitely abolished. For the future, said the Emperor, papers on practical subjects were to be set at the public examinations, and while the classics were to remain as a basis for the literary curriculum, candidates for the public service would be expected to display a knowledge of the history of other countries and of contemporary politics. It was at this juncture that the President of the Board of Rites, Hsü Ying-k'uei (who, though a Cantonese, was a stalwart Conservative), was denounced by the Censors Sung Po-lu and Yang Shen-hsiu for obstructing the decreed reforms. They begged the Emperor to "display his divine wrath by immediately reducing Hsü to the rank of a fourth class official as a warning to other offenders."

"We have noted," they said, "Your Majesty's zeal in the cause of reform and your gracious desire to promote improved education and friendly relations with foreign Powers. The Board of Rites is in charge of all the colleges in the Empire and the Tsungli Yamên directs our policy.

Hsü Ying-k'uei, President of the Board of Rites and a Minister of the Tsungli Yamên, is a man of second-rate ability, arrogant, ignorant, and hopelessly obstinate. Your Majesty, being deeply conscious of the vital need for permanent and radical reform, and anxious to encourage men of talent, has instituted a special examination in political economy, but Hsü Ying-ku'ei has dared to cast disparagement on your Majesty's orders and has openly stated that such an examination is a useless innovation. It is his intention to allow as few candidates as possible to pass this examination so as to render it unpopular. He is similarly opposing every one of your Majesty's proposed reforms. He vilifies western learning in conversation with his *protégés*, and is the sworn foe of all progressive scholars. Your Majesty's chief complaint is that such scholars are too few in number, but Hsü Ying-ku'ei's chief hope is to suppress the few there are."

"In the Tsungli Yamên a single phrase wrongly expressed may well precipitate a war; so important are the duties there to be performed that no one unacquainted with foreign affairs, and the ways of those who seek to injure us, can possibly render effective service to the State. Hsü Ying-ku'ei is far from being a distinguished Chinese scholar; nevertheless he despises European learning. His boundless conceit is a menace to our country's interests and dignity. It seems to us a monstrous thing that a man of this stamp should be employed at the Tsungli Yamên, and that his removal from the Board would be of incalculable benefit. He deserves to be removed from office for blocking reform and impeding the execution of your Majesty's plans, if only as a warning to reactionary officials, who are all a danger to their country. If your Majesty will reduce him to the fourth official rank we shall escape the ridicule of foreign nations, and the cause of reform will be greatly advanced."

On receipt of the above Memorial, Kuang-Hsü commanded Hsü Ying-ku'ei to submit a personal explanation of his conduct. The following is the text of his Memorial in reply, which shows K'ang Yu-wei in a light less favourable than that in which his admirers represented him:—

"I feel that because of my uprightness I have made myself enemies, and I am grateful to your Majesty for thus allowing me to defend myself. The Censors accuse me of thinking disparagingly of your Majesty's orders. How can they know what is in my mind? Their accusations are evidently worthless. Li Hung-chang and myself were strongly in favour of the original scheme for instituting an examination for political economy. I observed, however, that great care must be exercised in carrying out this new idea, and that the selection for office of too many successful candidates might endanger the main object of the reform. While in no way desiring to make the standard prohibitively high, I was determined not to court popularity by consenting to making the path of these candidates too easy. How can these Censors know that we are opposed to the proposals of reform before our Memorials have seen the light? Their remarks are based on pure conjecture and prejudice. Moreover, many of your Majesty's Decrees in no way concern the Board of Rites, *e.g.*, the contemplated reform of military examinations and the abolition of sinecures in the army. Again, the Memorialists accuse me of vilifying western learning in conversation with my *protégés*, and of being the sworn foe of progressive scholars. As a native of Canton province, I have had no little experience of foreign affairs, and have constantly had occasion to recommend for employment men well versed in the arts and sciences of the west; for instance, Hua T'ing-chun, for his knowledge of marksmanship, and Fang Yao for his skill in the manufacture of guns. With all my *protégés* my constant object has been to encourage them to acquire a thorough knowledge of current politics and to eschew forms of learning that are ornamental and useless.

"When the Censors accuse me of being the foe of scholars, they evidently refer to K'ang Yu-wei. As a native of my province K'ang was well known to me in his youth as a worthless fellow. After taking his degree and returning to his home, he was for ever inciting people to litigation; his reputation was evil. On coming to Peking he made friends with the Censors and intrigued with certain persons in high office, making great capital of his alleged knowledge of European science, in the hope of obtaining a lucrative post. On three occasions he tried to secure an interview with me, but I knew the man too well, and declined to receive him. He then founded a society at the Canton Guild-house, enrolling over two hundred members; but I caused it to be suppressed, fearing that disturbances would come of it. Hence K'ang's hatred of me. When your Majesty summoned him to audience, he boasted to his fellow-provincials that high promotion was in store for him; he was keenly disappointed at getting nothing higher than a clerkship in the Tsungli Yamên. He has been spreading lies about me and inciting the Censors to attack me in the hope of ousting me, one of his chiefs, from my position. That is quite in keeping with his character. The Grand Secretary, Li Hung-tsao, used to say that the flaunting of western knowledge was used only too often by persons who had no real education therein; persons who hoodwinked the public and were accepted at their own valuation. K'ang Yu-wei has got hold of many wild and fantastic ideas, and is trying to make a reputation for himself by plagiarising hackneyed articles from European newspapers and disparaging our country's ancient institutions. His proposals are utterly unpractical, and his motives will not bear investigation. If he is retained at the Tsungli Yamên, instead of being cashiered and sent back to Canton, as he deserves, he will inevitably bring about complications by the betrayal of State secrets. If he remains in Peking he and his associates will assuredly plot together for evil, their only object being to promote party strife and to foment intrigues.

"The danger with which his revolutionary tendencies threaten the State is indeed a most serious matter, and the Censors are, for once, quite right in describing me as his sworn foe.

"The Censors also accuse me of despising European learning. At audience with your Majesty I have frequently laid stress on the importance of opening mines, building ships and providing munitions of war; it is therefore known to your Majesty how baseless is this charge. But since the negotiations which followed the seizure of Kiaochao Bay, the transaction of the Tsungli Yamên's business has become increasingly difficult, nor will our position be improved by this futile wrangling. I would, therefore, humbly ask your Majesty to relieve me of my duties at the Yamên, so that calumny may be hushed and that I may cease to occupy a position for which I am eminently unfitted. This is my humble prayer."

The Emperor was greatly incensed at Hsü Ying-ku'ei's out-spoken denunciation of K'ang Yu-wei, but could not as yet sum-mon up courage to offend the Empress Dowager by dismissing from office one who enjoyed her favour and protection. Tzŭ Hsi perused both Memorials and was secretly impressed by Hsü's warning in regard to the revolutionary tendencies of the reform-ers. From that day, though openly unopposed to reform, she became suspicious of K'ang's influence over the Emperor, but preferred to bide her time, never doubting that, at a word from her, Kuang-Hsü would dismiss him. She gave a special audience to Wang Wen-shao, who had come from Tientsin after handing over the Chihli Viceroyalty to Jung Lu. Wang stoutly supported Hsü Ying-ku'ei's attitude of caution in regard to several of the Emperor's proposed measures. Following upon this audience, the Emperor issued a Decree permitting Hsü to retain his posts, but warning him to show more energy in future both at the Board of Rites and at the Tsungli Yamên. Hsü regarded this as a decided triumph, due to Tzŭ Hsi's protection, and became more than ever opposed to innovations; this attitude was strengthened when Huai Ta Pu, his Manchu colleague at the Board of Rites and a first cousin of Tzŭ Hsi, came out as a strong supporter of the ultra-Conservatives.

The Emperor's next Decree provided for the reorganisation of the effete Manchu troops of the Metropolitan Province and for the founding of colleges and high schools in the provinces, to correspond to the Peking University.

A reactionary Memorial by the Censor Wen T'i[1] charged his colleagues Sung Po-lu and Yang Shen-hsiu with making their personal jealousy of Hsü Ying-ku'ei an excuse for deluding the Emperor and setting him at variance with the Empress Dowager. This greatly angered His Majesty, who promptly had the offend-er dismissed from the Censorate for stirring up that very party

---

1. In 1901, this official begged Tzŭ Hsi, just before her departure from K'ai-Feng fu for Peking, not to return thither, on the ground that her Palace had been polluted by the presence of the foreign barbarians.

strife which his Memorial professed to denounce. Wen T'i, thus rebuked, induced Huai Ta Pu to go out to the Summer Palace and endeavour to enlist the Old Buddha's sympathy in his behalf. She, however, declined to move in the matter, having at the moment no specific ground of complaint against the Emperor and preferring to give the Progressives all the rope they wanted; but she caused Yü Lu, one of her old *protégés*, to be appointed to the Grand Council, and this official kept her regularly informed of everything that occurred in Peking. He belonged to the Kang Yi faction of extremists and disapproved of reform with all the dogged stupidity of his class. Later, in 1900, as Viceroy of Chihli, he rendered no little assistance to Kang Yi's schemes for massacring all foreigners, and was a noted leader of the Boxer movement. With three reactionaries on the Council of the stamp of Kang Yi, Wang Wen-shao and Yü Lu, there was small chance of any genuine opportunity or honest purpose of reform, whatever the Emperor might choose to decree, but before the Conservatives could assume the offensive, they had to win over Tzŭ Hsi definitely and openly to their side, and with her Jung Lu.

At about this time Kuang-Hsü reprimanded another Censor for a trifling error in caligraphy, the incorrect writing of a character.[1] Nevertheless, a week later, a Decree was issued, clearly showing the influence of K'ang Yu-wei, in which it was ordered that caligraphy should no longer form a special subject at the public examinations. "In certain branches of the public service neat handwriting was no doubt of great value, but it would in future be made the subject of special examinations for the appointment of copyists."

On the 8th day of the 6th Moon, a Decree ordered arrangements to be made for the publication of official Gazettes all over the Empire, and K'ang Yu-wei was placed in charge of the Head Office at Shanghai. These Gazettes were to be official newspapers,

---

1. The Emperor prided himself on being a great stickler in such matters, and many of the younger officials feared him on account of his quick temper and martinet manner in dealing with them.

and their object was the extension of general knowledge. They were to receive Government subsidies; copies were to be regularly submitted for the Emperor's perusal; opinions were to be freely expressed, and all abuses fearlessly exposed. K'ang Yu-wei was directed to draw up Press regulations in this sense.

On the 23rd of the 6th Moon, another vigorous Decree exhorted the official class to turn its attention seriously to reforms. Herein the Emperor declared that the procrastination hitherto displayed was most disheartening. "Stagnation," said the Edict, "is the sign of grave internal sickness; hopeless abuses are bred from this palsied indifference. An earnest reformer like Ch'en Pao-chen, the Governor of Hupei, becomes a target for the violent abuse of officials and gentry. Henceforward I would have you all sympathise with my anxiety and work earnestly together, so that we may profit by our past reverses and provide for a brighter future."

Another Decree ordered the institution of naval colleges as a step preliminary to the reconstruction of China's fleet. Railway and mining bureaus were established in Peking, and the Cantonese reformer, Liang Ch'i-Ch'ao, was given charge of a Translation Department, to publish standard foreign works on political economy and natural science, a grant of one thousand taels per mensem being allowed to cover his expenses.

But an innovation more startling than all these, broke upon the upholders of the old *régime* in a Decree issued in response to a Memorial by Jung Lu, who was all in favour of reform in military matters. It was therein announced that the Emperor would escort the Empress Dowager by train to Tientsin on the 5th day of the 9th Moon, and there hold a review of the troops. The Conservatives were aghast at the idea of their Majesties travelling by train, but Tzŭ Hsi, who had always enjoyed riding on the miniature railway in the Winter Palace, was delighted at the prospect of so novel an excursion. But if Manchu propriety was shocked at this proposal, a still heavier blow was dealt it by the next Decree, which abolished a number of obsolete and useless Government

offices and sinecures, fat jobs which, for generations, had maintained thousands of idlers in the enjoyment of lucrative squeezes, a burden on the State.

This Decree was loudly denounced as contrary to the traditions of the Manchu Dynasty, and from all sides came urgent appeals to the Old Buddha to protect the privileges of the ruling
class, and to order its cancellation. Yet another bolt fell two days
later, when all the high officials of the Board of Rites, including
Hsü Ying-ku'ei and the Empress Dowager's kinsman, Huai Ta Pu,
were summarily cashiered for having suppressed a Memorial by
the Secretary, Wang Chao. In this document it was suggested that
the Emperor, in company with the Empress Dowager, should
travel abroad, beginning with Japan and concluding with a tour
in Europe. Realising that "the craft of Demetrius was in danger,"
nearly all the Conservatives holding high office proceeded in a
body to the Summer Palace and told the Empress Dowager that
the only hope of saving the country lay in her resumption of the
supreme power. The Old Buddha bade them wait—the sands
were running out, but she was not yet ready to move.

K'ang Yu-wei, realising that there was danger ahead, took advantage of what he mistook for indecision on the part of Tzŭ Hsi
to induce the Emperor to rebel against her authority. Once more
he assured Kuang-Hsü that her professed sympathy for reform
was all a sham, and that, on the contrary, it was she herself who
was the chief obstacle to China's awakening, her influence being
really the prime factor in the country's corruption and lethargy.
Why should she be permitted to waste millions of Government
funds yearly in the upkeep of her lavish establishment at the
Summer Palace? He advised the Emperor by a *coup de main* to
surround her residence, seize her person, and confine her for the
rest of her days on a certain small island in the Winter Palace
lake. Thereafter he should issue a Decree recounting her many
misdeeds and proclaiming his intention never again to permit
her to have any part in the Government. This conversation was
held in a private apartment of the Palace, but there is every

reason to believe that it was reported to Tzŭ Hsi by one of the eunuch spies employed by Li Lien-ying for that purpose. The Emperor foolishly allowed himself to be led into approval of this plot, but decided to await the Court's proposed trip to Tientsin before putting it into execution. He knew that to ensure success for the scheme he must be able to command the services of the troops, and he realised that so long as Jung Lu was in command of the foreign-drilled forces of Chihli, he would never consent to their lifting a finger against his life-long benefactress. Herein, in the Emperor's opinion, lay the main obstacle that confronted him. The real danger, that lay in Tsŭ Hsi's enormous personal influence and fertility of resource, he appears to have under-rated, mistaking her inaction for indecision.

For the moment he continued to issue new Edicts, one ordering the making of macadamised roads in Peking, another the enrolment of militia for purposes of national defence, while a third authorised Manchus to leave Peking, should they so wish, to earn their living in the provinces. On the 27th of the 7th Moon, appeared the last of his important Reform Decrees — a document pathetic in the light of subsequent events.

"In promoting reforms, we have adopted certain European methods, because, while China and Europe are both alike in holding that the first object of good government should be the welfare of the people, Europe has travelled further on this road than we have, so that, by the introduction of European methods, we simply make good China's deficiencies. But our Statesmen and scholars are so ignorant of what lies beyond our borders that they look upon Europe as possessing no civilisation. They are all unaware of those numerous branches of western knowledge whose object it is to enlighten the minds and increase the material prosperity of the people. Physical well-being and increased longevity of the race are thereby secured for the masses.

"Is it possible that I, the Emperor, am to be regarded as a mere follower after new and strange ideas because of my thirst for reform? My love for the people, my children, springs from the feeling that God has confided them to me and that to my care they have been given in trust by my illustrious Ancestors. I shall never feel that my duty as Sovereign is fulfilled until I have raised them all to a condition of peaceful prosperity. Moreover, do not the foreign Powers surround our Empire, committing frequent acts of aggression? Unless we learn and adopt the sources of their strength, our plight cannot be remedied. The cause of my anxiety is not fully appreciated by my people, because the reactionary element deliberately misrepresents my objects, spreading the while baseless rumours so as to disturb the minds of men. When I reflect how deep is the ignorance of the masses of the dwellers in the innermost parts of the Empire on the subject of my proposed reforms, my heart is filled with care and grief. Therefore do I hereby now proclaim my intentions, so that the whole Empire may know and believe that their Sovereign is to be trusted and that the people may co-operate with me in working for reform and the strengthening of our country. This is my earnest hope. I command that the whole of my Reform Decrees be printed on Yellow paper and distributed for the information of all men. The District Magistrates are henceforward privileged to submit Memorials to me through the Provincial Viceroys, so that I may learn the real needs of the people. Let this Decree be exhibited in the front hall of every public office in the Empire so that all men may see it."

But the sands had run out. Tzŭ Hsi now emerged from "the profound seclusion of her Palace" and Kuang-Hsü's little hour was over.

XIV

THE *COUP D'ÉTAT* OF 1898

IN August 1898 — at the end of the 7th Moon — the position of
affairs in the Palace (known only to a few) was that the Empress
Dowager had been won over to the reactionary party; she was
postponing a decisive step, however, until she and the Emperor
made their proposed visit to Tientsin in the 9th Moon. It was
her intention there to confer with Jung Lu before resuming the
Regency, because of the unmistakable hostility towards her then
prevailing in the southern provinces, which she wished to allay,
as far as possible, by avoiding any overt measures of usurpation
until her preparations were made. On the 1st of the 8th Moon,
the Emperor, who was then in residence at the Summer Palace,
received in audience Yüan Shih-k'ai, the Judicial Commissioner
of Chihli, and discussed with him at great length the political
needs of the Empire. Yüan (then in his fortieth year) had owed
his rapid advancement to the protection of the great Viceroy Li
Hung-chang; nevertheless, among his rivals and enemies there
were many who attributed the disastrous war with Japan in 1894
to his arbitrary conduct of affairs as Imperial Resident in Corea.
There is no doubt that his reports and advice on the situation at
Seoul precipitated, if they did not cause, the crisis, leading the
Chinese Government to despatch troops into the country in the

face of Japan's desire and readiness for war, and thus to the extinction of China's sovereignty in the Hermit Kingdom; but the
fact had not impaired Yüan's personal prestige or his influence at
Court. As a result of this audience the Emperor was completely
won over by Yüan's professed interest in the cause of reform, and
was convinced that in him he had secured a powerful supporter.
His Majesty had already realised that he must now reckon with
the Old Buddha's uncompromising opposition; quite recently
she had severely rebuked him for even noticing K'ang Yu-wei's
suggestion that he should act more on his own authority. Jung
Lu, he knew, would always loyally support his Imperial mistress;
and there was not one prominent Manchu in the Empire, and, as
far as Peking was concerned, hardly a Chinese, who would dare
to oppose the Old Buddha, if once she declared herself actively
on the side of reaction. The only two high officials in Peking on
whom he could confidently reckon for sympathy and support
were the Cantonese Chang Yin-huan, and Li Tuan-fen, a native of
Kueichou. But if he could obtain control of the Northern foreign-
drilled army, the reactionary party might yet be overthrown. To
secure this end it was essential that Jung Lu, the Governor-General of Chihli and Commander-in-Chief of the foreign-drilled
forces, should be put out of the way, and this before the Empress
could be warned of the plot. The Emperor therefore proposed
to have Jung Lu put to death in his Yamên at Tientsin, and then
swiftly to bring a force of 10,000 of his disciplined troops to the
capital, who would confine the Empress Dowager to the Summer Palace. At the same time the most prominent reactionaries
in Peking, *i.e.*, Kang Yi, Yü Lu, Huai T'a Pu and Hsü Ying-ku'ei
were to be seized at their residences and hurried off to the prison
of the Board of Punishments. This was the scheme suggested by
K'ang Yu-wei, the Censor Yang Shen-hsiu, and the secretaries of
the Grand Council, T'an Ssu-t'ung, Lin-Hsü, Yang Jui, and Liu
Kuang-ti. At this first audience Yüan Shih-k'ai was informed
of the Emperor's determination to maintain and enforce his reform policy, and was asked whether he would be loyal to his

sovereign if placed in command of a large force of troops. "Your servant will endeavour to recompense the Imperial favour," he replied, "even though his merit be only as a drop of water in the ocean or a grain of sand in the desert; he will faithfully perform the service of a dog or a horse while there remains breath in his body."

Completely reassured by Yüan's words and earnest manner and his apparently genuine zeal for reform, the Emperor straightway issued the following Decree:

"At the present time army reform is of all things most essential, and the judicial commissioner of Chihli, Yüan Shih-k'ai, is an energetic administrator and thoroughly earnest in the matter of training our forces. We therefore accord him the rank of Expectant Vice-President of a Board and place him in special charge of the business of army reform. He is to memorialise from time to time regarding any measures which he may desire to introduce. Under the present conditions of our Empire it is of the first importance that our defences be strengthened, and it behoves Yüan Shih-k'ai therefore to display all-possible energy and zeal in the training of our troops, so that an efficient army may be organised, and the Throne's determination to secure homogeneous forces be loyally supported."

At this first audience there had been no mention of the proposed removal of Jung Lu. Scarcely had Yüan left the Jen Shou (Benevolent Old Age) Palace Hall, than the Empress Dowager summoned him to her own apartments, and closely questioned him as to what the Emperor had said. "By all means let the army be reformed," said the Old Buddha; "the Decree is sensible enough, but His Majesty is in too great a hurry, and I suspect him of cherishing some deep design. You will await a further audience with him, and then receive my instructions."

The Empress then sent for the Emperor, and informed him that he must have K'ang Yu-wei placed under arrest for speaking disrespectfully of her private life and morals.

She refrained from informing him that she knew of his design to deprive her of power, and she was so far unaware of the extent of the plot against herself and Jung Lu. She reproached him, however, in general terms for his evident and increasing lack of filial duty towards herself. The Emperor meekly promised to comply with her wishes as to K'ang Yu-wei's arrest, but late that same evening, while the Empress Dowager was entertaining herself at a water picnic on the K'un Ming Lake, he despatched his confidential eunuch, Sung Yu-lien, into Peking with the following Decree, drafted in His Majesty's own unformed and childish handwriting:

"On a previous occasion we commanded the Secretary of the Board of Works, K'ang Yu-wei, to take charge of the Government Gazette Bureau at Shanghai. We learn with astonishment that he has not yet left Peking. We are well aware of the crisis through which the Empire is passing, and have been anxious on this account to obtain the services of men well versed in political economy, with whom to discuss improved methods of government. We granted one audience to K'ang Yu-wei (sic: as a matter of fact K'ang was received by His Majesty on several occasions) because of his special knowledge, and we appointed him to take charge of the Government Gazette Bureau for the reason that newspapers are one of the most important factors in national education and progress. His duties are evidently of no light responsibility, and funds having been specially raised for this enterprise, we command him now to betake himself with all despatch to Shanghai; he shall on no account procrastinate any longer."

K'ang Yu-wei received the Decree, realised its significance, and left Peking by the first train next morning, arriving safely at Tongku, where he boarded a coasting steamer for Shanghai.[1] When the Empress heard of his departure she was furious, and telegraphed to Jung Lu to arrest K'ang, but for some unexplained

1. K'ang's subsequent escape under British protection, in which one of the writers was instrumental, is graphically described in despatch No.401 of Blue Book No.1 of 1899.

reason (the instructions reached him before K'ang could have arrived at Tientsin) Jung Lu took no steps to do so. At this time he was unaware of the plot against his life, or he would hardly have shown such magnanimity. K'ang Yu-wei never gave him any credit for it and has always denounced Jung Lu as second only in villainy to the Empress Dowager, an arch enemy of reform and reformers. As a matter of fact Jung Lu was one of the high officials who originally recommended K'ang to the notice of the Emperor, and till the day of his death he always alluded to himself jocularly as one of the *K'ang T'ang*, or K'ang Yu-wei party, to the great amusement of the Old Buddha, who would jokingly ask him what news he had of his friend K'ang, the traitor and rebel. That morning, the 2nd of the Moon, audience was given to the reformer Lin Hsü and to Yüan Shih-k'ai, who again assured the Emperor of his complete devotion. His Majesty then left for the Forbidden City, intending to carry out his plans against the Empress from there rather than from the Summer Palace, where nearly every eunuch was a spy in her service.

It is evident that, so far, the Emperor by no means despaired of his chances of success, as two Decrees were issued next morning, one ordering the teaching of European languages in the public schools, and the other requiring purer administration on the part of district magistrates.

On the morning of the 5th, Yüan Shih-k'ai had a final audience, before leaving for Tientsin. His Majesty received him in the Palace of Heavenly Purity (Ch'ien Ch'ing Kung) of the Forbidden City. Every precaution was taken to prevent the conversation being overheard. Seated for the last time on the great lacquered Dragon Throne, so soon to be reoccupied by the Empress Dowager, in the gloomy throne room which the morning light could scarcely penetrate, His Majesty told Yüan Shih-k'ai the details of the commission with which he had decided to entrust him. He was to put Jung Lu to death and then, returning immediately to the capital with the troops under his command, to seize and imprison the Empress Dowager. The Emperor gave him a small arrow, the symbol of his authority to carry out the Imperial orders, and bade him proceed with all haste to Tientsin, there to arrest Jung Lu in his Yamên and see to his instant decapitation. Kuang Hsü also handed him a Decree whereby, upon completion of his mission, he was appointed Viceroy of Chihli *ad interim*, and ordered to Peking for further audience.

Yüan promised faithful obedience, and, without speaking to anyone, left Peking by the first train. Meantime the Old Buddha was due to come in from the I-ho Yüan to the Winter Palace that morning at 8 o'clock, to perform sacrifice at the altar to the God of Silkworms, and the Emperor dutifully repaired to the Ying Hsiu Gate of the Western Park, where the Lake Palace is situated, to receive Her Majesty as she entered the precincts.

Yüan reached Tientsin before noon, and proceeded at once to Jung Lu's Yamên. He asked Jung Lu whether he regarded him as a faithful blood brother. (The two men had taken the oath of brotherhood several years before.) "Of course I do," replied the Viceroy. "You well may, for the Emperor has sent me to kill you, and instead, I now betray his scheme, because of my loyalty to the Empress Dowager and of my affection for you." Jung Lu, apparently unaffected by the message, merely expressed surprise that the Old Buddha could have been kept in ignorance of all these things, and added that he would go at once to the capital and see the Empress Dowager that same evening. Yüan handed him the Emperor's Decree, and Jung Lu, travelling by special train, reached Peking soon after 5 P.M.

He went directly to the Lake Palace, and entered the Empress's residence, boldly disregarding the strict etiquette which forbids any provincial official from visiting the capital without a special summons by Edict, and the still stricter rules that guard the *entrée* of the Palace. Unushered he entered the Empress's presence, and kowtowing thrice, exclaimed, "Sanctuary, your Majesty!" "What sanctuary do you require in the Forbidden precincts, where no harm can come to you, and where you have no right to be?" replied the Old Buddha. Jung Lu proceeded to lay before her all the details of the plot. Grasping the situation and rising immediately to its necessities with the courage and masculine intelligence that enabled her to overcome all obstacles, she directed him to send word secretly to the leaders of the Conservative party, summoning them to immediate audience in the Palace by the Lake. (The Emperor was still in the Forbidden City.) In less than two hours the whole of the Grand Council, several of the Manchu princes and nobles (Prince Ch'ing, with his usual fine "flair" for a crisis, had applied for sick leave and was therefore absent) and the high officials of the Boards, including the two Ministers whom the Emperor had cashiered (Hsü Ying-ku'ei and Huai Ta Pu) were assembled in the presence of the Empress. On their knees, the assembled officials besought her to resume the reins of government and to save their ancient Empire from the evils of a barbarian civilisation. It was speedily arranged that the guards in the Forbidden City should be replaced by men from Jung Lu's own corps, and that, in the meantime, he should return to his post in Tientsin and await further orders. The conference broke up at about midnight. The Emperor was due to enter the Chung Ho Hall of the Palace at 5.30 the next morning to peruse the litany drawn up by the Board of Rites, which he was to recite next day at the autumnal sacrifice to the Tutelary Deities. After leaving that hall, he was seized by the guards and eunuchs, conveyed to the Palace on the small island in the middle of the lake (the "Ocean Terrace") and informed that the Empress Dowager would visit him later.

The following Decree was thereupon issued by the Empress Dowager in the Emperor's name:

"The nation is now passing through a crisis, and wise guidance is needed in all branches of the public service. WE ourselves have laboured diligently, night and day, to perform OUR innumerable duties, but in spite of all OUR anxious energy and care WE are in constant fear lest delay should be the undoing of the country. WE now respectfully recall the fact that Her Imperial Majesty the Empress Dowager has on

two occasions since the beginning of the reign of H.M. T'ung-Chih, performed the functions of Regent, and that in her administrations of the
Government she displayed complete and admirable qualities of perfection which enabled her successfully to cope with every difficulty that
arose. Recollecting the serious burden of the responsibility WE owe to
OUR ancestors and to the nation, WE have repeatedly besought Her Majesty to condescend once more to administer the Government. Now she
has graciously honoured US by granting OUR prayer, a blessing indeed
for all OUR subjects. From this day forth Her Majesty will transact the
business of Government in the side hall of the Palace, and on the day
after to-morrow WE ourselves at the head of OUR Princes and Ministers
shall perform obeisance before Her in the Hall of Diligent Government.
The Yamêns concerned shall respectfully make the arrangements necessary for this ceremonial. The words of the Emperor."

Another Decree followed close upon the above, cashiering the
Censor Sung Po-lu, on the ground of his generally evil reputation
and recommendation of bad characters (*i.e.*, the reformer Liang
Ch'i-ch'ao). The Empress had a special grudge against this Censor because he had ventured to impeach her morals in a recent
memorial, but as he had taken no part in the conspiracy against
her person she spared his life.

Tzŭ Hsi in due course proceeded to the "Ocean Terrace," accompanied only by Li Lien-ying, who had been ordered to replace the Emperor's eunuchs by creatures of his own. (Kuang
Hsü's former attendants were either put to death or banished to
the post roads.) A Manchu who heard an account of the interview
from Duke Kuei Hsiang, Tz'u Hsi's younger brother, is our authority for what occurred at this dramatic meeting. The Empress
Dowager bluntly informed Kuang Hsü that she had decided to
spare his life and, for the present at any rate, to allow him to
retain the throne. He would, however, be kept henceforward under strict surveillance, and every word of his would be reported
to her. As to his schemes of reform, which at first she had encouraged, little dreaming to what depths of folly his infatuate

CIRCULAR THRONE HALL IN THE GROUNDS OF THE LAKE PALACE LOOTED BY ALLIED TROOPS IN 1900.

PAVILION ON LAKE TO THE WEST OF FORBIDDEN CITY.

presumption would lead him, they would all be repealed. How dared he forget what great benefits he owed her, his elevation to the throne and her generosity in allowing him to administer the government, he a poor puppet, who had no right to be Emperor at all, and whom she could unmake at will? There was not, she said, a single Manchu in high place but wished his removal, and urged her to resume the Regency. True, he had sympathisers among the Chinese, traitors all; with them she would deal in due course. Kuang Hsü's secondary consort (the Chen Fei or Pearl Concubine, the only one of his wives with whom he seems to have been on affectionate terms) knelt then before Tzŭ Hsi, imploring her to spare the Emperor further reproaches. She actually dared to suggest that he was, after all, the lawful Sovereign and that not even the Empress Dowager could set aside the mandate of Heaven. Tzŭ Hsi angrily dismissed her from the Presence, ordering her to be confined in another part of the Palace, where she remained until, in 1900, there came an opportunity in which the vindictive Empress took summary revenge on the presumptuous concubine.[1]

The Empress Consort, with whom Kuang Hsü was hardly on speaking terms, was commanded to remain with him. She, as Tzŭ Hsi's niece, could be trusted to spy upon the Emperor and report all his doings. He was allowed to see no one but her and the eunuchs in attendance, except in the presence of the Empress Dowager.

To the end of his life Kuang Hsü blamed Yüan Shih-k'ai, and him alone, for having betrayed him. To Yüan he owed his humiliation, the end of all his cherished plans of government and the twenty-three months of solitary confinement which he had to endure on the "Ocean Terrace." Almost his last words, as he lay dying, were to bid his brothers remember his long agony and promise to be revenged upon the author of his undoing. Of Jung Lu he said that it was but natural that he should consider first his

---

1. She was thrown down a well, by Tzŭ Hsi's orders, as the Court prepared for flight after the entrance of the allied forces into Peking. (*Vide infra.*)

duty to the Empress Dowager and seek to warn her; and, after all, as he had planned Jung Lu's death, he could hardly expect from him either devotion or loyalty. The Old Buddha's resentment was also natural; he had plotted against her and failed. But Yüan Shih-k'ai had solemnly sworn loyalty and obedience. The Emperor never willingly spoke to him again, even when, as Viceroy of Chihli, Yüan came to the height of his power.

To-day Yüan lives in retirement, and under the constant shadow of fear; for the Emperor's brother, the Regent, has kept his promise. Such are the intricate humanities of the inner circle around and about the Dragon Throne, the never-ending problem of the human equation as a factor in the destinies of peoples.

XV

TZǓ HSI RESUMES THE REGENCY
(1898)

KUANG Hsü's reign was over; there remained to him only the Imperial title. He had had his chance; in the enthusiasm of youth and new ideas he had played a desperate game against the powers of darkness in high places, and he had lost. Once more, as after the death of T'ung-Chih, Tzǔ Hsi could make a virtue of her satisfied ambitions. She had given her nephew a free hand, she had retired from the field, leaving him to steer the ship of State: if he had now steered it into troublous and dangerous seas, if, by common consent, she were again called to take the helm, this was the doing of Heaven and no fault of hers. She could no more be blamed for Kuang Hsü's folly than for the vicious habits and premature death of her son, which had brought her back to power 23 years before. It was clear (and there were many voices to reassure her of the fact) that the stars in their courses were working for the continuance of her unfettered authority, and that any trifling assistance which she might have given them would not be too closely scrutinised.

Kuang Hsü's reign was over; but his person (frail, melancholy tenement) remained, and Tzǔ Hsi was never enamoured of half measures or ambiguous positions. From the day when the pitiful monarch entered his pavilion prison on the "Ocean Terrace," she began to make arrangements for his "mounting the Dragon" and "visiting the Nine Springs" in the orthodox classical manner, and for providing the Throne with another occupant whose youth, connections and docility would enable her to hold the Regency indefinitely. Nevertheless, because of the turbulent temper of the southern provinces and possible manifestations of Europe's curious sympathy with the Emperor's Utopian dreams, she realised the necessity for proceeding with caution and decorum. It was commonly reported throughout the city in the beginning of October that the Emperor would die with the end of the Chinese year.

Kuang Hsü was a prisoner in his Palace, doomed, as he well knew; yet must he play the puppet Son of Heaven and perform each season's appointed posturings. On the 8th day of the 8th Moon he appeared therefore, as ordered by his attendants, and in the presence of his whole Court performed the nine prostrations and other proper acts of obeisance before Her Majesty Tzŭ Hsi, in recognition of his own nonentity and her supreme authority. In the afternoon, escorted by a strong detachment of Jung Lu's troops, he went from the Lake Palace to sacrifice at the Altar of the Moon. Thus, pending the *coup-de-grâce*, the wretched Emperor went through the empty ceremonies of State ritual; high priest, that was himself to be the next victim, how bitter must have been his thoughts as he was borne back with Imperial pomp and circumstance to his lonely place of humiliation!

Tzŭ Hsi then settled down to her work of government, returning to it with a zest by no means diminished by the years spent in retreat. And first she must justify the policy of reaction to herself, to her high officials, and the world at large. She must get rid of offenders and surround herself with men after her own heart.

A few days after the Autumn festival and the Emperor's melancholy excursion, Her Majesty proceeded to remind the Imperial Clansmen that their position would not protect them against the consequences of disloyalty; she was always much exercised

(remembering the Tsai Yüan conspiracy) at any sign of intriguing amongst her Manchu kinsmen. In this case her warning took
the form of a Decree in which she sentenced the "Beileh" Tsai
Ch'u[1] to perpetual confinement in the "Empty Chamber" of the
Clan Court. Tsai Ch'u had had the audacity to sympathise with
the Emperor's reform schemes; he had also had the bad luck to
marry one of Tzǔ Hsi's nieces and to be upon the worst of terms
with her. When therefore he advised the Emperor, in the beginning of the Hundred Days, to put a stop, once and for all, to the
Old Buddha's interference in State affairs, the "mean one of his
inner chamber" did not fail to report the fact to Her Majesty, and
thus to enlist her sympathies and activities, from the outset, on
the side of the reactionaries.

At the time immediately following the *coup d'état*, public opinion at the Capital was divided as to the merits of the Emperor's proposed reforms and the wisdom of their suppression, but the political instincts of the tribute-fed metropolis are, generally speaking,
dormant, and what it chiefly respects is the energetic display of
power. So that, on the whole, sympathy was with the Old Buddha.
She had, moreover, a Bismarckian way of guiding public opinion,
of directing undercurrents of information through the eunuchs
and tea-house gossip, in a manner calculated to appeal to the instincts of the *literati* and the *bourgeois*; in the present instance stress
was laid on the Emperor's lack of filial piety, as proved by his plotting against his aged and august aunt (a thing unpardonable in the
eyes of the orthodox Confucianist), and on the fact that he enjoyed
the sympathy and support of foreigners — an argument sufficient
to damn him in the eyes of even the most progressive Chinese.
It came, therefore, to be the generally accepted opinion that His
Majesty had shown deplorable want of judgment and self-control,
and that the Empress Dowager was fully justified in resuming

---

1. It is interesting to note that this Manchu Prince (Tsai Ch'u) was released from prison by
the present Regent, the Emperor's brother, and was appointed to the command of one of
the Manchu Banner Corps on the same day, in January 1909, that Yüan Shih-k'ai was dismissed from the viceroyalty of Chihli. The Emperor's party, as opposed to the Yehonala
Clan, heartily approved of his reinstatement.

control of the government. This opinion even came to be accepted and expressed by those Legations which had originally professed to see in the Emperor's reforms the dawn of a new era for China. So elastic is diplomacy in following the line of the least resistance, so adroit (in the absence of a policy of its own) in accepting and condoning any *fait accompli*, that it was not long before the official attitude of the Legations — including the British — had come to deprecate the Emperor's unfortunate haste in introducing reforms, reforms which every foreigner in China had urged for years, and which, accepted in principle by the Empress since 1900, have again been welcomed as proof of China's impending regeneration. In June 1898, the British Minister had seen in the Emperor's Reform Edicts proof that "the Court had at last thoroughly recognised a real need for radical reform." In October, when the Chief Reformer (K'ang Yu-wei) had been saved from Tzǔ Hsi's vengeance by the British Consul-General at Shanghai and conveyed by a British warship to the protection of a British Colony (under the mistaken impression that England would actively intervene in the cause of progress and on grounds of self-interest if not of humanity), we find the tide of expediency turned to recognition of the fact that "the Empress Dowager and the Manchu party were seriously alarmed for their own safety, and looked upon the Reform movement as inimical to Manchu rule"! And two months later, influenced no doubt by the impending season of peace and good will, the Marquess of Salisbury is seriously informed by Sir Claude Macdonald that the wives of the foreign Representatives, seven in all, had been received in audience by the Empress Dowager on the anniversary of her sixty-fourth birthday, and that Her Majesty "made a most favourable impression, both by the personal interest she took in all her guests and by her courteous amiability."[1] On which occasion the puppet Emperor was exhibited, to comply with the formalities, and was made to shake hands with all the ladies. And so the curtain was rung down, and the Reform play ended, to the satisfaction of all (or nearly

---

1. *Vide* Blue Book China No.1. of 1899, letters Nos. 266, 401, and 426.

all) concerned.

Nevertheless, the British Minister and others, disturbed at the persistent rumours that "the Empress Dowager was about to proceed to extreme steps in regard to the Emperor,"[1] went so far as to warn the Chinese Government against anything so disturbing to the European sense of fitness and decency. Foreign countries, the Yamên was told, would view with displeasure and alarm his sudden demise. When the news of the British Minister's intervention became known in the tea-houses and recorded in the Press, much indignation was expressed: this was a purely domestic question, for which precedents existed in plenty and in which foreigners' advice was inadmissible. The Emperor's acceptance of new-fangled foreign ideas was a crime in the eyes of the Manchus, but his enlistment of foreign sympathy and support was hateful to Manchus and Chinese alike.

Matters soon settled down, however, into the old well-worn grooves, the people satisfied and even glad in the knowledge that the Old Buddha was once more at the helm. In the capital the news had been sedulously spread—in order to prepare the way for the impending drama of expiation—that Kuang Hsü had planned to murder Her Majesty, and his present punishment was therefore regarded as mild beyond his deserts.[2] Scholars, composing essays appropriate to the occasion, freely compared His Majesty to that Emperor of the T'ang Dynasty (A.D. 762) who had instigated the murdering of the Empress Dowager of his day. Kuang Hsü's death was therefore freely predicted and its effects discounted; there is no doubt that it would have caused little or no comment in the north of China, however serious its consequences might have been in the south. The public mind having been duly prepared, the Empress Dowager, in the name of the prospective victim, issued a Decree stating that the Son of Heaven

---

1. *Vide* Blue Book China No.1. of 1899, letters Nos. 266, 401, and 426.
2. As an example of Chinese official methods: the Shanghai Taotai when requesting the British Consul-General's assistance to arrest K'ang Yu-wei, did not hesitate to say that the Emperor was dead, murdered by the Chief Reformer. *Vide* Blue Book No.1 of 1899, letter No. 401.

was seriously ill; no surprise or apprehension was expressed, and the sending of competent physicians from the provinces to attend His Majesty was recognised as a necessary concession to formalities. "Ever since the 4th Moon," said this Decree (*i.e.*, since the beginning of the hundred days of reform), "I have been grievously ill; nor can I find any alleviation of my sickness." It was the *pro forma* announcement of his impending despatch, and as such it was received by the Chinese people.

Amongst the doctors summoned to attend His Majesty was Ch'en Lien-fang, for many years the most celebrated physician in China. The following account of his experiences at the capital and the nature of his duties, was supplied by himself at the time, to one of the writers, for publication in *The Times*.

"When the Edict was issued calling upon the provincial Viceroys and Governors to send native doctors of distinction to Peking to advise in regard to the Emperor's illness, Ch'en Lien-fang received orders from the Governor at Soochow to leave for the north without delay. This in itself, apart from the uncongenial and unremunerative nature of the duty (of which Ch'en was well aware), was no light undertaking for a man of delicate physique whose age was over three score years and ten; but there was no possibility of evading the task. He according left his large practice in the charge of two confidential assistants, or pupils, and, having received from the Governor a sum of 6,000 taels for travelling expenses and remuneration in advance, made his way to Peking and reported for duty to the Grand Council. When he arrived there, he found three other native physicians of considerable repute already in attendance, summoned in obedience to the Imperial commands. Dr. Déthève, of the French Legation, had already paid his historical visit to the Emperor, and his remarkable diagnosis of the Son of Heaven's symptoms was still affording amusement to the Legations. The aged native physician spoke in undisguised contempt both of the French doctor's comments on the case and of his suggestions for its treatment. His own description of the Emperor's malady was couched in language not unlike that which writers of historical novels attribute to the physicians of Europe in the Middle Ages; he spoke reverently of influence and vapours at work in the august person of his Sovereign, learnedly of heat-flushings and their occult causes, and plainly of things which are more suited to Chinese than to British readers. Nevertheless, his description pointed clearly to disease of the respiratory organs which he said had existed for over twelve years to general debility, and to a feverish condition which he ascribed to mental anxiety combined with physical weakness. Before he left Peking (about the middle of November) the fever had abated and the patient's symptoms had decidedly improved; the case was, however, in his opinion, of so serious a nature that he decided to leave it, if possible, in the hands of his younger *confrères* — an object which by dint of bribing certain Court officials he eventually achieved. Asked if he considered the Emperor's condition critical, he replied oracularly that if he lived to see the Chinese New Year his strength would thereafter return gradually with the spring, and the complete restoration of his health might be expected.

"Some few days after his arrival in Peking, Ch'en was summoned to audience by orders conveyed through a member of the Grand Council; the Emperor and the Dowager Empress were awaiting his visit in a hall on the south side of the Palace. The consultation was curiously indicative of the divinity which hedges about the ruler of the Middle Kingdom; suggestive, too, of the solidity of that conservatism which dictates the inner policy of China. Ch'en entered the presence of his Sovereign on his knees, crossing the apartment in that position, after the customary kowtows. The Emperor and the Dowager Empress were seated at opposite sides of a low table on the dais, and faced each other in that position during the greater part of the interview. The Emperor appeared pale and listless, had a troublesome irritation of the throat, and was evidently feverish; the thin oval of his face, clearly defined features, and aquiline nose gave him, in the physician's eyes (to use his own words), the appearance of a foreigner. The Empress, who struck him as an extremely well-preserved and intelligent-looking woman, seemed to be extremely solicitous as to the patient's health and careful for his comfort. As it would have been a serious breach of etiquette for the physician to ask any questions of His Majesty, the Empress preceded to describe his symptoms, the invalid occasionally signifying confirmation of what was said by a word or a nod. During this monologue, the physician, following the customary procedure at Imperial audiences, kept his gaze concentrated upon the floor until, at the command of the Empress, and still kneeling, he was permitted to place one hand upon the Emperor's wrist. There was no feeling of the pulse; simply contact with the flat of the hand, first on one side of the wrist and then on the other. This done, the Empress continued her narrative of the patient's sufferings; she described the state of his tongue and the symptoms of ulceration in the mouth and throat, but as it was not permissible for the doctor to examine these, he was obliged to make the best of a somewhat unprofessional description. As he wisely observed, it is difficult to look at a patient's tongue when his exalted rank compels you to keep your eyes fixed rigidly on the floor. The Empress having concluded her remarks on the case, Ch'en was permitted to withdraw and to present to the Grand Council his diagnosis, together with advice as to future treatment, which was subsequently communicated officially to the Throne. The gist of his advice was to prescribe certain tonics of the orthodox native type and to suggest the greatest possible amount of mental and physical rest."[1]

The aged physician's oracular forecast was justified. The Emperor lived to see the New Year and thereafter to regain his strength, a result due in some degree to the Empress Dowager's genuine fear of foreign intervention, but chiefly to her recognition of the strength of public opinion against her in the south of China and of the expediency of conciliating it. In the Kuang provinces there was no doubt of the bitterly anti-Manchu feeling aroused by the execution of the Cantonese reformers: these turbulent southerners were fierce and loud in their denunciations of the Manchus and all their works, and it would not have required much to fan the flames of a new and serious rebellion. The south was well aware, for news travels swiftly in China, that the Emperor's life was in danger and that the close of the

1. From *The Times* of 31st March, 1899.

year was the time fixed for his death, and from all sides protests and words of warning came pouring from the provinces to the capital, addressed not only to the metropolitan boards but to the Throne itself. Amongst these was a telegram signed by a certain Prefect of Shanghai named Ching Yüan-shan, who, in the name of "all the gentry, scholars, merchants and public of Shanghai," referred to the Edict which announced the Emperor's illness and implored the Empress, the Clansmen and the Grand Council to permit his sacred Majesty to resume the government "notwithstanding his indisposition," and to abandon all thoughts of his abdication. He described the province of Kiangsu as being in a state of suppressed ferment and frankly alluded to the probability of foreigners intervening in the event of the Emperor's death. Tzŭ Hsi was much incensed with this courageous official, not because he actually accused her of premeditating murder, but because he dared threaten her with its consequences. She gave orders that he be summarily cashiered, whereupon, fearing further manifestations of her wrath, he fled to Macao. But his bold words undoubtedly contributed to saving the Emperor's life.

Of all the high provincial authorities, one only was found brave and disinterested enough to speak on behalf of the Emperor; this was Liu K'un-yi, the Viceroy of Nanking. He was too big a man to be publicly rebuked at a time like this and Tzŭ Hsi professed to admire his disinterested courage; but she was highly incensed at his action, which contrasted strongly with the astute opportunism of his colleague, the scholarly magnate Chang Chih-tung, Viceroy of Wuch'ang, who had been an ardent advocate of the reformers so long as the wind blew fair in that quarter. Only six months before he had recommended several progressives (amongst them his own secretary, Yang Jui) to the Emperor's notice, and just before the storm burst he had been summoned to Peking by Kuang Hsü to support His Majesty's policy as a member of the Grand Council. No sooner had the Empress Dowager declared herself on the side of the reactionaries, however, and the Emperor had failed in his attempt to win over Yüan Shih-k'ai and his troops, than Chang telegraphed to the Old Buddha warmly approving her policy, and urging strong measures against the reformers. The advice was superfluous; Tzŭ Hsi, having put her hand to the plough, was not the woman to remove it before her work was well done.

On the 11th day of the 8th Moon, she summoned Jung Lu to the capital to assist her in stamping out the reform movement. The Board of Punishments had just sent in a memorial urging the appointment of an Imperial Commission for the trial of K'ang Yu-wei's colleagues. Tzŭ Hsi, in reply, directed them to act in consultation with the Grand Council and to cross-examine the prisoners "with the utmost severity." At the same time she ordered the imprisonment in the Board's gaol of Chang Yin-huan,[1] the Emperor's trusted adviser and friend who, she observed, "bears an abominable reputation." This Edict took occasion to state that the Throne, anxious to temper justice with mercy, would refrain from any general proscription or campaign of revenge," although fully aware that many prominent scholars and officials had allowed themselves to be corrupted by the reformers."

The Empress's next step, advised by Jung Lu, was to issue a Decree, in the name of the Emperor, in which she justified the policy of reaction and reassured the Conservative party. The document is an excellent example of her methods. While the Emperor is made to appear as convinced of the error of his ways, all blame for the "feelings of apprehension" created by the reform movement is relegated to "our officials' failure to give effect to our orders in the proper way," so that everybody's "face" is saved. The following abridged translation is of permanent interest, for

---

1. Chang Yin-huan, who had been created a Knight Commander of St. Michael and St. George in connection with Queen Victoria's Jubilee celebration, was subsequently put to death, after banishment to Turkestan. An order given by Prince Tuan at the commencement of the Boxer crisis was the immediate cause of his execution.

  Another reformer named Hsü Chih-ching was condemned to imprisonment for life in the Board of Punishments under this same Decree; he was released by the Allies in August 1900, when he proceeded at once to T'ai-Yuan fu, and handed himself over to justice, disdaining to accept his release at the hands of foreigners. This incident is typical of the Chinese officials' attitude of mind and of their reverence for the Decrees of the head of the State.

the same arguments are in use to-day and will undoubtedly be required hereafter, when the Manchus come to deal with the impending problems of Constitutional Government:—

"The original object of the Throne in introducing reforms in the administration of the government was to increase the strength of our Empire and to ameliorate the condition of our subjects. It was no sudden whim for change, nor any contempt for tradition that actuated us; surely our subjects must recognise that our action was fully justifiable and indeed inevitable. Nevertheless, we cannot shut our eyes to the fact that feelings of apprehension have been aroused, entirely due to the failure of our officials to give effect to our orders in the proper way, and that this again has led to the dissemination of wild rumours and wrong ideas amongst the ignorant masses of the people. For instance, when we abolished six superfluous government boards, we did so in the public interest, but the immediate result has been that we have been plagued with Memorials suggesting that we should destroy and reconstruct the whole system of administration. It is evident that, unless we explain our policy as a whole, great danger may arise from the spread of such ideas, and to prevent any such result we now command that the six metropolitan departments which we previously abolished be re-established exactly as before. Again, our original intention in authorising the establishment of official newspapers, and allowing all and sundry of our subjects to address us, was to encourage the spread of knowledge and to improve our own sources of intelligence. Unfortunately, however, the right of addressing the Throne has been greatly abused, and the suggestions which have reached us in this way have not only been trivial and useless on many occasions, but have recently shown a tendency towards revolutionary propaganda. For this reason the right to memorialise the Throne will in future be strictly reserved in accordance with the established and ancient custom. As for official newspapers, we have come to the conclusion that they are quite useless for any purposes of the government, and that they only lead to popular discontent; they are therefore abolished from this day forth. The proper training grounds for national industry and talent are Colleges, and these are to go on as before, it being the business of the local officials, acting upon public opinion in their respective districts, to continue the improvement of education on the lines laid down; but there is to be no conversion of temples and shrines into schools, as was previously ordered, because this might lead to strong objection on the part of the people. Generally speaking, there shall be no measures taken contrary to the established order of things throughout the Empire. The times are critical, and it behoves us, therefore, to follow in government matters the happy mean and to avoid all extreme measures and abuses. It is our duty, without prejudice, to steer a middle course, and it is for you, our officials, to aim at permanence and stability of administration in every branch of the government."

Jung Lu was now raised to membership of the Grand Council, and given supreme command of the northern forces and control of the Board of War; he thus became the most powerful official in the Empire, holding a position for which no precedent existed in the annals of the Manchu Dynasty. He had once more proved loyal to the Empress and faithful to the woman whom he had served since the days of the flight to Jehol; and he had his reward. It was natural, if not inevitable, that the part played by Jung Lu in the crisis of the *coup d'état* should expose him to severe criticism, especially abroad; but, from the Chinese official's point of view, his action in supporting the Empress Dowager against her nephew, the Emperor, was nothing more than his duty, and as a statesman he showed himself consistently moderate, sensible, and reliable. The denunciations subsequently poured upon him by the native and foreign Press at the time of the Boxer rising were the result, partly of the unrefuted falsehoods disseminated by K'ang Yu-wei and his followers, and partly of the Legations' prejudice (thence arising) and lack of accurate information. As will hereafter be shown, all his efforts were directed towards stemming the tide of that fanatical outbreak and restraining his Imperial mistress from acts of folly. Amidst the cowardice, ignorance and cruelty of the Manchu Clansmen his foresight and courage stand out steadily in welcome relief; the only servant of the Throne during

Tzŭ Hsi's long rule who approaches him in administrative ability and disinterested patriotism is Tseng Kuo-fan (of whose career a brief account has already been given). From this time forward until his death (1903) we find him ever at Tzŭ Hsi's right hand, her most trusted and efficient adviser; and her choice was well made. As will be seen in a later chapter, there was a time in 1900, when the Old Buddha, distraught by the tumult and the shouting, misled by her own hopes, her superstitious beliefs and the clamorous advice of her kinsfolk, allowed Prince Tuan and his fellow fanatics to undermine for a little while Jung Lu's influence. Nevertheless (as will be seen by the diary of Ching Shan) it was to him that she always turned, in the last resort, for counsel and comfort; it was on him that she leaned in the dark hour of final defeat, and he never failed her. She lived to realise that the advice which he gave, and which she sometimes neglected, was invariably sound. Amidst all the uncertainties of recent Chinese history this much is certain, that the memory of Jung Lu deserves a far higher place in the esteem of his countrymen and of foreigners than it has hitherto received. Unaware himself of many of the calumnies that had been circulated about him at the time of the Court's flight, he was greatly hurt, and his sense of justice outraged, by the cold reception given him by the Legations after the Court's return to Peking. Thereafter, until his death, he was wont to say to his intimate friends that while he would never regret the stand he had taken against the Boxers, he could not understand or forgive the hostility and ingratitude shown him by foreigners. "It was not for love towards them," he observed, on one occasion recorded, "that he had acted as he did, but only because of his devotion to the Empress Dowager and the Manchu Dynasty; nevertheless, since his action had coincided with the interests of the foreigner, he was entitled to some credit for it."

The Empress Dowager consulted long and earnestly with Jung Lu as to the punishment to be inflicted upon the reformers. He advocated strong measures of repression, holding that the prestige of the Manchu Dynasty was involved. The six prisoners were examined by the Board of Punishments, and Jung Lu closely questioned them as to K'ang Yu-wei's intentions in regard to the Empress Dowager. Documents found in Kang's house had revealed every detail of the plot, and upon the Grand Council recommended the execution of all the prisoners. There being no doubt that they had been guilty of high treason against Her Majesty, it seemed clearly inadvisable to prolong the trial, especially as there was undoubtedly a risk of widening the breach between Manchus and Chinese by any delay in the proceedings, at a time when party spirit was running high on both sides. The Old Buddha concurred in the decision of the Grand Council, desiring to terminate the crisis as soon as possible; accordingly, on the 13th day of the Moon, the reformers were executed. They met their death bravely, their execution outside the city being witnessed by an immense crowd. It was reported that amongst the papers of Yang Jui were found certain highly compromising letters addressed to him by the Emperor himself, in which the Empress Dowager was bitterly denounced. There was also a Memorial by Yang impeaching Her Majesty for gross immorality and illicit relations with several persons in high positions, one of whom was Jung Lu; this document had been annotated in red ink by the Emperor himself. It quoted songs and ballads current in the city of Canton, referring to Her Majesty's alleged vicious practices, and warned the Emperor that, if the Manchu dynasty should come now to its end, the fault would lie as much with Tzŭ Hsi and her evil deeds as was the case when the Shang dynasty (of the 12th Century B.C.) fell by reason of the Emperor Chou Hsin's infatuation for his concubine Ta Chi, whose orgies are recorded in history. Yang Jui had compared the Empress Dowager's life at the Summer Palace with the enormities committed by this infamous concubine in her palace by the "Lake of Wine"; small wonder then, said Tzŭ Hsi's advocates in defence of drastic measures, that, having seen for herself, in the Emperor's own handwriting, that these treasonable utterances met with his favour and support, Her Majesty was vindictively inclined and determined to put an end, once and for all, to his relations with the Reform party.

The edict which ordered the execution of the Reform leaders was drafted by the Empress Dowager herself with the aid of Jung Lu, but with cynical irony it was issued in the name of the Emperor. It was written in red ink as an indication of its special importance, a formality usually reserved for decrees given by the Sovereign under his own hand. After laying stress upon the necessity for introducing reforms in the country's administration, and on the anxiety felt by the Throne in regard to the increasing difficulties of government, this Decree proceeded to state that K'ang Yu-wei and his followers, taking advantage of the necessities of the moment, had entered into a rebellious conspiracy, aiming at the overthrow of the Throne itself; fortunately, their treacherous intentions had been disclosed, and the whole plot revealed. The Decree continued as followed: —

"We are further informed that, greatly daring, these traitors have organised a secret Society, the objects of which are to overthrow the Manchu dynasty for the benefit of the Chinese. Following the precepts of the Sages, We, the Emperor, are in duty bound to propagate filial piety as the foremost of all virtues, and have always done so, as our subjects must be fully aware. But the writings of K'ang Yu-wei were, in their tendency, depraved and immoral; they contain nothing but abominable doctrines intended to flout and destroy the doctrines of the Sages. Originally impressed by his knowledge of contemporary politics, we appointed him to be a Secretary of the Tsungli Yamên, and subsequently gave him charge of the establishment of the proposed official newspaper at Shanghai; but instead of going to his post, he remained for the purposes of his evil conspiracies at Peking. Had it not been that, by the protecting influences of our ancestors, his plot was revealed, appalling disasters must undoubtedly have followed. K'ang himself, the moving spirit in this conspiracy, has fled from justice, and we rely upon the proper authorities to see to it that he be arrested, and that capital punishment be inflicted upon him."

The Decree then proceeded to award the death penalty to K'ang Yu-wei's colleague, Liang Ch'i-ch'ao, a scholar of the highest repute, who subsequently found a refuge in Japan, and there edits a newspaper of high and well-deserved reputation. Next in order of importance were the three Secretaries of the Grand Council, who were awaiting the result of their trial in the Board of Punishments. The Edict added that any delay in their execution might, in the opinion of the Grand Council, lead to a revolutionary movement, and for this reason further formalities of justice in regard to all six prisoners were dispensed with, and their summary decapitation ordered.

After disposing of K'ang Yu-wei's followers and accomplices, the Decree once more emphasises the heinous guilt of their leader: —

"Our dynasty." it says, "rules in accordance with the teachings of Confucius. Such treason as that of K'ang Yu-wei is abhorred by gods and men alike. Surely the elemental forces of nature must refuse to protect such a man,[1] surely all humanity must unite in the extermination of such noisome creatures. As to those of his followers who, for the most part, were led away by his immoral doctrines, their number is legion, and the Throne has taken note of their names, but the Imperial clemency is all-abounding, and we have decided to go no further with our enquiries into these treasonable plottings. Let all concerned now take warning by Kang's example. Let them conscientiously follow the doctrines of the Sages, and turn their hearts to wisdom in devotion to the Throne."

Despite the Throne's "all abounding clemency" and Tzŭ Hsi's declared intention to take no steps beyond the execution of the six reform leaders, her "divine wrath" continued to be stirred up by the recollection of the personal attacks that had been made against her. Following immediately upon the Decree above

---

1. On the occasion of her seventieth birthday (1904), the Empress Dowager promulgated a general amnesty for all those who had taken part in the Reform Movement of 1898, excepting only the leaders K'ang Yu-wei and Liang Ch'i-ch'ao, who were expressly excluded from grace, and Dr. Sun Yat-sen, who was a fugitive from justice on other counts.

quoted, came another whereby Chang Yin-huan was sentenced to banishment to the New Dominion on a vague charge of the usual classical type. His real offence lay in that he had denounced the Empress Dowager for extravagance, and she was the more embittered against him because the British Minister had presumed to intervene with a plea for his life.

In another Decree the proposed visit to Tientsin was cancelled, at the earnest request of Jung Lu, who dreaded the possibility of an attempt on the life of the Empress Dowager. Her feminine curiosity had been stirred by the prospect of a visit to the Treaty port and a change from the seclusion of Peking, but she yielded to the advice of the Commander-in-Chief. At the same time military reorganisation was pressed forward with the greatest energy, and the occasion was taken to bestow *largesse* on the Chihli troops.

Upon Jung Lu coming to Peking Yü Lu was appointed to succeed him as Viceroy of Chihli. This bigoted official enjoyed in a large measure the confidence of the Empress Dowager. Unusually ignorant, even for a Manchu, and totally devoid of ability, he was subsequently responsible for the growth of the Boxer movement in and around Tientsin. At this particular crisis, however, distrust of the Chinese was rife, and the Old Buddha felt that the presence of a Manchu Viceroy to control the Metropolitan Province was necessary to prevent any organised movement by the revolutionaries.

There now remained unpunished in Peking only one high official who had been in any way publicly associated with the reformers, *i.e.*, Li Tuan-fen, President of the Board of Ceremonies. After waiting a few days and finding that his case was not referred to in any of the Edicts, he applied in a Memorial to the Throne that the offence which he had committed (in recommending K'ang Yu-wei and other reformers for government employment) should be suitably punished. The Memorial is in itself a most interesting document, as it throws light on several characteristic features of the internal economy of the Chinese

Government. The writer, after admitting his guilt, and expressing astonishment that it has not been brought home to him,
placed on record his gratitude for the clemency thus far exercised, and asked that, as his conscience gave him no peace, Her
Majesty might be pleased to determine the penalty for his guilt,
"to serve as a warning to all officials who may be led to recommend evil characters to the notice of the Throne." Tzŭ Hsi's reply
was equally interesting, and was issued, as usual, in the name of
the Emperor: —

"We have read the Memorial of Li Tuan-fen. This official has enjoyed
our special favour; nevertheless, it was he who recommended to our
notice that base traitor, Kang Yu-wei, and he repeated his recommendations at more than one subsequent audience. His present action in
admitting his guilt after the conspiracy has been exposed indicates a certain amount of low cunning on his part, which makes it quite impossible
for us to treat him with further leniency. He is therefore to be cashiered
forthwith and banished to the New Dominion, where he will be kept
under close observation by the local authorities."[1]

The whole episode and correspondence are strongly suggestive of the sport of a cat with a mouse.

By this time the violent measures of the reactionary party
had aroused a storm of indignation in the South, where societies were being organised in support of His Majesty Kuang Hsü.
Newspapers published in the foreign settlements at Shanghai
repeated daily the wildest and bitterest denunciations against
Her Majesty and Jung Lu, the latter being specially singled out
for attack. The writers of these articles, evidently inspired by the
fugitive reform leaders, declared that the movement in Peking
was essentially anti-Chinese, and that it would undoubtedly end
in the appointment of Manchus to all important posts in the Empire. On the other hand, anti-foreign disturbances were foment-
ed in several provinces by those who believed that the Empress

---

1. Li Tuan-fen returned from exile in Turkestan under the amnesty of 1904.

Dowager would be gratified by these manifestations of public feeling. This state of affairs was undoubtedly fraught with serious danger, to which the attention of the Empress Dowager was drawn in a very plain-spoken Memorial by a Censor and Imperial Clansman named Hui Chang.

The memorialist congratulated the Throne upon the energetic and successful suppression of K'ang Yu-wei's treason, an achievement which would redound for ever to the fame of the Old Buddha. He then referred to the position of affairs in South China as follows: —

"Of late many rumours have been in circulation, due to the fact that the criminals executed by order of the Throne are all Chinese, and your Majesties are therefore accused of desiring to promote the interests of Manchus at the expense of your Chinese subjects. Although it should be well known and recognised that our dynasty has never held the balance unevenly between Manchus and Chinese, yet the followers of K'ang Yu-wei are undoubtedly taking advantage of these rumours, and the result threatens the State with danger."

The writer, after referring to the general futility of Edicts, then advised that special honours should be accorded to a few selected Chinese of undoubted loyalty and orthodoxy, by which means public opinion would be reassured. He justly observed that, if those who had been guilty of high treason had been made to suffer the penalty, those who had been consistently loyal should be suitably rewarded. He advised that all those who, during the past few months, had sent in Memorials denouncing the reform movement and rebuking the corrupt tendencies of the so-called new scholarship, should be advanced in the public service. Finally, he made the significant observation, that loyalty and patriotism when displayed by Chinese subjects are of greater value to the integrity of the Empire than these virtues when displayed by Manchus, an indication of statecraft likely to appeal to the acute intelligence of the Old Buddha. The Empress Dowager's reply, while ostensibly in the nature of a rebuke, was marked by unusual evasiveness on the subject actually at issue. She laid stress only on the strict impartiality of the Throne's decision, professing to be animated by feelings of abstract justice, and to be free from all manner of prejudice, whether against Manchus or Chinese. The Memorialist was, however, shortly afterwards promoted, and as a proof of her impartiality, the Empress Dowager proceeded, on the same day, to dismiss half-a-dozen high officials, one of whom was a Manchu; and on the ground that Jung Lu himself had recommended one of the reformers for employment, she ordered that he too be referred to the Board of Civil Appointments for the determination of a suitable penalty. This was merely "saving face."

Stirred, as usual, to activity by anything in the nature of criticism, Her Majesty now issued Decrees in rapid succession. One of these declared the necessity for adequate protection of foreigners in the interior and for the Legations in Peking; another took the form of a homily to the Provincial Authorities in regard to the selection of subordinate officials. A third called for advice from the Provincial Viceroys and Governors, but they were told, at the same time, to avoid criticising on party grounds because "the Throne was fully aware of the motives which usually inspire such attacks."

Subsequently, the Empress Dowager took occasion in a homily on the whole art of government, to place on record a defence of her policy as head of the Manchus in China. The following extract from this Decree is worth quoting: —

"The test of good government has always been the absence of rebellion; a State which takes adequate measures for self-defence can never be in serious danger. By the accumulated wisdom of six successive Sovereigns, our dynasty has succeeded in establishing a system of government, based on absolute justice and benevolence, which approaches very nearly to perfection. It has been our pleasure to grant immediate relief in times of flood and famine. When rivers burst their banks, our first thought has ever been the safety of our people. Never have we resorted to conscription, or to the levying of *corvées*. We have always excluded Chinese women from service as subordinates in the Palace. Surely such evidences of benevolent solicitude merit the hearty co-operation of all our subjects, and entitle us to expect that all our people, high and low, should peacefully pursue their business in life, so that all men, even the humblest labourers, may enjoy the blessings of peace. Is it any wonder then, that our soul is vexed when abominable treachery and the preaching of rebellion have been permitted to exist and to be spread broad-cast; when high officials, lacking all proper principles, have dared to recommend traitors to the Throne, in furtherance of their own evil designs? When we think of these things, our righteous indignation almost overwhelms us; nevertheless, we have granted a general amnesty, and will enquire no further into these base plottings."

The Decree concluded with the usual exhortation to the official class, and an appeal for the exercise of ideal virtue.

Her Majesty's next step was to reinstate certain leading reactionaries, whom the Emperor had recently dismissed, notably Hsü Ying-kuei, who had denounced the reformer Wang Chao. The Emperor's party was now completely broken up, and he was left without supporters or friends in Peking. The Manchu Treasurer of Kansuh (Tseng Ho) was the last high official to speak in favour of the reform movement, or rather of one of its chief advocates, and, by so doing, to bring down upon him the wrath of the Old Buddha. The Memorial which brought about his summary dismissal from office, never again to be re-employed, referred in terms of regret to the disgrace of Weng T'ung-ho, the Emperor's tutor.

Her Majesty next turned her attention to the provinces, and administered a severe rebuke to Liu K'un-yi, who, on grounds of ill-health, had asked to be relieved of the Nanking Viceroyalty. Her Majesty, reminding him in the classical phraseology of the high favours showered upon him by the Throne, directed him to abstain from frivolous excuses and to continue in the performance of his duties, exercising more diligence therein, and more care in his selection of subordinate officials.

The audacity of Weng T'ung-ho continued to rankle sorely in Her Majesty's mind, and to allow him to continue to live in honourable retirement in his native place without loss of rank or other punishment was not in accordance with her ideas of fitness; nor was it likely that Jung Lu, who had always borne a grudge against the Imperial tutor, would do anything to mitigate her wrath against him. In a Decree, issued in the name of the Emperor, she once more vented her spite on this aged and inoffensive scholar, in a manner highly characteristic of her temperament. The Edict is sufficiently interesting to justify the following quotation:–

"When Weng T'ung-ho acted as our Imperial tutor, his method of instruction left much to be desired; he never succeeded in explaining the inner meaning of classical or historical subjects, but would spend his time endeavouring to gain our favour and distract our attention by showing us curios and pictures. He would endeavour also to ascertain our views on current events and matters of policy by discussing questions of general contemporary interest. During the war with Japan, for instance, he would at one time profess to advocate peace, and again he would be all for war, and finally he even advised us to flee from our capital. He had a habit of exaggerating facts in order to make them coincide with his own views, and the result of the foolish and wrongful performance of his duties is now to be seen in a situation almost irreparable. In the spring of last year he was all in favour of reform, and secretly recommended to us K'ang Yu-wei as a man whose ability, he said, exceeded his own one hundred fold. We, being anxious above all things to strengthen our Empire at a time of national danger, reluctantly yielded to K'ang Yu-wei's advice in regard to reform. He, however, took advantage of our complaisance to plot treason. For this Weng T'ung-ho is primarily to blame, and his guilt is too great to be overlooked. Besides this, he has incurred our displeasure in several other ways; for instance, he would allow himself to show annoyance if we disagreed with his recommendations, and would even attempt to browbeat us. At such times his language was most improper, and the recollection of his bullying propensities remains in our mind most unpleasantly. In a previous Decree we ordered him to vacate his post and return to his native place, but for his many offences this in itself is no adequate punishment. We now order that he be cashiered, never again to be re-employed, and that henceforth he be held under close supervision of the local authorities and prohibited from creating trouble, as a warning to all double-minded officials for the future."[1]

Weng T'ung-ho lived in his family home (Chang Shu in Kiangsu) until June, 1904, beloved and respected by all who knew him. He was by no means a nonentity like most of the aged officials near the Throne, but rather a person of considerable force of character, and after his dismissal lived always in the hope that he might yet return to serve the Emperor and the cause of reform upon the death of the Old Buddha. Meanwhile, he became a source of considerable trouble and anxiety to the District Magistrate of his native place, as he made it his practice to call on that official three times a month, and, in the guise of a suppliant, to address him, thus, on his knees: "You have orders from the Throne secretly to keep watch over my conduct, and I therefore now attend, as in duty bound, to assist you in carrying out these orders." As the Magistrate could never be certain that the once all-powerful Grand Secretary might not return to power, his own position was evidently one of considerable embarrassment, especially as the Weng family was the most important of the whole neighbourhood. In the intervals of baiting local officials, the Grand Secretary spent his time in scholarly retirement, and a volume of the letters written by him at this period has since been published; they show the man in a most attractive light, as a scholar and a poet; his light and easy style, combined with a

---

1. Weng T'tung-ho has been posthumously restored to his full rank and titles by a Decree of the present Regent. Thus is the Emperor tardily justified and the pale ghosts of his followers continue to suffer, even in Hades, the chances and changes of Chinese official life!

tendency to mysticism and philosophic speculation, has always been highly appreciated by the *literati*. As his fortune had not been taken from him, his old age was probably happier in his native place than had it been exposed to the intrigues and hard work of official life at the Capital; and he died in the enjoyment of a reputation for patriotism and intelligence which extended far beyond his native province, and which, since his death, has greatly increased.

The Empress Dowager, realising that the loyalty of the *literati* had been greatly shaken by the Emperor's abolition of the old system of classical studies and public examinations, proceeded to reverse His Majesty's decision in a Decree which thoroughly delighted the Conservative Party. Scholars throughout the country praised it in unmeasured terms, as a striking example of the Old Buddha's acute reasoning powers. To a certain extent it may be admitted that the new system of examinations introduced by the Emperor had led, at the outset, to abuses which were absent under the old classical system, where the anonymity of candidates was a cardinal principle. Her Majesty dealt with the question as follows: —

"The ancient system whereby our Dynasty has selected the scholars at public examinations by means of essays taken from the Four Books, is based on the principle that the foundation of all education lies in expounding the fundamental doctrines of our national Sages and the Standard Commentaries on the Confucian doctrine. For over two centuries this system has worked most satisfactorily, and it is only quite lately that certain meretricious tendencies have sprung up in connection therewith, and that candidates at these examinations have succeeded in obtaining degrees by the use of parrot-like repetitions and empty catch-words. The fault has been wrongly attributed to the system; it is in reality due to incapable examiners, who have allowed these abuses to creep in. Critics have failed to realise the truth in this matter, and have allowed themselves to abuse the system, going as far as to assert that the classical subjects in themselves are of no practical value. They forget that the classical essays set at these examinations are merely a first stage, a test for entrance upon an official career, and that, if the candidate is really a man of ability, the fact that he has been made to compose verses in accordance with the time-honoured methods of the T'ang and Sung dynasties will never prevent him from making his way in the world. But should he be a man in whom there exists already a tendency towards rash and unorthodox principles, it may safely be said that to set him essays on subjects of contemporary interest for the purposes of this examination would only serve to aggravate the evil and further to demoralise his nature. For these reasons, therefore, I now definitely decree that, for the future, the old system shall be restored, and that public examinations shall henceforward consist of themes and extracts from the Classics. A special examination for students of political economy, lately authorised, has been shown to be productive of evil, and is therefore abolished. It is the wish of the Throne that these public examinations shall be in reality a sound test of merit. Examiners and candidates alike should avoid meretricious adornments of style, and endeavour to conform strictly to the classical models. We desire, of course, that studies of a practical nature should be continued, but these had best be conducted under the guidance of local officials. It is certainly desirable that agriculture, and the promotion of industrial and commercial enterprises, should be placed on a more effective basis of organisation, but owing to difficulties of inter-communication and voluminous correspondence, it is inadvisable that these matters should be centralised at Peking. Let Bureaux be established at the various provincial capitals, and let a beginning be made at Tientsin, as a test case and an example for the rest of the Empire. The Peking Bureau is hereby abolished."

Souvent femme varie, and the mind of Tzŭ Hsi never ran consistently for long in the same groove. Anxious always as to her popularity with all parties in the State, and with a view to adjusting that nice equilibrium of conflicting forces which constituted the pride of her statecraft and the strength of her rule, we find her next issuing a Decree which set forth the principles by which she professed to be guided. This Decree reflects a certain amount of anxiety and a doubt as to whether the punishment inflicted on the leading reformers might not be severely criticised by the outside world. Her Majesty therefore decrees:—

"From times of remote antiquity it has always been recognised that the perfect Government is that which is based on consistent maintenance of the doctrines of the Sages, but, in practice, the exigencies of any particular crisis must always justify modification of these principles, so that there can be no such thing as final and absolute adherence to any particular principle or method. Recently there have been introduced certain energetic measures of reform intended to put an end to the many and increasing abuses which admittedly exist all over the Empire; but certain evil-disposed persons have made these reforms the excuse for a revolutionary movement. These we have punished, so that the flood of treason and rebellion has been stemmed. This does not mean, however, that we shall fail to initiate and enforce all such measures, whether of a liberal or conservative nature, as may be necessary in the interest and for the welfare of our subjects. Was ever any man deterred from eating for fear lest a mouthful should choke him? There can surely be no real misapprehension in the public mind in the face of all the Decrees which we have issued on this subject, but we regret to note a marked lack of coherent opinion on the subject amongst our official advisers, for, at the time when these treasonable schemes were rife, we received scarcely any Memorials alluding to this national danger, and no suggestions for meeting it. It was only when the plot had been discovered and suppressed that certain attempts were made to acquire merit by those who thought they had fathomed the motives which had actuated our action. These misguided persons overlooked the important fact that it is the public interest, and the public interest only, which guides the policy of the Throne in matters of administration. The path we pursue is that of the just mean, diverging neither to right nor left. Once more would we admonish you, our officials throughout the Empire, bidding you purify your hearts and get rid, once and for all, of these false distinctions between reaction and reform. Let your Memorials consider only the needs of each day and each case as they come, and cease to submit haphazard schemes on the chance of their meeting with our personal approval."

Her Majesty next turned her attention to the necessities and distressing condition of her people at large, and ordered that measures should once more be taken to prevent the constant destruction of life and property by the Yellow River in Shantung Province. She was under no delusion as to the nature of the measures taken in the part to remedy "China's Sorrow" which, from time immemorial has been the happy hunting ground of peculating officialdom; nor could she expect that her stereotyped exhortations to virtue in this matter would afford her subjects any particular gratification. Her Majesty alluded to the fact that "frequent repairs to the banks of the Yellow River had not appeared to produce any permanent results," but the remedy which she applied, viz., a consultation between the Grand Council and the various Ministries with the Censorate, was not very reassuring. Nor was her subsequent decision to send Li Hung-chang, to estimate on the spot the sum required for the construction of effective river conservancy works, calculated to convince the public of the sincerity of her benevolent intentions.

As in the days immediately following her first assumption of power after the overthrow of the Tsai Yüan conspiracy in 1861, the Empress Dowager at this period displayed remarkable activity in every direction, as is shown by the number of her Decrees at this period. After dealing with the Yellow River, she turned her attention to another permanent and crying evil, which for centuries has weighed heavily upon the lower classes of the Chinese people, viz., the interminable delay and heavy cost of legal proceedings and the hardships thus inflicted on all who may be compelled to seek justice at the hands of Chinese officials.

Her Majesty, in her Edict on the subject, showed a very close knowledge of the abuses with which, indeed, all Chinese are fully acquainted, but which official documents usually ignore. It is no doubt largely to her frankness in cases of this kind that the Old Buddha's widespread reputation for good nature and tender-heartedness may be ascribed. Throughout the country, but especially in the north, it has always been the opinion of the peasantry and of the merchant class, that the Old Buddha was, if anything, too tender-hearted, and that her extreme mildness of disposition, though no doubt laudable, was on many occasions a source of danger. To her untimely "benevolence" the populace in Peking in 1900 undoubtedly ascribed the fact that the foreigners and native Christians were not massacred *en masse* before the arrival of the relief expedition. In this Decree on the subject of lawsuits, Her Majesty states that she has recently learned that legal proceedings are frequently hung up for several months at a time, and that innocent persons have been detained in custody for indefinite periods pending enquiry.

"Every sort of extortion is apparently practised in these courts, and their gaolers deliberately obstruct the hearing of cases unless they are heavily bribed. But if one member of a family is thrown into prison, it is evident that his whole household must suffer. Who would willingly enter upon legal proceedings, unless suffering from injustice too grievous to be borne, when the myrmidons of the law are able thus to ill-treat claimants? At the root of the whole evil lies the fact that the magistrates wilfully delay their business, being deaf to the needs of the people. From our hearts we pity them, and we now decree that regulations shall at once be drawn up for the expediting of outstanding cases. Any delay in this matter will involve heavy penalties."

Again, another Edict thus reflects the benevolence of the "Divine Mother" and her desire to conciliate public opinion: —

"In the majority of recent cases of summary executions in the provinces, the culprits have been guilty of robbery under arms. However heinous the offences of such criminals, they really deserve our sincere pity. The excuse generally given for their folly is that they have been forced into crime by starvation; under such conditions men are apt to forget that their evil acts will bring upon them the death penalty. These criminals are hardy men and resolute; if they could only be turned from their evil ways to service in our Army or to agriculture, they might become good citizens: how preferable such a result to seeing them cast into prison and finally dismembered? Apart from this consideration, the crimes which they commit involve their parents and families, a thought sufficient in itself to disturb their conscience for ever. Here, in the remote seclusion of our Palace, we think only of our people's welfare, and we long for the time when virtue may prevail and punishment become a thing of the past. We therefore now implore you, our children, to remember how real is our sympathy in all your troubles; strive then to be virtuous citizens, and cease from acts of violence which only bring trouble and misery in their train. Let this our Decree be made known to the most remote districts of our Empire, so that all may be aware of our solicitude and tender regard for our people."

The Empress Dowager was much incensed at the sympathy for the Emperor shown by foreigners both in China and abroad, a sympathy which was reflected for a time in the attitude of the British Minister and other members of the Diplomatic Body at Peking. Adopting, however, that policy of "conciliation pending a fitting opportunity for hostilities," which (as will be seen in another place) she had learned from study of the classics, she invited the wives of the foreign Ministers and other Legation ladies to an audience in the Palace at the beginning of the winter, and treated them with such courtesy and consideration that she won their hearts in a day. That her friendliness was entirely assumed, we have learned from her own statements, and there is no doubt that, from this time forward, she came more and more under the influence of the chief reactionary Kang Yi, who, during the absence of Jung Lu on leave, was able to persuade her that the first essential towards improving the country's military resources was the organisation of bands of militia throughout the Empire. By missionaries who were close observers of events in Shantung and other headquarters of this patriotic movement, it was soon realised that this military activity was directed primarily against foreigners, and owed its origin in the first instance to the Empress Dowager's approval of Kang Yi's policy of violent reaction.

The following Decree, promulgated towards the close of the year may, in a certain sense, be regarded as the beginning and the charter of the Boxer Movement; it was undoubtedly inspired by Kang Yi and his party.

"There has never been a time when the relations between Sovereign and people could safely dispense with a good understanding and certain general common objects. It is of course for the local Magistrates to initiate measures in all questions of local importance, but no successful national policy can be maintained unless the gentry and the lower classes co-operate with the Government. If we consider, for example, the question of food-supply reserves, the organisation of police, the drilling of militia or train-bands, and so forth: they may seem very ordinary matters, but if they are efficiently handled they may be made of the very greatest value to the nation; for by making due provision against famine, the people's lives are protected, and similarly, by the organisation of local police, protection is afforded against bandits. As to the train-bands, they only require to undergo regular training for a sufficient period to enable us to attain to the position of a nation in arms. At any crisis in our country's affairs their services would then be available and invaluable.

"We therefore decree that a beginning be now made in the Provinces of Chihli, Mukden, and Shantung, where all the local authorities must admonish the gentry and common people, so that these measures may be carried out with the utmost energy. Where any organisation already exists for the purposes mentioned, it need only be remodelled, and brought into line with the general system. Let steps be taken first at the provincial capitals, and extended thence throughout the Provinces. Eventually it is our intention that the system adopted shall be enforced throughout the Empire, on the basis of the new regulations adopted in these three Provinces."

The rest of the Decree consists of the usual exhortations and warnings, and is of no particular interest. It is not certain from this document that the Empress herself understood clearly the forces that were about to be let loose in these so-called military train-bands, and her subsequent vacillation in regard to the Boxers would seem to afford an indication, if not proof, that she acted impulsively and without full knowledge, under the influence of Kang Yi. But the question rapidly increased in importance, so that a few days later we find Her Majesty issuing a second Decree, which shows that the potential power of the train-bands as a national force was gradually impressing itself upon her mind, where, as we know, the hope of revenge on foreigners was ever latent. In this second Decree occurs the following passage:—

"Recent events have caused me the greatest grief and anxiety; by day and by night, in the seclusion of my Palace, my thoughts dwell on these matters, and my one object is now to secure the tranquillity and prosperity of my subjects by the organisation of adequate military forces. My purposes, set forth in numerous Decrees, regarding the organisation of a strong army, the improvement of communications, and the formation of train-bands and militia, aim all at strengthening the Empire and promoting the contentment of my people."

After reiterating the substance of former Decrees, Her Majesty proceeds pathetically to complain "that they have to a large extent been ignored, or merely transmitted by one provincial authority to another, descending from the Governor to the District Magistrate through the usual routine channels, and eventually pigeon-holed as so much waste paper." She admits frankly that this method of treating Imperial Decrees is quite usual, and that it has the sanction of tradition, but she insists that the time has come for a change, and therefore now directs that all her Decrees are in future to be printed on special Imperial yellow paper, and their contents made known throughout the length and breadth of the Empire.

After further earnest exhortations to patriotism, and to that keen sense of duty which alone can develop efficiency in the public service, she directs that the local officials should keep closer touch with the gentry and the elders of the people, and that officers in command of military forces are to explain clearly to the rank and file the objects which Her Majesty has in view in deciding upon military organisation.

The Decree concludes with the following words:—

"If in times of peace my people are prepared to face all possible dangers, and to put away from them selfish and ignoble ease, they will find that, when the hour of trial comes, their common resolution is in very truth a tower of strength, which shall not fail to bring about its due reward. By this means shall the foundations of our Empire be strengthened, and its prestige increased, and thus shall my purposes be fulfilled, for which I have issued to you this solemn admonition."

This Decree was followed by another, in the classical manner, exhorting the troops to practise patriotism, which calls for no especial notice, and certainly produced no more conspicuous effect than her repeated warnings to the provincial Mandarins and her appeals for more energy and intelligence in the public service. Certain writers have pointed to the numerous and plain-spoken Decrees issued by Tzŭ Hsi at this period, as proof that her heart was really set upon effectively reforming the country's administration, but it is always difficult for foreigners, and even for Chinese outside the Palace, to form any concise idea as to the inner meaning of these lucubrations, and how much of them was, on any particular occasion, to be taken as something outside of the traditional and stereotyped utterances of the Throne. It is certain that she herself failed to exercise the personal influence and example that would have convinced the world of her sincerity, and that she did nothing to put her house of the Forbidden City in order or to do away with the manifest and notorious abuses at her Court.

The Old Buddha concluded this remarkable display of literary and political activity by returning once more to the grievance which rankled most deeply, viz., that the chief conspirator against her sacred authority and person had made good his escape. Professing to believe that the heinousness of K'ang Yu wei's crimes was not fully realised by her people, she issued another Decree on the subject, in December, as follows: —

"T'an Chung-lin, Viceroy of Canton, has memorialised stating that he has brought to light, by searches at K'ang Yu-wei's birthplace, a large quantity of documents, chiefly correspondence between the members of K'ang's party, together with certain seals, made of stone; all of which he has forwarded for our personal inspection. These letters contain a mass of treasonable matter. In one place the suggestion is actually made that T'an Ssu-t'ung (one of the reformers executed) should be nominated as President of the Chinese Republic! The writers ignore the present Dynasty even in dating their correspondence, and use instead a chronology which begins with the birth of Confucius; one of them has actually had the unbounded audacity to describe the present Dynasty as 'perfectly useless.' Abominable wickedness of this kind shows that these men were something worse than ordinary rebels and parricides. Their correspondence implicates an enormous number of persons, but, as the Throne desires to show mercy and to refrain from any further enquiry into this matter, the whole correspondence has now been burnt by our orders.

"When first we stated in our Decrees the nature of the treasonable conspiracy that K'ang Yu-wei had organised and of his revolutionary programme, it was our object to nip rebellion in the bud. But it would appear, from information which has reached us, that certain misinformed people still hold to the opinion and express it, that K'ang Yu-wei was nothing worse than an over-zealous reformer. We mention therefore this matter of the correspondence of these traitors, as proving beyond possibility of doubt that K'ang Yu-wei was indeed a base and unnatural malefactor, and we feel convinced that our loyal subjects, from the highest to the lowest, realising this truth, will now relegate his revolutionary utterances to their proper position of insignificance. Thus shall right principles triumph and the wrong be wiped out."

Thus was Tzŭ Hsi established in her pride of place and thus were sown the seeds of that great upheaval which was soon to shake the Empire to its foundations.

XVI

THE GENESIS OF THE BOXER
MOVEMENT

THE history of the Boxers has been so fully written, and so many excellent accounts given of the origins and contributing factors of the movement, that any further reference to the matter may seem superfluous. Nevertheless, the following extracts from a letter addressed by Jung Lu to his friend Hsü Ying-kuei, the Viceroy of Fukien, may throw some new light, not only on the causes of the growth of the movement in Chihli but also on the character, private opinions and political methods of the Empress Dowager's favourite and trusted adviser. It was written in the early part of July 1900.

"The Boxers started in eighteen villages of the Kuan district of Shantung and they were originally called the 'Plum Blossom Fists.' When Li Ping-heng was Governor of the Province (1895) he did not forbid their proceedings, but, on the contrary, proceeded to enrol them as Militia. Last summer there were several conflicts between these Boxers and the Imperial troops, but the Military commander was cashiered by order of the Governor for his action and all the Boxer prisoners were released. Their leader at this time openly described himself as a descendant of the Ming Emperors and the female branch of his society called 'Red Lamp

Light' was named after him. Last autumn, thus encouraged, the movement spread into Chihli. The magistrate at Chingchou put out a proclamation warning the people not to believe in their so-called magic arts; he said these Boxers were only the 'White Lily Sect' under another name. This magistrate was a good friend to the French missionaries, and the Viceroy, hearing of the incident, enquired into the matter and promptly had him dismissed. This caused me great regret, for both Wang Wen-shao and I had known the man well, when we held the Chihli Viceroyalty, and respected him.

"At the end of the 9th Moon of last year there were Boxers openly displaying huge banners in Chihli, on which was written, 'The Gods assist us to destroy all foreigners; we invite you to join the patriotic Militia.' At one place a Buddhist abbot was the head of the Society and he led on the mob, burning the Christian chapel there. Subsequently, while they were burning converts' houses at Liupa, the magistrate came out and attacked them with his troops. The soldiers opened fire and the Boxers retreated, but their priest leaders were captured, and some thirty or forty were shot dead. This ought to have demonstrated to the people at large how nonsensical were the stories about the invulnerability of these mountebanks: our soldiers dealt with them as easily as if they had been trussing chickens! There were charms and forms of incantation found on the persons of the priests who, after an examination by the magistrate, were summarily executed.

"The provincial treasurer, T'ing Yung,[1] was largely responsible for the beginning of the trouble. I hear that about ten days ago he sent for all his subordinates to attend at his Yamên, and the Prefect of Hsüanhua,[2] who was passing through, came to pay his respects with the others. This man said, 'in the reign of Chia Ch'ing there were heterodox cults of this kind, and the Emperor ordered them to be suppressed.' T'ing Yung replied, 'circumstances alter

---

1. This official was eventually decapitated by the allies, as one of the originators of the Boxer rising.
2. This Prefect of Hsüanhua was subsequently promoted by the Empress Dowager, when passing through that city, at the beginning of the flight from Peking.

cases. Why should you now refer to those days?' The Prefect answered him, 'It is quite true that the calendar is no longer the same as it was at that time, but the enlightened principles laid down by our sacred ancestors should be a guidance to us for ever.' T'ing had of course nothing to say, and could only glare at him in silence and change the conversation.

"When first I read Her Majesty's decree of the 21st June in which she orders us to form train-bands of these brave Boxers, describing them as patriots of whom large numbers are to be found, and should be enrolled, in every province, I lay awake all the next night thinking over this matter. Unable to sleep, more than once I sprang from my bed restless and excited with mixed feelings of joy and fear. The idea of enlisting these patriotic volunteers to repel the aggression of the foreigner is undoubtedly a good one, and, if carefully worked out and directed by firm discipline and good leadership, it might no doubt be of the very highest utility. But if otherwise handled, these men will inevitably get out of hand, and the only result will be chaos and disaster. You will, no doubt, agree with me, my old friend and colleague, that the motive which inspires these Boxers is a patriotic one. So great is the ill-feeling that exists between the mass of our people and the converts to Christianity that we have been unavoidably dragged to the very verge of hostilities, and our Government has embarked upon a desperate course 'of inviting the enemy to meet us in battle before the walls of our capital.' It is as if we were treading on naked swords without flinching; there can be no question as to the enthusiasm and ardour in our cause.

"But, at the beginning of the movement, these Boxers were afraid to come together in large numbers lest the Imperial troops should attack and destroy them; from this alone we may reasonably infer that they are not devoid of the common instinct of fear. By themselves they cannot be fully trusted, but it seems to me (though you may consider the idea absurd) that one might profitably use them to inspire, by their fanaticism, the martial ardour of our regular troops. As a fighting force they are absolutely useless, but their claims to supernatural arts and magic might possibly be valuable for the purpose of disheartening the enemy. But it would be quite wrong, not to say fatal, for us to attach any real belief to their ridiculous claims, or to regard them as of any real use in action. Even if there were any truth in these tales of magic they must necessarily be founded in heresy, and you know full well that Chinese history records numerous instances of such superstitious beliefs ending in rebellions against the reigning Dynasty. You recently telegraphed me advising me not to be unduly anxious, because in your opinion the Boxers acquitted themselves exceedingly well in the fights at Tientsin and Taku on the 20th June. I am not so sure of this myself; in any case it is well to bear in mind that there is a very great difference between the fighting capacity and temperament of the natives of the north and south of China.[1] All the southern provinces are teeming with secret and revolutionary societies, salt smugglers, and other kinds of desperadoes; so much tinder, which any spark may kindle into flames of disturbance at any moment. These southern people are gamblers and disorderly characters by profession, but they are certainly not animated by any patriotic instinct, and if you were to enlist any large number of them as a military force, it would be just like organising bands of jackals and wolves to fight tigers. The result would be that while none of the tigers would be destroyed, millions of your own people, who may be likened to sheep, would suffer miserably. On the other hand these northern Boxers are not inspired by any lust of plunder, but by a species of religious frenzy. Now, as you know, northerners are dull and obstinate by nature, while the southerners are alert but unreliable, so that it is difficult, if not impossible, to arrive at any fixed policy or joint action in dealing with them together. Was it not because of this characteristic of the southerners that the Grand Council was so indignant in 1894, when, in fighting against the Japanese, our men feared them worse than tigers, and, recognising their own hopeless inferiority, threw down their

---

1. Hsü, to whom Jung Lu was writing, was a Cantonese by birth, and was at this time Viceroy of Foochow.

weapons and would not face the enemy?

"These Boxers are not trained troops, but they are ready to fight, and to face death. It is indeed a very gratifying surprise to see any of our people display courage, and to witness their enthusiasm for paying off old scores against the foreigner; but if, inspired by the sight of these brave fellows, we imagine for a moment that the whole Empire is going to follow their example, and that we shall thus be enabled to rid ourselves of the accursed presence of the foreigner, we are very much mistaken, and the attempt is foredoomed. My advice therefore to your Excellency, is not to hesitate in disobeying the Edict which commanded you to raise these train-bands. I do not hesitate to give you this advice and to assure you that you run no risks in following it. You should, of course, act with great discretion, but the main thing is to prevent the Throne's Decree becoming an excuse for the banding together of disorderly characters. I write this private letter under stress of much natural apprehension, and you will therefore pray forgive the haste and confusion of its contents, and I trust that you will favour me in due course with your reply.

(Signed)   JUNG LU.

XVII

THE DIARY OF HIS EXCELLENCY CHING SHAN

[NOTE. — Ching Shan, a Manchu of the Plain Yellow Banner Corps, was born in 1823. In 1863 he became a Metropolitan Graduate and Hanlin Compiler, especially distinguished as a scholar in Sung philosophy. In the following year he was appointed a Junior Secretary of the Imperial Household (Nei wu fu), rising to Senior Secretary in 1869 and Comptroller in 1879. His father, Kuang Shun, had held the post of Comptroller-General under the Emperor Tao-Kuang, with whom he was for years on terms of intimacy; he was a kinsman of the Empress Dowager's family and in close touch with all the leading Manchu nobles. Ching Shan had therefore exceptional opportunities of knowing all the gossip of the Court, of learning the opinions and watching the movements of the high officials, Chinese and Manchu, who stood nearest to the Throne. After holding office in several of the Metropolitan Boards, he retired in 1894. He was tutor to Prince Tuan, Duke Tsai Lan, and other sons of Prince Tun (younger son of the Emperor Tao-Kuang), and therefore intimately associated with the leaders of the Boxer movement.

Seen even against the lurid background of the abomination of desolation which overtook Peking in August 1900, Ching Shan's fate was unusually tragic. Above the storm and stress of battle and sudden death, of dangers from Boxers, wild Kansuh soldiery and barbarian invaders, the old scholar's domestic griefs, the quarrels of his women folk, his son's unfilial behaviour, strike a more poignant note than any of his country's fast pressing misfortunes. And with good cause. On the 15th August, after the entry of the allied forces into Peking and the flight of the Empress Dowager, his wife, his senior concubine, and one of his daughters-in-law committed suicide. He survived them but a few hours, meeting death at the hands of his eldest son, En Ch'un, who pushed him down a well in his own courtyard. This son was subsequently shot by British troops for harbouring armed Boxers.

The Diary was found by the translator in the private study of Ching Shan's house on August 18th and saved, in the nick of time, from being burnt by a party of Sikhs. Many of the entries, which cover the period from January to August 1900, refer to trivial and uninteresting matters. The following passages are selected chiefly because of the light they throw on the part played by the Empress Dowager in that tragedy of midsummer madness — on the strong hand and statecraft of the woman, and on the unfathomable ignorance which characterises to-day the degenerate descendants of Nurhachu. It should be explained that Ching Shan (景善), who retired from office in 1894, must be distinguished from Ching Hsin (敬信), who died about 1904. The latter was also a Manchu and a favourite of Tzǔ Hsi, well known to foreigners at the capital. He held various high posts, rose to be a Grand Secretary, and remained in Peking after the flight of the Court, in charge of the Palace. It was he who escorted the Diplomatic Body through the deserted halls of the Forbidden City in September 1900. He was highly respected by all who knew him.

Ching Shan, though of similarly high rank, was personally quite unknown to foreigners, but a short note on his career (and another on that of Ching Hsin) will be found in the "List of the Higher Metropolitan and provincial officials" periodically compiled by the Chinese Secretariat of the British Legation; Edition of 1902, Kelly and Walsh, Shanghai.]

25th Year of Kuang Hsü, 12th Moon, 25th Day (25th January, 1900). — Duke Tsai Lan came to see me, his old tutor, to-day. He has much to tell me concerning the "Patriotic Harmony" train-bands (I

Ho Tuan) which have been raised in Shantung by Yü Hsien, the Governor. Later, he described yesterday's audience at the Palace; in addition to the Grand Secretaries, the Presidents of Boards and the Ministers of the Household, the "Sacred Mother" received Prince Kung, his uncles Tsai Ying and Tsai Lien and Prince Tuan. The Old Buddha announced her intention of selecting a new Emperor. She said: "The nation has shown resentment and reproached me for putting Kuang Hsü on the Throne, he being of the wrong generation; furthermore, he himself has shown great lack of filial duty to me notwithstanding the debt of gratitude he owed me for my kindness in thus elevating him. Has he not plotted against me with traitors from the south? I now propose therefore to depose him and to place a new Emperor on the Throne, whose accession shall take place on the first day of the New Year. It should be for you Ministers now to consider what title should be given to Kuang Hsü upon his abdication. There is a precedent for his removal from the Throne in the case of the Emperor Ching T'ai of the Ming Dynasty who was reduced to the rank of Prince and whose brother was restored to the Throne after eight years of captivity among the Mongols." There was dead silence for some time in the Hall of Audience. At last the Grand Secretary Hsü T'ung suggested as appropriate the title of "Hun-te-Kung," which means, "The Duke of Confused Virtue"—or well-meaning bungler:—it had been given by the Mongol Dynasty to a deposed Sung Emperor. The Old Buddha approved. She then declared to the assembly that her choice of the new Emperor was already made; it had fallen upon the eldest son of Prince Tuan, whose great devotion to Her Majesty's person was well known. Henceforward Prince Tuan should be in constant attendance at the Palace to supervise the education of his son. At this point the Grand Secretary Sun Chia-nai[1] craved permission to speak. He implored the Empress not to depose the Emperor; of a certainty there would be rebellion in the Southern provinces. The choice of a new Sovereign rested with her, but it could only be done after "ten thousand years had

---

1. A note on the career and character of this courageous official is given in the Appendix.

elapsed" (*i.e.*, after the death of the present Emperor). The "Motherly Countenance" showed great wrath; turning on Sun Chia-nai, she bade him remember that this was a family council to which she only admitted Chinese as an act of grace. She had already notified the Emperor of her intention, and he had no objections to offer. The Empress then ordered all present to repair to the Hall of Diligent Government there to await her and the Emperor, and upon their coming to witness the draft of the Decree appointing the Heir Apparent. The formal announcement of his accession to the throne would be postponed until the first day of the New Year.

They proceeded therefore to the entrance of the appointed Hall, and in a few minutes the Empress's chair appeared at the gateway, when all knelt and kowtowed three times. A number of eunuchs accompanied her, but she bade them remain without. She sent Major-domo Li Lien-ying to request the Emperor's presence; he came in his chair, alighting at the outer gate and kowtowed to the Empress, who had taken her seat on the main throne within. She beckoned him to come to the Hall, and he knelt again, all officials still kneeling outside. "*Chin lai, pu yung kuei hsia*" (Come in, you need not kneel), called Her Majesty. She bade him sit down, and summoned next the princes and ministers—some thirty in all—to enter. Again the Old Buddha repeated her reasons for the step she was taking. The Emperor only said "What Your Majesty suggests is quite proper and in accordance with my views." At this the Grand Secretary Jung Lu handed to the Empress the Decree which the Grand Council had drafted.[1] She read it through and forthwith ordered its promulgation. Nothing was said to "The Lord of Ten Thousand Years" as to his being deposed; only the selection of the Heir Apparent was discussed. The Grand Council then remained for further audience, but the Princes were ordered to withdraw, so that Duke Lan does not know what passed thereafter. The Emperor seemed dazed, as one in a dream.

---

1. The Decree is given at the end of this chapter.

THE "BEILEH" TSAI YING, SON OF PRINCE KUNG (CASHIERED BY TZU HSI FOR
PRO-BOXER PROCLIVITIES), AND HIS SON.

30th Day (30th January, 1900). — To-day Liu Shun shaved my head; he leaves to-night for his home at Pao-ti-hsien there to spend the new year. My eldest son, En Ch'u, is pressing me to give him fifty taels to buy an ermine cloak; he is a bad son and most undutiful. Chi Shou-ch'ing came to see me to-day; he has moved to "Kuai Pang" Lane. He tells me that his father-in-law, Yü Hsien, is to be made Governor of Shansi. The Old Buddha has received him in audience since his removal from the Governorship of Shantung on account of the murder of a French[1] missionary, and praised him for the honesty and justice of his administration. She does not approve of the Big Sword Society's proposed extermination of foreigners, because she does not believe they can do it; Yü Hsien goes often to Prince Tuan's palace, and they have many secret interviews. Prince Tuan declares that if he were made President of the Tsung-li Yamên he would make short work of all difficulties with foreigners. He is a violent man and lacking in refinement.

1st Day of 26th Year of Kuang Hsü (31st January, 1900). — To-day I am 78 years of age and my children mock me for being deaf. They are bad sons and will never rise so high as their father has done. When I was their age, between 20 and 30, the Emperor Tao-Kuang had already praised my scholarship and presented me with a complimentary scroll bearing a quotation from the writings of the philosopher Chu.

This year will witness many strange events; the people all say so. The eighth month is intercalary which, in a year that has "Keng" for its cyclical character, has ever been an evil omen. The New Emperor was to have been proclaimed to-day under the title of "Heng-Ching" — all pervading prosperity — but my son En Lin tells me that the new year sacrifices were performed by the Ta-A-Ko (heir apparent) at the Palace of Imperial Longevity, acting only as Deputy for the Emperor Kuang Hsü. The Ta-A-Ko is a boy of fourteen; very intelligent, but violent-tempered. He

---

1. The victim was British, not French — viz., the Rev. Mr. Brooks, killed on 31st December, 1899, just after Yu Hsien's removal had been arranged.

walked on foot to the Palace Hall from the Coal Hill Gate.

5th Moon, 5th Day: The Dragon Festival (1st June, 1900).[1] —
Arose at six o'clock and was washing my face in the small inner
room, when Huo Kuei, the gatekeeper, came in with the card
of Kang Yi, the Grand Secretary, and a present of ten pounds of
pork, with seasonable greetings. I was not aware that he had already returned from his journey to Chu Chou, whither he had
gone with Chao Shu-ch'iao to examine and report on the doings
of the "patriotic train bands" (*i.e.* Boxers). He sends word by the
messenger that he will call upon me this morning.

My sons En Ch'u and En Shun are going to-day to a theatrical performance at Chi Shou-ch'eng's residence. My youngest
son, En Ming, is on duty at the Summer Palace, where, for the
next four days, the Old Buddha will be having theatricals. I am
surprised that Kang Yi is not out there also. No doubt he only
returned to Peking last night, and so does not resume his place
on the Council till to-morrow morning.

The Hour of the Monkey (3 P.M.). — Kang Yi has been here and
I persuaded him to stay for the mid-day meal. He is a worthy
brother-in-law, and, though twenty years younger than I am, as
wise and discreet a man as any on the Grand Council. He tells
me that several hundred foreign devil troops entered the City
yesterday evening. He and Chao Shu-ch'iao arrived at Peking
at 4.30 P.M., and immediately set to composing their memorial
to the Empress Dowager about the heaven-sent Boxers, for presentation to-morrow morning. Prince Tuan has five days' leave
of absence: Kang Yi went to see him yesterday evening. While
they were discussing the situation, at the Prince's own house,
there came a Captain of Prince Ch'ing's bodyguard with a message. Saluting Prince Tuan, he announced that about 300 foreign
soldiers had left Tientsin in the afternoon as reinforcement for
the Legation Guards. Prince Ch'ing implored Prince Tuan not to
oppose their entry, on the ground that a few hundred foreigners,
more or less, could make no difference. He trusted that Prince

---

1. Between January and June the entries are of no particular interest.

H.M. The Empress Dowager, and Ladies of the Court (1903).

Daughters of H.E. Yü Keng   Wife of H.E. Yü Keng, ex-Minister to Paris
H.M. Tzŏ Hsi

Second wife of late Emperor.

Tuan would give orders to his Corps (the "Celestial Tigers" Force) not to oppose the foreign devils. It was the wish of the Old Buddha that they should be permitted to guard the Legations. Prince Tuan asked for further details, and the Captain said that Prince Ch'ing had received a telegram from the Governor-General of Chihli (Yü Lu) to the effect that the detachment carried no guns. At this Prince Tuan laughed scornfully and said "How can the few resist the many? What indeed will a hundred puny hobgoblins, more or less, matter?" Kang Yi, on the contrary, tells me that he strongly urged Prince Tuan to issue orders to Chung Li, the Commandant of the city, to oppose the entry of the foreign troops, but it appears that Jung Lu had already ordered their admission. Kang Yi is much incensed with Jung Lu about this, and cannot understand his motives. It seems that towards the close of last year Prince Tuan and Jung Lu had agreed to depose the Emperor and to put the Heir Apparent on the Throne, and Tuan confesses that, were it not for Jung Lu's great influence with the Old Buddha she would never have agreed to select his son as Heir Apparent. But now Jung Lu is for ever denouncing the Boxers and warning the Empress against encouraging and countenancing them. Prince Tuan and Kang Yi despair of ever being able to induce her to support the Boxers whole-heartedly so long as Jung Lu is against them. As an example of her present attitude, Prince Tuan told Kang Yi one day lately that his son, the Ta-a-ko, had dressed himself up as a Boxer and was going through their drill in the Summer Palace grounds with some eunuchs. The Old Buddha saw him and promptly gave orders that he be confined to his rooms. She also reprimanded the Grand Secretary, Hsü T'ung, for not keeping a better watch on his pupil and for permitting such unseemly behaviour, as she called it.

After leaving Prince Tuan's house, Kang Yi had gone out of the city by the Ch'ien Men and had seen the foreign troops pass in. The people muttered curses, he says, but no one molested them. What does it matter? None of them will ever leave the city. Kang Yi's journey to Chu-chou has convinced him that the whole province stands together as one man; even boys in their teens are drilling. Not a doubt of it; the foreigner will be wiped out this time! At Chu-chou the Departmental Magistrate, a man named Kung, had arrested several Boxer leaders, but Kang Yi and Chao Shu-ch'iao ordered them to be released and made them go through their mystic evolutions and drill. It was a wonderful sight, scarcely to be believed; several of them were shot, some more than once, yet rose uninjured from the ground. This exhibition took place in the main courtyard of the Magistrate's Yamên, in the presence of an enormous crowd, tight pressed, as compact as a wall. Chao Shu-ch'iao remembers having seen many years ago, in his native province of Shensi, a similar performance, and it is on record that similar marvels were seen at the close of the Han Dynasty, when Chang Chio headed the Yellow Turban insurrection against the Government and took many great cities with half a million of followers. They were said to be under the protection of the Jade Emperor[1] and quite impervious to sword-thrusts. Kang Yi and Chao Shu-Ch'iao will memorialise the Empress to-morrow, giving the results of their journey and begging her to recognise the "patriotic train-bands" as a branch of the army. But they should be placed under the supreme command of Prince Tuan and Kang Yi, as Jung Lu, the Commander-in-Chief of the Northern army, is so incredulous as to their efficacy against foreign troops.

Although Major Domo Li Lien-ying is a warm supporter of the Boxers, and never wearies of describing their feats to the Old Buddha, feats which he himself has witnessed, it is by no means certain that the "kindly Mother" will heed him so long as Jung Lu is opposed to any official encouragement of the movement. And, besides, the nature of the Empress is peace-loving; she has seen many springs and autumns. I myself know well her refined and gentle tastes, her love of painting, poetry, and the theatre. When in a good mood she is the most amiable and tractable of women, but at times her rage is awful to witness. My father was

---

1. The Supreme Deity of the Taoists and tutelary spirit of the Boxers.

Comptroller-General of the Imperial Household, and it was his lot on one occasion to experience her anger. This was in the sixth year of Tung Chih (1868), when she learned that the chief eunuch, "Hsiao An'rh,"[1] had been decapitated in Shantung by the orders of the Co-Regent, the late "Empress Dowager of the East." She accused the Comptrollers of the Household of being leagued together in treachery against her, as they had not told her of what was going on she declared that Prince Kung was plotting against her life, and that all her attendants were associated in his treason. It was years before she forgave him. All An's fellow-eunuchs were examined under torture by the Department responsible for the management and discipline of the Household. When the chief eunuch's betrayer was discovered by this means, he was flogged to death by her orders in the Palace. But nowadays the Old Buddha's heart has softened, even towards foreigners, and she will not allow any of them to be done away with. One word from her would be sufficient to bring about their immediate and complete destruction, so that neither dog nor fowl be left alive, and no trace be left of all their foreign buildings. Kang Yi stayed with me about two hours and left to go and see Prince Tuan, who was expecting Major Domo Li Lien-ying to come into the city this afternoon.

K'un Hsiu, Vice-President of the Board of Works, called to see me. He tells me that Prince Ch'ing habitually ridicules the Boxers in private conversation, declaring them to be utterly useless, and unworthy of even a smile from a wise man. In public, however, he is most cautious — last week when the Old Buddha asked his opinion of them he replied by vaguely referring to the possible value of train-bands for protection of the Empire.

9 P.M. — My son En Ch'u has returned from Chi Shou-ch'eng's theatricals; everyone was talking, he says, of Jung Lu's folly in allowing the foreign troops to enter the city yesterday. Chi's father-in-law, Yü Hsien, has written to him from Shansi saying that for the present there are but few Boxers enrolled in that province,

---

1. A nickname of An Te-hai, *vide supra* p.92 *et seq.*

but he is doing his best to further the movement, so that Shansi may unite with the other provinces of the north "to destroy those who have aroused the Emperor's wrath." By common report, Yüan Shih-k'ai has now become a convert to Christianity: if he too were to suppress the movement in Shantung, not death itself could expiate his guilt.

En Chu's wife is most undutiful; this evening she has had a quarrel with my senior concubine, and the two women almost came to blows. Women are indeed difficult to manage; as Confucius has said, "Keep them at a distance, they resent it; treat them familiarly, and they do not respect you." I am seventy-eight years of age and sore troubled by my family; their misconduct is hard for an old man to bear.

12th Day of the 5th Moon (June 8th, 1900). — My son, En Ming, came in this morning about midday; as Officer of the Bodyguard he had been in attendance on the Empress coming in from the Summer Palace. Jung Lu had been there yesterday morning and had had a long audience with Her Majesty. He gave her details of the burning of the railway by the Boxers. She was seriously alarmed and decided to return at once to the Winter Palace on the Southern Lake. It seems she cannot make up her mind as to the Boxers' invulnerability. Jung Lu has again applied for leave. When he is absent from the Grand Council, Kang Yi and Ch'i Hsiu have the greatest influence with her. En Ming says that on the way to the city she kept urging the chair-bearers to hurry, and seemed out of sorts — nervously fanning herself all the time. At the Ying Hsiu gate of the Winter Palace the Emperor and the Heir Apparent were kneeling to receive her. No sooner had she reached the Palace than she summoned Prince Tuan to audience, which lasted a long time. It is a pity that the Old Buddha will not decide and act more promptly. The Emperor never speaks at audience nowadays, although Her Majesty often asks him for his opinion. Tung Fu-hsiang accompanied the Court into Peking; he denounced Jung Lu at audience to-day, telling the Empress that if only the Legations were attacked, he would undertake to demolish them in five days; but that Jung Lu, by failing to support the Boxers, was a traitor to the Dynasty. The Empire, said he, would be endangered unless the present opportunity were seized to wipe off old scores against the foreigner. Tung is a coarse, foul-spoken fellow, most violent in his manner towards us Manchus. Kang Yi hates him, but for the present is only too willing to make use of him.

14th day of the 5th Moon (June 10th). — Grand Councillor Ch'i Hsiu called to-day — he showed me the draft of a Decree breaking off all relations with foreigners, which he had prepared for the Empress's signature; so far, however, she has given no indication of agreeing to make war against them. In the afternoon I went to Duke Lan's residence — to-day being his wife's birthday. There are more than a hundred Boxers living in his outer courtyard, most of them country-folk, under the command of a Banner Captain named Wen Shun. Among them are five or six lads of thirteen or fourteen who will fall into a trance, foam at the mouth, then rise up and grasp wildly at anything that comes within their reach, uttering the while strange uncouth noises. Duke Lan believes that by their magic arts they will be able to guide him, when the time comes, to the houses of Christian converts (*lit.* Secondary Devils). He says that his wife goes often to the Palace and that she has told the Old Buddha of these things. The "Ta Kung Chu" (Princess Imperial and adopted daughter of the Empress Dowager) has over two hundred and fifty Boxers quartered at the Palace outside the Hou Men, but she has not dared to tell the Empress Dowager. Her brother, the "Prince" Tsai Ying, is also learning this drill. Truly it is a splendid society! The Kansuh braves are now entering the Chinese city, and thousands of people are preparing to leave Peking.

16th day of the 5th Moon (June 12th). — Jung Lu attended the Grand Council this morning. Prince Li, the Senior Councillor, did not dare to tell the Empress that a foreign devil[1] had been killed yesterday by the Kansuh braves just outside the Yung-Ting

---

1. The Chancellor of the Japanese Legation, Mr. Sugiyama.

Gate. Jung Lu was called to the audience chamber after Prince Li had retired, and Kang Yi believes that he urged her to order Tung Fu-hsiang to leave the city with his troops and at the same time to issue an Edict, bestowing posthumous honours on the murdered foreigner. None of the other Grand Councillors were summoned to audience; when Jung Lu left the presence, he returned straightway to his own house and spake no word to any of his colleagues. It is rumoured that more foreign troops are coming to Peking, and that the Empress Dowager will not permit them to enter the city. In this Jung Lu agrees with her. He has advised that all foreigners shall be allowed to leave Peking, but that it is contrary to the law of nations to attack the accredited representatives of foreign Powers.

18th Day of the 5th Moon (June 14th). — Yesterday, just before nightfall, En Ch'u came in to tell me that several hundred Boxers had entered the Ha-Ta Gate. I was sorry that my lameness prevented me from going out to see them, but I sent Hao Ching-ting to report. Well indeed, is it, that I have lived to see this day; almost every foreign building except the Legations had been burnt to the ground. Throughout the night flames burst forth in every quarter of the city; a grand sight! Kang Yi has sent me a message to say that he and Duke Lan went to the Shun Chih (S.W.) Gate at about the third watch to encourage and direct the Boxers who were burning the French Church. Hundreds of converts were burnt to death, men, women and children, and so great was the stench of burning flesh that Duke Lan and Kang Yi were compelled to hold their noses. At dawn Kang Yi went to the Palace to attend the Grand Council. Major Domo Li Lien-ying told him that the Old Buddha had watched the conflagrations from the hillock to the west of the Southern Lake, and had plainly seen the destruction of the French Church at the Shun Chih Men. Li Lien-ying had told her that the foreigners had first fired on the crowd inside the Ha-Ta Gate, and that this had enraged the patriotic braves who had retaliated by slaughtering the converts. It seems that Hsü T'ung is unable to get out of his house because the foreign devils have barricaded the street; the Old Buddha is anxious about him and has commanded Prince Ch'ing to ask the foreign Legations to let him pass out. She is amazed at the Boxers' courage, and Kang Yi believes that she is about to give her consent to a general attack upon the Legations. Nevertheless, Li Lien-ying has warned him that exaggerated praise of the Boxers arouses her suspicions, and that, with the exception of Jung Lu, all the Grand Councillors are afraid to advise her. Her Majesty is moving into the Palace of Peaceful Longevity in the Forbidden City, as all these alarms and excursions disturb her sleep at the Lake Palace.

21st Day of the 5th Moon (June 17th). — A great fire has been raging all to-day in the southern city. Those reckless Boxers set fire to a foreign medicine store in the Ta Sha-lan'rh, and from this the flames spread rapidly, destroying the shops of the wealthy goldsmiths and assayers. Rightly says the Canon of History, "When fire rages on the Kun Lun ridge, common pebble and precious jade will be consumed together." The Boxers themselves are worthy men, but there are among them many evil doers whose only desire is plunder; these men, wearing the Boxer uniform, bring discredit upon the real "patriotic braves." The outer tower of the Ch'ien Men having caught fire, the Empress ordered Jung Lu to send Banner troops on to the wall so as to prevent any ruffians entering the Tartar City by the Ta Ch'ing Gate.

In the afternoon my married niece came over to see her aunt: she has been greatly alarmed by the uproar and fighting near her home, so they are moving to her father-in-law's house in the northern city.

I hear that Prince Tuan has now persuaded the Old Buddha to appoint him President of the Tsung Li Yamên; also that she has authorised him to require all foreigners to leave Peking, but they are to be protected against any attacks by the Boxers. My old friend, Ch'i Hsiu, has been made a Minister of the Tsung Li Yamên, also Na T'ung, the Sub-Chancellor of the Grand Secretariat. The latter memorialised lately advising the Throne to

declare war before the foreign Powers could send reinforcements; the Old Buddha has placed him in the Tsung Li Yamên
to assist Prince Tuan and Chi Hsiu in arranging for the foreigners' departure from the city. Prince Ch'ing still says nothing for
or against the Boxers. Jung Lu has offered to escort the foreign
Ministers half-way to Tientsin, but he stipulates that the Viceroyalty of Chihli must be taken from Yü Lu. My wife was taken
seriously ill this evening; she kept on muttering incoherently
and rolling about on the k'ang as if in great pain. We sent for Dr.
Yung, who applied acupuncture.

24th Day of the 5th Moon (June 20th). — Yesterday, at mid-day,
Yü Lu's memorial reached the Throne. He says that the foreign
devils have actually demanded the surrender of the Taku forts,
and he begs the Empress Dowager to declare war on them forthwith, to make them atone for their insolence and treachery. A
special meeting of the Grand Council was immediately called.
The Old Buddha was very wroth, but said she would postpone
her decision until to-day, when all the Princes, Presidents and
Vice-Presidents of the Boards and Ministries, and the Lieuten-
ant-Generals of Banners, would meet in special audience. Prince
Tuan, Ch'i Hsiu and Na T'ung showed her a despatch from the
foreign Ministers couched in most insolent language demanding
her immediate abdication, the degradation of the Heir Apparent, and the restoration of the Emperor.[1] The Ministers also asked
that the Emperor should allow 10,000 foreign troops to enter Peking to restore order. Kang Yi came to tell me that never had he
seen the Old Buddha so angry, not even when she learned of
K'ang Yu-wei's treason. "How dare they question my authority!"
she exclaimed. "If I can bear this, what must not be borne? The
insults of these foreigners pass all bounds. Let us exterminate
them before we eat our morning meal."[2]

The wrath of the Old Buddha is indeed beyond control; neither Jung Lu, nor any other can stop her now. She has told Jung

---

1. This was a forgery.
2. A quotation from the "Book of Odes."

Lu that if he wishes, he may still offer to escort the foreign Ministers to Tientsin, but she will give no guarantee for their safety on the journey because of their monstrous suggestion that she should abdicate. She does not absolutely desire their death, but says that the consideration she showed them in allowing the Legation guards to enter the city, and her solicitude in restraining the Boxers, have been ill-requited. "It were better," says she, "to go down in one desperate encounter than to surrender our just rights at the bidding of the foreigner."

Though only a woman, Her Majesty Tzŭ Hsi has all the courage of a man, and more than the ordinary man's intelligence.

24th Day of the 5th Moon: The Hour of the Cock, 5-7 P.M. (20th June). — I have just returned from visiting my brother-in-law, the Grand Secretary Kang Yi; he told me all about this morning's audience. At the hour of the Tiger (3-5 A.M.) the Grand Council assembled in the Palace by the Lake, and were received by the Old Buddha in the Pavilion of the Ceremonial Phœnix. All were there, Prince Li, Jung Lu, Kang Yi, Wang Wen-shao, Ch'i Hsiu, and Chao Shu-ch'iao, but the Emperor was absent. This was a special audience, preparatory to the general audience of all the Princes and Ministers, and its object was to give the Grand Council an opportunity of laying before Her Majesty any new facts or opinions bearing upon the situation.

With tears in his eyes, Jung Lu knelt before Her Majesty; he confessed that the foreigners had only themselves to blame if China declared war upon them, but he urged her to bear in mind that an attack on the Legations, as recommended by Prince Tuan and the rest of the Council, might entail the ruin of the ancestral shrines of the Dynasty, as well as the altars of the local and tutelary Gods. What good purpose, he asked, would be served by the besieging nay, even by the destruction, of this isolated handful of Europeans? What lustre could it add to the Imperial arms? Obviously, it must be waste of energy and misdirected purpose.

The Old Buddha replied that if these were his views, he had better persuade the foreigners to leave the city before the attack began; she could no longer restrain the patriotic movement, even if she wished. If therefore, he had no better advice than this to offer, he might consider himself excused from further attendance at the Council.

Jung Lu thereupon kowtowed thrice and left the audience hall to return to his own house. Upon his departure, Ch'i Hsiu drew from his boot the draft of the Decree which was to declare war. Her Majesty read it and exclaimed, "Admirable, admirable! These are exactly my views." She asked each Grand Councillor in turn for his opinion, and they declared unanimously in favour of hostilities. It was now the hour appointed for the general audience and Li-Lien-ying came in to conduct her Majesty to her own apartments to take tea before proceeding to the "Hall of Diligent Government."

All the leading members of the Imperial Clan were kneeling at the entrance to the Hall, awaiting their Majesties' arrival: the Princes Kung, Ch'un and Tuan; the "Beilehs" Tsai Lien and Tsai Ying; Duke Lan and his brother the "Beitzu" Ying; Prince Ch'ing and the five Grand Councillors; the Princes Chuang, Su and Yi; the Presidents, Chinese and Manchu, of the six Boards and the nine Ministries; the Lieutenants-General of the twenty-four Banner divisions; and the Comptrollers of the Imperial Household. Their Majesties arrived together in chairs, borne by four bearers. The Emperor alighted first, and knelt as the "benign mother" left her palanquin and entered the Hall, supported by the Chief Eunuch Li Lien-ying, and by his immediate subordinate, Ts'ui Chin. The Emperor was ghastly pale, and it was observed that he trembled as he took his seat on the Lower Throne by the Empress Dowager's side.

The Old Buddha first called on all present to draw near to the Throne; then, speaking with great vehemence, she declared that it was impossible for her to brook these latest indignities put upon her by the foreigners. Her Imperial dignity could not suffer it. Until yesterday, until, in fact, she had read the dispatch addressed to the Tsungli Yamên by the Diplomatic Body, it had been her intention to suppress the Boxers; but in the face of their insolent proposal that she should hand over the reins of government to the Emperor, who had already proved himself quite unfitted to rule, she had been brought to the conclusion that no peaceful solution of the situation was possible. The insolence of the French Consul at Tientsin Tu Shih-lan (Du Chaylard), in demanding the surrender of the Taku Forts was bad enough, but not so grievous an affront as the Ministers' preposterous proposal to interfere with her personal prerogatives as Sovereign. Her decision was now taken, her mind resolved; not even Jung Lu, to whom she had always looked for wise counsel, could turn her from this purpose. Then, addressing more directly the Chinese present, she bade them all to remember that the rule of her Manchu House had conferred many and great benefits upon the nation for the past two hundred and fifty years, and that the Throne had always held the balance fairly in the benevolent consideration for all its subjects, north and south alike. The Dynasty had scrupulously followed the teachings of the Sages in administering the government; taxation had been lighter than under any previous rulers. Had not the people been relieved, in time of their distress, by grants from the Privy Purse? In her own reign, had not rebellions been suppressed in such a manner as to earn the lasting gratitude of the southern provinces? It was therefore now their duty to rally to the support of the Throne, and to assist it in putting an end, once and for all, to foreign aggression. It had lasted too long. If only the nation were of one mind, it could not be difficult to convince these barbarians that they had mistaken the leniency of the past for weakness. That leniency had been great; in accordance with the principle which prescribes the showing of kindness to strangers from afar, the Imperial House had ever shown them the greatest consideration. The Emperor K'ang Hsi had even allowed them liberty to propagate their religion, an act of mistaken benevolence which had been an increasing cause of regret to his successors. In matters of vital principle, she said, these foreigners ignore the sacred doctrines of the Sages; in matters of detail, they insult the customs and cherished beliefs of the Chinese people. They have trusted in the strength of their arms, but to-day China can rely upon millions of her brave and patriotic volunteers. Are not even striplings taking up arms for the defence of their country? She had always been of the opinion that the allied armies had been permitted to escape too easily in the tenth year of Hsien Feng (1860), and that only a united effort was then necessary to have given China the victory. To-day, at last, the opportunity for revenge had come.

Turning to the Emperor, she asked for his opinion. His Majesty, after a long pause, and with evident hesitation, urged her to follow Jung Lu's advice, to refrain from attacking the Legations, and to have the foreign Ministers escorted in safety to the coast. But, he added, it must be for her to decide. He could not dare to assume any responsibility in the matter.

The junior Chinese Member of the Council, Chao Shu-ch'iao then spoke. He begged the Old Buddha to issue her orders for the immediate extermination of every foreigner in the interior, so as to avoid the danger of spies reporting on the nature and extent of the patriotic movement. Her Majesty commanded the Grand Council to consider this suggestion and to memorialise in due course for an Edict.

After him, however, each in his turn, the Manchu Li-shan, and the Chinese Hsü Ching-ch'eng and Yüan Ch'ang implored the Empress not to declare war against the whole world. China, they said, could not possibly escape defeat, and, even if the Empire should not be partitioned, there must arise great danger of rebellion and anarchy from within. Yüan Ch'ang even went so far as to say that he had served as a Minister of the Tsungli Yamên for two years and that he had found foreigners to be generally reasonable and just in their dealings. He did not believe in the authenticity of the despatch demanding the Empress's abdication, which Prince Tuan professed to have received from the Diplomatic Body; in his opinion, it was impossible that the Ministers should have dared to suggest any such interference with China's internal affairs.

At this Prince Tuan arose and angrily asked the Empress

whether she proposed to listen to the words of a Chinese traitor? Her Majesty rebuked him for his loud and violent manner of speaking, but ordered Yüan Ch'ang to leave the Audience Hall. No one else dared to say anything.

She then ordered the promulgation of the Decree, for immediate communication to all parts of the Empire; at the same time announcing her intention of sacrificing at the ancestral shrines before the commencement of hostilities. Prince Chuang and Duke Lan were appointed joint Commanders-in-Chief of the Boxers, but Tzŭ Hsi gave them clearly to understand that if the foreign Ministers would agree to take their departure from Peking this afternoon Jung Lu was to do his best to protect them as far as Tientsin. Finally, the Empress ordered the Grand Council to report themselves at mid-day for further orders. All were then permitted to retire with the exception of Prince Tuan and Duke Lan; these remained in special audience for some time longer. Hsü T'ung was present at the general audience, having made good his escape from the Legation quarter, and was congratulated by Her Majesty on his safety.

They say that Duke Lan told the Empress of a vision in which, the night before, he had seen Yü Huang, the Jade Emperor. To him, and to his company of Boxers while drilling, the god had appeared, and had expressed his satisfaction with them and their patriotic movement. The Old Buddha observed that the Jade Emperor had appeared in the same manner at the beginning of the reign of the Empress Wu of the T'ang Dynasty (the most famous woman ruler in Chinese history); the omen, she thought, showed clearly that the gods are on the side of China and against the barbarians.

When, at the hour of the Sheep (1 P.M.) Kang Yi returned to the Palace, he found Prince Ch'ing in the anteroom of the Grand Council, greatly excited. It seems that En Hai,[1] a Manchu sergeant, had just come to his residence and reported that he had

---

1. This man's subsequent arrest and execution are described in a Censorate memorial at the end of this chapter.

shot and killed two foreigners whom he had met, riding in sedan chairs that morning, just opposite the Tsungpu Street. As orders had been issued by Prince Tuan and Ch'i Hsiu to the troops that all foreigners were to be shot wherever met, and as one of these two was the German Minister, he hoped that Prince Ch'ing would recommend him for special promotion. Prince Tuan had already heard the news and was greatly pleased. Prince Ch'ing and Kang Yi discussed the matter and decided to inform the Empress Dowager at once. Kang Yi did not think that the death of one foreign devil, more or less, could matter much, especially now that it had been decided to wipe out the Legations entirely, but Prince Ch'ing thought differently and reiterated his opinion that the killing of an accredited Envoy is a serious matter. Until now, only missionaries and their converts had been put to death, but the murder of a Minister could not fail to arouse fierce indignation, even as it did in the case of the British negotiator[1] who was captured by our troops in the 10th year of Hsien-Feng (1860).

The Grand Council then entered the presence. Prince Li, as the senior member of the Council, told the Old Buddha the news, but added that the foreigners had brought it on themselves because they had first fired on the people. Upon hearing this Her Majesty ordered Jung Lu to be summoned in haste, but Kang Yi, being extremely busy with his work of providing supplies for the Boxers, did not await his arrival.

Now, even as I write, they tell me that bullets are whizzing and whistling overhead; but I am too deaf to hear them. En Ch'u says that already the Kansuh braves have begun the attack upon the Legations and that Jung Lu's endeavours to have the foreigners escorted to a place of safety have completely failed.

Liu Shun has just come in and asked for leave to go home for a week. People are leaving the city in all directions and in great numbers.

24th Day of the 5th Moon: the Hour of the Dog, 7-9 P.M. (June 20th, 1900).—En Ming has just come in to inform me that a

---

1. Mr. (later Sir Harry) Parkes.

foreign devil[1] has been captured by Tung Fu-hsiang's troops. They were taking him, wounded, to Prince Chuang's Palace, prodding at him with their bayonets; and he was babbling in his foreign tongue. He will be decapitated, and his captors will receive good rewards (Prince Ch'ing has just been given command of the gendarmerie). "The rut in which the cart was overturned is just ahead." Let this be a warning to those puny barbarian ruffians, the soldiery encamped at the very gates of the Palace. (*This alludes to the proximity of the Legations to the Palace enclosure.*) Jung Lu was all ready to escort the foreigners to Tientsin; he had with him over 2,000 Manchu troops. Doubtless he means well, but the Old Buddha now says that she will not prevent the Kansuh braves from destroying the Legations. If the foreigners choose to leave with Jung Lu, let them do so, and they will not be attacked; but if they insist upon remaining, then their punishment be upon their own heads, and "let them not say they were not forewarned."

Duke Lan sent over to invite me to breakfast with him to-morrow; he is sore pressed with business cares just now; nevertheless, he and his brothers always treat their old teacher with politeness and respect. Though bellicose by nature, he is singularly gentle and refined. Chi Pin[2] sent over to ask whether we would like to move to his house in the north of the city, because the noise of the firing is very great in our quarter, but I am so deaf that I hear not a sound of it all.[3]

Chi Pin is writing to his father-in-law, Yü Hsien, about the audience in the Palace.

Duke Lan writes to tell me that this evening * * * * informed Prince Tuan and Chi Hsiu that, by the orders of that rascally Chinaman, Yüan Ch'ang, the corpse of the foreign devil had been coffined. * * * * wanted Prince Tuan to have the corpse decapitated

---

1. Professor James.
2. Mentioned above under full name of Chi Shou-ch'eng. Chi Pin was his "hao" or intimate personal name.
3. Ching Shan's house was just inside the Tung An Gate of the Imperial City, about a quarter of a mile to the north of the present Legation area boundary.

and the head exhibited over the Tung An Gate. Yüan Ch'ang defends his action, saying that he knew the German Minister personally at the Tsung Li Yamên, and he cannot bear the idea of leaving his body uncoffined. Mencius says, "It is common to all men to feel pity. No one can see a child fall into a well without a shudder of commiseration and horror." But these Chinese traitors of ours are compassionate to the enemies of our glorious Kingdom, and the foes of our ancient race. It is passing strange!

25th Day of the 5th Moon: the Hour of the Monkey, 3-5 P.M. (June 21st). — My chair-bearers have fled from the city, so to-day I had to use my cart to go to Duke Lan's residence. Prince Tuan and the Grand Secretary, Kang Yi, were there; also Chung Li, lately Commandant of the gendarmerie, and the "Beileh": Tsai Lien. Prince Tuan had seen the Old Buddha this morning; their Majesties have moved from the Palace by the lake into the Forbidden City. As the Empress Dowager was crossing the road which runs between the Gate of the Hsi Yuan (Western Park) and the Hsi Hua Gate of the Forbidden City she saw that a number of Boxers had lined up on each side of the street as a Guard of Honour for the "Sacred Chariot." She presented them with 2,000 taels, congratulating their commander, Prince Chuang, on their stalwart appearance. Said the Old Buddha to Prince Tuan, "The foreigners are like fish in the stew-pan. For forty years have I lain on brushwood and eaten bitterness because of them, nursing my revenge like Prince Kou Chien of the Yüeh State (5th Century B.C.). Never have I treated the foreigners otherwise than generously; have I not invited their womenfolk to visit the Lake Palace? But now, if only the country will stand together, their defeat is certain."

I think Prince Tuan hopes that the Old Buddha will now have the Ta-A-Ko proclaimed Emperor; but unfortunately the Nanking Viceroy, Liu K'un-yi, has much influence over her in this matter. When he was in Peking this spring, in the second moon, he solemnly warned her against the Boxers and ventured even to remonstrate at the Ta-A-Ko being made Heir Apparent. Were it not for Liu K'un-yi, he would have been Emperor long since;

therefore Prince Tuan has a very bitter hatred against him. Liu told the Old Buddha at his second audience that if H.M. Kuang Hsü were deposed, the people of his province would assuredly rise in rebellion. What concern is it of theirs who reigns in the Capital? His present Majesty's reign has brought many misfortunes to the nation; it is high time that it came to an end. Why does not Prince Tuan enter the Palace and proclaim his son Emperor? Tung Fu-hsiang's Kansuh braves and the Prince's own Manchu soldiery would surely rally round him. But if Jung Lu opposed them the Old Buddha would side with him. His wife[1] is for ever in the Palace.

26th Day of the 5th Moon (June 22nd). — I went this morning to Prince Li's palace in the western quarter of the city. I had to go in my small cart, because my chair-bearers have either run away to their homes in the country or had joined the Boxers. My two sons, En Ch'u and En Ming, have been making arrangements to quarter one hundred Boxers in our outer courtyard, and it seems that we shall have to supply them with food. Although it cannot be denied that everyone should join in this noble work of exterminating the barbarians, I grudge, nevertheless, spending money in these hard times even for the Boxers, for rice is now become as dear as pearls, and firewood more precious than cassia buds. It may be that, in my old age, I am becoming like that Hsiao Lung, brother to the founder of the Liang Dynasty, who was so miserly that he stored up his money in heaps. On every heap of a million cash he would place a yellow label, while a purple label marked each hoard of ten millions. It is recorded of him, that his relatives abused him for this habit; as for me, my sons would like to get at my money, but they cannot.

I find Prince Li much depressed in his mind; his treasure vaults contain vast wealth; as senior member of the Grand Council, moreover, he feels a weight of responsibility that is too much

---

1. This favourite companion of Tzŭ Hsi was really Jung Lu's secondary consort, who was only raised to the rank of *la premiere légitime* after his first wife's death in September, 1900. She survived him and continued to exercise great influence with the Old Buddha.

for him. His abilities are certainly small, and I have never yet understood why the Old Buddha appointed him to succeed Prince Kung as senior Councillor. He tells me of a stormy meeting at the Grand Council this morning; it seems that Her Majesty is greatly annoyed with Liu K'un-yi for sending in a telegram strongly denouncing the Boxers. He has also telegraphed privately to Jung Lu, imploring him to check their rebellion, but no one knows what answer Jung Lu has made.

In his telegram to the Empress Dowager, which came forward by express couriers from Pao-ting-fu, the Viceroy declares that he would be more than ready to march north with all his troops if it were to repel a foreign invasion, but he firmly declines to lend his forces for the purpose of massacring a few helpless foreigners. Commenting on this, the Empress Dowager quoted the words of the Classic Historical Commentary (Tso Chüan): "The upper and lower jaws mutually assist each other; if the lips shrivel, then must the teeth catch cold." Thereby she meant to imply that even such, in its close interdependence, is the relation between the northern and southern parts of our Empire, and no one should know this better than Liu K'un-yi, after his experiences at the time of the Taiping Rebellion.

The Old Buddha has directed Prince Chuang, as head of the city gendarmerie, to issue a proclamation offering Tls. 50 for every head of a male barbarian brought in, Tls. 40 for that of a woman, and Tls. 30 for that of a child.

While I was still talking with Prince Li, Jung Lu came over in his sedan chair to visit his kinsman. He looks very tired, and walks with a limp. He was loud in denouncing the Boxers, who, he says, are quite incapable of doing any good. They had even now dared to shout abuse at him while passing the "Houmen," calling him a Chinese traitor. I could not help thinking that Jung Lu deserved the name, but I did not say so. He is a strong man, the strongest of all the Manchus, and I greatly fear that his influence may yet be able to wreck all our hopes.

Returning to my house, I heard that the Princes Tuan and

Chuang were sending troops to surround the French Cathedral, which is defended by a few foreign soldiers only, and which should, therefore, be easily captured. Prince Li's palace is within a stone's throw of the cathedral, and to enter the Forbidden City he has to pass just south of it, through the "Hsi-Hua" gate. Although greatly disturbed by the impending hostilities in his neighbourhood, he fears to move to a quieter locality, lest, in his absence, his treasure vaults should be plundered. No doubt the cathedral will fall in a few days.

My courtyard is now full of Boxers and Kansuh soldiery; I can no longer call my house my own. How I loathe these cursed foreigners for causing all this disturbance!

The same Day: at the Hour of the Dog (7-9 P.M.). — I learn that Jung Lu has just sent off a courier with a telegram, which Yüan Shih-k'ai is to send on to the Viceroys of Canton, Nanking and Wuch'ang. Prince Li has sent me a copy, which I am to keep secret; it reads as follows: —

"With all respect I have received your telegrams. Where one weak people dares to oppose ten or more powerful nations, the inevitable result can only be complete ruin. It has always been maintained as a fixed principle with civilised nations, that, in the event of war between any two Powers, their respective Envoys should be treated with respect. Can it now be that this our great inheritance, founded by our remote ancestors at so great a cost of toil and danger, is to be endangered, and suddenly brought to ruin, by these false workers of magic? Shall the fate of the Dynasty be staked on a single throw? It requires no peculiar sagacity to see that these Boxers' hopes of success are nothing but the shadow of a dream. It is true and undeniable, that, from their Majesties on the Throne down to the very lowest of our people, all have suffered from the constant aggression of foreigners and their unceasing insults. For this reason these patriotic train-bands have been organised, claiming a divine mission of retaliation; but the present crisis is all-serious, and although I have used every effort to explain its dangers, I have laboured in vain. I am sick and suffering from lameness, but since I obtained leave of absence I have already submitted seven separate memorials denouncing these Boxers. Seeing that they produced no result, I have now left my sick bed, in order, if possible, to explain the situation clearly to their Majesties; and this also has been in vain.

"All the Princes and Ministers of State who surround the Throne now cry out against me with one voice, as your Excellencies can readily believe. I dare not quote in this place the words of Her Majesty, but I may say that the whole of the Imperial family have joined the Boxers, and at least two-thirds of our troops, both Manchu and Chinese, are with them. They swarm in the streets of our capital like a plague of locusts, and it will be extremely difficult to disperse them.

"Even the divine wisdom of Her Majesty is not sufficient to stand against the will of the majority. If Heaven is not on our side, how can I oppose its will? For several days past I have been pondering night and day on some way out of our difficulties, some forlorn hope of escape. Therefore yesterday morning (June 20th) I arranged for a meeting with the foreign Ministers at the Tsung Li Yamên, with a view to providing a safe conduct for the entire foreign community, with my own troops, to Tientsin. This course appeared to me to hold out some reasonable chances of success, but Prince Tuan's soldiery slew the German Minister, and since then the situation continues to develop from hour to hour with such extraordinary rapidity that words fail me to describe it. On my side, in the discussions of the Grand Council and the Chamberlains of the Presence, are Prince Ch'ing and Wang Wen-shao, but the former, following his usual practice, has applied for leave, and Her Majesty will have nothing to do with him; so that these two are of no real assistance to me. I have no fear of death, but I grieve at the thought of the guilt which will be recorded against me in history; Heaven knows that I am overwhelmed with grief and shame. I have received great favours at the hands of the Throne, and can only now pray to the spirits of the Dynastic ancestors to protect our Empire. The situation here is well-nigh lost, but it remains for your Excellencies to take all possible steps for the protection of your respective provinces. Let each do his utmost, and let proper secrecy be maintained." Signed "Jung Lu, with tears in his eyes."

It is reported from the Grand Council that Chang Chih-tung has telegraphed to Her Majesty, assuring her of his devotion and loyalty, and asking whether he should come north with his troops to help in the work of destroying the barbarians. Chang is a time-server, and loves not the Emperor;[1] we have not forgotten how he approved the Decree appointing an Heir Apparent, and how he would have been a party to His Majesty's removal from the Throne, justifying himself on quibbling grounds of legality and precedents as to the lawful succession. He trims his sails according to the wind of the moment, and has no courage of fixed principles, like Liu K'un-yi. I despise the latter's views in opposing the Boxers, but no one can help admiring his upright character.

(At this point the diarist proceeds to give a full account of the rise and spread of the Boxer movement, describing in detail their magic rites, their incantations, and their ceremonies of initiation. The facts have nearly all been published before, so that most of this portion of the Diary is here omitted. It is chiefly interesting as showing to what heights of superstition even the most educated of the Manchus, including the Empress Dowager, could go. We give one example only of the farrago of gibberish which, believed in high quarters, nearly brought about the end of the Dynasty.)

The Boxers also possess a secret Talisman, consisting of a small piece of yellow paper, which they carry on their persons when going into battle. On it is drawn, in vermilion paint, a figure which is neither that of man nor devil, demon nor saint. It has a head, but no feet; its face is sharp-pointed, with eyes and eyebrows, and four halos. From the monster's heart to its lower extremities runs a mystic inscription, which reads: "I am Buddha of the cold cloud; before me lies the black deity of fire; behind is Laotzu himself." On the creature's body are also borne the characters for Buddha, Tiger, and Dragon. On the top left-hand corner are the words "invoke first the Guardian of Heaven," and on the right-hand corner, "invoke next the black gods of pestilence."

---

1. A short biographical note on Chang Chih-tung will be found in the Appendix.

The Empress Dowager has learned this incantation by heart, and repeats it seventy times daily, and every time that she repeats it the chief eunuch (Li Lien-ying) shouts: "There goes one more foreign devil." The Boxers determine the fate of their victims by a curious test, which consists of burning a ball of paper, and seeing whether the ashes ascend or remain upon the ground. They may believe that it is the spirits who decide, but, as a matter of fact, these balls of paper are sometimes made of thinner material, which naturally leave a lighter ash that is easily caught up in the air; whereas, when they use thick paper, the ashes seldom rise. Some of the balls are also more tightly rolled than others, and it is quite evident that the ashes of the loose ones have a much better chance of blowing away than those which are tightly rolled. Similarly, when they set fire to any place, they profess to be guided by their gods, and they say that fire leaps forth at the point of their swords in any quarter which the spirits desire to have destroyed. As a matter of fact, however, there is deception practised in this also, for when they wish to burn any place for purposes of plunder they have it sprinkled in advance with kerosene oil, and if no oil is available, they even pile up brushwood around it, upon which they drop a lighted match secreted upon their persons.

27th Day of the 5th Moon (June 23rd). — The foreign barbarian of whom I have written[1] was executed this morning at the hour of the Hare (6 A.M.) and his head is now exhibited in a cage, hanging from the main beam of the "Tung-An" gate. It had to be put in a cage, as there was no queue to hang it by. The face has a most horrible expression, but it is a fine thing, all the same, to see a foreigner's head hung up at our palace gates. It brings back to memory the heads that I saw outside the Board of Punishments in the tenth year of Hsien-Feng (1860), but there were black devils among those. Jung Lu tried to save the barbarian's life, and even intended to rescue him by force, but the Princes Tuan and Chuang had determined upon his death, and they had him executed before Jung Lu knew it, so that, when his men arrived

---

1. *Vide* under June 20th.

upon the scene, the foreigner's head had already parted company from his body. The Princes had him kneeling before them yesterday for several hours on a chain, and all the time he kept on imploring them to spare his life; his groans were most painful to hear. The Old Buddha has been informed of his death, and she gave orders that Tls. 500 be distributed to the soldiers who had captured him, *i.e.* a reward ten times greater than that which was promised in the proclamations.

The Boxers who occupy my courtyard tried to take away my cigars from me, but subsequently relented and allowed me to keep them because of my extreme old age. Nothing of foreign origin, not even matches, may be used nowadays, and these Boxer chiefs, Chang Te-ch'eng and Han Yi-li, both of whom are common and uneducated men, are treated with the greatest respect even by Princes of the blood: a curious state of affairs indeed!

Duke Tsai Lan came to see me this afternoon. He tells me an extraordinary story how that the Heir Apparent called the Emperor a "Devil's pupil" this morning, and, when rebuked for it, actually boxed His Majesty's ears. The Emperor then reported the facts in a memorial to Her Majesty, who flew into a towering rage, and gave orders to the eunuch Ts'ui to administer twenty sharp strokes of the whip on the Heir Apparent's person. Prince Tuan is much enraged at this, but he is horribly afraid of Her Majesty, and, when she speaks to him, "he is on tenter-hooks, as if thorns pricked him, and the sweat runs down his face."

T'ung Fu-hsiang told the Empress Dowager yesterday that the Legations have come to the end of their tether. From a rockery on some high ground in the Forbidden City gardens, the Old Buddha could see the flames bursting from the Legation quarter, and was more than once assured that final destruction had come upon the foreigners at last. But later in the afternoon, Hsü Ching-ch'eng was received in audience, when he presented a memorial which he and Yüan Chang had drawn up, denouncing the Boxers; he told Her Majesty that it was not the Legations, but the Han Lin Academy, that was in flames, the Kansuh soldiery having set fire to it in the hope that the conflagration might spread and thus enable them to force a way into the Legation. Her Majesty was greatly disappointed and displeased, severely blaming Tung Fu-hsiang, and she sent for Jung Lu and talked with him in private for a long while.

Good news has come in to-day of victorious fighting at Tientsin; Yü Lu reports that many foreigners were slain in their attack on the Taku forts, and several of their warships sunk. Practically the whole of the foreign community of Tientsin had been annihilated, he says.

Many hundreds of Chinese Christians were put to death to-day just outside Prince Chuang's palace. The judges who convicted them were Prince Chuang, Yi Ku, Fen Che, and Kuei Ch'un. There was no mercy shown, and a large number of innocent people perished with the guilty. The Empress is essentially a kind-hearted woman, and she was greatly shocked to hear of this wholesale massacre. She was heard to say that if the Catholics would only recant and reform, a way of escape might very well be provided for them.

29th Day of the 5th Moon (June 25th). — To-day about sixty of the Boxers, led by the Princes Tuan and Chuang, and the "Beilehs" Tsai Lien and Tsai Ying, marched to the Palace at 6 o'clock in the morning to search there for converts. Coming to the gate of the Palace of Peaceful Longevity, where their Majesties were still abed, they noisily clamoured for the Emperor to come out, denouncing him as a friend of foreigners. Prince Tuan was their spokesman. I heard of the incident from Wen Lien, Comptroller of the Household, who was on duty this morning; he was amazed at the foolhardy effrontery of Prince Tuan, and thought that he had probably been drinking. On hearing the noise outside and the shouts of the Boxers clamouring to kill all "Devil's pupils," the Old Buddha, who was taking her early tea, came out swiftly and stood at the head of the steps, while the Princes and the Boxer leaders swarmed in the courtyard below her. She asked Prince Tuan whether he had come to look upon himself as the Emperor;

if not, how dared he behave in this reckless and insolent manner? She would have him know that she, and she alone, had power to create or depose the Sovereign, and she would have him remember that the power which had made his son Heir Apparent could also wipe him out in a moment. If he and his fellow Princes thought that because the State was at a crisis of confusion they could follow their own inclinations in matters of this kind, they would find themselves very seriously mistaken. She bade them depart, and refrain from ever again entering the palace precincts, except when summoned to her presence on duty. But they would first prostrate themselves and ask His Majesty's pardon for their insolent behaviour. As a slight punishment for their offences, she further commanded that the Princes be mulcted of a year's allowances. As to the Boxer chiefs, who had dared to create this uproar in her hearing, they should be decapitated upon the spot, and Jung Lu's guards, who were on duty at the outer gates, were ordered to carry this sentence into immediate effect. Her Majesty is so greatly incensed against the Boxers at this moment that everyone thinks that Jung Lu will now be able to put a stop to the attacks on the Legations. The Emperor was much alarmed at this incident, and when it was over humbly thanked Her Majesty for so benevolently protecting him.

Later; 9 P.M. — The Old Buddha has suddenly determined, in her rage against Prince Tuan and his followers, to put a stop to the fighting in Peking, and she now agrees that Jung Lu shall proceed to the Legations to discuss terms of peace. At 6 P.M. today all firing stopped, and Jung Lu, at the head of his troops, proceeded to the bridge which lies on the north of the Legation quarter. The foreigners came out from their hiding-places and commenced to parley; they were shown a board, and on it the words written: "Orders have now been received from the Empress Dowager to afford due protection to the Legations." Jung Lu hoped to be able to induce the foreign Ministers to confer with him for the purpose of restoring order. For three hours not a shot has been fired; but En Ming has just come in to tell me that

THE TA-A-KO, SON OF PRINCE TUAN, THE BOXER LEADER.
Appointed Heir-Apparent in January, 1900. Appointment rescinded November, 1901.

the situation has again changed, and that the Old Buddha has heard such good accounts of the defeat of the foreign relief force on its way to Peking that she is once more determined to give the Boxers their head and "to eat the flesh and sleep on the skins" of the foreign devils.

4th Day of the 6th Moon: at the Hour of the Dog, 7 P.M. (June 30, 1900). — Kang Yi called to-day, and remained with me for the evening meal. He tells me that Tung Fu-hsiang called in person this morning on Jung Lu at his residence, and asked him for the loan of the heavy artillery which is under his orders. Jung Lu is said to have ample armaments in stock in the city, the property of the Wu Wei-chün (Military Defence Corps) sufficient to knock every foreign building to pieces in a few hours.

Tung was kept waiting at Jung Lu's door for over an hour; when finally admitted, he began to bluster, whereupon Jung Lu feigned sleep. "He gave no consent, but leant on his seat and slumbered."[1] Tung then expostulated with Jung Lu for his rudeness, but the Commander-in-chief only smiled, and brought the interview to an end by remarking that Tung's only way to get the guns would be to persuade the Old Buddha to give him Jung Lu's head with them. "Apply for an audience at once," he said. "She believes you to be a brave man and will certainly comply with any request you may make."

Tung Fu-hsiang left in a towering rage, and made straight for the Forbidden City, although the hour for audiences was long since past. At the gate of the Hall of Imperial Supremacy (Huang Chi-tien) he made a loud disturbance, bidding the eunuchs inform Her Majesty that the Kansuh Commander-in-chief was without, desiring audience. It so happened that the Old Buddha was engaged in painting a design of bamboos on silk, and she was highly displeased at being thus disturbed. Tung was ushered in, however, and fell on his knees. "Well," said Her Majesty, "I suppose that you have come to report the complete destruction of the Legations? This will be the tenth time since the end of

---

1. A quotation from Mencius.

last Moon." "I have come," replied Tung Fu-hsiang, "to ask Your Majesty's permission to impeach the Grand Secretary Jung Lu as a traitor and the friend of barbarians. He has the guns which my army needs; with their aid not a stone would be left standing in the whole of the Legation quarter. But he has sworn never to lend these guns, even though Your Majesty should command it." Angrily the Old Buddha replied, "Be silent. You were nothing but a brigand to begin with, and if I allowed you to enter my army it was only to give you an opportunity of atoning for your former misdeeds. Even now you are behaving like a brigand, forgetting the majesty of the Imperial Presence. Of a truth, your tail is becoming too heavy to wag. Leave the Palace forthwith, and do not let me find you here again unless summoned to audience."

Kang Yi declares that we shall never take the Legations so long as Jung Lu continues to exercise his present great influence at Court. Li Shan, who is also a great favourite of the Empress Dowager, is now on the side of those who would make peace with the foreigners, and has been impeached for it by Na T'ung.

The following proclamation is now placarded all over the city, in accordance with the Empress Dowager's orders issued to Prince Chuang. They say that she means to pay the rewards from her own privy purse:

"REWARDS.

"Now that all foreign churches and chapels have been razed to the ground, and that no place of refuge or concealment is left for the foreigners, they must unavoidably scatter, flying in every direction. Be it therefore known and announced to all men, scholars and volunteers, that any person found guilty of harbouring foreigners will incur the penalty of decapitation. For every male foreigner taken alive a reward of 50 taels will be given; for every female 40 taels, and for every child 30 taels; but it is to be clearly understood that they shall be taken alive, and that they shall be genuine foreigners. Once this fact has been duly authenticated, the reward will be paid without delay. A special proclamation, requiring reverent obedience."

Much larger rewards than these were paid in the tenth year of Hsieng-Feng (1860) for the heads of barbarians, but of course in those days they were comparatively rare, whereas now, alas, they have become as common as bees!

This morning an important trial took place outside the gate of Prince Chuang's palace; Yi Ku, Fen Che, and Kuei Ch'un presided. Over nine hundred people were summarily executed by the Boxers, in some cases before any proofs whatsoever had been substantiated in regard to their alleged connection with foreigners. Helpless babes even were amongst the slain. Fen Che is nothing more than a butcher and the Old Buddha remonstrated with Prince Chuang for not keeping the Boxers in better order.

8th Day of the 6th Moon, 11 A.M. (July 4th). — Yü Hsien's son-in-law, Chi Shou-ch'eng, came and talked with me for a long while. The bombardment of the city was going on all the time he was here, and to the south of my house, close to the Imperial City Wall, the troops of Li Ping-heng were mounting cannon on an elevated platform. They are all still very wroth with Jung Lu, who refuses to lend his guns, and his troops are so faithful to him that it is impossible to bribe them to disobey him. Jung Lu's courage is really extraordinary; he said of himself lately, that "in the days of the wicked Ruler (meaning Prince Tuan) he bided his time on the shores of the bleak North Sea, awaiting the purification of the Empire."[1] I am told that Prince Tuan has taken possession of one of the Imperial Seals, so as to be able to proclaim his son Emperor at the first favourable opportunity; but if the Old Buddha finds this out, as most probably she will, there is trouble ahead for Prince Tuan.

Chi Shou-ch'eng tells me that Yü Hsien has sent in a memorial to the Empress Dowager with reference to the missionaries in Shansi. Ten days ago she had sent him a secret Decree, saying, "Slay all foreigners wheresoever you find them; even though they be prepared to leave your province, yet must they be slain." It seems that the Old Buddha ordered that this Decree should be

---

1. Quotation from Mencius.

sent to every high provincial official in the Empire, but it is now reported that Tuan Fang, the acting governor of Shensi, and Yü Chang, governor of Honan, together with the high officials in Mongolia, received the Edict in a very different form, for the word "slay" had been changed to "protect." It is feared that some treacherous minister is responsible for this, but no one dares inform Her Majesty. To Yü Hsien's latest memorial, she has made the following reply, which has been sent by the fastest express riders to T'ai-yüan fu: "I command that all foreigners — men, women, and children, old and young — be summarily executed. Let not one escape, so that my Empire may be purged of this noisome source of corruption, and that peace may be restored to my loyal subjects." Chi Shou-ch'eng tells me that Yü Hsien's bitterness against foreigners is inspired by his wife, of whom he is greatly afraid. He himself has earned golden opinions in T'ai-yüan during his short administration, and has a high reputation for even-handed justice. He says also that this last Decree gave pleasure to Prince Chuang; Jung Lu tried to stop it, asking the Old Buddha what glory could China expect to gain by the slaughter of women and children. "We should become the laughing-stock of the world," he said, "and the Old Buddha's widespread fame and reputation for benevolence would be grievously injured." "Yes," replied the Empress Dowager, "but these foreigners of yours wish to see me deposed, and I am only paying off old scores. Ever since the days of Tao-Kuang this uproarious guest within our borders has been maltreating his hosts, and it is time that all should know who is the real master of the house."

Yesterday afternoon the Empress Dowager crossed over to the Lake Palace for a water picnic, attended by several ladies of the Court. The continuous bombardment of the French cathedral eventually made her head ache, so she despatched a chamberlain to the officer commanding at the Hsi-Hua Gate, ordering them to cease firing until her return to the Forbidden City.

11th Day of the 6th Moon (7th July). — Yü Lu has sent in a ridiculous memorial, reporting the capture of four camels, as well as

REPRODUCTION OF PICTURE PAINTED ON SILK,
BY HER MAJESTY TZU HSI.

the killing of many foreigners, in Tientsin. Jung Lu has advised him to cease attacking the foreign Settlements. Talking of Jung Lu, I hear that Tung Fu-hsiang recently hired a Manchu soldier to assassinate him, but, instead of doing so, the man betrayed the plot to Jung Lu. This soldier turns out to be a brother of that En Hai who slew the foreign devil (Baron von Ketteler), and Tung thought therefore that he would gladly do anything to assist in destroying the Legations. But he is a clansman of Jung Lu's banner, and, like Yü Kung-ssŭ, whom Mencius called the best archer in Wei, "he could not bear to slay the old Chief who had taught him the arts of war." Jung Lu has again memorialised the Old Buddha, reminding her of that well-known saying in the Spring and Autumn annals,[1] which lays down that the persons of foreign Envoys are always inviolate within the territories of any civilised State. This attack on the Legation, he says, is worse than an outrage; it is a piece of stupidity which will be remembered against China for all time. Her Majesty appeared to think that, because a small nation like the Transvaal could conquer a great Power like England, China must necessarily be even more successful in fighting the whole world; but there was no analogy between the two cases. If peace were to be made at once, the situation might still be saved; but if the Legations were demolished, there must be an end of Manchu rule. He warned Her Majesty solemnly, and she appears to be gradually coming to look at things from his point of view. These Boxers can certainly talk, but they do very little.

Bad news has reached the palace to-day of the fighting around Tientsin, and Her Majesty is most anxious about it, though she still refuses to believe that the foreign brigands can possibly enter Peking.

15th Day of the 6th Moon (11th July). My neighbour Wen Lien, Comptroller-General of the Imperial Household, tells me that the Old Buddha is in a furious rage. She finds the heat trying, and yesterday she turned on the Heir Apparent and snubbed him badly for impertinence; he had asked if he might be permitted to escort

---

1. History of events under the Chou dynasty, by Confucius; one of the Five Classics.

her to Jehol, leaving the Emperor to settle matters with his foreign friends in Peking. One of the young eunuchs tried to mollify her by reporting, whenever the report of a gun was heard, that another foreign devil had been killed, but as the Old Buddha observed, "there has been enough firing for the past few weeks to kill off every foreigner in China several times, and so far there is hardly anything to show for it."

17th Day of the 6th Moon (13th July). — Jung Lu asked Her Majesty yesterday what she would do if the Boxers were defeated, and if Peking were captured by the foreigners. In reply, she quoted to him the words of Chia Yi, a sophist of the Han dynasty, in reference to the Court's diplomatic dealings with the Khan of the Hans: —

"If the Emperor wishes to gain the allegiance of other countries, he can only do so by convincing their rulers that he possesses the three cardinal virtues of government, and by displaying the five allurements.

These allurements are: (1) Presents of chariots and rich robes, to tempt the eye; (2) rich food and banquets, to tempt the palate; (3) musical maidens, to tempt the ear; (4) fine houses and beautiful women, to tempt the instinct of luxury; and (5) the presence of the Emperor at the table of the foreign ruler, to tempt his pride.

The three cardinal virtues of government are: (1) to simulate affection; (2) to express honeyed sentiments; and (3) to treat one's inferiors as equals."

Two years ago, said the Empress, she had invited the foreign ladies to her Court, and had noticed their delight at the reception she gave them, although she well knew that their sympathies were with the Emperor, and against her. She would again allure them to her side with rich gifts and honeyed words.[1]

---

1. How well and successfully she did it, has been told in Miss Catherine A. Carl's book, *With the Empress Dowager of China*. The painting of her portrait for the St. Louis exhibition was in itself an example of Tzŭ Hsi's "cardinal virtues of government," which she practised with conspicuous success on the simple-minded wife of the American Minister, Mrs. Conger. (*Vide* Cordier, *Relations de la Chine*, Vol. III., p. 423.)

20th Day of the 6th Moon (16th July). — Bad news from Yü Lu;
Tientsin has been captured by the foreigners, who now swarm
like locusts. Not one of the Grand Councillors dared to carry the
news to Her Majesty, so Prince Tuan went in boldly, and informed
her that the foreign devils had taken the city, because the Boxers
had been negligent in the performance of their prescribed rites;
Peking, however, would always be perfectly safe from invasion.
Early this morning Jung Lu had informed the Old Buddha that
he had ascertained beyond doubt that the document, which pur-
ported to come from the Foreign Ministers, demanding her abdication, was a forgery. It had been prepared by Lien Wen-chung, a
Secretary of the Grand Council, at Prince Tuan's orders. The Old
Buddha was therefore in no soft mood; angrily she told Prince
Tuan that, if the foreigners entered Peking, he would certainly
lose his head. She was quite aware of his motives; he wanted to
secure the Regency, but she bade him beware, for, so long as she
lived, there could be no other Regent. "Let him be careful, or his
son would be expelled from the palace, and the family estates
confiscated to the throne." His actions had indeed been worthy
of the dog's[1] name he bore. Prince Tuan left the palace, and was
heard to remark that "the thunderbolt had fallen too quickly for
him to close his ears."

Jung Lu has won over all the military commanders except
Tung Fu-hsiang and his staff, and they have come to a general understanding that the bombardment of the Legations must cease.
Jung Lu has explained, as his reason for not allowing the heavy
artillery to be used, that it would inevitably have inflicted serious damage on the Imperial shrines and the Ancestral temple.

The Old Buddha is sending presents to the Legations, water-
melons, wine, vegetables, and ice, and she has expressed a wish
that Prince Ch'ing should go and see the Foreign Ministers.

They say that Hsü Ching-ch'eng is secretly communicating

---

1. The second character of Prince Tuan's name contained the radical sign for *dog*, and was
given him by the Emperor Hsien-Feng, because he had been begotten during the period
of mourning for his parent Tao-Kuang; it being an offence, under Chinese law, for a son
to be begotten during the twenty-seventh months of mourning for father or mother.

with the Legations.

A messenger with twelve dispatches from the Legations was captured to-day and taken to Prince Chuang's Palace. Three of the twelve were in cipher and could not be translated by the Tsung Li Yamên interpreter, but from the others it was learned that the foreigners had lost over a hundred killed and wounded and that their provisions were running very low.

Chi Shou-ch'eng has gone to T'ai-yüan fu to see Yü Hsien, his father-in-law. The latter has memorialised the Throne, reporting that he cunningly entrapped all the foreigners, cast them into chains and had every one decapitated in his Yamên. Only one woman had escaped, after her breasts had been cut off, and had hidden herself under the City wall. She was dead when they found her.

Rain has fallen very heavily to-day. Liu Ta-chiao brought me 8 lbs. of pork from the Palace kitchen, and I sent a large bowl of it to my married sister. Towards evening a detachment of cavalry, with several guns, passed my door. They were Li Ping-heng's men, on their way to mount these guns on a platform above the Forbidden City wall, as a precaution against sorties by the foreigners. There has been heavy firing all night, and it is reported that foreign devils have been seen in the neighbourhood of the Ha-Ta Men.

21st Day of the 6th Moon (17th July). — A lovely day. I walked over to call on Prince Li and Duke Lan. The latest rumour is that Yü Lu's troops are in flight and harrying the country side. They are said to be clamouring for their pay, which is months in arrears, and have plundered both Tungchou and Chang Chia-wan most thoroughly. Both the eastern gates of the City are now kept closed, and the northern gate (Anting men) is only opened occasionally.

Yang Shun, the gate-keeper, has returned from his home at Pao-ti hsien, east of Peking, where he reports things fairly quiet.

Li Ping-heng's troops are reported to have won a great victory and driven the barbarians to the sea. Nevertheless, heavy firing was heard to the south-eastward this afternoon.

Duke Lan has gone out with a large force of Boxers to search for converts reported to be in hiding in the temple of the Sun.

27th Day of the 6th Moon (23rd July). — This morning Yüan Ch'ang and Hsü Ching-ch'eng handed in the third of their Memorials against the Boxers, in which they recommend the execution of several members of the Grand Council. Their valour seems to be more laudable than their discretion, especially as the Old Buddha is disposed once more to believe in the Boxers as the result of Li Ping-heng's audience with her yesterday. He came up from Hankow, and has now been appointed joint Commander, with Jung Lu, of the army of the North. He confidently assured her of his ability to take the Legations by storm, and repeatedly said that never again would the tutelary deities of the Dynasty suffer her to be driven forth, in humiliation, from her capital.

I went across to Duke Lan's house this morning and found Prince Tuan and Li Ping-heng there. They were busy planning a renewed attack on the Legations, and Li was strongly in favour of mining from the Hanlin Academy side. He has advised the Empress Dowager that a mine should be sprung, as was done lately at the French Cathedral, and he is convinced that in the ensuing confusion the foreigners would be easily overwhelmed.

After reading the latest Memorial of Hsü and Yuan, the Old Buddha observed, "These are brave men. I have never cared much for Hsü, but Yüan behaved well in 1898 and warned me about K'ang Yu-wei and his plotting. Be that as it may, however, they have no business to worry me with these persistent and querulous questions. The Throne itself is fully competent to judge the character of its servants, and it is a gross misconception of duty for 'the acolyte to stride across the sacred vessels and show the priest how to slaughter the sacrificial beasts.'[1] Desiring to deal leniently with the Memorialists, I command that my censure be communicated to them and that they take heed to refrain in future from troubling my ears with their petulant complainings."

---

1. A classical allusion, in common use, equivalent to "Ne sutor ultra crepidam."

3rd Day of the 7th Moon (28th July). — The Old Buddha places much confidence in Li Ping-heng. Yesterday he and Kang Yi discovered that the word "to slay," in Her Majesty's Decree ordering the extermination of all foreigners, had been been altered to "protect" by Yüan Ch'ang and Hsü Ching-ch'eng. I have just seen Kang Yi, and he says that Her Majesty's face was divine in its wrath. "They deserve the punishment meted out to Kao Ch'u-mi,"[1] she said, "their limbs should be torn asunder by chariots driven in opposite directions. Let them be summarily decapitated." An Edict was forthwith issued, but no mention is made in it of the alteration of the Decree, as this is a matter affecting the nation's prestige; the offenders are denounced only for having created dissensions in the Palace and favoured the cause of the foreigner. Both were executed this morning; my son, En Ming, witnessed their death. It is most painful to me to think of the end of Yüan Ch'ang, for he had many sterling qualities; as for Hsü, I knew him in the days when we were colleagues at the Grand Secretariat, and I never had a high opinion of the man. His corruption was notorious. Just before the sword of the executioner fell, Yüan remarked that "he hoped that the Sun might soon return to its place in the Heaven, and that the usurping Comet might be destroyed." By this he meant that Prince Tuan's malign influence had led the Empress Dowager to act against her own better instincts. Duke Lan, who was superintending the execution, angrily bade him be silent for a traitor, but Yüan fearlessly went on, "I die innocent. In years to come my name will be remembered with gratitude and respect, long after you evil-plotting Princes have met your well-deserved doom." Turning then to Hsü, he said, "We shall meet anon at the Yellow Springs.[2] To die is only to come home." Duke Lan stepped forward as if to strike him, and the headsman quickly despatched them both.

8th Day of the 7th Moon (3rd August). — I have had much trouble with my eldest son to-day. He has been robbing me lately of

---

1. A traitor whose crime and punishment are recorded in the Spring and Autumn Annals.
2. A classical expression, meaning the Spirit-world.

large sums, and when I rebuked him he had the audacity to reply that my duty to the Throne would make my suicide a fitting return for the benefits which I have received at its hands.

Li Ping-heng has gone to the front to rally the troops and check the foreigners' advance. He has impeached Jung Lu but the Old Buddha has suppressed the Memorial. The Emperor thanked Jung Lu for his services, and the Commander-in-Chief replied that he of all the servants of the Throne never expected to receive praise from His Majesty, considering the events of the past two years.[1]

11th Day of the 7th Moon (5th August). — The Old Buddha has commanded Jung Lu to arrange for escorting the foreigners to Tientsin, so that the advance of the Allies may be stopped. In this connection, I hear that not many days ago, * * * * persuaded Ch'i Hsiu to have a letter sent to the Foreign Ministers, inviting them to come, without escort of troops, to an interview with the Tsung Li Yamên, his idea being to have them all massacred on the way. Ch'i Hsiu thought the suggestion excellent, but, although several letters have been sent proposing it, the Ministers decline to leave the Legations. Meanwhile, there have been several fresh attacks on the Legations during the past few days.

A foreign devil, half naked, was found yesterday in Hatamen Street. He kowtowed to everyone he met, high class or low, imploring even the rag-pickers to spare his life and give him a few cash. "We shall all be massacred soon," he said, "but I have done no wrong." One of Jung Lu's sergeants seized him and took him to the Commander-in-Chief's residence. Instead of decapitating him, Jung Lu sent him back. This shows, however, the desperate straits to which the foreigners are reduced.

15th Day of the 7th Moon (9th August). — Bad news from the South. Yü Lu's forces have been defeated and the foreigners are approaching nearer every day. The Old Buddha is meditating flight to Jehol, but Jung Lu strongly urges her to remain, even if the Allies should enter the City. Duke Lan scoffs at the idea of

---

1. Referring to his part in the *coup d'état* of 1898.

their being able to do so. One comfort is that, if they do come, they will not loot or kill. I remember well how good their discipline was forty years ago. I never stirred out of my house and not one of the barbarians ever came near it. We had a little difficulty about getting victuals, but the foreigners hardly came into the city, and did us no harm.

16th Day of the 7th Moon (10th August). — My old colleague, Li Shan, whose house adjoins the French Cathedral, has been accused of making a subterranean passage and thus assisting the foreigners with supplies. He has been handed over to the Board of Punishments by Prince Tuan, without the knowledge of the Empress Dowager, together with Hsü Yung-yi and Lien Yuan. Prince Tuan has long had a grudge against Hsü for having expressed disapproval of the selection of the Heir Apparent. As to Lien, they say that his arrest is due to * * * *, and his offence is that he was on terms of intimacy with Yüan Ch'ang. All three prisoners were decapitated this morning. Hsü Yung-yi was older than I am (seventy-nine) and his death is a lamentable business indeed. But he went to his death calmly and without complaint when he learned that the Empress Dowager knew nothing of the matter and that it was Prince Tuan's doing alone. "The power of the usurper," said he, "is short-lived. As for me, I am glad to die before the foreigners take Peking." The Old Buddha will be very wrath when she hears that two Manchus have thus been put to death. Li Shan and Jung Lu were old friends.

A certain General Liu, from Shansi, assured the Empress this morning that he would undertake to demolish the Legations in three days, and this would so alarm the allies that their advance would certainly be stopped. A furious bombardment has just begun.

The Boxers have proved themselves utterly useless. I always said they never would do anything.

18th Day of the 7th Moon (12th August}. — The foreigners are getting nearer and nearer. Yü Lu shot himself with a revolver on the 12th at Ts'ai Ts'un. He had taken refuge in a coffin shop, of

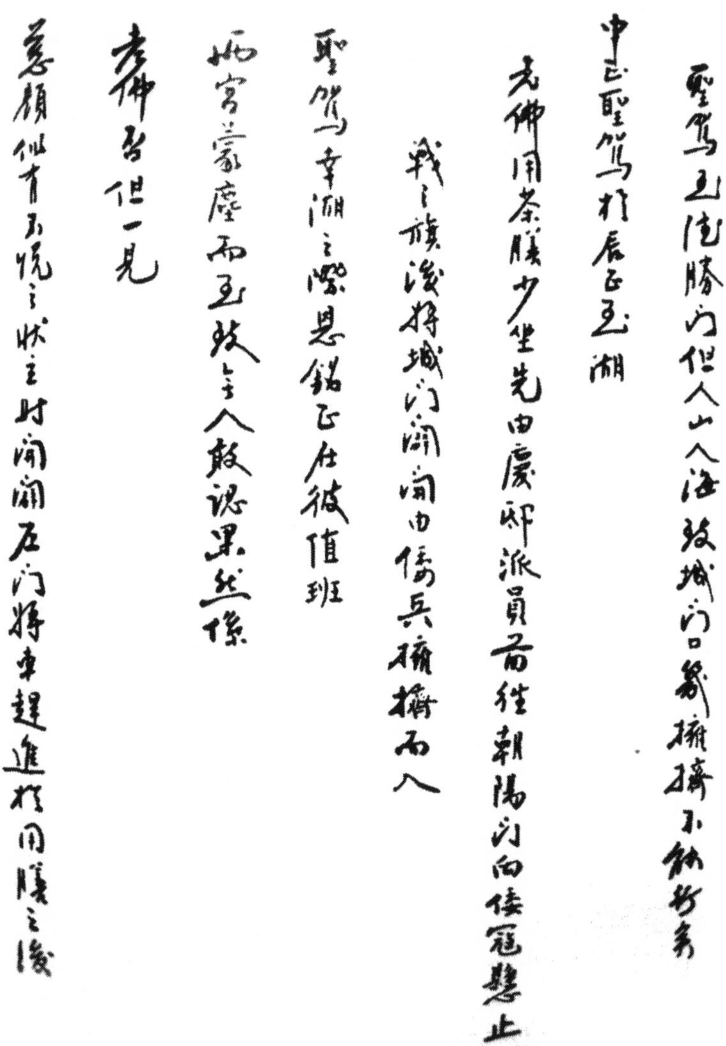

聖駕玉輦勝以但人山人海玻城内口爲擁擠不能前行各

中正聖駕停於辰正玉湖

先佛用茶膳少坐先由慶邸派員前往朝陽河向倭寇懇止

戰之旗後將城内開闢由僑兵稍擠而入

聖駕幸湖之際恩銘正在彼值班

兩宮蒙塵而玉玫主人敢诶巣兰係

李佛答但一見

意顧似有不悦之狀主財開闢石内將車輦進於用膳之後

all ill-omened places! His troops had been utterly routed thrice, at Pei Tsang, Yang Ts'un and at Ts'ai Ts'un. Li Ping-heng reached Ho-hsi wu on the 14th, but in spite of all his efforts to rally our forces, the two divisional leaders, Chang Ch'un-fa and Ch'en Tse-lin, refused to fight. Li Ping-heng therefore took poison. Jung Lu went to-day to break the news to the Old Buddha: sovereign and Minister wept together at the disasters which these Princes and rebels have brought upon our glorious Empire. Jung Lu refrained from any attempt at self-justification; he is a wise man. The Old Buddha said she would commit suicide and make the Emperor do the same, rather than leave her capital. Jung Lu besought her to take his advice, which was to remain in Peking and to issue Decrees ordering the decapitation of Prince Tuan and his followers, thus proving her innocence to the world. But she seems to cling still to a hope that the supernatural powers of the Boxers may save Peking, and so the furious bombardment of the Legations continues.

Eight audiences have been given to-day to Jung Lu and five to Prince Tuan. All the other members of the Grand Council sat with folded hands, suggesting nothing.

20th Day (14th August], 5 P.M. — Tungchou has fallen and now the foreigners have begun to bombard the city. The Grand Council has been summoned to five meetings to-day in the Palace of Peaceful Longevity: Her Majesty is reported to be starting for Kalgan. At the hour of the Monkey (4 P.M.) Duke Lan burst into the Palace, unannounced, and shouted, "Old Buddha, the foreign devils have come!" Close upon his footsteps came Kang Yi, who reported that a large force of turbaned soldiery were encamped in the enclosure of the Temple of Heaven. "Perhaps they are our Mahommedan braves from Kansuh," said Her Majesty, "come to demolish the Legations?" "No," replied Kang Yi, "they are foreign devils. Your Majesty must escape at once, or they will murder you."

Later, midnight. — There has just been an Audience given to the Grand Council in the Palace, at which Kang Yi, Chao Shu-ch'iao and Wang Wen-shao were present. "Where are the others?" said the Old Buddha. "Gone, I suppose, everyone to his own home, leaving us here, Mother and Son,[1] to look after ourselves as best we may. At all events, you three must now accompany me on my journey." Turning to Wang Wen-shao, she added: "You are too old, and I could not bear the thought of exposing you to such hardships. Make such speed as you can and join me later." Then to the other two she said, "You two are good riders. It will be your duty never to lose sight of me for an instant. Wang Wen-shao replied, "I will hasten after Your Majesty to the best of my ability." The Emperor, who seemed surprisingly alert and vigorous, here joined in, "Yes, by all means, follow as quickly as you can." This ended the audience, but the actual hour of Her Majesty's departure remains uncertain. Jung Lu's attendance was impossible because he was busy trying to rally our forces.

21st Day (15th August). — Wen Lien tells me that the Old Buddha arose this morning at the Hour of the Tiger (3 A.M.) after only an hour's rest, and dressed herself hurriedly in the common blue cloth garments of a peasant woman, which she had ordered to be prepared. For the first time in her life, her hair was done up in the Chinese fashion. "Who could ever have believed that it would come to this?" she said. Three common carts were brought into the Palace; their drivers wore no official hats.

All the Concubines were summoned to appear before Her Majesty at 3.30 A.M.; she had previously issued a decree that none of them would accompany her for the present. The Pearl Concubine, who has always been insubordinate to the Old Buddha, came with the rest and actually dared to suggest that the Emperor should remain in Peking. The Empress was in no mood for argument. Without a moment's hesitation, she shouted to the eunuchs on duty, "Throw this wretched minion down the well!" At this the Emperor, who was greatly grieved, fell on his knees in supplication, but the Empress angrily bade him desist, saying that this was no time for bandying words. "Let her die at once,"

---

1. The expression is figurative.

she said, "as a warning to all undutiful children, and to those 'hsiao' birds[1] who, when fledged, peck out their own mother's eyes." So the eunuchs Li and Sung took the Pearl Concubine and cast her down the large well which is just outside the Ning Shou Palace.

Then to the Emperor, who stood trembling with grief and wrath, she said: "Get into your cart and hang up the screen, so that you be not recognised" (he was wearing a long gown of black gauze and black cloth trousers). Swiftly then the Old Buddha gave her orders. "P'u Lun, you will ride on the shaft of the Emperor's cart and look after him. I shall travel in the other cart, and you, P'u Chün (the Heir Apparent) will ride on the shaft. Li Lien-ying, I know you are a poor rider, but you must shift as best you can to keep up with us." At this critical moment it seemed as if the Old Buddha alone retained her presence of mind. "Drive your hardest," she said to the carters, "and if any foreign devil should stop you, say nothing. I will speak to them and explain that we are but poor country folk, fleeing to our homes. Go first to the Summer Palace." Thereupon the carts started, passing out through the northern gate of the Palace (The Gate of Military Prowess) while all the members of the Household and the Imperial Concubines prostrated themselves, wishing their Majesties a long life. Only the three Grand Councillors followed on horseback, a rendezvous having been arranged for other officials at the Summer Palace. My neighbour Wen Lien, the Comptroller of the Household, followed their Majesties at a distance, to see them safely out of the city. They left by the "Te-sheng-men," or Gate of Victory, on the north-west side of the city, where for a time their carts were blocked in the dense mass of refugees passing out that way.

4 P.M. — The Sacred Chariot of Her Majesty reached the Summer Palace at about 8 A.M. and Their Majesties remained there an hour. Meanwhile, at 6 A.M., Prince Ch'ing, just before starting for the Summer Palace, sent a flag of truce to the Japanese Pigmies

---

1. A species of owl — classical reference.

who were bombarding the city close to the "Chi Hua" Gate on the east of the city. The gate was thrown open and the troops swarmed in.

My son En Ming was on duty at the Summer Palace with a few of his men, when the Imperial party arrived, all bedraggled and dust-begrimed. The soldiers at the Palace gate could not believe that this was really their Imperial mistress until the Old Buddha angrily asked whether they failed to recognise her. The carts were driven in through the side entrance, and tea was served. Her Majesty gave orders that all curios, valuables, and ornaments were to be packed at once and sent off to Jehol; at the same time she despatched one of the eunuchs to Peking to tell the Empress[1] to bury quickly every scrap of treasure in the Forbidden City, hiding it in the courtyard of the Ning Shou Palace.

The Princes Tuan, Ching, Na, and Su joined Their Majesties at the Summer Palace; a few Dukes were there also, as well as Wu Shu-mei and Pu Hsing of the higher officials. About a dozen Secretaries from the different Boards, and three Clerks to the Grand Council, accompanied the Court from this point. General Ma Yu-k'un, with a force of 1,000 men escorted Their Majesties to Kalgan, and there were, in addition, several hundreds of Prince Tuan's "Heavenly Tiger" Bannermen, fresh from their fruitless attacks on the Legations. Jung Lu is still endeavouring to rally his troops.

I have just heard of the death of my old friend, Hsü T'ung, the Imperial Tutor and Grand Secretary. He has hanged himself in his house and eighteen of his womenfolk have followed his example. He was a true patriot and a fine scholar. Alas, alas! From all sides I hear the same piteous story; the proudest of the Manchus have come to the same miserable end. The betrothed of Prince Ch'un, whom he was to have married next month, has committed suicide, with all her family. It is indeed pitiful.[2]

1. Consort of Kuang-Hsü, now Empress Dowager, known by the honorific title of Lung-yü.
2. Prince Ch'un subsequently married Jung Lu's daughter, by special command of the Empress Dowager.

Thus, for the second time in her life, the Old Buddha has had to flee from her Sacred City, like the Son of Heaven in the Chou Dynasty, who "fled with dust-covered head." The failure of the southern provinces to join in the enterprise has ruined us. Prince Tuan was much to blame in being anti-Chinese. As Confucius said, "By the lack of broad-minded tolerance in small matters, a great design has been frustrated." After all, Jung Lu was right — the Boxers' so-called magic was nothing but child's talk. They were in reality no stronger than autumn thistledown. Alas, the bright flower of spring does not bloom twice!

My wife and the other women, stupidly obstinate like all females, intend to take opium. I cannot prevent them from doing so, but, for myself, I have no intention of doing anything so foolish. Already the foreign brigands are looting in other quarters of the city, but they will never find my hidden treasure, and I shall just remain here, old and feeble as I am. My son, En Ch'u, has disappeared since yesterday, and nearly all my servants have fled. There is no one to prepare my evening meal.

(Here the Diary ends. The old man was murdered by his eldest son that same evening; all his women folk had previously taken poison and died.)

Vermilion Decree of H.M. Kuang Hsü, 24th day, 12th Moon of 25th year (January, 1900), making Prince Tuan's son Heir Apparent.

"In days of our tender infancy we succeeded by adoption to the Great Inheritance, and were favoured by the Empress Dowager, who graciously 'suspended the curtain' and administered the Government as Regent, earnestly labouring the while at our education in all matters. Since we assumed the reins of government, the nation has passed through severe crises, and our sole desire has been to govern the Empire wisely in order to requite the material benevolence of Her Majesty as well as to fulfil the arduous task imposed on us by His late Majesty.

"But since last year our constitution has been sore-stricken with illness, and we have undergone much anxiety lest the business of the State should suffer in consequence. Reflecting on the duty we owe to our sacred ancestors and to the Empire, we have therefore besought Her Majesty to administer the Government during the past year. Our sickness has so far shown no signs of improvement, and it has prevented us from performing all the important sacrifices at the ancestral shrines and at the altars of the gods of the soil.

"And now at this acute crisis, the spectacle of Her Majesty, labouring without cease in the profound seclusion of her Palace, without relaxation or thought of rest, has filled us with dismay. We can neither sleep nor eat in the anxiety of our thoughts. Reflecting on the arduous labours of our ancestors from whom this great Heritage has descended to us, we are overwhelmed by our unfitness for this task of government. We bear in mind (and the fact is well known to all our subjects) that when first we succeeded by adoption to the Throne, we were honoured with a Decree from the Empress Dowager to the effect that so soon as we should have begotten an heir, he should become the adopted son of His Majesty T'ung-Chih. But our protracted sickness renders it impossible for us to hope for a son, so that His late Majesty remains without heir. This question of the succession is of transcendent importance, and our grief, as we ponder the situation, fills us with feelings of the deepest self-abasement, and renders illusive all hope of our recovery from this sickness.

"We have accordingly prostrated ourselves in supplication before our Sacred Mother, begging that she may be pleased to select some worthy person from among the Princes of the Blood as heir to His Majesty T'ung-Chih, in order that the Great Inheritance may duly revert to him. As the result of our repeated entreaties Her Majesty has graciously consented, and has appointed P'u Chün, son of Prince Tuan, as heir by adoption to His late Majesty. Our gratitude at this is unbounded, and obediently we obey her behests, hereby appointing P'u Chün to be

DAUGHTERS OF A HIGH MANCHU OFFICIAL OF THE COURT.

Heir Apparent and successor to the Throne. Let this Decree be made known throughout the Empire."

Seldom has history seen so tragically pathetic a document. It was not only a confession of his own illegality and an abdication, but his death-warrant, clear writ for all men to read. And the poor victim must perforce thank his executioner and praise the "maternal benevolence" of the woman whose uncontrollable love of power had wrecked his life from the cradle.

Memorial from the Censorate at Peking to the Throne at Hsi-an, describing the arrest of En Hai, the murderer of the German Minister, Baron von Ketteler.[1]

This Memorial affords a striking illustration of the sympathy which animated, and still animates, many of those nearest to the Throne in regard to the Boxers and their anti-foreign crusade, and their appreciation of the real sentiments of the Empress Dowager, even in defeat. It also throws light on the Chinese official's idea of heroism in a soldier.

"A spy in Japanese employ, engaged in searching for looted articles in the pawnshops of the district in Japanese military occupation, found among the unredeemed pledges in one shop a watch bearing Baron von Ketteler's monogram. The pawnbroker said that it had been pledged by a bannerman named En Hai, who lived at a carters' inn of the Tartar city. This spy was a man named Te Lu, a writer attached to the Manchu Field Force, of the 8th squad of the 'Ting' Company. He went at once and informed the Japanese, who promptly sent a picquet to the inn mentioned. Two or three men were standing about in the courtyard, and the soldiers asked one of them whether En Hai was there. 'I'm the

---

1. This Memorial was never published officially, and Tzŭ Hsi refrained from issuing a Rescript thereto; it was forwarded by an official with the Court at Hsi-an to one of the vernacular papers at Shanghai, which published it.

man,' said he, whereupon they took him prisoner. Under examination, En was perfectly calm and showed no sort of emotion.
The presiding Magistrate enquired 'Was it you who slew the German Minister?' He replied 'I received orders from my Sergeant to
kill every foreigner that came up the street. I am a soldier, and I
only know it is my duty to obey orders. On that day I was with
my men, some thirty of them, in the street, when a foreigner
came along in a sedan chair. At once I took up my stand a little to
the side of the street, and, taking careful aim, fired into the chair.
Thereupon the bearers fled; we went up to the chair, dragged
the foreigner out, and saw that he was dead. I felt a watch in
his breast pocket and took it as my lawful share; my comrades
appropriated a revolver, some rings and other articles. I never
thought that this watch would lead to my detection, but I am
glad to die for having killed one of the enemies of my country.
Please behead me at once.'

"The interpreter asked him whether he was drunk at the time.
He laughed and said, 'Wine's a fine thing, and I can put away
four or five catties at a time, but that day I had not touched a
drop. Do you suppose I would try to screen myself on the score
of being in liquor?' This En Hai appears to have been an honest
fellow; his words were brave and dignified, so that the bystanders all realised that China is not without heroes in the ranks of her
army. On the following day he was handed over to the Germans,
and beheaded on the scene of his exploit. We, your Memorialists, feel that Your Majesties should be made acquainted with his
meritorious behaviour, and we therefore report the above facts.
We are of opinion that his name should not be permitted to fall
into oblivion, and we trust that Your Majesties may be pleased to
confer upon him honours as in the case of one who has fallen in
battle with his face to the foe."

XVIII

IN MEMORY OF TWO BRAVE MEN

THE Memorial of the Censors given in the last chapter, recording the arrest and execution of the Manchu soldier who shot the German Minister defenceless in his chair, took occasion to congratulate the Empress and the nation on possessing such brave defenders; and to do the man justice, he met his end with a fine courage. But with fuller knowledge and a clearer insight, the scholars of the Empire might well put forward claims to real heroism, moral courage of the rarest kind, in the case of Yüan Ch'ang and Hsü Ching-ch'eng, the two Ministers who, as we have shown, so nobly laid down their lives for what they knew to be their country's highest good. So long as China can breed men like these, so long as the Confucian system contains moral force sufficient to produce Stoic scholars of this type, the nation has no cause to despair of its future. We make no apology for insisting on the claims of these two men to our grateful admiration, or for reproducing their last Memorials, in which they warned the Old Buddha of her folly, and, by denouncing the Boxers, braved all the forces of anarchy and savagery which surged about the Dragon Throne. Already their good name stands high in the esteem of their countrymen. *Et prevalebit*: their courage and unselfish patriotism have been recognised by their canonisation in the Pantheon of China's worthies, under an Edict of the present Regent.

Shortly after their execution the following circular letter *pour faire part* was addressed by the sons of Yüan Ch'ang to the relatives and friends of the family: —

Notice sent by the Yüan family to their relatives regarding the death of Yüan Ch'ang, September, 1900.

After the usual conventional formulæ of grief and self-abasement, this circular letter proceeds as follows: —

"We realise that it was because of his outspoken courage in resisting the evil tendencies of the times that our parent met his untimely death, and we now submit the following report of the circumstances for the information of our relatives and friends.

"When, in the 5th Moon of this year, the Boxer madness commenced, our late father, in his capacity as a Minister of the Foreign Office, felt extremely anxious in regard to the situation, and his anxiety was shared by his colleague, Hsü Ching-ch'eng. On three occasions when the Princes and Ministers were received in audience, my father expressed his opinion to the Throne that the Boxers were utterly unreliable. 'I have been in person,' he said, 'to Legation Street, and have seen the corpses of Boxers lying on all sides. They had most certainly been shot, proving that their unholy rites availed them nothing. They should be exterminated and not used as Government forces.' On hearing this advice, the Emperor, turning to Hsü Ching-ch'eng, enquired whether China is strong enough to resist the foreigners or not, and other questions bearing on the position of the Foreign Powers abroad. Hsü replied without hesitation that China was far too weak to think of fighting the whole world. His Majesty was so much impressed by what he had heard that he caught hold of Hsü by the sleeve and seemed much distressed. Hsü sorrowfully left the presence, and proceeded with our father to draft the first of their joint Memorials.

"Later on, when the bombardment of the Legations was in full swing, our father observed to Hsü, 'This slaughtering of Envoys is a grave breach of all international law. If the Legations are destroyed and the Powers then send an expedition to avenge them, what will become of our country? We must oppose this folly, you and I, even at the risk of our lives.' So they put in their second Memorial, which never appeared in the Gazette, but which so frightened the Boxer princes and Ministers that they slackened for a while in their attacks on the foreigners. The preservation of the Legations on this occasion was really due to this Memorial, and from this moment the enemies of Hsü and our father became more than ever bent on revenge.

"In the last few days of the 6th Moon (July 15th to 25th) the foreign armies were massing for their march on Peking, and our father said to Hsü, 'We are only waiting for death. Why should we delay it any longer?' So they handed in their third Memorial. In this document they declared that the situation was becoming desperate, that even the Princes of the Blood and the Ministers of the Grand Council had come to applaud these Boxers, and to assist in deceiving their Majesties. There was only one way left to avoid dire peril and hold back the foreign armies, and that was to put an end to these Boxers, and to do this it was necessary to begin by beheading their leaders among the Princes and Ministers. Having sent in this Memorial, our father said to our mother 'Things have now come to such a pass that, whether I speak out or keep silence, my death is certain. Rather than be murdered by these treacherous Ministers, I prefer to die at the hands of the public executioner. If only by my death I can convince the Throne of the peril of the situation, I shall die gladly.'

"We all crowded round our father and wept. Calmly he spake to us, saying, 'I am giving my life for the State. What other thought have I now? You must decide for yourselves whether you will remain in Peking or return to our home in the south.' He then gave us a solemn admonition in regard to our duties of loyalty and patriotism.

"On the second day of the 7th Moon, (July 27th) he was arrested and taken to the Board of Punishments. Next day, at 1 P.M., 'his duty was finally consummated.' The execution ground was crowded with a mob of Boxers. Angrily some of them asked him why he had borne a grudge, and spoken evil, against the 'Patriotic Harmony Militia.' Our father mockingly answered 'A statesman speaks out in obedience to a sense of duty. How should such as you understand?'

"We were informed by the gaolers that our father and Hsü had chatted quietly and contentedly in prison. They had asked for paper and ink, and had written over twenty sheets, but this document was found by the Boxers and burned. Was it, we wonder, a valedictory Memorial to the Throne, or a last mandate to their families? We cannot say, and we shall never know. Alas, alas, that we, undutiful sons as we are, should have to bear this crowning sorrow! We have failed in our duty both as sons and as men. Our mother still survives, and our father's burial remains to be attended to, so that we feel bound to go on, drawing the breath of pain, so as to perform our duty to our lamented sire. On the 8th of this Moon we propose to carry his remains to a place of temporary sepulture in the Garden of 'Wide Friendship' at Hangchow, and shall escort our mother to her home. We shall set up the tablet of our father in a building adjoining his temporary grave, and there weep and lament."

If to meet an undeserved doom with high courage is heroism, then these men were indeed heroes. In reading their Memorials — and especially the last of them — one is inevitably and forcibly reminded of the best examples in Greek and Roman history. In their high-minded philosophy, their instinctive morality and calm contemplation of death, there breathes the spirit of Socrates, Seneca and Pliny, the spirit which has given European civilisation its classical models of noble fortitude and many of its finest inspirations, the spirit which, shorn of its quality of individualism, has been the foundation of Japan's greatness. In the last

of these three Memorials, their swan-song, there rings the true
heroic note, clear-seeing, earnest and fearless. The first, though
forwarded in the name of Yüan alone, was drafted conjointly
with Hsü Ching-ch'eng. Hsü, well-known in diplomatic circles
by his having been Minister in St. Petersburg and Berlin, had
not the same high reputation for personal integrity and disinterested patriotism as his friend, but whatever his former failings,
he made full amends by the unflinching nobility of purpose that
led to his death.

Yüan Ch'ang's First Memorial against the Boxers,
Dated 20th June, 1900.

"Ever since the 16th day of the Moon (June 12th), when the
Boxers first burst into Peking, your Majesties have been giving audience daily to all the Princes and Ministers of State. The
weight of the nation's sorrow has afflicted your Sacred Persons,
and you have sought the advice of us, your humble servants,
in your anxious desire that a policy may be devised whereby
peace should be restored to the shrines of your ancestors and to
the Chinese people. But we have failed so far to avert calamity,
and thus to bring comfort to our sorrowing Sovereigns: grievous indeed are our shortcomings, which fill us with shame and
dismay.

"Humbly I recall to your Majesties' memories a Decree which
was issued in the 7th Moon of the 13th year of Chia-Ch'ing. Therein it is recorded that, in the provinces of Shantung and Honan,
a dangerous conspiracy had been organised by evil-doers under
the name of the 'Eight Diagram' Society. These latter day Boxers
are, in fact, merely the descendants of the 'White Lily' sect, and
your Majesties have already decreed their extermination. It was
only last year that the District Magistrate of Wu Chiao, in Shantung, drew up a memorandum giving a very full account of this
sect, and two months ago the Governor of Shantung (Yüan Shih-
k'ai), replying to your Majesties' enquiries, reported that these

Boxers were in no way deserving of Imperial favour, and could never be enrolled as Government troops. No statement could be more explicit. Furthermore, the ex-Governor, Yü Hsien, reporting in connection with the case of a leader of this sect named Chu Hung-teng, or 'Chu of the Red Lamp,' stated that this impostor claimed to be a descendant of the Ming Dynasty; he had so worked upon the ignorant people that the whole district was in a state of unrest, and these treasonable proceedings increased and spread until the Imperial forces arrested and executed the ringleaders. Their purely mythical claims to invulnerability were clearly disproved by the fact that their execution presented no difficulties.

"When seeking information on this subject last year, I was informed by General Ch'eng Wen-ping that five years ago (in 1895) he was stationed at a post on the Chihli frontier, infested by robbers, who there went by the name of the 'Golden Bell' Society, and were brothers of the 'Golden Lamp.' On one occasion some fifty of these men desired to join General Ch'eng's forces, but upon his putting their alleged powers to the test, by firing bullets at them and stabbing them with swords, blood flowed in the most natural manner, so that these magic workers died. I mention the fact to show the absurdity of this superstition; it proves, beyond doubt, that the organisers of these Societies are dangerous and treasonable rogues, harbouring evil designs against the Dynasty, especially when they claim to be descendants of the Mings. They have, however, collected an enormous following, and should be dealt with as rebels, which they undoubtedly are.

"Last year, in the 11th Moon, 13th day, your Majesties granted me audience, and I reported the above facts, adding that the alleged anti-Christian propaganda of these Boxers was merely a pretext, and that their treasonable aims justified their immediate extermination. Subsequently Yüan Shih-k'ai, then newly appointed Governor, did his duty in suppressing the movement, so that several Boxer societies were broken up or destroyed. Once more peace reigned, so that the gentry and *literati* of the province, who for a time had believed in the Boxers and had accused the Governor of ruthless methods, were forced to admit that he had acted rightly and that they had been misled. Who could have supposed that the suppression of the movement in Shantung would be followed by its spreading and increasing in Chihli? The Viceroy (Yü Lu) must undoubtedly be blamed for this; he has allowed the canker to grow without check, playing the part of an indifferent spectator. Latterly, after these Boxers had murdered the Magistrate of Lai Shui, the Viceroy appeared to realise, for the first time, that their professed campaign against the Christians was merely a cloak for rebellion. He telegraphed, therefore, recommending their suppression. But there were differences of opinion at Court, and nothing was decided. Other districts became speedily affected with the evil, and for no other reason than that the rebels of Lai Shui had escaped without punishment. They grew bolder and bolder, until finally they tore up the railway lines and destroyed the telegraphs throughout the province, although both are Government property, upon which vast sums of the public money have been spent. Deplorable, indeed, that one morning's work of rebels should witness the loss of millions of taels! They have also destroyed many Christian churches, for which the State will have to pay heavily hereafter.

"I humbly submit that this fierce outbreak of the Boxers against Christians is a matter of deadly peril to the Empire. By our laws, Magistrates are expected to administer justice without fear or favour; there is no distinction to be made between Christians and non-Christians, and it should certainly not be permitted that evil-doers should pursue their ends on any plea of religious zeal. And now, within the last few days, these rebels have even dared to invade our Capital, and their armed mob profanes the very chariot wheels of the Throne. Arson and murder are their work; they have burned the churches and attacked the Legations. Your Majesties' Palace is shaking to its foundations, as by an earthquake. For such deeds there is no penalty but death; clemency in such a case were folly.

"On the 20th day of this Moon they set fire to more than a thousand shops outside the Main Gate, so that the wealthiest quarter of the city is now a hideous desert. Nine out of every ten inhabitants are fleeing from the city, and hardly a shop remains open. There is no money forthcoming from the provinces wherewith to pay our troops. Words cannot describe the utter desolation prevailing on all sides. In allowing these rioters to stalk through the land, breathing slaughter and plunder, we were making ourselves a byeword and an object of derision throughout the civilised world. The ministers of the foreign Powers, alarmed by the Boxers' wild threats, have been compelled, by the necessities of their situation, to bring up Legation guards, but these only amount to four hundred and ten men altogether, and the object of their coming is clearly not offensive, but defensive only.

"On the 16th day (June 12th) Ch'i Hsiu and other members of the Grand Council were instructed by your Majesty (the Empress Dowager) to have compliments and expressions of sympathy sent to the foreign Ministers and their wives. This act of benevolent courtesy was gratefully recognised. They were fully alive to the bountiful measure of protection thus extended to them in your Majesty's clemency; it penetrated to their very marrow. The Ministers then informed your Majesty that their Legation guards have been brought up solely as a precaution, and they have no thought of interfering in the domestic affairs of our country. They give the most solemn assurances, invoking the sun as witness and pointing to heaven, that, so soon as these disturbances are at an end, their troops will immediately be withdrawn. There is no reason to suspect them of any treachery or evil purpose. It should be our immediate aim to rid the Tartar city of the presence of these rebels, in order not only to reassure the minds of our own people, but to relieve the anxiety of the foreigners. If we do this, there will be no further talk of the foreign Powers sending more troops; if we crush the rebellion ourselves, there would be no need of foreign co-operation to that end. Surely the wisdom of this course is self-evident." (*Here follow certain suggestions for Police and military measures.*)

"If it be objected that the destruction of so vast a number of Boxers is impracticable, I venture to reply that the present situation has been entirely brought about by a few ringleaders, and that the majority of the Boxers are simply ignorant peasantry. If, on the other hand, it be maintained that these rebels are in possession of magical secrets which confer upon them supernatural powers, I would venture to remind your Majesties of Chang Chio's 'Yellow Turban' sect, which flourished towards the end of the Han Dynasty, and of the historic case of P'an Kuang, the 'head-breaker' of the Yuan Dynasty; both of these men, though possessing supernatural powers, nevertheless lost their heads. One of the principal reasons for the alleged invulnerability of these Boxer bandits is that in the day time they lie low; it is at night that they display activity, and call upon their deities to succour them. All the magical arts which they profess — their incantations, charms, invocations of spirits, table-turning, and the 'five demon' trick — are merely cheap devices of useless sorcery. Let them encounter any lethal weapon, let them be struck by cannon or rifle bullet, and they fall dead upon the spot. Can it be seriously maintained that they are really safe from bullets when it is notorious that a large number of them were shot by the foreign troops on the 17th day of this Moon (June 13th), when they began their attack upon the Legations? Only yesterday over forty Boxers were shot dead in Shuai Fu lane,[1] and their altar was destroyed.

"The population of Peking numbers close upon a million, and, with the exception of these wretched mobs or Boxers, they are all loyal to the Throne and law-abiding. The capture and execution of these Boxers would vindicate the majesty of the law, and tranquillise the minds of the people; the courage of the rebels would wane as that of the respectable community increased.

---

1. A lane four hundred yards north of the glacis which now surrounds the Legation quarter.

Once rid Peking of the Boxers, and the Legations will gratefully recognise the efficacy of your Majesty's divine protection, and their feelings towards you will be as towards a second Creator. The reinforcements of the foreign guards could then reasonably be stopped, or withdrawn, at an early date, there being clearly no further necessity for their presence.

"In conclusion it is written in the Book of Ceremonies of the Chou Dynasty 'that the existence of anarchy in a State necessitates the adoption of the death penalty'; also in the Canon of History it is written 'that there is a time when the infliction of capital punishment becomes a sacred duty.' It would therefore appear to be clearly proved that these Boxers should properly be exterminated, and that any further continuance of procrastination or of evasive measures, such as their enrolment in the army, will be utterly unavailing. The foreign Powers are strong, and their indignation has reached extreme limits. Should they now unite in measures of retaliation, indescribable disasters await us. Instead of allowing the foreigners to suppress the Boxers, which would mean much fighting and bloodshed in and around Peking, the slaughter of many innocent persons ('jade and common stone perishing together in one catastrophe'), let us rather suppress the movement ourselves, and thus close the mouths of our detractors and those who criticise our Empire. Thus only will the ancestral shrines escape desecration, and the people enjoy untold benefits.

"The Grand Secretary, Jung Lu, is patriotic and loyal. If your Majesties will but grant him full powers, success will speedily be attained. Diplomatic difficulties can easily be overcome by careful attention to the exigencies of the moment. Urging upon your Majesties the essential fact that in undivided control of authority lies our only safeguard against dire catastrophe, I now beg humbly to submit this my Memorial, laying bare my innermost feelings, and ask that your Majesties' divine wisdom may consider and decide the matter."

The Second Memorial of Yüan Ch'ang and Hsü Ching-ch'eng,
July 8th.

"Ever since, on the 24th day of last Moon, the German Minister von Ketteler was killed by the Boxers, the latter have been besieging the Legations, and the Kansuh troops under Tung Fu-hsiang have been their willing accomplices in perpetrating every kind of evil. Countless is the number of our people, residing near the Legations, who have suffered death at their hands. Practically every house in the eastern quarter of the city, whether public or private property, has been mercilessly plundered.

"The Boxers originally proclaimed that their mission was to pay off old scores against the Christians; they then proceeded to include the Legations in their attacks. From the Legations they have extended their sphere of activity, directing their operations against our officials and the common people. That a mutinous soldiery and mobs of rebels should be permitted to run riot over our Capital, and work their evil will upon the people, is indeed a circumstance unparalleled in our history.

"When the siege began it was their boast that, within twenty-four hours, not a single Legation would remain standing, nay more, Tung Fu-hsiang has repeatedly boasted that they are already nothing more than a heap of ashes. As a matter of fact, however, nearly a month has passed, and whereas scarcely a foreign soldier has been killed, the entire Legation quarter lies strewn with the corpses of these Boxers. Where now the proud boast, with which they deluded simple folk, that their magic arts rendered them immune from bullet wounds? If, after a month's effort, fifty thousand bandits are unable to capture a few Legations garrisoned by less than four hundred foreigners, we can form a fairly accurate estimate of their value and prowess. Who would ever dream of using the services of such heroes to check foreign aggression?

"It may perhaps be suggested that genuine Boxers would show very different results in their country's service, and that those who have been guilty of murder and arson are not really Boxers at all, but outsiders and charlatans, having no legitimate connection with the cult. But we submit that if the society has been so disorganised as to be divided into real and counterfeit members, and if the latter are permitted with the tacit consent of the former, to commit every kind of atrocity, it seems clear that the genuine Boxer himself is a thoroughly disreputable person.

"Moreover, the Throne has expressly forbidden them to take up arms and to continue their devastation with fire and sword; they have been ordered to disband and leave Peking. Nevertheless, they ignore these orders and continue in their wicked ways. Whether genuine or counterfeit, these Boxers vie with one another in flouting the law of the land. Their incorrigible wickedness renders them one and all deserving of death; the leniency shown them has but increased their arrogance, and the number of these evil-doers has grown by reason of the tolerance extended to them.

"In a previous Memorial we urged that the Grand Secretary Jung Lu should be given full powers, with instructions to adopt such severe measures as might be necessary for the suppression of this movement, but your Majesties declined to follow our advice. To-day the danger has grown infinitely greater, and we feel it therefore our bounden duty to lay before your Sacred intelligence our crude and humble views even though, in doing so, we incur the risk of death for our temerity. We bear in mind the words of the Spring and Autumn classic, 'in time of war the persons of Envoys are inviolate.' By the international law of European countries, foreign Ambassadors are regarded as semi-sacred personages: whosoever treats them wrongfully commits a wrong against the State which they represent. If these Boxer bandits be permitted to destroy the Legations and to slay the foreign Ministers, the Powers will undoubtedly consider this a monstrous outrage, and will unitedly make any sacrifice in order to avenge it. The foreign troops at present in Peking are but few in number, but there are great armies to take their place. That China should attempt to fight the entire world means, in our humble opinion, not the defeat only, but the complete annihilation of the Empire. For the past sixty years China has made treaties with Foreign Powers, and has permitted European missionaries to come amongst us for the propagation of their religion. It is true that their converts take advantage of their position to act unjustly to their fellow-countrymen and to insult them. It is true that they frequently rely upon missionary protection to secure their evil ends, but it is also true that our local officials often treat these matters with apathy and injustice. The non-Christians are therefore filled with resentment and indignation against the Christians, a result very largely due to lack of ability and energy on the part of the Government officials. This is the case at present; we are but reaping the harvest of past faults. Your Memorialists do not venture to suggest that the cause of this ill-feeling against the Christians lies chiefly with the common people, but it cannot be denied that China loses dignity in the eyes of the world while our Government remains indifferent to these continual feuds between Christians and non-Christians. It is inadmissible that the local officials should excuse themselves for inaction on the plea that they cannot maintain order. For example, if two neighbours in a village are on bad terms, and a clan fight takes place between their respective families and followers, and if, as the result, property is destroyed and lives lost in the fray, reparation will be claimed by the aggrieved party, not from the actual fighters, but from the heads of the other clan, with whom rests the responsibility for law and order. In matters of State the same principle holds good.

"The religions of Europe may be divided into Catholic and Protestant; the priests of the former sect are known as "spiritual fathers" while the latter are called "pastors." These Boxer brigands class all foreign religions alike, making no difference between sect and sect; but the Russians are of the Greek church, while the Japanese are Buddhists. Neither of these nations has hitherto sent missions to the interior of China, a fact which these

Boxers completely ignore. To them, the mere sight of a foreign costume, or the hearing of words in a foreign tongue, immediately evokes their war cry of "hairy devils," who must be exterminated. It is clear that all right principles of conduct render such an attitude unjust, while our weakness as a nation renders it inexpedient; and we would ask your Majesties to remember that China has also sent its Envoys on foreign missions. If the Powers, enraged by the massacre of their Envoys, should retaliate by killing ours, will it not be said that China has dealt the fatal blow to her own Ministers by the hand of another? Your Majesty, the Empress Dowager, has just sent presents to the foreign Legations — fruit, vegetable, flour and rice — in order to 'display your beneficence to the strangers from afar.'[1] Nevertheless these Boxer brigands, trusting in their arrogant Commander (Tung Fu-hsiang) as a tower of strength, continue their attacks upon the Legations. If the foreigners come to suspect the Throne of hypocritical displays of friendliness while secretly encouraging this bombardment, who will hereafter believe any statement that may be put forward as to your innocence and disapproval of all this carnival of slaughter, however earnestly you may proclaim it to a doubting world?

"If, on the other hand, the Legations successfully maintain their resistance until peace is eventually restored, then the foreign Envoys, who have received your Majesty's bounty, will naturally feel bound, in common gratitude, to advise their Governments that the Boxers alone were responsible for the siege, which no foresight could have prevented, and that your Majesties are to be acquitted of all blame for the growth of this movement. By a wise course of action at this juncture, the suspicions of foreign Powers may be lulled, and a very great advantage gained at very little trouble to ourselves. It will thus be easy to restore harmonious relations. But if the Legations are utterly destroyed and every foreign Minister put to the sword, by what means can the outside world ever learn of your Majesty's present thoughtful

---

1. Quotation from Confucius.

generosity? It will be quite vain to hope that, without supporting evidence, the Throne will ever be able to persuade the foreign Powers of its innocence. They are now pouring in troops on the plea of suppressing the rebellion on behalf of China. There are many who believe that this is merely an excuse for obtaining a permanent foothold on Chinese territory; only the most credulous persons believe in the sincerity of the professed motives of foreigners. We, your Memorialists, have not wisdom sufficient to fathom their real object, but we maintain that these lawless Boxer mobs should long since have been wiped out of existence. Why should it be necessary to wait until foreign Powers demand their extermination, and, above all, why wait until those Powers take in hand themselves a matter with which we should have dealt?

"Thoroughly convinced that China's only hope of preserving her integrity lies in the preservation of the Legations, we now ask that a strong Decree be issued, censuring Tung Fu-hsiang and commanding the withdrawal of his troops from Peking; he should under no circumstances be permitted to approach the Legation quarter any more. It should be clearly laid down that any of these Boxers or of their followers who may continue the attack on the Legations will at once be executed. By withdrawing the support of the Government troops from the Boxers, the destruction of the latter will be greatly facilitated. At the same time we earnestly request that Jung Lu be authorised to expel every Boxer from Peking within a given limit of time, so as to save the State from a danger which is 'scorching its very eyebrows,' and to prevent any recurrence of these troubles.

"We are aware that the clear light of Heaven is temporarily obscured by this very plague of locusts, and that our plain speaking may very well be our own undoing. But since, in all humility, we realise that China is like a sick man whose every breath may be his last, our fear in speaking weighs less heavily with us than our sense of duty. Therefore, knowing that we face death in so doing, we submit this our Memorial, and humbly beg that your Majesties may honour us by perusing it."

*Extract from the third and last of the three Memorials by Yüan Chang
and Hsü Ching-Ch'eng, 23rd July, 1900.*

"We, your Memorialists, now humbly desire to point out that
it is more than a month since our sacred Capital was given over
to anarchy, a state of affairs which has reacted throughout the
entire Empire. We now stand confronted by the prospect of a war
with the whole civilised world, the conclusion of which can only
be an unparalleled catastrophe.

"In the reign of Hsien-Feng the Taiping and Mahomedan rebels devastated more than ten provinces, and the uprising was not
quelled until ten years had passed. In the reign of Chia-Ch'ing
the rebellion of the 'White Lily' sect laid waste three or four provinces. It is recorded in the history of these wars that, only after
the most heroic efforts, and with the greatest difficulty, the Imperial armies succeeded in restoring order. But these rebellions, in
comparison with the present Boxer rising, were mere trifling ailments: the State to-day stands threatened with mortal sickness.
For on the former occasions everyone, from the Throne downwards to the lowest of the people, was fully aware that the Taipings were rebels; but to-day some of the highest in the land look
upon the Boxers as patriots, so that even those who know them
to be rebels are afraid to confess the truth. Our folly is bringing
down upon us the ridicule and hatred of every foreign country.
When this movement began, these men were ignorant peasants,
unversed in military matters; they drew after them large numbers of criminals by proclaiming as their watchword 'Prop up the
Dynasty and slay the foreigner.' But what is the rational interpre-
tation of this watchword? If we are to take it as meaning that every native of China who treads the soil of our country and lives
on its fruits should be imbued with feelings of deep gratitude for
the benevolent and virtuous rule which the present Dynasty has
maintained for over two centuries, and would gladly repay the
bounty of the Throne by fighting for its protection, we heartily
endorse the sentiment. But if it means that, at a great crisis in our

national history, it is the mob alone that has power sufficient to 'prop up' our tottering fortunes and restore tranquillity, should we not remember that he who can 'prop up' can also throw down, and that the power which 'props up' the Dynasty may overthrow it to-morrow? What is this then but treasonable language, and who so greatly daring as to utter sentiments of this kind?

"We, your Memorialists, unworthy as we are, fully realise that the foreigners, who make their nests in the body of our State, constitute a real danger. But the way to deal with the situation is to reform the administration in the first place, and in the meanwhile to deal most cautiously with all questions of foreign policy. We must bide our time and select a weak opponent; by this means our strength might in due course be displayed, and old scores paid off.

"If foreign nations had gratuitously invaded our country, we should be the first to welcome as loyal patriots everyone who should take up arms and rush into the fray, however feeble his efforts. But to-day, when the Throne's relations with foreign States were perfectly friendly, this sudden outcry of 'Slay the foreigner' is nothing but a wanton provocation of hostilities on all our frontiers. Foolishness of this kind is calculated to destroy our Empire like a child's toy. Besides, when they talk of slaying the foreigner, do they mean only the foreigners in China, or the inhabitants of every State within the five Continents? The slaughter of Europeans in China would by no means prevent others taking their places. But if the meaning of this watchword is that they propose to make a clean sweep of every non-Chinese inhabitant on the face of the earth, any fool can see the utter impossibility of their programme. It seems almost incredible that Yü Hsien, Yü Lu and other Viceroys should not be capable of realising such simple facts as these. Yü Lu in particular has gathered around him the Boxer chiefs, and treats them as honoured guests. Thousands of the most notorious villains throng into his official residence, and are freely admitted on presenting a card bearing the title of 'Boxer.' These men sit by the side of the Viceroy on his judgment-seat, bringing the authority of the Throne into contempt, and insulting the intelligence of all educated men. Abominable scoundrels like the Boxer chiefs, Chang Te-ch'ang and Han Yi-li, men formerly infamous throughout their province, and now known in Peking itself as a scourge, have actually been recommended for official posts in a public Memorial to the Throne! Never has there been a case of a Viceroy so flagrantly hoodwinking his Sovereign.

"In regard to Yü Lu's Memorials reporting his military success at Tientsin, we have caused careful inquiry to be made from many refugees, and they one and all deny the truth of these reports. On the contrary they unanimously assert that many thousands of our troops have been slain by the foreigners, and they even go so far as to say that the capture of the Taku Forts is entirely attributable to the fact that Yü Lu first permitted the Boxers to attack the foreign Settlements. Their indignation against Yü Lu may possibly lead them into some slight exaggeration in these statements, but, in our opinion, the Viceroy's bombastic reports are of a piece with Tung Fu-hsiang's braggart lies, when he tells your Majesties that he has destroyed the Legations and annihilated their defenders. Tung Fu-hsiang is nothing but a Kansuh robber, who, after surrendering to the Imperial forces and obtaining some credit in their ranks, attained his present position by the exceptional favours of the Throne. He should have requited your Majesty's bounty better than by associating himself with treasonable rogues and behaving like a common footpad. His present actions may very well foreshadow some dastardly design hidden in his wolf-heart.

"Yü Lu is one of the highest officials in the Empire, and very different from military men of the Tung Fu-hsiang type. It is hard to explain his blear-eyed stupidity. No doubt he has been led astray by the deceitful representations of your Majesty's Ministers, who have even led the Throne to depart from the path of wisdom formerly followed. It is these Ministers who are entirely to blame.

"The Grand Secretary, Hsü T'ung, was born stupid; he knows

nothing of the needs and dangers of our times. Grand Councillor Kang Yi, an obstinate bigot, herds with traitors and fawns on rebels; Ch'i Hsiu is arrogant and obstinate; while Chao Shu-ch'iao, the President of the Board of Punishments, is crafty-hearted and a master of sycophancy.

"After the first entry of the Boxers into Peking, your Majesties held a special audience, at which all the Princes and Ministers were present, and our advice was asked in regard to the adoption of a policy of encouragement or repression. Your Memorialists replied that the Boxers were anything but patriots and were of no use against foreigners; at the same time we earnestly begged that war should not be lightly declared against the whole world. It was on this occasion that Hsü T'ung, Kang Yi, and the rest of them actually dared to rebuke us in the presence of the Throne. Now, if it were a fact that a hundred thousand newly sharpened swords might suffice to overcome our enemies, we, your Memorialists, by no means devoid of natural feelings of patriotism, would welcome the day when these foreigners might once for all be smitten hip and thigh. But if such a result can by no means be achieved under existing conditions, then it is not we who deserve the name of traitors, but those Ministers who, by their errors, have led the State to the brink of disaster.

"When, in the 5th Moon, your Majesties ordered Kang Yi and Chao Shu-ch'iao to proceed to Cho Chou and order the Boxers to disperse, the latter forced these Ministers to go down upon their knees and burn incense before their altar while they chanted their nonsensical incantations. Chao Shu-ch'iao knew perfectly well the degrading folly of this performance, and openly lamented his part in it; but he had not courage sufficient to contradict Kang Yi, who believed in the Boxers' magic, so that, upon his returning, he joined Kang Yi in reporting to the Throne that the Boxers had all dispersed. But if they have been dispersed, how comes it now that their numbers have been so greatly increased? And how does the Throne propose to deal with Ministers who dare to memorialise in this haphazard manner?

"Tientsin has already fallen, and the foreign troops draw nearer every day. So far, no magical arts of the Boxers have availed us
anything, and it is our deliberate opinion that, within a month,
the enemy will be knocking at the gates of our Capital. We ask
your Majesties to consider the dire consequences of the situation, and the possibility of the desecration of the shrines of your
sacred ancestors. Our minds are filled with horror at the thought
of what may occur. But in the meantime Hsü T'ung, Kang Yi, and
the rest of them laugh and talk together. The ship is sinking, but
they remain splendidly unconcerned, just as if they believed in
the Boxers as a tower of refuge. From such men, the State can
no more derive council than from idiots and drunkards. Even
some of the highest in the land, your Majesty's own Ministers
and members of the Grand Council, have bowed the knee before the Boxers. Many a Prince's palace and a ducal mansion has
been converted into a shrine for the Boxer cult. These Boxers are
fools, but they have been clever enough all the same to befool
Hsü T'ung, Kang Yi, and their followers. Hsü T'ung, Kang Yi,
and the rest of them are fools, but they in their turn have contrived to befool the Princes and Nobles of the Imperial clan. All
our calamities may be directly traced to these Ministers, to Hsü
T'ung, Kang Yi, and the rest of them, and unless your Majesties
will order their immediate decapitation, thereby vindicating the
majesty of the law, it is inevitable that every official in and near
the Court must accept the Boxer heresies, and other Provincial
Governors, following the lead of Yü Lu and Yü Hsien, will adopt
and spread them.

"And not only on Hsü T'ung, Kang Yi, and their followers
should the Imperial wrath fall, but also upon those in high places
whose midsummer madness has led them to protect and encourage the Boxers. Their close relationship to your Majesties, or their
position as Imperial clansmen, should in no wise protect them
from the penalty of their guilt. Thus only can the foreigners be
led to recognise that this Boxer madness, this challenge to the
world in arms, was the work of a few misguided officials, and in

no sense an expression of the intentions or wishes of the Throne. War will then immediately give way to peace, and the altars of our gods will remain inviolate. And when these things have come to pass, may your Majesties be pleased to order the execution of your Memorialists, so that the spirits of Hsü T'ung, Kang Yi, and their associates may be appeased. Smilingly should we go to our death, and enter the realms of Hades. In a spirit of uncontrollable indignation and alarm, we present this Memorial with tears, and beg that your Majesties may deign to peruse it."

XIX

SIDELIGHTS ON TZǓ HSI'S STATECRAFT

YÜAN Ch'ang and Hsü Ch'ing-ch'eng were not alone in warning Her Majesty of the danger and folly of her Boxer proclivities. At the beginning of the crisis Liu K'un-yi, the aged Viceroy of Nanking, sorely distressed at the suicidal policy into which she had been led, wrote and despatched, by telegram and swift couriers, a Memorial, in which he implored her to put a stop to the attacks on the Legations. Tzǔ Hsi's reply to this document clearly reveals the indecision which characterised her at this period, her hopes of revenge on the hated foreigner struggling ever with her fears of impending disaster. The diary of Ching Shan has shown us the woman under the fierce stress of her conflicting emotions and swiftly-changing impulses, of those moods which found their alternating expression in the ebb and flow of the struggle around the Legations for more than a month after she had received and answered the southern Viceroy's Memorial. Of his unswerving loyalty she had no more doubt than of that of Jung Lu, and his ripe wisdom had stood her in good stead these many years. Nevertheless, his advice could not turn her from the path of revenge, from her dreams of power unrestrained. All it could effect, aided, no doubt, by the tidings of the Allies' capture of the Taku Forts, was to cause her to prepare possible by-paths and bolt-holes of escape and exoneration. To this end she addressed direct appeals, a tissue of artless fabrications, to the Sovereigns and chief rulers of the Great Powers, and proceeded next to display her sympathy with the besieged Ministers in the Legations by presents of fruits and vegetables, to which she subsequently referred with pride as convincing proof of her good faith and good will. Her Majesty, in fact, was induced to hedge, while never abandoning hope that Prince Tuan and his Boxers would make good their boast and drive the barbarians into the sea.

The Viceroy's Memorial is chiefly interesting as an example of that chief and unalterable sentiment which actuates the Chinese *literati* and has been one of the strongest pillars of Manchu rule, namely, that the Emperor is infallible, a sentiment based on the fact that complete and unquestioning loyalty to the Throne is the essential cornerstone of the whole fabric of Confucian morality, filial piety, and ancestral worship. While deprecating the Imperial folly, the Viceroy is therefore compelled to ascribe it to everyone but Her Majesty, and to praise the Imperial wisdom and benevolence.

His Memorial is as follows: —

"The present war is due to bandits spreading slaughter and arson on the pretext of paying off a grudge against Christianity; thus we are face to face with a serious crisis. The Powers are uniting to send troops and squadrons to attack China on the plea of protecting their subjects and suppressing this rebellion. Our position is critical and the provinces are naturally bound to look now to their defences. I have already made the necessary preparations, so that if those hordes of foreigners do invade us, we shall resist them with all our might. I feel that our Sovereigns are displaying glorious virtue and that your Majesties are as bountiful as the Almighty. Your indulgence to the men from afar indicates the boundless magnanimity and good faith which animate all your actions.

"At present, the first essential is to make the Throne's embarrassments, which have led up to the present situation, widely known, as well as the quality of consistent kindness with which you are imbued. By so doing, rebels will be deprived of any pretext for further rioting.

"At the beginning of the war, my colleagues and I issued a proclamation bidding the people go about their avocations as usual, and not to give heed to suspicious rumours. A petition has now reached me from Chinese residents abroad to urge effective protection for foreigners in China, so that there may be no risk of revenge being taken on themselves. The language used is very strong, and we have taken advantage of the visit of the foreign Consuls, who suggested certain measures for the protection of missionaries and merchants, to give orders to the Shanghai Taotai to come to an arrangement with them in regard to the preservation of peace in the Yangtsze valley, and at Soochow and Hangchow. This arrangement will hold good so long as they do not invade the region in question. The Consuls have telegraphed to their respective Governments, and I to our Ministers abroad, explaining fully this arrangement. The Germans, owing to the murder of their Minister, were disposed to oppose it, but finally, under compulsion from their colleagues, gave their consent also.

"I respectfully quote your Majesties' decree of the 29th of the 5th Moon (June 25th): 'The foreign Ministers are now in a desperately dangerous position; we are still doing our best to protect them.' The decree proceeds to direct us to guard well our respective provinces and to take such steps as policy may dictate at this emergency. Again, on the 3rd of the 6th Moon (June 29th), your decree to our Ministers abroad states 'We are now sending troops to protect the Legations, but we are weak and can only do our best. You are to carry on the business of your missions abroad as usual.'

"In other words, the Throne is inflicting stern and exemplary punishment on those foreigners in Tientsin who provoked hostilities, while doing its utmost to protect those innocent foreign officials, merchants and missionaries who were not responsible for those attacks. Your benevolence and the majesty of your wrath are displayed simultaneously, manifested as brightly as the sun and moon.

"We have again and again implored you to protect the foreign Ministers: this is the one all-important step which must on no account be deferred a day, not only because your Majesties' own anxiety recognises its necessity, but because the crisis now forces it upon you.

"The Ministers abroad, Yang Ju and his colleagues, have telegraphed to the effect that our first duty is to protect the lives of the foreign Ministers and of all foreigners in China. I therefore humbly ask you to send competent troops to protect the Legations in Peking, and by so doing to protect the lives of your own Envoys abroad. I also urge you to instruct the provincial authorities to protect all foreigners within their respective jurisdictions, and thereby to protect our Chinese subjects residing in foreign lands. My anxiety is intense."

To this memorial Tzŭ Hsi replied, by express courier and telegram, as follows:—

"Your memorial has reached us. The Throne was reluctant lightly to enter upon hostilities, as we have already informed the several foreign Governments and the various provincial authorities. We have also issued several decrees ordering protection for the Ministers and foreign residents all over China. Hence our ideas seem to be identical with your own.[1] Happily all the Ministers, except Baron von Ketteler, are perfectly well and quite comfortable; only a day or two ago we sent them presents of fruits and viands, in order to show our commiseration. If the Powers now dare to invade your provinces, you must all protect your territories and resist with all your might. Even though at the moment peace may prevail, you must make most strenuous preparations against possible emergencies. In a word, we will not willingly be the aggressors. You are to inform our various Legations abroad of our calm and kindly feelings towards all foreigners, so that they may think out some plan of a peaceful settlement, in the general interest. It is highly desirable that you give no ready ear to vague rumours which are calculated only to lead to further lack of unity. This decree is to be conveyed by special courier, at six hundred *li* (two hundred miles) a day."

A few days before this Decree, *i.e.*, on the 1st of July, Her Majesty

---

1. Tzŭ Hsi was addicted to gentle sarcasm of this kind in Decrees.

had drafted with her own pen an explanatory decree for the edification of the foreign Powers, recounting how the Throne had been led into its present unpleasant situation. It is interesting to note that, ten days before, she had offered rewards for the heads of foreigners in Peking and had sent orders to Yü Hsien to kill every foreigner in Shansi, which he did. But Tzǔ Hsi had studied her classics and knew from her own experience how easily dissension and jealousies could be created among the barbarians.

"Owing to a succession of most unfortunate circumstances, rapidly and confusedly following each other, we are utterly at a loss to account for the situation which has brought about hostilities between China and the Powers. Our representatives abroad are separated from us by wide seas, and besides have no special knowledge of the facts, and they are therefore unable to explain to the respective Foreign Offices the real state of the Chinese Government's feelings. We therefore desire now to place before you the following detailed statement of the facts.

"In the Provinces of Chihli and Shantung there has arisen a certain class of disorderly characters who, in their respective villages, have been wont to practise the use of the quarter-staff and pugilism, combining these exercises with certain magic arts and incantations. Owing to the failure of the local Magistrates to detect and stop these proceedings, the result has been that gradually a state of unrest has shown itself throughout that region until, all of a sudden, the Boxer movement assumed serious proportions. They spread even to Peking, where they were regarded as possessed of supernatural powers, so that they gained vast numbers of followers and universal sympathy. Following in their train the disorderly people of the lower sort raised a cry of 'Death to the Christians!' following upon which, in the middle of the 5th Moon, they proceeded to carry their words into deeds, and to slaughter the converts. The churches were burned, the whole city was in an uproar, and the population passed completely out of our control.

"When the first rumours of the coming disaster were noised abroad, the Legations asked our consent to bring up special guards, which consent, in view of the special necessities of the case, was readily given.

In all some five hundred foreign troops came to Peking, which in itself shows plainly the friendly disposition of the Throne towards all foreign nations. Under ordinary circumstances the foreign Legations and their guards do not come in contact with the local Chinese authorities, and have no relations with them, friendly or otherwise; but since the arrival of these troops, the soldiers have not confined themselves to the duty of protecting the Legations, but have gone upon the city walls and have even patrolled the outlying parts of the capital, with the result that shots have been exchanged and blood has been shed. Indeed, so great are the liberties which they have taken in the course of their walks abroad, that on one occasion they actually endeavoured to force their way into the Forbidden City, which, however, they failed to do. For these reasons great and widespread indignation has been excited against them, and evil-doers have seized the opportunity to commit deeds of slaughter and arson, waxing daily bolder. At this stage the Powers endeavoured to bring up[1] reinforcements from Tientsin, but these were cut to pieces on their journey from the sea, and the attempt was perforce abandoned. By this time the rebels in the two provinces had become so intermingled with the people that it was impossible to identify them. The Throne was by no means averse to give orders for their suppression, but had we acted with undue haste, the result might have been a general conflagration, and our efforts to protect the Legations might have ended in a dire calamity. If we had proceeded to destroy the rebels in the two provinces, no single missionary or native Christian would have been left alive in either, so that we had to proceed cautiously in this dilemma.

"Under these circumstances we were compelled to suggest the temporary withdrawal of the Legations to Tientsin, and we were proceeding to make the necessary arrangements to this end when the German Minister was unfortunately murdered one morning on his way to the Tsungli Yamên. This incident placed the rebel leaders in a desperate position, like that of the man who rides a tiger and who hesitates whether it be more dangerous for him to continue his ride or to jump off. It became then inexpedient that the proposed withdrawal of the Legations to Tientsin should proceed. All we could do we did, which

---

1. Admiral Seymour's expedition.

was to enforce urgent measures for the due protection of the Legations in every emergency. To our dismay, on the 16th ultimo, certain foreign naval officers from the squadron outside Taku had an interview with the Commandant of the forts, demanding their surrender, and adding that, if their demand were refused, they would take them by force on the following day. The Commandant was naturally unable to betray the trust confided to him, and the foreigners accordingly bombarded the forts and captured them after a vigorous resistance. A state of war has thus been created, but it is none of our doing; besides, how could China be so utterly foolish, conscious as she is of her weakness, as to declare war on the whole world at once? How could she hope to succeed by using the services of untrained bandits for any such a purpose? This must be obvious to the Powers.

"The above is an accurate statement of our situation, explaining the measures unavoidably forced upon China to meet the situation. Our representatives abroad must carefully explain the tenor of this decree to the Governments to which they are accredited. We are still instructing our military Commanders to protect the Legations, and can only do our best. In the meantime you, our Ministers, must carry on your duties as usual, and not pose as disinterested spectators."

Supplementing this Decree, the Empress, possibly instigated by some of the master-minds of the Grand Council, proceeded to prepare the way for a time-honoured, and invariably successful, device of Chinese statecraft, namely, the creation of dissension and jealousy between the Powers, and to this end she addressed telegrams to the Emperor of Russia, Queen Victoria, the Emperor of Japan, and other rulers. It is typical of the infantile *naïveté* of Chinese officials in such matters of foreign policy, that copies of these extraordinary messages, intended solely to mislead public opinion abroad, should have been sent in to the (still besieged) Legations with the cards of Prince Ch'ing, and the Ministers of the Tsungli Yamên.[1] It is certain that these artless telegrams, as well as the conciliatory instructions subsequently sent to China's

---

1. See Dr. Smith's "China in Convulsion".

representatives abroad, were but the outward and visible signs of Tzŭ Hsi's inward and spiritual misgivings caused by the fall of the Taku Forts, the capture of the native city of Tientsin, and the massing of the armies of the Allies for the advance on her capital. If possible, she would therefore make friends in advance among the humane, and invariably gullible, sovereigns of Europe, making good use of her knowledge of their little weaknesses in matters of foreign policy, and be ready to pose in due course as the innocent victim of circumstance and fate. But "in the profound seclusion of her Palace" she continued to hope against hope for the Boxers' promised victories and the fall of the Legations which she was so carefully "protecting."

And here let us briefly digress. Students of modern Chinese history, desirous of applying its latest lessons to future uses, will no doubt observe, that in advising the Throne either for peace or war, all Chinese and Manchu officials (no matter how good or bad from our point of view, how brave or cowardly, how honest or corrupt) agree and unite in frankly confessing to their hatred of the foreigner and all his works. This sentiment, loudly proclaimed by the simple-minded braggart Boxers, is politely re-echoed by the *literati*, and voiced with equal candour by the picked men of the Government, men like Yüan Shih-k'ai, Jung Lu, and Liu K'un-yi. Those who pose as the friends of foreigners merely advocate dissimulation as a matter of expediency. The thought should give us pause, not only in accepting at their current value the posturings and pronouncements of the *monde diplomatique* at Peking, and the reassurances given as to our excellent relations with such-and-such officials, but it should also lead us to consider what are the causes, in us or in them, which produce so constant and so deep a hatred? If we study the Memorials of high Chinese officials for the past fifty years, the same unpleasant feature presents itself at every turn. We may meet with exceptional cases, here and there, like Yüan Ch'ang, who will profess respect for the European, but even his respect will be qualified and never go to the length of intimate friendship.

Our perennial gullibility, that faculty which makes the Chinese classical "allurements" invariably successful with the foreigner, accounts, no doubt, to some extent for the Chinese official's contempt for our intelligence, and for our failure to learn by experience. It is fairly certain that the Boxers of to-morrow will be pooh-poohed (if not applauded) in advance by our Chinese Secretariats, as they were in 1900. But for the Chinese official's unchanging hostility towards us, no such explanation offers, and it is perhaps, therefore, most satisfactory to our *amour propre* to assume that his attitude is dictated by feelings similar to those which inspired Demetrius of the Ephesians, ostensibly fearful for the cult of Diana, but in reality disturbed for his own livelihood.

To return. The following are translations of the telegrams sent under date 3rd July, by order of the Empress Dowager, to the Emperor of Russia, Queen Victoria, and the Emperor of Japan. The text of those which were sent at the same time to the Presidents of the French and American Republics, and which were dated, curiously enough, on the 19th of June (the Taku Forts fell on the 16th), have been published in Monsieur Cordier's most accurate and painstaking work, *Les Relations de la Chine*, Vol. III.

Telegram dated 3rd July: —

"To the Emperor of Russia: — Greeting to your Majesty! For over two hundred and fifty years our neighbouring Empires have enjoyed unbroken relations of friendship, more cordial than those existing between any other Powers.

"Recent ill-feeling created between converts to Christianity and the rest of our people have afforded an opportunity to evil-disposed persons and rebels to create disturbances, and the result has been that the foreign Powers have been led to believe that the Throne itself is a party to their proceedings and is hostile to Christianity. Your Majesty's representative at my Court (M. de Giers) has actually requested our Foreign Office to suppress the rebellion and thus to allay the suspicions of the Powers. But at the time that he made this request, Peking was thoroughly infested with rebels, who had stirred up the people and gained for themselves no small prestige. Not only our soldiery but the mass of the people were burning for revenge against those who practised the foreign religion, and even certain Princes of our Imperial Clan joined in the movement, declaring that there was no room in the Celestial Kingdom for Christianity and the ancient religions of the soil. My chief anxiety has been lest any precipitate action on the part of the Government might lead to some dire catastrophe (*i.e.*, the destruction of the Legations), and I feared, too, that the anti-foreign movement might break out simultaneously at the Treaty Ports in the South, which would have made the position hopeless. I was doing my utmost to find a way out of the dilemma when the foreign Powers, evidently failing to realise the difficulties of our situation, precipitated matters by the bombardment and capture of the Taku Forts: now we are confronted with all the dire calamities of war, and the confusion in our Empire is greater than ever before. Amongst all the Powers, none has enjoyed such friendly relations with China as Russia. On a former occasion I deputed Li Hung-chang to proceed to your Majesty's capital as my special Envoy; he drew up on our behalf and concluded with your country a secret Treaty of Alliance, which is duly recorded in the Imperial Archives.

"And now that China has incurred the enmity of the civilised world by stress of circumstances beyond our power to control, I must perforce rely upon your country to act as intermediary and peacemaker on our behalf. I now make this earnest and sincere appeal to your Majesty, begging that you may be pleased to come forward as arbitrator, and thus to relieve the difficulties of our situation. We await with anxiety your gracious reply."

On the same day the Empress Dowager addressed Her Majesty Queen Victoria in a telegram which was sent in the Emperor's name and forwarded through the Chinese Minister in London. Its text runs as follows: —

"To your Majesty, greeting! — In all the dealings of England with the Empire of China, since first relations were established between us, there has never been any idea of territorial aggrandisement on the part of Great Britain, but only a keen desire to promote the interests of her trade. Reflecting on the fact that our country is now plunged into a dreadful condition of warfare, we bear in mind that a large proportion of China's trade, seventy or eighty per cent., is done with England: moreover, your Customs duties are the lightest in the world, and few restrictions are made at your sea-ports in the matter of foreign importations; for these reasons our amicable relations with British merchants at our Treaty Ports have continued unbroken for the last half century, to our mutual benefit.

"But a sudden change has now occurred and general suspicion has been created against us. We would therefore ask you now to consider that if, by any conceivable combination of circumstances, the independence of our Empire should be lost, and the Powers unite to carry out their long plotted schemes to possess themselves of our territory, the results to your country's interests would be disastrous and fatal to your trade. At this moment our Empire is striving to the utmost to raise an army and funds sufficient for its protection; in the meanwhile we rely upon your good services to act as mediator, and now anxiously await your decision."

Again, in the name of the Emperor and through the Chinese Minister at Tokio, the following message was addressed to the Emperor of Japan:—

"To your Majesty, greeting!—The Empires of China and Japan hang together, even as the lips and the teeth, and the relations existing between them have always been sympathetic. Last month we were plunged in deep grief when we learned of the murder of the Chancellor of your Legation in Peking; we were about to arrest and punish the culprits when the Powers, unnecessarily suspicious of our motives, seized the Taku Forts, and we found ourselves involved in all the horrors of war. In face of the existing situation, it appears to us that at the present time the Continents of Europe and Asia are opposed to each other, marshalling their forces for a conflict of irreconcilable ambitions; everything therefore depends upon our two Asiatic Empires standing firm together at this juncture. The earth-hungry Powers of the West, whose tigerish eyes of greed are fixed in our direction, will certainly not confine their attention to China. In the event of our Empire being broken up, Japan in her turn will assuredly be hard pressed to maintain her independence. The community of our interests renders it clearly imperative that at this crisis we should disregard all trifling causes of discord, and consider only the requirements of the situation, as comrade nations. We rely upon your Majesty to come forward as arbitrator, and anxiously await your gracious reply to this appeal."

These remarkable effusions have been inscribed in the annals of the Dynasty, by order of Her Majesty, those same annals from which all her Boxer Edicts have been solemnly expunged for purposes of historic accuracy. One cannot but hope that, in process of time, consideration of facts like these may cure European diplomacy and officialdom generally of its unreasoning reverence for the Chinese written character, a species of fetish-worship imbibed from the native pundit and aggravated by the sense of importance which knowledge of this ancient language so frequently confers.

These Imperial messages throw into strong relief the elementary simplicity of China's foreign policy, a quality which foreigners frequently misunderstand, in the general belief that the Oriental mind conceals great depths of subtlety and secret information. Looking at these documents in the light of the known facts of China's political situation at that moment, and stripping them of all artificial glamour, it becomes almost inconceivable that any Government should publish to the world and file in its archives such puerile productions. But it is frequently the case that this very kindergarten element in Chinese politics is a stumbling-block to the elaborate and highly specialised machinery of European diplomacy, and that, being at a loss how to deal with the suspiciously transparent artifices of the elderly children of the Waiwupu, the foreigner excuses and consoles himself by attributing to them occult faculties and resources of a very high order. If one must be continually worsted, it is perhaps not unwise to attribute to one's adversary the qualities of Macchiavelli, Talleyrand and Metternich combined. As far as British interests are concerned, one of the chief lessons emphasised by the events of the past ten years in China is, that the reform of our diplomatic machinery (and particularly of the Consular service) is urgently needed, a reform for which more than one British Minister has vainly pleaded in Downing Street.

XX

THE FLIGHT FROM PEKING AND
THE COURT IN EXILE

THE diarist, Ching Shan, has described in detail the flight of the Empress Dowager and Emperor from Peking, before dawn, on the morning of the 15th August. From an account of the Court's journey, subsequently written by the Grand Secretary, Wang Wen-shao, to friends in Chekiang, and published in one of the vernacular papers of Shanghai, we obtain valuable corroboration of the diarist's accuracy, together with much interesting information.

Wang Wen-shao overtook their Majesties at Huai-lai on the 18th August; for the past three days they had suffered dangers and hardships innumerable. On the evening of the 19th they had stopped at Kuanshih (seventy *li* from Peking), where they slept in the Mosque. There the Mahommedan trading firm of "Tung Kuang yü" (the well-known contractors for the hire of pack animals for the northern caravan trade) had supplied them with the best of the poor food available—coarse flour, vegetables, and millet porridge—and had provided mule litters for the next stage of the journey. As the troops of the escort had been ordered to remain at some distance behind, so long as there was any risk of pursuit by the Allies' cavalry, their Majesties' arrival was unannounced, and their identity unsuspected. As they descended from their carts, travel-stained, weary, and distressed, they were surrounded by a large crowd of refugee idlers and villagers, eager for news from the capital. An eye-witness of the scene has reported that, looking nervously about him, the Emperor said, "We have to thank the Boxers for this," whereupon the Old Buddha, undaunted even at the height of her misfortunes, bade him be silent.

Next day they travelled, by mule litter, ninety *li* (thirty-two miles), and spent the night at Ch'a-Tao, just beyond the Great Wall. Here no preparations of any kind had been made for their reception, and they suffered much hardship, sleeping on the brick platform (*k'ang*) without any adequate bedding. But the Magistrate of Yen-Ch'ing chou had been able to find a blue sedan-chair for Her Majesty, who had thus travelled part of the day in greater comfort. Also at midday, stopping to eat at Chü-yung kuan, Li Lien-ying, the chief eunuch, had obtained a few tea cups from the villagers.

On the 16th they travelled from Ch'a-Tao to Huai-lai, a hard stage of fifty *li*. Some of the officials and Chamberlains of the Court now joined their Majesties, so that the party consisted of seventeen carts, in addition to the Old Buddha's palanquin and the Emperor's mule litter. As the *cortège* advanced, and the news of their flight was spread abroad, rumours began to be circulated that they were pretenders, personating the Son of Heaven and the Old Buddha, rumours due, no doubt, to the fact that Her Majesty was still wearing her hair in the Chinese manner, and that her clothes were the common ones in which she had escaped from the Forbidden City. In spite of these rumours the Magistrate of Huai-lai, a Hupeh man (Wu Yung), had received no intimation of their Majesties' coming, and, when the Imperial party, accompanied by an enormous crowd, entered his Yamên, he had no time to put on his official robes, but rushed down to receive them as he was. After prostrating himself, he wanted to clear out the noisy and inquisitive rabble, but the Old Buddha forbade him, saying, "Not so; let them crowd around us as much as they like.

It amuses me to see these honest country folk." Here, after three days of coarse fare, the Empress Dowager rejoiced once more in a meal of birds'-nest soup and sharks' fins, presented by the Magistrate, who also furnished her with an outfit of woman's clothing and suits for the Emperor and the Heir Apparent, for all of which he received Her Majesty's repeated and grateful thanks.

It was here, at Huai-lai, while the Court was taking a day's rest, that Wang Wen-shao came up with them. He was cordially, even affectionately, greeted by the Old Buddha, who condoled with him on the hardships to which he had been exposed, and insisted on his sharing her birds'-nest soup, which, she said, he would surely enjoy as much as she had done after so many and great privations. She rebuked the Emperor for not greeting the aged Councillor with warm thanks for his touching devotion to the Throne.

From Huai-lai, Prince Ch'ing was ordered to return to Peking to negotiate terms of peace with the Allies. Knowing the difficulties of this task, he went reluctantly; before leaving he had a long audience with Her Majesty, who assured him of her complete confidence in his ability to make terms, and bade him adopt a policy similar to that of Prince Kung in 1860.

Wang Wen-shao's account of the first part of the Court's journey is sufficiently interesting to justify textual reproduction.

"Their Majesties fled from the palace at the dawn of day in common carts. It was only after their arrival at Kuan-shih that they were provided with litters. The Emperor and Prince P'u Lun rode on one cart until their arrival at Huai-lai, where the District Magistrate furnished a palanquin, and later on, at Hsüan-hua, four large sedan chairs were found for the Imperial party. It was at this point that the Emperor's Consort overtook their Majesties.

"So hurried was the flight that no spare clothes had been taken; the Empress Dowager was very shabbily dressed, so as to be almost unrecognisable, the Chinese mode of hair-dressing producing a very remarkable alteration in her appearance. On the first night after leaving Peking, they slept, like travellers of the lowest class, on the raised brick platform of the inn, where not even rice was obtainable for the evening meal, so that they were compelled to eat common porridge made of millet. In all the disasters recorded in history, never has there been such a pitiful spectacle.

"It was only after reaching Huai-lai that their condition improved somewhat, but even then the number of personal attendants and eunuchs was very small, and not a single concubine was there to wait upon the Old Buddha. For the first few days' flight, neither Prince Li, nor Jung Lu, nor Ch'i Hsiu (all of them Grand Councillors), were in attendance so that Her Majesty nominated Prince Tuan to serve on the Council. She reviled him at the outset severely, reproaching him for the misfortunes which had overtaken the Dynasty, but as time went on, as he shared with her the privations and troubles of the day's journey, she became more gracious towards him. This was to some extent due to the very great influence which Prince Tuan's wife exercised at Court.

"When I reached Huai-lai, the Court consisted of the Princes Tuan, Ching, Na, Su, and P'u Lun, with a following of high officials led by Kang Yi, and some twenty Secretaries. General Ma's troops and some of the Banner Corps of Prince Tuan formed the Imperial escort; and they plundered every town and village on their line of march. This, however, is hardly remarkable, because all the shops had been closed and there were no provisions to be purchased anywhere.

"To go back for a few days. Yü Lu (Viceroy of Chihli) shot himself in a coffin shop at a place south of the Hunting Park, and Li Ping-heng took poison after the defeat of his troops at T'ungchow. The Court's flight had already been discussed after the first advance of the Allies from T'ungchow towards Peking; but the difficulty in providing sufficient transport was considered insuperable. On the 19th of the Moon a steady cannonade began at about midnight, and, from my house in Magpie Lane, one could note, by the volume of sound, that the attack was steadily advancing closer to the city, and eventually bullets came whistling as thick as hail. The bombardment reached its height at about noon on the 20th, when news was brought that two gates of the Imperial City had been taken by storm. I was unable to verify this report. It was my turn for night duty at the Palace, but after the last audience, I was unable to enter the Forbidden City, as all its gates were barred. It was only at 7 A.M. on the 21st inst. (August 15th) that I was able to gain admittance to the Forbidden City, and then I learned that their Majesties had hurriedly fled. On the previous day five urgent audiences with the Grand Council had been held; at the last of these only Kang Yi, Chao Shu ch'iao, and myself were present. Sadly regarding us, the Old Buddha said, 'I see there are only three of you left. No doubt all the rest have fled, leaving us, mother and son, to our fate. I want you all to come with me on my journey.' Turning to me she then said, 'You are too old. I would not wish you to share in all this hardship. Follow us as best you can later on.' The Emperor expressed his wishes in the same sense.

"By this time it was nearly midnight, and they still hesitated about leaving the city; judge then of my surprise to learn that, at the first streak of dawn, their Majesties had left the city in indescribable disorder and frantic haste. I could not return to my house that day because all the gates of the Imperial City were closed, but at 10 A.M. on the following day, I made my way out of the Houmen.[1] On my way I came across Jung Lu; he had fainted in his chair, and had been forsaken by his cowardly bearers. He said: 'This is the end. You and I never believed in these Boxers; see now to what a pass they have brought the Old Buddha. If you see Her Majesty, tell her that I have gone to rally the troops, and that, if I live, I will join her later on.'

"After leaving Jung Lu, I made my way to a little temple which lies midway between the North and the North-West Gates of the city, and there I rested a while. It was the opinion of the Abbot in charge that the foreigners would burn every temple of the city, as all of them had been used by the Boxers for their magic rites, and he said that, in times of dire peril such as this, it was really inconvenient for him to offer any hospitality to visitors. Just at this moment news was brought us that the foreign troops were on the wall of the city, between the two gates nearest to us, and that they were firing down upon the streets; the city was already invested, but the foreigners were not molesting civilians, though they were shooting all 'braves' and men in uniform. As the priest

---

1. The North Gate of the Imperial City.

declined to receive me, I sought refuge at the house of a man named Han, retainer in the Imperial Household, who lived close by. All my chair-bearers and servants had fled. Shortly after noon I heard that one might still leave Peking by the Hsi-chih Men; so leaving everything — carts, chairs, and animals — where they were, I started off at dusk on foot with such money and clothing as I had on my person. The road ahead of me was blocked by a dense crowd of refugees. I took the road by the Drum Tower, skirting the lakes to the north of the Imperial City. Towards evening a dreadful thunderstorm came on, so I took refuge for the night with the Ching family. The bombardment had ceased by this time, but the whole northern part of the Imperial City appeared to be in flames, which broke out in fresh places all through the night. At three in the morning we heard that the West Gates were opened, and that the City Guards had fled, but that the foreigners had not yet reached that part of the city.

"I had intended to travel by cart, but the disorganised troops had by this time seized every available beast of burden. My second son, however, was luckily able to persuade Captain Liu to fetch one of my carts out from the city, and this was done after several narrow escapes. I had left Peking on foot, but at the bridge close to the North-West Gate I found this cart awaiting me, and with it my second son, who was riding on a mule, and the five servants who remained to us following on foot. When we reached Hai-Tien (a town which lies close to the Summer Palace) every restaurant was closed, but we managed to get a little food, and then hurried on after their Majesties to Kuan-shih, where we passed the night. Next day, continuing our journey, we learned that their Majesties were halting at Huai-lai, where we overtook them on the 24th day of the Moon. We expect to reach T'ai-yüan fu about the middle of next week.

"The dangers of our journey are indescribable. Every shop on the road had been plundered by bands of routed troops, who pretend to be part of the Imperial escort. These bandits are ahead of us at every stage of the journey, and they have stripped the country-side bare, so that when the Imperial party reaches any place, and the escort endeavour to commandeer supplies, the distress of the inhabitants and the confusion which ensues are really terrible to witness. The districts through which we have passed are literally devastated."

From Huai-lai the Court moved on to Hsüan-hua fu, a three days' march, and there remained for four days, resting and preparing for the journey into Shansi. The Border Warden at Sha-ho chên had provided their Majesties with green (official) sedan chairs, and the usual etiquette of the Court and Grand Council was being gradually restored. Her Majesty's spirits were excellent, and she took a keen interest in everything. At Chi-ming yi, for instance, she was with difficulty dissuaded from stopping to visit a temple on the summit of an adjoining hill, in honour of which shrine the Emperor Kanghsi had left a tablet carved with a memorial inscription in verse.

At Hsüan-hua fu there was considerable disorder, but the Court enjoyed increased comforts; thanks to the zeal and energy of the local Magistrate (Ch'en Pen). Here the Old Buddha received Prince Ch'ing's first despatch from Peking, which gave a deplorable account of the situation.

The Court left Hsüan-hua on the 25th August (its numbers being increased by the Emperor's Consort with a few of her personal attendants) and spent the night at a garrison station called Tso-Wei. The deplorable state of the country was reflected in the accommodation they found there; for the guards had fled, and the official quarters had all been plundered and burnt, with the exception of two small rooms, evil-smelling and damp. There was no food to be had, except bread made of sodden flour. One of the two available rooms was occupied by the Old Buddha, the other by Kuang Hsü and his Consort, while all the officials of the Court, high and low, fared as best they might in the stuffy courtyard. For once the venerable mother's composure deserted her. "This is abominable," she complained; "the place swarms with insects, and I cannot sleep a wink. It is disgraceful that I should have come to such a pass at my time of life. My state is worse even than that of the Emperor Hsüan-Tsung of the T'ang Dynasty, who was forced to fly from his capital, and saw his favourite concubine murdered before his very eyes." An unsubstantiated report that the Allies had plundered her palace treasure vaults was not calculated to calm Her Majesty, and for a while the suite went in fear of her wrath.

On August 27th the Court crossed the Shansi border, and spent the night at T'ien-chen hsien. The local Magistrate, a Manchu, had committed suicide after hearing of the fall of Moukden and other Manchurian cities; and the town was in a condition of ruinous disorder. Their Majesties supped off a meal hastily provided by the Gaol Warder. But their courage was restored by the arrival of Ts'en Ch'un-Hsüan,[1] an official of high intelligence and courage, who greatly pleased the Old Buddha by bringing her a gift of eggs and a girdle and pouch for her pipe and purse.

On the 30th August the Court lay at Ta-t'ung fu, in the Yamên of the local Brigadier-General. They stayed here four days, enjoying the greatly improved accommodation which the General's efforts had secured for them.

On September 4th, they reached the market town of T'ai-yüeh, having travelled thirty-five miles that day, and here again they found damp rooms and poor fare. But Her Majesty's spirits had recovered. On the 16th, while crossing the hill-pass of the "Flighting Geese," Her Majesty ordered a halt in order to enjoy the view. "It reminds me of the Jehol Country," she said. Then, turning to the Emperor. "After all, it's delightful to get away like this from Peking and to see the world, isn't it?" "Under happier circumstances, it would be," replied Kuang Hsü. At this point Ts'en Ch'un-hsüan brought Her Majesty a large bouquet of yellow flowers, a present which touched her deeply: in return she sent him a jar of butter-milk tea.

On the 7th, the only accommodation which the local officials had been able to prepare at Yüan-p'ing was a mud-house belonging to one of the common people, in which, by an oversight, several empty coffins had been left. Ts'en, arriving ahead of the party,

---

1. At that time Governor-designate of Shensi. He had come north with troops to defend the capital.

was told of this, and galloped to make excuses to Her Majesty and take her orders. Happily, the "Motherly Countenance" was not moved to wrath, and "the divine condescension was manifested." "If the coffins can be moved, move them," she said; "but so long as they are not in the main room, I do not greatly mind their remaining." They were all removed, however, and the Old Buddha was protected from possibly evil influences.

On the 8th September, at Hsin Chou, three Imperial (yellow) chairs had been provided by the local officials, so that their Majesties' entrance into T'ai-yüan fu, on the 10th, was not unimposing. The Court took up its residence in the Governor's Yamên (that same bloodstained building in which, six weeks before, Yü Hsien had massacred the missionaries). Yü Hsien, the Governor, met their Imperial Majesties outside the city walls, and knelt by the roadside as the Old Buddha's palanquin came up. She bade her bearers stop, and called to him to approach. When he had done so, she said: "At your farewell audience, in the last Moon of the last year, you assured me that the Boxers were really invulnerable. Alas! You were wrong, and now Peking has fallen! But you did splendidly in carrying out my orders and in ridding Shansi of the whole brood of foreign devils. Everyone speaks well of you for this, and I know, besides, how high is your reputation for good and honest work. Nevertheless, and because the foreign devils are loudly calling for vengeance upon you, I may have to dismiss you from office, as I had to do with Li Ping-heng: but be not disturbed in mind, for, if I do this, it is only to throw dust in the eyes of the barbarians, for our own ends. We must just bide our time, and hope for better days."

Yü Hsien kowtowed, as in duty bound, nine times, and replied: "Your Majesty's slave caught them as in a net, and allowed neither chicken nor dog to escape: yet am I ready to accept punishment and dismissal from my post. As to the Boxers, they have been defeated because they failed to abide by the laws of the Order, and because they killed and plundered innocent people who were not Christians."

This conversation was clearly heard by several bystanders, one of whom reported it in a letter to Shanghai. When Yü Hsien had finished speaking, the Old Buddha sighed, and told her bearers to proceed. A few days later she issued the first of the Expiatory Decrees by which Yü Hsien and other Boxer leaders were dismissed from office, but not before she had visited the courtyard where the hapless missionaries had met their fate, and cross-examined Yü Hsien on every detail of that butchery. And it is recorded, that, while she listened eagerly to this tale of unspeakable cowardice and cruelty, the Heir Apparent was swaggering noisily up and down the courtyard, brandishing the huge sword given him by Yü Hsien, with which his devil's work had been done. No better example could be cited of this remarkable woman's primitive instincts and elemental passion of vindictiveness.

Once more, during the Court's residence at T'ai-yüan, did the Old Buddha and Yü Hsien meet. At this audience, realising the determination of the foreigners to exact the death penalty in this case, and realising also the Governor's popularity with the inhabitants of T'ai-yüan, she told him, with unmistakable significance, that the price of coffins was rising, a plain but euphemistic hint that he would do well to commit suicide before a worse fate overtook him.

Her Majesty was much gratified at the splendid accommodation provided for her at T'ai-yüan, and particularly pleased to see all the gold and silver vessels and utensils that had been made in 1775 for Ch'ien Lung's progress to the sacred shrines of Wu-T'ai shan; they had been polished up for the occasion and made a brave show, so that the "Benevolent Countenance" beamed with delight. "We have nothing like this in Peking," she said.

Jung Lu joined the Court on the day after its arrival at T'ai-yüan, and was most affectionately welcomed by the Old Buddha, to whom he gave a full account of his journey through Chihli and of the widespread devastation wrought by the Boxers. He had previously sent in the following Memorial which clearly

reflects those qualities which had endeared him to his Imperial
Mistress, and which so honourably distinguished him from the
sycophants and classical imbeciles of the Court:—

"At dawn, on the 21st day of the 7th Moon (15th August) your
Majesty's servant proceeded to the Gate of Reverend Peace (inside the
Palace), and learned that your Majesties' sacred chariot had left for the
West. While there I came across Ch'ung Ch'i,[1] the President of the Board
of Revenue, and we were proposing to hurry after your Majesties, when
we learned that the North-Eastern and Northern Gates of the city had
fallen. So we left Peking by another gate, my first object being to try and
rally some of the troops. But after several conferences with Generals
Sung Ch'ing and Tung Fu-hsiang, I was forced to the conclusion that
our repeated defeats had been too severe, and that, in the absence of
large reinforcements, there was no hope of our being able to take the
field again. Our men were in a state of complete panic and had lost
all stomach for fighting. I therefore left and came on to Pao-t'ing fu,
and lodged there with Chung Ch'i in the "Water Lily" Garden. All night
long he and I discussed the situation, hoping to see some way out of
the misfortunes which had overtaken the State. Ch'ung Ch'i could not
conceal the bitterness of his grief, and on the morning of the next day
he hanged himself in one of the outer courtyards, leaving a letter for me
in which was enclosed his valedictory Memorial to your Majesties, together with a set of verses written just before his death. These I now forward for your Majesty's gracious perusal, because I feel that his suicide
deserves your pity, just as his high sense of duty merits your praise. He
was indeed a man of the purest integrity, and had all the will, though,
alas, not the power, to avert the misfortunes which have befallen us. He
had always looked upon the magic arts of the Boxers with profound
contempt, unworthy even of the effort of a smile from a wise man. At
this critical juncture, the loss of my trusted colleague is indeed a heavy
blow, but I am compelled to remember that the position which I hold,
all unworthily, as your Majesty's Commander-in-Chief, necessitates my

---

1. Tutor of the Heir Apparent, father-in-law of the Emperor T'ung-Chih; his daughter, the
Empress Chia-Shun (A-lu-te), had committed suicide in 1875 (*vide supra*).

bearing the burden of my heavy responsibilities so long as the breath of life is in my body.

"Such makeshift arrangements as were feasible I made for the temporary disposal of Ch'ung Ch'i's remains, and I now forward the present Memorial by special courier to your Majesty, informing you of the manner of his decease, because I hold it to be unfitting that his end should pass unnoticed and unhonoured. Your Majesty will, no doubt, determine on the posthumous honours to be accorded to him.

"It is now my intention to proceed, with what speed I may, to T'ai-yüan fu, there to pay my reverent duty to your Majesty and to await the punishment due for my failure to avert these calamities."

In reply to this Memorial, Tzǔ Hsi conferred high posthumous honours upon Ch'ung Ch'i, praising his loyalty and honesty.

Jung Lu proceeded on his journey, but at a town on the Chi-hli border his wife took ill and died. She had only joined him at Pao-t'ing fu. The Old Buddha welcomed him with sincere affection upon his arrival at T'ai-yüan and raised his secondary wife, the Lady Liu, to the rank of "Fu Jen" or legitimate consort. (This lady had always had great influence with the Empress Dowager, which increased during the exile of the Court, and became most noticeable after the return to Peking.)

Tzǔ Hsi asked Jung Lu for his advice as to her future policy. Bluntly, as was his wont, he replied "Old Buddha, there is only one way. You must behead Prince Tuan and all the rest of the Princes and Ministers who misled you and then you must return to Peking."

An incident, vouched for by a high Manchu official attached to the Court, illustrates the relations at this time existing between the Emperor, the Empress Dowager, and Jung Lu. When the latter reached T'ai-yüan fu, Kuang-Hsü sent a special messenger to summon him. "I am glad you have come at last," said His Majesty. "I desire that you will have Prince Tuan executed without delay."

"How can I do so without the Empress Dowager's orders?"

he replied. "The days are past when no other Decree but your Majesty's was needed."[1]

Jung Lu's position, but for the high favour of the Empress Dowager, would have been full of danger, for he was disliked by reactionaries and reformers alike; surrounded by extremists, his intuitive common sense, his doctrine of the "happy mean" had made him many enemies. Nor could he lay claim to a reputation for that "purest integrity" which he had so greatly admired in his colleague Ch'ung Ch'i. At T'ai-yüan fu, he was openly denounced to the Old Buddha for having connived in the embezzlements of a certain Ch'en Tsê-lin, who had been robbing the military Treasury on a grand scale. Jung Lu had ordered that his defalcations be made good, but subsequently informed the Throne that the money had been captured by the Allies, and the accusing Censor did not hesitate to say that the price of his conversion (brought to his quarters by the hands of a sergeant named Yao) had been forty thousand taels of silver, twenty pounds of best birdnests, and four cases of silk. The Empress Dowager shelved the Memorial, as was her wont, though no doubt she used the information for the ultimate benefit of her privy purse. Jung Lu also received vast sums of money and many valuable presents on his birthday, and at the condolence ceremonies for the death of his wife, so much so that he incurred the fierce jealousy of the chief eunuch Li Lien-ying, who was doing his best at this time to re-feather his own nest, despoiled by the troops of the Allies.

At T'ai-yüan fu, so many officials had joined the Court that intrigues became rife; there was much heartburning as to precedence and status. Those who had borne the burden and heat of the day, the dangers and the hardships of the flight from Peking, claimed special recognition and seniority at the hands of their Imperial Mistress. Each of these thought they should be privileged above those of equal rank who had only rejoined the Court when all danger was past, and still more so above those who were now hurrying up from the provinces in search of advancement.

---

1. An allusion to Kuang-Hsü's order for Jung Lu's summary execution in September 1898.

The chief topic of discussion at audience, and at meetings of the Grand Council, was the question of the Court's return to Peking, or of the removal of the Capital to one of the chief cities of the South or West. Chang Chih-tung had put in a Memorial, strongly recommending the city of Tang-Yang in Hupei, on account of its central position. One of the arguments gravely put forward by the "scholarly bungler" for this proposal was, that the characters "Tang-Yang" (which mean "facing south") were in themselves of good augury, and an omen of better days to come, because the Emperor always sits with his face to the south. Chang's enemies at Court saw in this idea a veiled hint that the Emperor should be restored to power.

But Jung Lu was now *facile princeps* in the Old Buddha's counsels, and at audience his colleagues of the Grand Council (Lu Ch'uan-lin and Wang Wen-shao) followed his lead implicitly. He never ceased to advise the Empress to return forthwith to Peking, and, when at a later date she decided on this step, it was rather because of her faith in his sound judgment than because of the many Memorials sent in from other high officials. During the Court's stay at T'ai-yüan fu, argument on this subject was continual, but towards the end of September rumours reached Her Majesty that the Allies were sending a swift punitive expedition to avenge the murdered missionaries; this decided her to leave at once for Hsi-an fu, where she would feel safe from further pursuit. The Court left accordingly on the 30th September; but as the preservation of "face" before the world is a fundamental principle, with Empresses as with slave-girls, in China, her departure was announced in the following brief Edict: —

"As Shansi province is suffering from famine, which makes it very difficult to provide for our needs, and as the absence of telegraphic communication there causes all manner of inconvenient delays, we are compelled to continue our progress westwards to Hsi-an."

The journey into Shensi was made with all due provision for the dignity and comfort of their Majesties, but the Empress was

MARBLE BRIDGE IN THE GROUNDS OF THE LAKE PALACE.

IN THE GROUNDS OF THE PALACE IN THE WESTERN PARK.

overcome by grief *en route* at the death of Kang Yi, chief patron of the Boxers, and the most bigoted and violent of all the reactionaries near the Throne. He fell ill at a place called Hou Ma, and died in three days, although the Vice-President of the Board of Censors, Ho Nai-ying, obtained leave to remain behind and nurse him. The Old Buddha was most reluctant to leave the invalid, and showed unusual emotion. After his death she took a kindly interest in his son (who followed the Court to Hsi-an) and would frequently speak to him of his father's patriotism and loyalty.

At Hsi-an fu the Court occupied the Governor's official residence, into which Her Majesty removed after residing for a while in the buildings formerly set apart for the temporary accommodation of the Viceroy of Kansuh and Shensi on visits of inspection. Both Yamêns had been prepared for Their Majesties' use; the walls had been painted Imperial red, and the outer Court surrounded with a palisade, beyond which were the quarters of the Imperial Guards, and the makeshift lodgings of the Metropolitan Boards and the officials of the nine Ministries on Palace duty. The arrangements of the Court, though restricted in the matter of space, were on much the same lines as in Peking. The main hall of the "Travelling Palace" was left empty, the side halls being used as ante-chambers for officials awaiting audience. Behind the main hall was a room to which access was given by a door with six panels, two of which were left open, showing the Throne in the centre of the room, upholstered in yellow silk. It was here that Court ceremonies took place. On the left of this room was the apartment where audiences were held daily, and behind this again were the Empress Dowager's bedroom and private sitting-room. The Emperor and his Consort occupied a small apartment communicating with the Old Buddha's bedroom, and to the west of these again were three small rooms, occupied by the Heir Apparent. The chief eunuch occupied the room next to that of the Old Buddha on the east side. The general arrangements for the comfort and convenience of the Court were necessarily of a makeshift and provisional character and the Privy Purse was for a time at a low ebb, so that Her Majesty was much exercised over the receipt and safe custody of the tribute, in money and in kind, which came flowing in from the provinces. So long as the administration of her household was under the supervision of Governor Ts'en, the strictest economy was practised; for instance, the amount allowed by him for the upkeep of their Majesties' table was two hundred taels (about £25) per day, which, as the Old Buddha remarked on one occasion, was about one-tenth of the ordinary expenditure under the same heading at Peking. "We are living cheaply now," she said; to which the Governor replied, "The amount could still be reduced with advantage."

Her Majesty's custom, in selecting the menus for the day, was to have a list of about one hundred dishes brought in every evening by the eunuch on duty. After the privations of the flight from Peking, the liberal supply of swallows' nests and *bêche-de-mer* which came in from the South was very much appreciated, and her rough fare of chickens and eggs gave way to *recherché* menus; but the Emperor, as usual, limited himself to a diet of vegetables. She gave orders that no more than half a dozen dishes should be served at one meal, and she took personal pains with the supply of milk, of which she always consumed a considerable quantity. Six cows were kept in the immediate vicinity of the Imperial apartments, for the feeding of which Her Majesty was charged two hundred taels a month. Her health was good on the whole, but she suffered from indigestion, which she attributed to the change of climate and the fatigues of her journey. For occasional attacks of insomnia she had recourse to massage, in which several of the eunuchs were well-skilled. After the Court had settled down at Hsi-an fu, Her Majesty was again persuaded to permit the presentation of plays, which she seemed generally to enjoy as much as those in Peking. But her mind was for ever filled with anxiety as to the progress of the negotiations with the foreign Powers at the Capital, and all telegrams received were brought to her at once. The news of the desecration of her Summer Palace had filled her with wrath and distress, especially when, in letters from the eunuch Sun (who had remained in charge at Peking), she learned that her Throne had been thrown into the lake, and that the soldiers had made "lewd and ribald drawings and writings": even on the walls of her bedroom. It was with the greatest relief that she heard of the settlement of the terms of peace, subsequently recorded in the Protocol of 7th of September, and so soon as these terms had been irrevocably arranged, she issued a Decree (June, 1901) fixing the date for the Court's return in September. This Decree, issued in the name of the Emperor, was as follows:

"Our Sacred Mother's advanced age renders it necessary that we should take the greatest care of her health, so that she may attain to peaceful longevity; a long journey in the heat being evidently undesirable, we have fixed on the 19th day of the 7th Moon to commence our return journey, and are now preparing to escort Her Majesty, viâ Honan."

One of the most notorious Boxer leaders, namely, Duke Kung, the younger brother of Prince Chuang, had accompanied the Court, with his family, to Hsi-an. The Old Buddha, realising that his presence would undoubtedly compromise her, now decided to send him away. His family fell from one state of misery to another; no assistance was rendered to them by any officials on the journey, and eventually, after much wandering, the Duke was compelled to earn a bare living by serving as a subordinate in a small Yamên, while his wife, who was young and comely, was sold into slavery. It was clear that the Old Buddha had now realised the error of her ways and the folly that had been committed in encouraging the Boxers. After the executions and suicides of the proscribed leaders of the movement she was heard on one occasion to remark: "These Princes and Ministers were wont to bluster and boast, relying upon their near kinship to ourselves, and we foolishly believed them when they assured us that the foreign devils would never get the better of China. In their folly they came within an ace of overthrowing our Dynasty. The only one whose fate I regret is Chao Shu-ch'iao. For him I am truly sorry."

The fate of Prince Chuang's brother showed clearly that both officials and people had realised the genuine change in the Empress Dowager's feelings towards the Boxers, for there was none so poor to do him honour.

Both on the journey to Hsi-an fu and on the return to the Capital, Her Majesty displayed the greatest interest in the lives of the peasantry and the condition of the people generally. She subscribed liberally to the famine fund in Shansi, professing the greatest sympathy for the stricken people. She told the Emperor that she had never appreciated their sufferings in the seclusion of her Palace.

During the Court's stay at Hsi-an fu the Emperor came to take more interest in State affairs than he had done at any time since the *coup d'état,* but although the Old Buddha discussed matters with him freely, and took his opinion, he had no real voice in the decision of any important matter. His temper continued to be uncertain and occasionally violent, so that many high officials of the Court preferred always to take their business to the Empress Dowager. One important appointment was made at this time by the Old Buddha at the Emperor's personal request, viz., that of Sun Chia-nai (ex-Imperial tutor) to the Grand Secretariat. This official had resigned office in January 1900 upon the selection of the Heir Apparent, which he regarded as equivalent to the deposition of the Emperor.[1] Subsequently, throughout the Boxer troubles, he had remained in his house at Peking, which was plundered, and he himself would undoubtedly have been killed, but for the protection given him by Jung Lu. At this time also, Lu Ch'uan-lin joined the Grand Council. When the siege of the Legations began, he had left his post as Governor of Kiangsu, and marched north with some three thousand men to defend Peking against the foreigners. Before he reached the Capital, however, it had fallen, so that, after disbanding his troops, he went for a

---

1. See biographical note, *infra* (Appendix).

few weeks to his native place in Chihli, and thence proceeded to join the Court at T'ai-yüan fu, where the Old Buddha received him most cordially. His case is particularly interesting in that he was until his death a member of the Grand Council,[1] and that, like many other high officials at Peking, his ideas of the art of government and the relative position of China in the world, remained exactly as they were before the Boxer movement. His action in proceeding to Peking with his troops from his post in the south is also interesting, as showing the semi-independent position of provincial officials, and the free hand which any man of strong views may claim and enjoy. The Viceroys of Nanking and Wuch'ang might dare to oppose the wishes of the Empress Dowager, and to exercise their own judgment as regards declaring war upon foreigners, but it was equally open to any of their subordinates to differ from them, and to take such steps as they might personally consider proper, even to the movement of troops. An official, one of the many provincial deputies charged with the carrying of tribute to the Court at Hsi-an, returning thence to his post at Soochow, sent to a friend at Peking a detailed description of the life of the Court in exile, from which the following extracts are taken. The document, being at that time confidential and not intended for publication, throws some light on the Court and its doings which is lacking in official documents: —

"The Empress Dowager is still in sole charge of affairs, and controls everything in and around the Court; those who exercise the most influence with her are Jung Lu and Lu Ch'uan-lin. Governor Ts'en, has fallen into disfavour of late. His Majesty's advisers are most anxious that she should return to Peking. She looks very young and well; one would not put her age at more than forty, whereas she is really sixty-four. The Emperor appears to be generally depressed, but he has been putting on flesh lately. The Heir Apparent is fifteen years of age; fat, coarse-featured, and of rude manners. He favours military habits of deportment and dress, and to see him when he goes to the play, wearing a felt cap

1. Deceased, 26th August 1910.

with gold braid, a leather jerkin, and a red military overcoat, one would take him for a prize-fighter. He knows all the young actors and rowdies, and associates generally with the very lowest classes. He is a good rider, however, and a very fair musician. If, at the play-houses, the music goes wrong, he will frequently get up in his place and rebuke the performer, and at times he even jumps on to the stage, possesses himself of the instrument, and plays the piece himself. All this brings the boy into disrepute with respectable people, and some of his pranks have come to the ears of the Old Buddha, who they say has had him severely whipped. His last offence was to commence an intrigue with one of the ladies-in-waiting on Her Majesty, for which he got into serious trouble. He is much in the company of Li Lien-ying (the chief eunuch), who leads him into the wildest dissipation.[1] My friend Kao, speaking of him the other day, wittily said, that 'from being an expectant Emperor, he would soon become a deposed Heir Apparent'; which is quite true, for he never reads, all his tastes are vicious, and his manners rude and overbearing. To give you an instance of his doings: on the 18th of the 10th Moon, accompanied by his brother and by his uncle, the Boxer Duke Lan, and followed by a crowd of eunuchs, he got mixed up in a fight with some Kansu braves at a theatre in the temple of the City God. The eunuchs got the worst of it, and some minor officials who were in the audience were mauled by the crowd. The trouble arose, in the first instance, because of the eunuchs attempting to claim the best seats in the house, and the sequel shows to what lengths of villainy these fellows will descend, and how great is their influence with the highest officials. The eunuchs were afraid to seek revenge on the Kansu troops direct, but they attained their end by denouncing the manager of the theatre to Governor Ts'en, and by inducing him to close every theatre in Hsi-an. Besides which, the theatre manager was put in a wooden collar, and thus ignominiously paraded through the streets of the city. The Governor was induced to take this action on the ground that Her Majesty, sore distressed at the famine in Shansi and the calamities which have overtaken China, was offended at these exhibitions of unseemly gaiety; and the proclamation which closed the play-houses, ordered also that restaurants and other

---

1. As he had done for Tzŭ Hsi's son the Emperor Tung-Chih.

places of public entertainment should suspend business. Everybody in the city knew that this was the work of the eunuchs. Eventually Chi Lu, Chamberlain of the Household, was able to induce the chief eunuch to ask the Old Buddha to give orders that the theatres be reopened. This was accordingly done, but of course the real reason was not given, and the Proclamation stated that, since the recent fall of snow justified hopes of a prosperous year and good harvests, as a mark of the people's gratitude to Providence, the theatres would be reopened as usual, 'but no more disturbances must occur.'

"The chief eunuch does not seem to be abusing his authority as much as usual at Hsi-an, most of his time and attention being given to the collection and safe keeping of tribute. If the quality and quantity received is not up to his expectations, he will decline to accept it, and thus infinite trouble is caused to the officials of the province concerned.

"A few days before the Old Buddha's sixty-fifth birthday in the 10th Moon, Governor Ts'en proposed that the city should be decorated, and the usual costly gifts should be presented to Her Majesty, but to this proposal Prince P'u T'ung took the strongest exception; 'China is in desperate straits,' he said, 'and even the ancestral shrines and birthplaces of the Dynasty are in the hands of foreign troops. How then could the Old Buddha possibly desire to celebrate her birthday? The thing is impossible.' The matter was therefore allowed to drop. But the Governor is certainly most anxious to make a name for himself, and, in spite of his blustering professions of an independent attitude, he does not disdain to curry favour with the chief eunuch and others who can serve him. They say that he has recently sworn 'blood brotherhood' with Hsin, the eunuch whose duty it is to announce officials at audiences. No doubt it is due to this distinguished connection that he has recently been raised to the rank of a Board President, and therefore entitled to ride in a sedan chair within the precincts of the Court, which, no doubt, he considers more dignified than riding in a cart.[1]

"Tung Fu-hsiang has returned to his home in Kansu, but his troops remain still at Hsi-an under the command of General Teng, who so

---

1. Amongst Chinese officials no characteristic is more common than their jealousy of each other and their promiscuous habit of backbiting and slandering.

greatly distinguished himself in the Mahomedan rebellion.

"It would seem that the Old Buddha still cherishes hopes of defeating the foreigners, for she is particularly delighted by a Memorial which has been sent in lately by Hsia Chen-wu, in which he recommends a certain aboriginal tribesman ('Man-tzu') as a man of remarkable strategic ability. He offers to lose his own head and those of all his family, should this Heaven-sent warrior fail to defeat all the troops of the Allies in one final engagement, and he begs that the Emperor may permit this man to display his powers and thus save the Empire."

XXI

HOW THE BOXER LEADERS DIED

CHINA'S officials may be said to be a class of individualists, incapable, as a rule, of collective heroism or any sustained effort of organised patriotism; but it is one of the remarkable features and results of her system of philosophy that the mandarins, even those who have been known publicly to display physical cowardice at critical moments, will usually accept sentence of death at the hands of their Sovereign with perfect equanimity, and meet it with calm philosophic resignation. The manner in which the Boxer leaders died, who were proscribed in the course of the negotiations for the peace Protocol at Peking, affords an interesting illustration of this fact; incidentally it throws light also on a trait in the Chinese character, which to some extent explains the solidity and permanence of its system of government, based as it is on the principle of absolute obedience and loyalty to the head of the State as one of the cardinal Confucian virtues.

Despite the repeated and unswerving demands of the foreign Powers that the death penalty should be inflicted upon the chief leaders and supporters of the Boxers, the Empress Dowager was naturally loth to yield, inasmuch as she herself had been in full sympathy with the movement. It was only after many and prolonged meetings with her chief advisers, and when she realised that in this course lay her only hope of obtaining satisfactory terms of peace, that she finally and most reluctantly consented, in February 1901, to the issue of a Decree (drafted by Jung Lu) in which she abandoned to their fate those who, with her full knowledge and approval, had led the rising which was to drive all foreigners into the sea. With the knowledge in our possession as to Her Majesty's complicity, and in some cases her initiative, in the anti-foreign movement, it is impossible to read this Decree without realising something of the ruthlessness of the woman and her cynical disregard of everything except her own safety and authority. Even so, however, Tzǔ Hsi could not bring herself at first to comply with all the demands of the Powers, evidently hoping by compromise and further negotiations to save the lives of her favourites, Prince Tuan, Duke Lan and Chao Shu-ch'iao. The Decree, issued in the Emperor's name, was as follows:—

"In the summer of last year, the Boxer Rebellion arose, which brought in its train hostilities with friendly Powers. Prince Ch'ing and Li Hung-chang have now definitely settled the preliminary conditions of the Peace Protocol. Reflecting on the causes of this disaster, we cannot escape the conclusion that it was due to the ignorance and arrogance of certain of our Princes and Ministers of State who, foolishly believing in the alleged supernatural power of the Boxers, were led to disobey the Throne and to disregard our express commands that these rebels should be exterminated. Not only did they not do this, but they encouraged and assisted them to such an extent that the movement gained hosts of followers. The latter committed acts of unprovoked hostility, so that matters reached a pass where a general cataclysm became inevitable. It was by reason of the folly of these men that General Tung, that obstinate braggart, dared to bombard the Legations, thus bringing our Dynasty to the brink of the greatest peril, throwing the State into a general convulsion of disorder, and plunging our people into uttermost misery. The dangers which have been incurred by Her Majesty the Empress Dowager, and myself are simply indescribable, and our hearts are sore, aching with unappeased wrath at the remembrance of our sufferings. Let those who brought about these calamities ask themselves what punishment can suffice to atone for them?

"Our former Decrees on this subject have been far too lenient, and we must therefore now award further punishments to the guilty. Prince Chuang, already cashiered, led the Boxers in their attack upon the French Cathedral and the Legations, besides which, it was he who issued a Proclamation in violation of all our Treaties. (This refers to the rewards offered for the heads of foreigners.) He too it was who, acting as the leader of the savage Boxers, put to death many innocent persons. As a mark of clemency unmerited by these crimes, we grant him permission to commit suicide, and hereby order that Ko Pao-hua shall supervise the execution of these our commands.

"Prince Tuan, already cashiered, was the leader and spokesman of the Imperial Clan, to whom was due the declaration of war against foreigners; he trusted implicitly in Boxer magic, and thus inexcusably brought about hostilities. Duke Lan, who assisted Prince Chuang in drawing up the proclamation which set a price on the head of every foreigner, deserves also that he be stripped of all his dignities and titles. But remembering that both these Princes are our near kinsmen, we mitigate their sentence to exile to Turkestan, where they will be kept in perpetual confinement. The Governor of Shensi, Yü Hsien, already cashiered, believed in the Boxers at the time when he held the Governorship of Shantung; when he subsequently came to Peking, he sang their praises at our Court, with the result that many Princes and Ministers were led astray by his words. As Governor of Shansi he had put to death many missionaries and native converts, proving himself to be an utterly misguided and bloodthirsty man. He was undoubtedly one of the prime causes of all our troubles. We have already decreed his banishment to Turkestan, and by this time he should already have reached Kansu. Orders are now to be transmitted for his immediate decapitation, which will be superintended by the Provincial Treasurer.

"As to the late Grand Secretary, Kang Yi, he also believed in the Boxers, and went so far as to set a price on the lives of foreigners so that, had he lived, he too would have been sentenced to death, but as matters stand, we order that he be posthumously deprived of his rank and summarily cashiered.

"We have already cashiered Tung Fu-hsiang. While permitted to retain his rank as a military official, he cannot escape a certain share of responsibility for the siege of the Legations, although his orders emanated from Princes and Ministers of State; and because of his ignorance of foreign affairs, slack discipline, and general stupidity, he certainly deserves severe punishment. But we cannot overlook the services he has rendered in the Kansu rebellion, and the good name which he bears amongst our Chinese and Mahomedan subjects in that province, so that, as a mark of our favour and leniency, we merely remove him from his post.[1]

"Ying Nien, Vice-President of the Censorate, was opposed to the issue of the proclamation which offered rewards for foreigners' heads, and for this he deserves lenient treatment, but he failed to insist strongly in his objections, and we are therefore compelled to punish him. He is hereby sentenced to be cashiered and imprisoned pending decapitation.[2]

"As regards the Grand Councillor Chao Shu-ch'iao, he had never, to our knowledge, shown any hostility to foreigners, and when we despatched him on a special mission to confer with the Boxers, the report which he submitted on his return showed no signs of sympathy with their proceedings.[3] Nevertheless, he was undoubtedly careless, and we therefore, acting in leniency, decree that he be cashiered and imprisoned pending decapitation.[4]

"The Grand Secretary Hsü T'ung and Li Ping-heng, our Assistant Commander-in-Chief, have both committed suicide, but as their behaviour has been very severely criticised, we order that they be deprived of their ranks; and all posthumous honours granted to them are hereby cancelled.

"The Ministers of the friendly Powers can no longer fail to recognise that the Boxer Rebellion was indeed the work of these guilty officials, and that it was in no way due to any action or wishes on the part of

---

1. It was because of Tung Fu-hsiang's great popularity in Kansu that Her Majesty, fearing another rebellion, hesitated to order his execution.
2. This sentence is equivalent to imprisonment for life.
3. See Ching Shan's Diary pages 262; also cf. pages 328.
4. The Empress Dowager was from the outset most anxious to screen and protect this official, for whom she had a great personal regard. On reviewing his case in the light of later information and current public opinion, it would appear that most of his actions were instigated, if not ordered, by Kang Yi, and that the decision of the foreign Ministers to insist upon his death was taken without any very definite information as to his share of guilt.

the Throne. In the punishment of these offenders we have displayed no leniency, from which all our subjects may learn how grave has been the recent crisis."

As the terms of this Decree still failed to satisfy the foreign Ministers, especially as regards the sentences passed on Prince Tuan and Duke Lan, another Decree, a week later, ordered that both these Manchu leaders should be imprisoned pending decapitation, a sentence which was eventually reduced to one of perpetual banishment to Turkestan. Posthumous decapitation, a grievous disgrace in the eyes of Chinese officials, was decreed as a further punishment upon Kang Yi, while Chao Shu-ch'iao and Ying Nien were ordered to commit suicide. Finally, the Grand Councillor Ch'i Hsiu, and a son of the Grand Secretary Hsü T'ung (who had closely followed in his father's footsteps as the most violent opponent of everything foreign), were sentenced to decapitation, and were duly executed at Peking.

In compliance with the last demands of the Foreign Ministers, a final Decree, the wording of which points clearly to reluctant action under compulsion, restored the ranks and honours of the five officials who had been executed for advising Her Majesty against the Boxers. To revise this sentence without leaving them under some imputation of blame would have involved most undesirable loss of "face," and the Decree therefore observes:—

"When we urged these officials, at a general audience of all our Ministers, to state their views definitely, so that we might judge fairly of the issues, they expressed themselves hesitatingly, and our evil-disposed Princes and advisers were thus able to take advantage of their apparent indecision. This was the cause of their undoing. They were impeached on all sides, and were eventually decapitated. We recall to mind the fact that these five officials always showed considerable ability in handling diplomatic questions, and, as a mark of our favour, we therefore restore to them their original rank."

The Death of Chao Shu-ch'iao. — This Grand Councillor, one of the Empress's favourite Ministers, whom to the last she endeavoured to protect from execution, was originally sentenced only to imprisonment for life. He was confined in the prison of the Provincial Judge at Hsi-an, where his family were allowed to visit him. On the day before the issue of the Decree which sentenced him to imprisonment, the Old Buddha had said, at a meeting of the Grand Council, "I do not really believe that Chao sympathised in the very least with the Boxers; the error that he made lay in under-estimating the seriousness of the movement." This was reported to Chao, who was naturally much elated, and believed that his life would surely be spared. A few days later, however, it was freely rumoured that the foreign Powers were insisting upon his decapitation, and the news created the greatest excitement throughout the city, which was his native place. Some three hundred of the chief men of the city having drawn up a monster petition, proceeded with it to the office of the Grand Council, and begged, in the name of the whole community, that his life be spared. The Grand Councillors were afraid to take the petition to Her Majesty, but, in reply to the deputation, the President of the Board of Punishments (who was related to Chao) declared that his execution would be an act of monstrous injustice.

On the first day of the New Year, these rumours took more definite shape, and on that day Her Majesty's audience with the Grand Council lasted from six to eleven in the morning; but even then no decision had been come to in regard to complying with the demand for Chao's execution. Throughout the neighbourhood of the Drum Tower the streets were packed with a huge crowd, who threatened that they would certainly rescue Chao if he were taken out for execution. So great was the clamour that the Grand Council feared a riot, and they determined, therefore, to beg Her Majesty to permit Chao to commit suicide. This was done, and Tzŭ Hsi reluctantly agreeing, issued the Decree at one o'clock on the following morning, which fixed the hour for reporting his death to Her Majesty at five o'clock in the afternoon of the same day. Governor Ts'en was ordered to proceed to the prison, and read the Decree to Chao, which he did in due form. After hearing it in silence to the end, Chao asked: "Will there be no further Decree?" "No," said Ts'en. "Surely, there must be," said Chao. At this his wife, intervening, said, "There is no hope; let us die together!" She then gave him poison, of which he took a little, but up till 3 P.M. it appeared to have had no effect whatsoever, for he seemed most vigorous, and discussed at great length with his family the arrangements to be made for his funeral. He was much exercised in mind at the effect which his death would have upon the health of his aged mother. All day long his room was crowded by friends and colleagues; the Governor had endeav-oured at first to prevent their coming, but had eventually yield-ed, so that the number of those present was very large. Chao, addressing them, said: "I have been brought to this pass entirely by the fault of Kang Yi." The Governor, observing that his voice sounded clear and firm, and that, at this hour, there were no signs of impending death about him, ordered one of the attendants to give him some opium to swallow. At 5 o'clock, the opium having apparently taken no effect, the attendants were ordered to give him a liberal dose of arsenic, after which he rolled over on to the ground, and lay there, groaning and beating his breast with his hands. Later, complaining of extreme pain, he asked that friction might be applied to his chest, but so strong was his constitution, and so determined his will, that even at 11 o'clock it was evident that there was still no little life left in him. The Governor was much disturbed and distressed, being well aware that the Old Buddha would require some adequate explanation of this long delay in the execution of her orders. "I was to report his death at 5 o'clock," said he, "the man will not die: what is to be done?" The attendants suggested that he should screw up some pieces of thick paper, dip them in strong spirit, and with them close the breathing passages; by this means he would be speedily suf-focated. Ts'en approved of the suggestion, and after five wads of paper had been inserted, death ensued. His wife, weeping bitterly, thereupon committed suicide. To the end, Chao could not believe that the Empress Dowager would allow his death, and for this reason it is probable that he purposely took an insufficient dose of opium in order to gain time for a reprieve.

The Death of Prince Chuang. — Prince Chuang, with his concubine and son, went to Tu Chou, in South Shansi, there to await the decision of the Empress Dowager as to his fate. He lodged in an official house of entertainment. When Ko Pao-hua, the Imperial Commissioner, brought thither the Decree commanding him to commit suicide, it was early in the morning; nevertheless, upon his arrival, crackers were fired, in accordance with etiquette, to greet him. The noise greatly irritated Prince Chuang, who turned savagely upon the attendants, and asked what they meant by making such a noise at such an hour. "An Imperial Commissioner has arrived," they said. "Has he come about me?" asked the Prince. "No," they replied, "he is merely passing through on business." When the Imperial Commissioner was ushered in, the Prince began to ply him with questions about the Court, to which Ko briefly replied. After talking for a little while Ko went off to inspect the premises, at the back of which he found an old temple, in which he selected an unoccupied room to be the scene of Prince Chuang's suicide. From a beam in the roof he hung a silken cord, and, after fastening it securely, he directed the Prefect and the District Magistrate to send some soldiers to keep order. Having made these preparations he returned to the presence of the Prince, and informing him that he had an Imperial Decree to read to him, ordered him to go down on his knees to hear it. The Prince, drawing himself up to his full height, said, "Is it my head that you want?" The Imperial Commissioner made no direct reply, but proceeded to read the Decree to the Prince, who reverently knelt.[1] When the Commissioner had finished, "So it is suicide," said the Prince, "I always expected they would not be content with anything less than my life. I greatly fear that even our Old Buddha will not be allowed

1. In accordance with prescribed custom.

to last much longer." He next asked the Imperial Commissioner to be permitted to bid farewell to his family, which was allowed him. At this moment, his concubine and his son, having learned of the Imperial Commissioner's business, entered the room. The Prince, addressing his son, said: "Remember that it is your duty to do everything in your power for your country; at all costs, these foreigners must not be allowed to possess themselves of the glorious Empire won for us by our ancestors."[1] His son, bitterly weeping, could not reply, while his concubine passed from frantic grief to a swoon. The Prince, unmoved, asked: — "Where is the death chamber?" The Imperial Commissioner replied: — "Will your Highness please to come to the empty room at the back of the house." When the Prince, following him, saw the silken cord hanging from the beam, he turned and said: — "Your Excellency has indeed made most admirable and complete arrangements." With these words he passed the cord around his neck, and in a very few minutes life was extinct.

The Death of Ying Nien. — Ying Nien was an arrant coward. On the day of the issue of the first Decree, ordering his imprisonment at Hsi-an, his family deserted him, and he remained all through the night, weeping, in great distress of mind. To his attendants he complained bitterly that Prince Ch'ing had not intervened to protect him. The next day was the New Year Festival, and as everybody was busy with preparations for the occasion, little heed was paid to him, and he spent the day weeping. Towards midnight his crying suddenly ceased, and on the following morning he was found by his servant, prone upon the ground, his face covered with mud, quite dead. He had choked himself by swallowing mud, but as the Decree ordering him to commit suicide had not actually been issued, the fact of his death was suppressed for forty-eight hours, after which Governor Ts'en was informed, and he reported it to the Old Buddha.

The Decapitation of Yü Hsien. — When the Decree, commanding his decapitation, reached Yü Hsien, he had already started

---

1. He was directly descended from Nurhachu, the conqueror of the Mings.

under escort for his place of banishment, but he was a sick man and could only totter weakly along. On learning the news, he appeared as one dazed, a very different man indeed from that fierce Governor of Shansi, who had displayed such bloodthirsty activity. On the day before his death he was very seriously ill, and when the time came, he was so weak that he had to be supported to the execution ground. On the previous day the leading citizens of Lan-chou fu expressed their desire to offer him a valedictory banquet, but he declined the honour with thanks, expressing his wish to spend his last day in quietude. He wrote a pair of scrolls as an expression of his gratitude for the courtesy thus shown to him, and the elders of the city decided and informed him that the execution ground would be decorated with red cloth, as for a festival, in his honour. Towards evening, notices were placarded in the principal streets, calling on the people to insist upon his being reprieved, but Yü Hsien knew that this was quite useless. He composed a statement of his actions in the form of an official proclamation, maintaining stoutly that his death was to be regarded as a glorious and patriotic end, and bidding the people on no account to interfere with the execution of his sentence. Finally he wrote, with his own hand, a pair of valedictory scrolls, the text of which was widely quoted after his death all over China. The first may be translated as follows:—

"The Minister dies for his Sovereign; wives and concubines die for their lord. Who shall say that this is unseemly? It is sad that my aged mother is ninety years of age, and my little daughter only seven. Who shall protect them in their old age and tender youth? How shall that filial piety be fulfilled which a man owes to his parent? The Sovereign commanded, and the Minister obeyed. I slew others; now, in my turn, am I slain. Why should I regret it? Only one cause for shame have I that I have served my Sovereign all these years, and have held high rank in three provinces, without displaying merit more conspicuous than a grain of sand in the desert or a drop of water in the ocean. Alas, that I should thus unworthily requite the Imperial bounty."

And the second reads: —

"The Minister has by his guilt incurred the sentence of decapitation. At this moment there is no thought in my mind except the hope that my death may be as glorious as my life has been honest.[1] I would far rather die than pine away the rest of my life in degrading imprisonment. I have ill-requited Her Majesty's kindness. Who shall now relieve her grief? I sincerely hope that you, the Statesmen who surround the Throne, may yet find means to restore our fallen fortunes, and that you will honourably fulfil your bounden duty in ministering to the distress of their Imperial Majesties."

On the following day, at one o'clock of the afternoon, Yü Hsien's head was severed from his body, in the presence of a great crowd, which greeted his end with sounds of lamentation.

The Death of Ch'i Hsiu. — Ch'i Hsiu was executed, together with Hsü Ching-yu, outside the wall of the Tartar city, in Peking, early one morning in February, 1901, the execution being witnessed by more than one European. When informed that he was to die, Ch'i Hsiu's only question was: "By whose commands?" and when told that a Decree had come from Hsi-an fu, he said, "It is by the will of the Empress Dowager; I die happy then, so long as it is not by order of the foreigners." This Grand Councillor had been arrested several months before by the Japanese, and Prince Ch'ing had been able to obtain his release on the ground that his aged mother was very ill; but when she subsequently died, he strongly advised Ch'i Hsiu "to make his filial piety coincide with his loyalty by committing suicide." Coming from Prince Ch'ing, the suggestion was one hardly to be misunderstood, but Ch'i Hsiu failed to act upon it, thereby incurring a certain amount of criticism.

---

1. This was no empty boast. Yü Hsien, cold-blooded fanatic that he was, bore a most honourable name for absolute integrity and contempt for wealth. He died in poverty, so miserable, that amongst all his clothes there was not one suit new enough to be fittingly used for his burial robes. His name is still held in high honour by the people of Shansi, who sing the praises of his Governorship, and who claim that his proud spirit it was which protected their Province from being invaded by the foreigners. They erected a shrine to his memory, but it was demolished to appease the foreign Powers.

XXII

THE OLD BUDDHA PENITENT

WHEN the wrath of the Powers had been appeased by the death and banishment of the leading Boxers, and when the Empress Dowager had come to realise that her future policy must be one of conciliation and reform, she proceeded first of all to adjust the annals of her reign for the benefit of posterity, in the following remarkable Edict (13th February, 1901):—

"In the summer of last year, the Boxers, after bringing about a state of war, took possession of our Capital and dominated the very Throne itself. The Decrees issued at that time were the work of wicked Princes and Ministers of State, who, taking advantage of the chaotic condition of affairs, did not hesitate to issue documents under the Imperial seal, which were quite contrary to our wishes. We have on more than one previous occasion hinted indirectly at the extraordinary difficulty of the position in which we were placed, and which left us no alternative but to act as we did. Our officials and subjects should have no difficulty in reading between the lines and appreciating our meaning.

"We have now punished all the guilty, and we hereby order that the Grand Secretariat shall submit for our perusal all Decrees issued between the 24th day of the 5th moon and the 20th day of the 7th moon (20th June to 14th August), so that all spurious or illegal documents may be withdrawn and cancelled. Thus shall historical accuracy be attained and our Imperial utterances receive the respect to which they are properly entitled."

Having thus secured the respect of posterity, Tzŭ Hsi proceeded to make the "amende honorable," (with due regard to the Imperial "face,") for so many of her sins as she was prepared to admit. In another Decree, in the name of the Emperor, which gives a Munchausen account of the Throne's part and lot in the crisis of 1900, and a pathetic description of her own and the Emperor's sufferings during the flight, she makes solemn confession of error and promise of reform. As an example of the manner in which history is made in China, the Edict is of permanent interest and value.

"A PENITENTIAL DECREE
"*26th day, 12th moon of Kuanghsü's 26th year*
(Feb. 13th, 1901).

"Last summer the Boxers sowed the seeds of rebellion, which led to our being involved in a war with friendly Powers. Thereafter, our Capital being thrown into a state of great disorder, we escorted the Empress Dowager, our mother, on a progress of inspection throughout the Western Provinces. To Prince Ch'ing and to the Grand Secretary Li Hung-chang we entrusted full powers, and bade them negotiate with the foreign Ministers for the cessation of hostilities and a Treaty of peace. These Plenipotentiaries having lately telegraphed to us the twelve principal clauses of the proposed protocol, we have consented thereto, but at the same time have instructed them carefully to scrutinise their various provisions in the light of China's ability to fulfil them.

"It having been accorded to us to retrieve our disastrous mistakes, we are in duty bound to promulgate this Penitential Decree, and to let every one of our subjects know how vast and harassing were the perplexities with which the Throne has been beset.

"There are ignorant persons who believe that the recent crisis was partly caused by our government's support of the Boxers; they must have overlooked our reiterated Decrees of the 5th and 6th moons, that the Boxers should be exterminated, and the Christians protected. Unfortunately these rebels and their evil associates placed us in a position from which it was impossible to escape; we exhausted every possible effort of strong remonstrance, appalled at the impending ruin of our Empire. Events moved swiftly until, on the 21st of the 7th moon, our Capital fell; on that day, both Her Majesty the Empress Dowager and ourselves decided to commit suicide in the presence of the tutelary deities of our Dynasty and the gods of the soil, thus making atonement and offering propitiation to the spirits of our nine Imperial ancestors. But, at the critical moment of dire lamentation and confusion, we were seized by our Princes and Ministers, and forcibly led away from that place where bullets fell like rain, and where the enemies' guns gathered thick as forest trees. Hastily, and with souls perturbed, we started on our Western tour. Were not all these disasters caused by the Boxers? The imminent danger of her sacred Majesty, the overwhelming ruin of our ancestors' inheritance, our prosperous Capital turned to a howling wilderness, its ravines filled with the dead bodies of our greatest men: how can it possibly be said that the Throne could protect the rebels who brought such disasters upon us?

"There was, however, an explicable cause for the Boxer movement and for its disastrous results." (*The Decree proceeds here to ascribe blame to local Magistrates for not administering even justice between Christians and non-Christians, and thus producing a state of discontent and unrest, which afforded opportunities to the Boxers. The latter received a further impetus by reason of the inefficiency of the Imperial troops sent to quell the first rising. Finally, references are made to the evil advice and ignorance of the highly placed clansmen and Ministers of State who favoured the Boxer cause. This Decree is in fact a complete justification of the views expressed in the three memorials by Yüan Chang and Hsü Ching-ch eng, for which these patriotic officials*

laid down their lives. After describing the entry of the Boxers into Pe-
king, and lamenting the position of the Throne as resembling "a tail
which is too big to wag," the Decree proceeds): — "Nevertheless, and
while the Legations were being besieged, we repeatedly directed
our Ministers of the Tsungli Yamên to put a stop to hostilities,
and at the same time to keep up communication with the foreign
Ministers, assuring them of our kindly and sympathetic regard.
This latter order, however, was not carried out because of the
continuous artillery and rifle fire between the besiegers and the
besieged, and it was impossible for us, under such conditions, to
insist upon its execution. Supposing, by some horrible fatality,
the Legations had actually fallen, how could China have hoped
to preserve her integrity? To the Throne's strenuous efforts is really due the avoidance of such a dreadful catastrophe, and the
gifts of wine, fruit and water-melons to the besieged Legations,
were an indication of Her Majesty's benevolent intentions. It was
but natural and right that the friendly Powers should appreciate
these our feelings, and the fact that at such a crisis they have respected the integrity of our Empire as a Sovereign State, goes to
prove that the Allies attribute no longer any blame to the Throne.
This, however, only adds to our wrath at the ignorance and violence of our offending subjects; when we look back upon the
past, we are filled with shame and indignation. We are convinced
that, in these peace negotiations, the foreign Powers will not attempt to extract from us more than we are able to concede. We
have ordered Prince Ch'ing and Li Hung-chang, negotiating this
Treaty, to continue patiently in friendly discussion, maintaining
all questions of vital principle, while recognising the special circumstances which attach to any given case. Foreign Powers are
lovers of justice, and they are bound to consider what China is
capable of doing if they wish to see this negotiation brought to
a successful conclusion. To this end we expect that our Plenipotentiaries will display their virtue of patriotism to the very best
of their ability.

"At the time of the terror in Peking, our provincial authorities were ordered to keep the peace in their respective provinces, and to take no part in provoking hostilities. If the Southern and Eastern parts of our Empire enjoyed full protection from disorders, the fact was solely due to our Decrees, which insisted upon the rigid maintenance of peace. The trade of foreign Powers was in no way injured, our Viceroys and Governors being able to preserve normal conditions in those parts of our Empire. As regards the Southern provinces, however, which are always talking loudly of strengthening their defences, it cannot be gainsaid that, upon the outbreak of any trouble, they fall into a state of hopeless confusion. Caring nothing for the innumerable difficulties which beset our Throne, they stand idly by, contenting themselves with delivering oracular opinions and catch-words, and they even go so far as to reproach their Sovereign, the father of his people. We would have them bear in mind that when our Imperial chariot departed in haste from the Forbidden City, the moaning of the wind and the cry of the heron overhead seemed to our startled ears as the tramp of an advancing enemy. As we fled through Ch'ang-ping chou northward to Hsüan-hua, we personally attended on the wants of the Empress Dowager. We were both clad in the meanest of garments, and to relieve our hunger we were scarcely able to obtain a dish of beans or porridge. Few of our poorest subjects have suffered greater hardships of cold and hunger than befell us in this pitiful plight. We wonder whether those who call themselves our faithful Ministers and servants have ever taken real thought of their bounden duty towards their afflicted and outraged Sovereigns?

"To sum up the matter in a word, is it not the case that, when either our Statesmen or our people are guilty of any offence, it is upon our Imperial persons that the blame must fall? In recalling this fact to mind, we do not desire to rake up bygone offences, but rather because it is our duty to warn our subjects against their repetition. For the past twenty years, whenever difficulties have arisen with foreign nations, it has been our duty to issue solemn warnings and reproofs. But the saying which is in common use, that we 'sleep on brushwood and taste gall' has, by lapse of time, become almost meaningless; when we talk of putting our house in order, and reforming our finances, the words have no real significance. The time of danger once over, favouritism and the neglect of public business go on as of old; as of old, money purchases rank, and the Throne continues to be persistently mis-led. Let our officials ask themselves in the silence of the night watches whether, even had there been no Boxer rebellion, China could possibly have become a great Power? Even before these disasters occurred there was great difficulty in maintaining our position as a nation, and now, after this awful visitation, it must be obvious to the dullest amongst us that our weakness and poverty have been greatly increased. To our Ministers of State, who have received high favour from the Throne, we would say that, at this time of our nation's history, it is essential to display new qualities of integrity and patriotism. Taxation should now be re-arranged in such a manner as to enable us to repay the foreign indemnities, while bearing in mind the poverty of the lower classes of the people. In the selection of officials, good character should be considered the first essential, and men of talent should be encouraged to the utmost.

"The whole duty of a Minister of State may be summed up in two words: to abolish corrupt tendencies, and to put off the abuses of former days. Justice and energy should be the principles guiding towards economical and military efficiency; on this the spirit of the nation and its future depend as upon its very life blood.

"For nearly thirty years our mother, the Empress Dowager, has laboured without ceasing to instruct us and train us in the right way, and now, at one blow, all the results of her labour are brought to nought. We cannot but remember the abomination of desecration which has overthrown our ancestral shrines and the temples of our gods. Looking to the North, we think upon our Capital ruined and profaned, upon the thousands of our highest officials whose families have lost their all, of the millions of our subjects whose lives and property have been sacrificed in this cataclysm. We can never cease to reproach ourselves: how then should we reproach others? Our object in issuing this solemn warning is to show that the prosperity or the ruin of a State depends solely upon the energy or apathy of its rulers and people, and that the weakness of an Empire is the direct result of rottenness in its administration. We desire to reiterate our commands that friendly relations with foreign Powers are to be encouraged, that at the same time our defences are to be strengthened, that freedom of speech and the employment of trustworthy servants are to be encouraged. We expect obedience to these commands, and sincere patriotism from our subjects. Earnestly the Empress Dowager and ourselves pray that it may be brought home to our Ministers of State, that only out of suffering is wisdom developed, and that a sense of duty insists upon unceasing effort. Let this Decree be made known throughout the entire Empire."

This Edict was issued in February, coincidently with Her Majesty's acceptance of the conditions imposed by the Powers in the peace negotiations at Peking. From that date until, in June, the terms of the Protocol were definitely settled by the plenipotentiaries, her attitude continued to be one of nervous apprehension, while the discomfort of life at Hsi-an, as well as the advice repeatedly given her by Jung Lu and the provincial Viceroys, combined to make her look forward with impatience to the day when she might set out for her capital.

There remained only one source of difficulty, namely, the presence of Prince Tuan's son, the Heir Apparent, at her Court. Tzŭ Hsi was well aware that she could hardly look for cordial relations with the representatives of the Powers at Peking, or for sympathy abroad, so long as this son of the Boxer chief remained heir to the Throne. It would clearly be impossible, in the event of his becoming Emperor, for him to consent to his father remaining under sentence of banishment, and equally impossible to expect the Powers to consent to Prince Tuan's rehabilitation and return.

Yet the youth had been duly and solemnly appointed to succeed to the Throne, a thing not lightly to be set aside. Once again the Old Buddha showed that the sacred laws of succession were less than a strong woman's will.

Politics apart, it was common knowledge that Tzŭ Hsi had for some time repented of her choice of Prince Tuan's ill-mannered, uncouth son as Heir Apparent. More than once had she been brought to shame by his wild, and sometimes disgraceful, conduct. Even in her presence, the lad paid little heed to the formalities of Court etiquette, and none at all to the dignity of his own rank and future position. Tzŭ Hsi was therefore probably not sorry of the excuse for deposing him from that high estate. In the Decree cancelling his title to the Throne, she observed that his father, Prince Tuan, had brought the Empire to the verge of ruin, and that the guilt which he had thus incurred towards his august ancestors could never be wiped out. In order to save the "face" of the Heir Apparent and her own, in a difficult position, the Edict describes him as being fully convinced of the impossibility of his succeeding to the Throne under existing conditions, and that he himself had therefore petitioned Her Majesty to cancel her previous decision. In granting this request and directing him to remove himself forthwith from the Palace precincts, the Empress conferred upon him the rank of an Imperial Duke of the lowest grade, excusing him at the same time from performance of any official duties in that capacity. By this decision she meant to mark the contempt into which the Heir Apparent had fallen, for the rank thus granted him was a low one, and, without any official duties or salary, he was condemned to a life of poverty and obscurity. This fallen Heir to the Dragon Throne is a well-known figure to-day in the lowest haunts of the Chinese City at Peking: a drunkard and disreputable character, living the life of a gambler, notorious only as a swashbuckler of romantic past and picturesque type, — one who, but for adverse fate and the accursed foreigner, would have been Emperor of China at this moment.

Having deposed him, the Empress let it be known that the selection of an heir to the disconsolate shade of T'ung-Chih would
be postponed "until a suitable candidate should be found," an
intimation generally understood to mean that the vital question
of providing an heir in legitimate and proper succession to the
Throne could not well be determined until China's foreign relations, as well as her internal affairs, had been placed upon a basis
of greater security. It is curious to note how, in all such utterances, it appears to have been tacitly understood that the Emperor
Kuang Hsü was a "bad life."

Thus, in exile, the Old Buddha wore philosophically the white
sheet of penance and burned the candle of expiation, preparatory to re-entering anon upon a new lease of power in that Peking
where, as she well knew, the memory of the foreigner is short
and his patience long. In June, 1901, the terms of peace were
settled; on the 7th September the Peace Protocol was solemnly
signed by the representatives of all the Powers, that "monument
of collective inefficiency" which was to sow the seeds of trouble
to last for many years to come. At Hsi-an "in the profound seclusion of the Palace" she knew remorse, not unstimulated by fear;
on the return journey to her capital (from 20th October, 1901, to
6th January, 1902), while preparing her arts and graces to capti-
vate the barbarian, she was still a victim to doubt and apprehension. Meanwhile, at Peking, the mandarin world, reassured by
the attitude of the peace negotiators and their terms, was fast
shedding its garments of fear and peacocking as of yore, in renewed assurance of its own indisputable superiority. Evidence
of this spirit was to be met with on all sides, gradually coming to
its fine flower in the subsequent negotiations for the revision of
the commercial Treaties, and bringing home once more, to those
who study these things, the unalterable truth of the discovery
made years ago by one of the earliest British representatives in
China, namely, that "this people yields nothing to reason and everything to fear."

One of the most remarkable instances of this revival of the

mandarin's traditional arrogance of superiority occurred, signifi-
cantly enough, in connection with the penitential mission of the
Emperor's brother, Prince Ch'un (now Regent) to Berlin, an episode which threatened for a moment to lead to a rupture between
Germany and China. By Article 1 of the Peace Protocol, Prince
Ch'un had been specially designated for this mission to convey
in person to the German Emperor the regrets of the Chinese Government for the murder of Baron von Ketteler. He left Peking for
the purpose on the 12th July, 1901, with definite instructions as to
the manner in which the Chinese Government's regrets were to
be expressed. The German Emperor's proposals as to the form of
ceremony to be followed in this matter were regarded by Prince
Ch'un as incompatible with his instructions, and it will be remembered that, after some hesitation on the part of the German
Government, the Chinese policy of passive resistance eventually
carried the day. The following telegraphic correspondence on
the subject is of permanent interest. Prince Ch'un (whose personal name is Tsai Feng) telegraphed from Germany on the 26th
September to the Peace Plenipotentiaries, Prince Ch'ing and Li
Hung-chang, as follows: —

"I have duly received the Grand Council's message, and note that I
am commanded to act as circumstances may require, and that a middle
course is suggested as expedient. I fully appreciate the intelligent caution of your policy, and fortunately had already taken steps to act in
the sense indicated. On the 14th of this moon the German Emperor had
given orders to stop preparations for the ceremony, but as I noticed that
the Royal train had not been withdrawn nor had his aide-de-camp left
my suite, I inferred that there was a possibility of his yielding the points
in dispute. Accordingly, after a long discussion of the situation with Yin
Ch'ang, I directed him to write in German to *Jeng-yintai*[1] requesting his
friendly intervention at the Foreign Office with a definite explanation
that China could not possibly agree that the mission should be received
kneeling, that Germany had nothing to gain on insisting upon such a

1. The Chinese rendering of a German name.

procedure, and that the only result of a fiasco would be to make both countries appear extremely ridiculous. I therefore begged that the Emperor should accede to my personal appeal and waive the point. At the same time I requested the German gentleman who acts as Chinese Consul for Bavaria to address the Foreign Office to the same effect, and with a request that we might enter upon discussion of the point. Four days later I directed Lü Hai-huan to return to his post at Berlin to make such arrangements as might be possible, and on the following day I telegraphed to him a summary of the Grand Council's views on the matter. In the afternoon of the 20th I received the Consul for Bavaria, who informed me that he had received a telegram from the Foreign Office inquiring when I proposed to start for Berlin, and hoping that I would do so speedily, as the Emperor had now consented to waive the question of our kneeling, but required that only Yin Ch'ang should accompany me when presenting the letter of regret, the remainder of my suite to remain in another place.

"The same evening I received a message from Lü Hai-huan, stating that the Emperor would undoubtedly receive me, and that, since all other difficult questions had been settled, His Majesty wished to leave for the country in a few days. Under these circumstances I did not consider it advisable to insist too strictly on minor details of etiquette, being pressed for time, and I therefore requested the German Emperor's Chamberlain to have a special train prepared for my journey. We reached Potsdam at 3 P.M. on the 21st[1]; I was met by a General sent by the Emperor with his state carriage. Myself and my suite were lodged in the Palace, where every attention was shown to us, and it was arranged that I should fulfil my mission on the following day, after depositing a wreath on the grave of the late Empress. On the morning of the following day I visited her tomb, and at noon the state carriage came to take me to the New Palace, where, after being ushered into the Emperor's presence, I read aloud Their Majesties' complimentary letter. The members of my suite were awaiting in an adjoining apartment. After the ceremony I was escorted back to my residence, and at 2 P.M. the Emperor came to call upon me. He was very cordial and remained talking with me for a long time. By

---

1. This is the Chinese date; the day of the audience was the 4th September.

His Highness Prince Tsai Hsün.
Brother of the late Emperor and Present Regent—recently head of the Naval Mission to
Europe and America.

his orders a steam launch was provided for me, in which I visited the Lake and Peacock Island; on the following day I saw a review of the troops, and was presented to the Empress. The Emperor begged me to remain longer in Berlin, suggesting that I should visit the arsenals and inspect the fleet under Prince Henry at Stettin. I could scarcely decline these polite attentions, and after visiting the Empress I took lodging in an hotel at Berlin. Thanks to the glorious prestige of our Empire, matters have thus been satisfactorily settled, and the knowledge that my mission has been satisfactorily carried out will, I hope, bring comfort to Their Imperial Majesties in their anxiety. I beg that you will memorialise the Throne accordingly. Tsai Feng."

The Empress Dowager was pleased to express her approval of the result of this mission, which in the eyes of the Chinese Government was undoubtedly one of those diplomatic triumphs which China appears to attain most easily when her material resources have completely failed. Reading the above despatch, it is difficult to realise that the Prince's mission had for its object the expiation of a brutal murder committed, with the full approval of the Chinese Government and Court, on the representative of a friendly nation. The opinion is commonly believed, held by the Legations at Peking, that the present Regent has learned much since he returned from that penitential mission to the German capital. During the present year his brothers have been engaged on missions ostensibly intended to acquire knowledge for the sorely-needed reorganisation of China's army and navy, missions which have been received with royal honours by almost every civilised Power; but there are many close observers of the changing conditions at Peking who see in these missions merely a repetition of farces that have often been played before, and an attempt to gain prestige in the eyes of the Chinese people for the Regent's family and the Court, rather than any definite intention or desire to reform the official system.

XXIII

THE RETURN OF THE COURT TO PEKING

THE state of mind of the Empress Dowager during the flight from the Capital, and subsequently while the Court remained in exile at Hsi-an, was marked by that same quality of indecision and vacillating impulse which had characterised her actions throughout the Boxer crisis and the siege of Peking. This may be ascribed partly to her advancing age and partly to the conflicting influences of astrologers and fortune-tellers, to whose advice she attached the greatest importance in all times of peril. We have dealt in another place with her marked susceptibility to omens and superstitious beliefs; its effect is most noticeable, however, at this stage of her life, and was conspicuous in matters of small detail throughout the return journey to Peking.

The influence of Jung Lu at Hsi-an, and that of Li Hung-chang at Peking, had been systematically exercised to induce Her Majesty to return to the Capital; but until the Peace Protocol conditions had been definitely arranged, and until she had been persuaded to decree adequate punishment upon the Boxer leaders, the predominant feeling in her mind was evidently one of suspicion and fear, as was shown when she ordered the hurried flight from T'ai-yüan fu to Hsi-an. The influence of Li Hung-chang, who, from the outset, had realised the folly committed by the Chinese Government in approving the attack upon the Legations, was exercised to create in the mind of Her Majesty a clearer sense of the folly of that policy. At the height of the crisis (21st July, 1900), realising that the foreign forces brought to bear upon China were steadily defeating both Boxers and Imperial troops, she appointed Li Hung-chang to be Viceroy of Chihli, and directed that he should proceed from Canton with all haste, there being urgent need of the services of a diplomat versed in foreign affairs. Her Majesty went so far as to suggest that he should proceed from Shanghai to Tientsin in a Russian vessel which "he might borrow for the purpose." Li Hung-chang's reply, telegraphed to Yüan Shih-k'ai for transmission to the Throne, while outwardly respectful, clearly implies that Her Majesty has been to blame for the disasters then occurring. "I am sincerely grateful," he says, "for Your Majesty's gratifying confidence in me, but cannot help recalling to mind the folly which has now suddenly destroyed that structure of reformed administration which, during my twenty years' term of office as Viceroy of Chihli, I was able to build up not unsuccessfully. I fear it will not be possible for me to resume the duties of this difficult post at a time of crisis like the present, destitute as I am of all proper and material resources." He proceeds even to criticise Her Majesty's suggestion as to his journey, observing that "Russia possesses no vessel at Shanghai, and would certainly refuse to lend if she had one, in view of the state of war now existing." Finally, he excuses himself for deferring his departure, on the ground that the British Minister had requested him not to leave until the foreign Ministers had been safely escorted from Peking to Tientsin. "I do not know," says he, "if any such arrangements for safely escorting them can be made," and therefore concludes by asking Yüan to inform the Throne that he will start northwards, journeying by land, "as soon as his health permits it." To this plain-spoken message from the great Viceroy, Tzǔ Hsi replied in two lines of equally characteristic directness: — Li Hung-chang is to obey our earlier Decree, and to make all haste northwards. The crisis is serious. Let him make no further excuses for delay."

In spite of these peremptory orders, Li Hung-chang, who had a very definite conception of his own predicament, remained at Shanghai, ostensibly negotiating, but in reality waiting, to see what would be the outcome of the siege of the Legations. He was interviewed by *The Times* correspondent at Shanghai on the 23rd of July, and then stated that he would not proceed to his post in the north until convinced by clear proofs that the Empress Dowager had seen the folly of her ways, and was prepared to adopt a conciliatory policy towards the outraged foreign Powers. At the end of July, when it became clear to him that the Court had determined on flight, he forwarded by special courier a very remarkable Memorial, in which he called the Throne to task in the plainest possible terms, and urged an immediate change of policy. This Memorial reached the Empress before her departure from Peking; certain extracts from it are well worth reproduction, as showing Li Hung-chang at his best, and displaying that quality of courageous intelligence which made him for twenty years the foremost official in China and a world-wide celebrity: —

"It is to be remembered that between this, our Empire of China, and the outer barbarians, hostilities have frequently occurred since the remotest antiquity, and our national history teaches that the best way to meet them is to determine upon our policy only after carefully ascertaining their strength as compared with our own, Since the middle of the reign of Tao-Kuang the pressure of the barbarians on our borders has steadily increased, and to-day we are brought to desperate straits indeed. In 1860 they invaded the Capital and burnt the Summer Palace; His Majesty Hsien-Feng was forced to flee, and thus came to his death. It is only natural that His Majesty's posterity should long to avenge him to the end of time, and that your subjects should continue to cherish undying hopes of revenge. But since that time, France has taken from us Annam, the whole of that dependency being irretrievably lost; Japan has fought us, and ousted us from Korea. Even worse disasters and loss of territory were, however, to follow: Germany seized Kiaochao; Russia followed by annexing Port Arthur and Talienwan; England demanded Wei-hei-wei and Kowloon, together with the extension of the Shanghai Settlements, and the opening of new treaty ports inland; and France made further demands for Kuang-Chou wan. How could we possibly maintain silence under such grievous and repeated acts of aggression? Craven would be the man who would not seek to improve our defences, and shameless would be he who did not long for the day of reckoning. I myself have enjoyed no small favours from the Throne, and much is expected of me by the nation. Needless for me to say how greatly I would rejoice were it possible for China to enter upon a glorious and triumphant war; it would be the joy of my closing days to see the barbarian nations subjugated at last in submissive allegiance, respectfully making obeisance to the Dragon Throne. Unfortunately, however, I cannot but recognise the melancholy fact that China is unequal to any such enterprise, and that our forces are in no way competent to undertake it. Looking at the question as one affecting chiefly the integrity of our Empire, who would be so foolish as to cast missiles at a rat in the vicinity of a priceless piece of porcelain? It requires no augur's skill in divination to foresee that eggs are more easily to be cracked than stones. Let us consider one recent incident in proof of this conclusion. Recently, in the attack by some tens of thousands of Boxers and Imperial troops upon the foreign Settlements at Tientsin, there were some two or three thousand foreign soldiers to defend them; yet, after ten days of desperate fighting, only a few hundred foreigners had been slain, while no less than twenty thousand Chinese were killed and as many more wounded. Again, there are no real defences or fortified positions in the Legations at Peking, nor are the foreign Ministers and their Legation staffs trained in the use of arms; nevertheless, Tung Fu-hsiang's hordes have been bombarding them for more than a month, and have lost many thousands of men in the vain attempt to capture the position.

"The fleets of the Allied Powers are now hurrying forward vast bodies of their troops; the heaviest artillery is now being brought swiftly to our shores. Has China the forces to meet them? Does she possess a single leader capable of resisting this invasion? If the foreign Powers send

100,000 men, they will easily capture Peking, and Your Majesties will then find escape impossible. You will no doubt endeavour once more to flee to Jehol, but on this occasion you have no commander like Sheng Pao to hold back the enemies' forces from pursuit; or, perhaps, you may decide to hold another Peace Conference, like that at Shimonoseki, in 1895? But the conditions to-day existing are in no way similar to those of that time, when Marquis Ito was willing to meet me as your Minister Plenipotentiary. When betrayed by the Boxers and abandoned by all, where will your Majesties find a single Prince, Councillor, or Statesman able to assist you effectively? The fortunes of your house are being staked upon a single throw; my blood runs cold at the thought of events to come. Under any enlightened Sovereign these Boxers, with their ridiculous claims of supernatural powers, would most assuredly have been condemned to death long since. Is it not on record that the Han Dynasty met its end because of its belief in magicians, and in their power to confer invisibility? Was not the Sung Dynasty destroyed because the Emperor believed ridiculous stories about supernatural warriors clad in miraculous coats of mail?

"I myself am nearly eighty years of age, and my death cannot be far distant; I have received favours at the hands of four Emperors. If now I hesitate to say the things that are in my mind, how shall I face the spirits of the sacred ancestors of this Dynasty when we meet in the halls of Hades? I am compelled therefore to give utterance to this my solemn prayer, and to beseech Your Majesties to put away from you at once these vile magic workers, and to have them summarily executed.

"You should take steps immediately to appoint a high official who shall purge the land of this villainous rabble, and who shall see to it that the foreign Ministers are safely escorted to the headquarters of the Allied Armies. In spite of the great heat, I have hurried northwards from Canton to Shanghai, where your Majesties' Decrees urging me to come to Peking have duly reached me. Any physical weakness, however serious, would not have deterred me from obeying this summons, but perusal of your Decrees has led me to the conclusion that Your Majesties have not yet adopted a policy of reason, but are still in the hands of traitors, regarding these Boxers as your dutiful subjects, with the result that unrest is spreading and alarm universal. Moreover, I am here in Shanghai without a single soldier under my command, and even should I proceed with all haste in the endeavour to present myself at your Palace gates, I should meet with innumerable dangers by the way, and the end of my journey would most probably be that I should provide your rebellious and turbulent subjects with one more carcass to hack into mincemeat. I shall therefore continue in residence here for the present, considering ways and means for raising a military force and for furnishing supplies, as well as availing myself of the opportunity of ascertaining the enemies' plans, and making such diplomatic suggestions as occur to me to be useful. As soon as my plans are complete, I shall proceed northwards with all possible speed."

The plain-spoken advice of Li Hung-chang was not without effect on the Empress Dowager. The Decrees issued by her in the name of the Emperor from Huai-lai on the 19th and 20th of August are the first indications given to the outside world that she had definitely decided on a policy of conciliation so as to render possible her eventual return to the capital—an event which, as she foresaw, would probably be facilitated by the inevitable differences and jealousies already existing among the Allies.

In the Edict of the 19th of August, after explaining that the whole Boxer crisis and the attack on the Legations was the result of differences between Christian and non-Christian Chinese, she querulously complains that the foreign Powers, although doubtless well meaning in their efforts to "exterminate the rebels," are behaving in a manner which suggests aggressive designs towards China, and which shows a lamentable disregard of proper procedure and friendliness. She *naïvely* observes that the Chinese Government had been at the greatest pains to protect the lives and property of foreigners in Peking, in spite of many difficulties, and expresses much surprise at such an evil return being made for her invariable kindness and courtesy. If it were not for the unbounded capacity of foreign diplomats, fully proved in the past, in the matter of credulity where Chinese statecraft is concerned, it would be difficult to regard utterances like these as the work of an intelligent ruler. But Tzŭ Hsi was, as usual, justified, for at the very time when these Decrees were issued, Russia was already using very similar arguments, and making excuses for the Chinese government, in pursuance of her own policy at Peking.

In the conclusion of the Decree above referred to, Her Majesty orders Jung Lu, Hsü T'ung and Ch'ung Ch'i to remain in Peking to act as peace negotiators, but she admits that, in dealing with foreigners supported by troops and flushed with success, it may be difficult for them at the outset to determine on a satisfactory line of procedure. She leaves it to these plenipotentiaries, therefore, to determine whether the best course would be to telegraph to the respective Foreign Offices of the countries concerned, or to consult with the Consuls-General at Shanghai (*sic*), with a view to obtaining friendly intervention! It could not escape so shrewd a person as Tzŭ Hsi that the atmosphere of Peking at this juncture was not likely to be favourable to her purposes, and that it would be easier to hoodwink the Foreign Offices and the Consuls at Shanghai than those who had just been through the siege.

A Decree of the following day, also in the name of the Emperor, is couched in a very different strain—a pathetic admission of the Throne's guilt, a plea for the sympathy of his people, and an exhortation to return to ways of wisdom. "Cleanse your hearts, and remove all doubt and suspicion from your minds, so as to assist us, the Emperor, in our shortcomings. We have been utterly unworthy, but the time is at hand when it shall be for us to prove that Heaven has not left us without sense of our errors and deep remorse." The whole document reads with an unusual ring of sincerity, accepting, in the name of the Emperor, full blame for all the disasters which had overtaken the country, while reminding the official class that the first cause of these calamities dates back to the time when they learned and adopted habits of inveterate sloth and luxury. From depths of contrition, the Edict admits fully the Throne's responsibility, "We, the Lord of this Empire, have failed utterly in warding off calamities from our people, and we should not hesitate for one moment to commit suicide, in order to placate our tutelary deities and the gods of the soil, but we cannot forget that duty of filial piety and service which we owe to our sacred and aged mother, the Empress Dowager."

The policy of reform is now clearly enunciated and outlined as an essential condition of the future government of the Empire. Provincial and metropolitan officials are ordered to proceed at once to join the Court, in order that the reform programme may be speedily initiated; the Yangtsze Viceroys are thanked for preserving order in accordance with "treaty stipulations," and Chinese converts to Christianity are once more assured of the Throne's protection and good-will.

These utterances of the Throne, which lost nothing in their presentation to the respective Powers by Prince Ch'ing and his colleagues, soon produced the desired effect, and reassured the Throne and its advisers as to their personal safety. Accordingly, early in September, we find all the Viceroys and high officials of the Provinces uniting in a Memorial, whereby the Court is urged to return at once to the Capital, advice which would never have been given had there been any question of violent measures being taken by the Allies against the Empress Dowager. At this time the question of the future location of the Chinese Capital was being widely discussed at Court, and there was much conflicting advice on the subject. The Viceroys' Memorial was drafted by Yüan Shih-k'ai and forwarded by him to Liu K'un-yi, at Nanking, for transmission; it definitely blames the Boxers and their leaders for the ruin which had come upon China, and rejoices at the thought that "the perplexities which embarrassed your Majesties in the past have now given place to a clearer understanding of the situation." Noting the possibility of the Court's leaving T'ai-yuan fu and making "a further progress" westwards to Hsi-an, the Memorialists deplore the idea and proceed to show that such a step would be unwise as well as inconvenient. As an example of the way in which Chinese Ministers of State deal with questions of high policy and strategy, the following extract from this Memorial is not without interest: —

"It is true that, in times past, our Capital has been shifted on more than one occasion of national danger, but in those days our enemies were not able to push their armies far into the interior of our country for indefinite periods, and were compelled to withdraw after brief expeditions. The position of affairs to-day, however, is very different, so that we can obtain no reliable guidance from precedents of history. As regards the province of Shensi, it has always been a centre of wars and rebellions; its people are poverty stricken, and there is no trade there. Seven centuries ago, Hsi-an was an Imperial city, but is now anything but prosperous. Its vicinity to Kansu and the New Dominion territories, infested with Mahomedan rebels and adjoining the Russian Empire, renders it most unsuitable as a site for your Majesties' Capital. Supposing that the Allies, flushed with success, should determine on an advance westwards, what is there to prevent them from doing so? If ten thousand miles of ocean have not stopped them, are they likely to be turned back from a shorter expedition by land?"

After referring to the fact that the cradle of the Dynasty and the tombs of its ancestors are situated near Peking, and that it is geographically best fitted to be the centre of Government, the Memorialists remind the Throne that the foreign Powers have promised to vacate Peking, and to refrain from annexing any territory if the Court will return. These ends, they say, will not be attained should the Court persist in its intention to proceed further westwards, since it is now the desire of the foreign Ministers that China's rulers should return to Peking. In the event of a permanent occupation of Peking by the Allies, the loss of Manchuria would be inevitable. The Memorialists predict partition and many other disasters, including financial distress, and the impossibility of furnishing the Throne with supplies at Hsi-an or any other remote corner of the Empire. If the Court's decision to proceed to Hsi-an is irrevocable, at least a Decree should now be issued, stating that its sojourn there will be a brief one, and that the Court will return to Peking upon the complete restoration of peaceful conditions. "The continued existence of the Empire must depend upon the Throne's decision upon this matter." The Memorial concludes by imploring their Majesties to authorise Prince Ch'ing to inform the foreign Ministers that the withdrawal of the allied armies will be followed by a definite announcement as to the Court's return.

In a further Memorial from the Viceroys and Governors, it is stated that the Russian Minister for Foreign Affairs had suggested to the Chinese Minister in St. Petersburg, that the location of the Capital at Hsi-an would certainly prove undesirable, in view of the poverty-stricken condition of the province, and that their Majesties would no doubt, therefore, proceed to Lan-chou fu, in Kansu. Referring to this interesting fact, the Memorialists observe: —

"Those who are in favour of establishing the Capital at Hsi-an profess to claim that the Yellow River and the T'ung Kuan Pass constitute natural and impassible frontiers against attack. They forget, however, that foreign nations possess artillery of very long range. At T'ung Kuan the Yellow River is less than two miles wide, and their guns will easily carry twice that distance. Your Majesties have nothing but the native artillery, and a few inferior foreign guns, and would never be able to hold the position. The foreigners would undoubtedly penetrate far into the interior, and control all the waterways, thus preventing transport and supplies. Even if one foreign Power were to find it difficult, there is no doubt that it would be easy for several of them acting together.

"Moreover, friendly Powers are entitled, by the law of civilised nations, to send their diplomatic representatives to our Capital. If peace be made, and the foreign Powers assent to the proposed change of capital, they will surely insist upon sending their envoys into Shensi. After their recent experiences, they will require to have foreign troops to guard their Legations, whose numbers must necessarily be large, in proportion to the distance from the coast. Foreign garrisons would thus have to be established at points in Honan, Shansi and Chihli, in order to maintain their line of communications, so that China would eventually be overrun by foreign troops. It is, therefore, plainly out of the question that the Court should leave Peking. In times of peace it might have been suggested, but to think of it after a disastrous war is impossible. The foreigners are acting in unison; China is completely disorganised. They have ample resources and reinforcements; China has none. If we have thoughts of fighting any foreign Power we must first form alliances with several others; in any case nothing can be done before an ample supply of ordnance and munitions of war has been accumulated. This is no time for considering such possibilities. We, your Memorialists, venture to suggest that Your Majesties have failed to take into consideration all these facts, and in impressing them upon you, we earnestly beg that you may now come to a wise decision."

Before coming to a decision, however, Tzŭ Hsi required to be fully assured that the foreign Powers would not insist on her abdicating the supreme power as one of the conditions of peace. Convinced on that point, the hesitation which she had previously shown in regard to returning to Peking dropped from her like a garment. It had been freely predicted by conservative officials and the *literati* that the Old Buddha would never again wish to see her desecrated capital or to visit the polluted shrines of her ancestors. In spite of her superstitious nature, however, she was far too level-headed and far-seeing a woman to attach supreme importance to sentimental considerations, or to allow them to weigh heavily in the balance when the question of her own rulership was at stake. The hesitation which she had shown and the attention which she had paid to the advice of those who, like Chang Chih-tung, desired her to establish a new capital in Central China, were primarily a question of "face." She would only return to Peking if guaranteed the full dignity and power of her former position. But as the peace negotiations proceeded, and as it became clear to her that along the well-worn path of international jealousies she might return unpunished, and even welcomed, to Peking, she proceeded to make preparations for an early return. Fully informed each day by Prince Ch'ing of the progress which her plenipotentiaries were making towards the completion of the Peace Protocol, and overjoyed at its terms, she waited only until the condition of the roads, always more or less impassable after the summer rains, had sufficiently improved to permit of comfortable travelling. During the delay necessitated by the collecting and packing of the enormous quantity of "tribute" collected by Her Majesty and the Court during their stay at Hsi-an, she received definite confirmation of the good news that her treasure vaults in the capital had not been plundered by the foreign troops — good news which increased her anxiety to return as quickly as possible to superintend its removal before any pilfering by the eunuchs should take place.

It was on the 24th day of the 8th Moon (20th October, 1901) that the long procession started from Her Majesty's temporary residence in the Governor's Yamên; followed by an enormous retinue, she commenced her journey by sacrificing to the God of War, the guardian spirit of her Dynasty (and, it may be added, patron of the Boxers), at a small temple outside the city gates. From this onward the Court advanced northward by easy stages of about twenty-five miles a day, resting first at Ho-nan fu; thence on to K'ai-feng, where her sixty-sixth birthday was celebrated and where she remained for some weeks. The travelling lodges and other arrangements for her comfort and convenience along the whole line of her route were in striking contrast to the squalor and privation which the Court had endured in the flight from Peking.

It was during her stay at K'ai-feng that the Peace Protocol was signed at Peking. It was also before her departure from that city, at the end of the 9th Moon, that Li Hung-chang died. His knowledge of foreign affairs and remarkable ability in negotiations had been of the greatest service to his Imperial mistress, and there is no doubt that the liberal terms granted to China by the victorious Allies were very largely due to his efforts. Her Majesty, while fully appreciating his ability, had never treated him with marked favour, and had always refused to appoint him to the Grand Council, giving as her excuse that she could not understand his dialect. Upon his death, however, she conferred upon him an honour which had never before been granted to any Chinese subject under the Dynasty, namely, that of having a shrine built to his memory at the capital itself, in addition to those erected in the provinces where he had borne office.

It was significant of her impartial and intelligent rulership that, although she had blamed him as originally responsible for the Japanese War and its disastrous results, she had never approved of the Emperor's hasty and vindictive action in removing him from the Viceroyalty of Chihli. Upon the signing of the Peace Protocol she conferred additional posthumous honours upon him, taking occasion at the same time, in an Imperial Decree, to congratulate and thank Prince Ch'ing, Yüan Shih-k'ai and others, who assisted in bringing about the settlement of peace terms. In particular she praised the loyalty of Jung Lu, "who had earnestly advised the annihilation of the Boxers, and who, in addition to other meritorious services on the Grand Council, had been chiefly instrumental in protecting the Legations."

After a series of magnificent theatrical entertainments in honour of her birthday, the Court left K'ai-feng and continued its journey to the capital. On the eve of her departure Her Majesty took occasion sternly and publicly to rebuke the Manchu Prefect, Wen T'i,[1] who had dared to advise her against returning to the capital, and to predict that the treacherous foreigners would certainly seize her sacred person—a useful piece of play to the gallery.

At the crossing of the Yellow River, which took place in beautiful weather, she sacrificed to the River God, in expiation and thanksgiving. The local officials had constructed a magnificent barge, in the form of a dragon, upon which she and the ladies

---

1. Wen T'i had been a censor in 1898, but was cashiered by the Emperor for being reactionary. Tzŭ Hsi restored him to favour after the *coup d'état.*

of the Court crossed the stream. It was noticed from this point onwards that wherever foreigners happened to be amongst the spectators of the Imperial *cortège*, she made a point of showing them particular attention and civility, and before her arrival in Peking she issued a Decree commanding that Europeans should not be prevented from watching the procession upon her arrival, and this in spite of the fact that, in accordance with the usual custom, the Legations had issued notices forbidding their nationals to appear in the streets during the passage of the Imperial *cortège*. Everything indicated, in fact, that Her Majesty now desired to conciliate the European Powers by all possible means, and if it be borne in mind that it was part of her deliberate policy thus to ingratiate herself with foreigners as a means of furthering her own future policy, her actions lose nothing of interest, while they gain something from the humorous point of view.

On crossing the borders of the Province of Chihli, Her Majesty issued a Decree, couched in almost effusive terms of friendliness, proclaiming that the Emperor would receive the foreign Ministers in audience immediately upon his return to the Palace, and that the reception would take place in the central Throne Hall of the sacred enclosure. Chinese, reading this Decree, and ignorant of the terms of the Peace Protocol which provided for this particular concession to the barbarian, would naturally regard it as a spontaneous mark of the Imperial clemency and goodwill. In the same Edict Her Majesty proclaimed her intention of receiving the Ministers' wives in person, intimating that she cherished most pleasant memories of past friendly intercourse with them. Here, again, we note fulfilment of a plan, deliberately conceived and formed upon the best classical models, "for dealing with strong and savage people."

At noon on the 6th of January, 1902, the Imperial party arrived by special train at the temporary station which had been erected close to the Southern walls of Peking, and adjoining the old terminus at Ma-chia pu. Large pavilions, handsomely decorated, had been erected near the station, in which the Old Buddha and the Emperor were to be received; they were furnished with a throne of gold lacquer, cloisonné altar vessels and many valuable pieces of porcelain. Several hundreds of the highest metropolitan officials were in attendance, and a special place had been provided for foreigners. As the long train of over thirty carriages drew up at the station, the keen face of the Old Buddha was seen anxiously scanning her surroundings from one of the windows of her car. With her were the young Empress and the Princess Imperial, while the chief eunuch, Li Lien-ying, was in attendance. Recognising Her Majesty, every official fell upon his knees, whilst Chi Lu, chief officer of the Household, officiously shouted to the foreigners to remove their hats (which they had already done). The first to emerge from the train was the chief eunuch, who proceeded forthwith to check the long list of provincial tribute and treasure, mountainous loads of baggage which had travelled with the Court from the start and under Her Majesty's close personal supervision. After the eunuch came the Emperor, evidently extremely nervous, who, at a sign from Her Majesty, hurried into his sedan-chair and was swiftly borne away, without a word or a sign of recognition to any of the officials in attendance. After his departure, the Empress came out and stood upon the platform at the end of her carriage. "Quite a number of foreigners are here, I see," she was heard to observe. She saluted them in accordance with the etiquette observed by Chinese women bowing and raising her crossed hands. Prince Ch'ing then advanced to greet Her Majesty, and with him Wang Wen-shao (who had succeeded Li Hung-chang as Peace Plenipotentiary). They invited Her Majesty to enter her chair: "There is no hurry," she replied. She stood for some five minutes in full view of the crowd, talking energetically with the bystanders, and looking extremely well and youthful for her age, until the chief eunuch returned and handed her the list of baggage and treasure, which she scanned with close attention and then returned to him with an expression of satisfaction.

After this, at the request of the Viceroy of Chihli (Yüan Shih-k'ai), the foreign manager and engineer of the railway were presented to her, and received her thanks for the satisfactory arrangements made throughout the journey. She then entered her chair, a larger and finer conveyance than that supplied to the Emperor, and was borne away towards the Palace; by her side ran one of her favourite eunuchs repeatedly calling Her Majesty's attention to objects of interest. Whenever foreigners were in sight he would inform Her Majesty of the fact, and by one he was heard distinctly to say: "Look! Old Buddha, look quickly at that foreign devil," whereupon the Empress smiled and bowed most affably. Passing through the Southern gate of the Chinese city, her bearers carried her straight to the large *enceinte* of the Tartar city wall at the Ch'ienmen, where stands the shrine dedicated to the tutelary God of the Manchus. Here crowds of foreigners were in waiting on the wall. Looking down on the courtyard towards the shrine, they saw the Old Buddha leave her chair and fall upon her knees to burn incense before the image of the God of War, whilst several Taoist priests chanted the ritual. Rising she next looked up towards the foreigners, smiling and bowing, before she was carried away through the gate into the precincts of the Forbidden City. No sooner had she reached the inner palace (the Ning Shou kung) at about 2 P.M., than she commanded the eunuchs to commence digging up the treasure which had been buried there at the time of her flight; she was gratified beyond measure to find that it had indeed remained untouched.

Next, with an eye not only upon her future relations with foreigners but also on public opinion throughout the Empire, she issued a Decree conferring posthumous honours on the "Pearl concubine," who, as it will be remembered, was thrown down a well by her orders on the morning of the Court's flight from the Palace. In this Decree Her Majesty praises the virtue and admirable courage of the dead woman, which "led her virtuously to commit suicide when unable to catch up the Court on its departure," unwilling as she was to witness the destruction and pollution of the ancestral shrines. Her trustworthy conduct was therefore rewarded by the granting of a posthumous title and by promotion of one step in rank in the Imperial harem. The Decree was generally regarded as fulfilling all reasonable requirements of atonement towards the deceased, for in China the dead yet live and move in a shadowy, but none the less real, hierarchy. Alive, a "Pearl concubine" more or less counted for little when weighed against the needs of the Old Buddha's policies; once dead, however, her spirit must needs be conciliated and compensated.

Many Europeans who had witnessed the arrival of the Empress Dowager, remained at the railway station to see the unloading of her long baggage train, a most interesting and instructive sight. First were discharged the yellow chairs of the young Empress and the Princess Imperial, and four green chairs with yellow borders for the principal concubines; the other ladies of the Court followed in official carts, two to each vehicle. There were about ninety of them altogether, and the arrangements for their conveyance were accompanied by no little noise and confusion, the loquacity of some of the elder ladies being most noticeable. After their departure the attention of the eunuchs and minor officials was directed to the huge pile of the Empress Dowager's personal baggage, which included her cooking utensils and household articles in daily use. This operation, as well as the removal of a very large quantity of bullion, (every case of which was marked with the name of the province or city that had sent it as tribute), was for a time superintended by the Grand Council. But as the work was enough to last for several hours, it was not long before, led by Jung Lu, they entered their chairs and left for the City. It was noticed that Jung Lu seemed very infirm, and was supported as he walked by two attendants of almost gigantic stature.

From Cheng-ting fu to Pao-ting fu, and thence to Peking, the Court travelled, for the first time in its history, by train. The following description of the journey is reprinted, by kind permission of the editor of *The Times*, from an article published in that paper in March, 1902. It shows an interesting side of the Empress Dowager's character, that of the thrifty mistress of her goods and chattels, and gives a clear-cut impression of that vigorous personality which devoted the same close attention to details of transport and domestic economy as to niceties of Court ceremonial or historical precedents on vital questions of State; characteristics which inevitably suggest a marked resemblance between the Old Buddha and *le petit Caporal.*

"Early on December 31st the Court arrived at Cheng-ting fu, escorted by a large body of cavalry and accompanied by an enormous suite of officials, eunuchs and servants. The baggage was carried by a train of carts, estimated by an eye-witness at three thousand. The eunuchs numbered between three and four hundred, and of cooks and other kitchen servants there were almost as many. To provide accommodation for such a mass of people was impossible, especially as all the best quarters in the town had already been occupied by the high officials who, with their retainers, had come from the north to welcome the Empress Dowager on her return. For three days the Court rested in Cheng-ting fu, during which time the scene was one of indescribable confusion; baggage, stacked haphazard, filled every available corner, eunuchs and servants camping around and upon it, stolidly enduring much physical discomfort with the apathy peculiar to Asiatics. Yet, so great was the cold (on the night of January 1st the thermometer stood at two degrees (Fahrenheit) below zero) that many of these wayfarers gave way to lamentations and tears. Officials of the lower and middle grades, unable to obtain a lodging, were compelled to pass these days in such makeshift shelter as they could find in the vicinity of the railway station, where swarmed a mob of undisciplined soldiery. On the second night a fire broke out in the stables of the Imperial residence, which, though eventually checked before much damage was done, added greatly to the general disorder, and might well have had serious results in the absence of all organisation and control. The definite announcement of the Court's intention to leave for Pao-ting fu on the 3rd of January was received with unmistakable relief by the hungry, motley crowd which represented the pomp and pride of Asia's greatest Empire.

"From the Yellow River to the railway terminus at Cheng-ting fu — a distance of about two hundred and fifty miles — the ever-growing Imperial procession had travelled almost continuously in chairs, litters, carts, and on horseback, affording a spectacle which recalled in many of its chief characteristics those of Europe's mediæval pageantry as described by Scott. Every Manchu Prince had a retinue of horsemen varying from thirty to a hundred in number; along the frost-bound, uneven tracks which serve for roads in Northern China, an unending stream of laden waggons creaked and groaned through the short winter's day, and on, guided by soldier torch-bearers, through bitter nights to the appointed stopping places. But for the Empress Dowager and the Emperor, with the Chief Eunuch and the ladies of the Court, there was easy journeying and a way literally made smooth. Throughout its entire distance the road over which the Imperial palanquins were borne had been converted into a smooth, even surface of shining clay, soft and noiseless under foot; not only had every stone been removed, but as the procession approached gangs of men were employed in brushing the surface with feather brooms. At intervals of about ten miles well-appointed rest-houses had been built, where all manner of food was prepared. The cost of this King's highway, quite useless, of course, for the ordinary traffic of the country, was stated by a native contractor to amount roughly to fifty Mexican dollars for every eight yards — say £1,000 a mile — the clay having to be carried in some places from a great distance. As an example of the lavish expenditure of the Court and its officials, in a land where squalor is a pervading feature, this is typical.

"The hour for leaving Cheng-ting fu was fixed by the Empress Dowager at 9.30 A.M. on January 3rd. It is significant of the character of this remarkable woman, now in her sixty-seventh year, that even in matters of detail she leaves nothing to chance, nothing to others; the long arm of her unquestioned authority reaches from the Throne literally to the servants' quarters. Without

creating any impression of fussiness, she makes a distinctly feminine personality felt, and the master-mind which has guided the
destinies of China for the last forty years by no means disdains
to concern itself in minor questions of household commissariat
and transport. It is impossible not to reflect what such a woman
might have been, what she might have done for her people, had
there come into her life some accident or influence to show her,
in their true light, the corruption, dishonesty, and cold-blooded
cruelty of her reign.

"The departure of the Court by a special train, long since prepared for its reception by the Belgian railway authorities and
Sheng Hsüan-huai, was fixed for 9.30 A.M. in accordance with
Her Majesty's orders; that Imperial and imperious lady, however, made her appearance at the station at seven o'clock, accompanied by the young Empress, the Imperial concubine, and the
ladies-in-waiting. The Emperor had preceded her, and upon her
arrival knelt on the platform to perform respectful obeisance, in
the presence of an interested crowd. The next two hours were
spent by the Empress, who showed no signs of fatigue, in supervision of the arrangements for despatching the vast accumula-
tion of her personal baggage, and in holding informal audiences
with various high dignitaries, military and civil, on the platform.
Amongst others she sent for M. Jadot, and spent some time in
friendly conversation with him, expressing great satisfaction at
the excellent arrangements made for her comfort, and pleasure at
exchanging the sedan chair for her luxuriously-appointed draw-
ing-room car. She took pains to impress upon the engineer-in-
chief the importance which she attached to keeping the Court's
baggage and effects within reach, evincing on this subject much
determination of a good-humoured kind.

"Eventually, after the despatch of four freight trains, her mind
was relieved of this anxiety, but it was to be clearly understood
that the same personal supervision would be exercised at Pao-
ting fu, for in no circumstances could the impedimenta be sent
on in advance to Peking. There is a touch of feminine nature in

this incident which can hardly fail to bring the Empress Dowager into some degree of kinship with her fellow-women in other lands; there is also an implied reflection on the honesty of persons in attendance on the Court which is not without significance.

"The scene upon the platform was one of remarkable interest. In utter subversion of all accepted ideas in regard to the seclusion and privacy in which the Chinese Court is supposed to live, move, and have its being, there was on this occasion—and indeed throughout the journey—no sign of either attempt or wish to guard Their Majesties from observation and intrusion. The crowd, quietly inquisitive, but showing no inclination to demonstration of any sort, came and went at its pleasure; Yüan Shih-kai's braves, who to the number of about a thousand travelled to Peking as the Empress Dowager's bodyguard, crowded around the Imperial party, invading even their railway carriages. While the ruler of the Empire held audience with some of its highest officials, none of their retainers were employed, as might have been expected, in keeping the people at a respectful distance; the scene, in fact, bore striking testimony to that democratic side of the Chinese character which cannot but impress itself on every foreign visitor to a Viceroy's or magistrate's Yamên; in the present instance, however, it must have been, for all concerned, a new and remarkable experience.

"To the native spectators, the ladies of the Court with their eunuch attendants were as much objects of interest as the foreign railway officials; the Imperial concubine, 'Chin' (or 'Lustrous') Kuei fei, a lively young person of pleasing appearance, attracting much attention. This lady, gaily clad and with lavishly painted face, bestowed upon everything connected with the train an amount of attention which augurs well for the future of railway enterprise in China, running from car to car and chatting volubly with the ladies-in-waiting. All the ladies of the Court wore pearls in profusion—those of the Empress being particularly fine—and all smoked cigarettes in place of the time-honoured water-pipe. Herein again, for the optimistically inclined, may be found a harbinger of progress. During the Empress Dowager's audiences, lasting sometimes over a quarter of an hour at a time, the Emperor stood close at her side; invariably silent, generally listless, though his expression when animated is described as conveying an impression of remarkable intelligence. The young Empress has good features, marred, in European eyes, by excessive use of paint; she, too, appeared to be melancholy, and showed but little interest in her surroundings. The Emperor and both Empresses were simply dressed in quiet coloured silks.

"The special train in which, punctually at 9.30 A.M., the rulers of China left for their capital consisted of a locomotive and twenty-one carriages, arranged in the following order: — Nine freight cars laden with servants, sedan chairs, carts, mules, &c.; a guard's van, for employés of the railway; two first-class carriages (Imperial Princes); Emperor's special carriage; first-class carriage for high officials in attendance (Jung Lu, Yüan Shih-k'ai, General Sung Ch'ing, Lu Ch'uan-lin, Governor Ts'en of Shansi, Ministers of the Household, and others); Empress Dowager's special carriage; special carriages of the young Empress and the Imperial concubine; two second-class carriages, for eunuchs in attendance; first-class carriage for the Chief Eunuch, and the 'Service' carriage of M. Jadot.

"The special carriages had been prepared at great expense under instructions issued by the Director-General of Railways, Sheng. Those of the Empress Dowager, the Emperor, and his consort, were luxuriously furnished with costly curios and upholstered in Imperial yellow silk; each had its throne, divan, and reception room. Heavy window curtains had been thoughtfully provided in the carriages intended for the ladies' use; they were not required, however, as none of the party showed any desire for privacy during the entire journey. While travelling, the carriage of the Empress Dowager was the general rendezvous of all the ladies, attended by their eunuchs, the Empress Dowager spending much of the time in conversation with the Chief Eunuch — of somewhat notorious character — and the Emperor.

"The Empress Dowager possesses in a marked degree a characteristic frequently observed in masterful natures: she is extremely superstitious. The soothsayers and astrologers of the Court at Peking enjoy no sinecure; on the other hand, more attention is paid to their advice than that which the average memorialist obtains, and the position of necromancer to the Throne is not unprofitable. On the present occasion the sages-in-ordinary had fixed the auspicious hour for the Sovereign's return to Peking at 2 P.M. on January 7th; M. Jadot was accordingly requested to make the necessary arrangements to this end, and the Empress Dowager repeatedly impressed upon him the importance which she attached to reaching the Yung-ting gate of the city at that particular hour. To do this, as the engineer-in-chief pointed out, would entail starting from Pao-ting-fu at 7 A.M., but the determined ruler of China was not to be put off by any such considerations. At 6 A.M. this wonderful woman arrived at the station; it was freezing hard, and the sand storm was raging violently; soldiers bearing lanterns and torches led the way for the chair-bearers, since the day had not yet dawned. The scene in all its details appeals powerfully to the imagination. Once more the baggage question monopolised the Empress Dowager's attention; her last freight train, laden with spoils of the southern provinces, preceded the Imperial train by only twenty minutes. It will be realised that the august lady's requirements in the matter of personal supervision of her property added responsibility of a most serious kind to the cares — at no time light — of the railway staff.

"An incident occurred at Pao-ting fu which throws a strong side-light upon the Empress Dowager's character. The high Chinese officials above mentioned, who travelled in the first-class carriage between the Emperor's special car and that of the Empress, finding themselves somewhat pressed for space, consulted the railway officials and obtained another first-class compartment, which was accordingly added to the train. Her Majesty immediately noticing this, called for explanations, which failed to meet with her approval. The extra carriage was removed forthwith,

Yüan Shih-k'ai and his colleagues being reluctantly compelled to resume their uncomfortably crowded quarters; to these Her Majesty paid a visit of inspection before leaving the station, making enquiries as to the travellers' comfort, and expressing complete satisfaction at the arrangements generally.

"At 11.30 A.M., punctual to the minute, the train arrived at Feng-T'ai, where the Luhan line from Lu Ko-ch'iao meets the Peking-Tien-tsin Railway; here the British authorities took charge. The Empress Dowager was much reassured by the excellence of the arrangements and the punctuality observed; nevertheless, she continued to display anxiety as to the hour of reaching Peking, frequently comparing her watch with railway time. To M. Jadot, who took leave of Their Majesties at Feng-T'ai, she expressed again the satisfaction she had derived from this her first journey by rail, promising to renew the experience before long and to be present at the official opening of communication between Hankow and the capital. She presented five thousand dollars for distribution among the European and Chinese employés of the line, and decorated M. Jadot with the order of the Double Dragon, Second Class.

"From Feng-T'ai the railway under British control runs directly to the main south gate of the Tartar city (Ch'ien-men), but it had been laid down by the soothsayers and astrologers aforesaid that, for good augury, and to conform with tradition, the Imperial party must descend at Machiapu and enter the Chinese city by the direct road to the Palace through the Yung-ting Men. At midday, therefore, leaving the railway, the Court started in chairs for the city, in the midst of a pageant as magnificent as the resources of Chinese officialdom permit. The scene has been described by European writers as imposing, but a Japanese correspondent refers to its *mise-en-scène* as suitable to a rustic theatre in his own country. Be this as it may, the Empress Dowager, reverently welcomed by the Emperor, who had preceded her, as usual, entered the city, from which she had fled so ignominiously eighteen months before, at the hour named by her spiritual advisers as propitious. Present appearances at Peking, as well as the chastened tone of Imperial Edicts, indicate that the wise men were right in their choice.

"It may be added, in conclusion, as a sign of the times, that the Empress Dowager's sleeping compartment, prepared under the direction of Sheng Hsüan-huai, was furnished with a European bed. *Per contra*, it contained also materials for opium smoking, of luxurious yet workmanlike appearance."

Within a week or so of the Court's return, the representatives of the foreign Powers were duly received in audience under the conditions named in the Peace Protocol. It was observed that the Old Buddha assumed, as of old, the highest seat on the Throne dais, the Emperor occupying a lower and almost insignificant position. At the subsequent reception of the Minister's wives, in the Pavilion of Tranquil Longevity, the wife of the Doyen of the Diplomatic Corps presented an address to "welcome Her Imperial Majesty back to her beautiful Capital." The document was most cordially, almost effusively, worded, and showed that the astute and carefully pre-arranged measures taken by the Empress to conciliate the foreign Powers by adroit flattery and "allurements" had already attained their desired effect. Already the horrors of the siege, the insults and the arrogance of 1900, were forgotten; already the representatives of the Powers were prepared, as of old, to vie with each other in attempts to purchase Chinese favour by working each against the other.

In receiving the address of the ladies of the Diplomatic Body, Her Majesty created a marked impression by the emotion with which she referred to her affectionate regard for Europeans in general and her visitors in particular. With every evidence of complete sincerity she explained that a "Revolution in the Palace" had compelled her to flee from Peking; she deeply regretted the inconvenience and hardships to which her good friends of the Foreign Legations had been so unfortunately subjected, and she hoped for a renewal of the old cordial relations. The foreign ladies left the audience highly satisfied with the Empress Dowager for her condescension, and with themselves at being placed in a position to display such magnanimity. This audience was the first of many similar occasions, and reference to the numerous works in which the social side of Her Majesty's subsequent relations with Europeans have been described will show that the Old Buddha had not greatly erred when she assured Jung Lu of the value of ancient classical methods in dealing with barbarians, and promised him that all would readily be forgiven and forgotten in the tactful exercise of condescending courtesies.

Life settled down then into the old grooves, and all went on as before in the Capital of China, the garrisons of the Allies soon becoming a familiar feature in the streets to which gradually the traders and surviving Chinese residents returned. Once more began the farce of foreign intercourse with the so-called Government of the Celestial Empire, and with it were immediately renewed all the intrigues and international jealousies which alone enable its rulers to maintain some sort of equilibrium in the midst of conflicting pressures.

The power behind the Throne, from this time until his death, was undoubtedly Jung Lu, but the Foreign Legations, still confused by memories and echoes of the siege, and suspicious of all information which did not conform to their expressed ideas of the causes of the Boxer Rising, failed to realise the truth, and saw in him a suspect who should by rights have suffered punishment with his fellow conspirators. But the actual facts of the case, and his individual actions as recorded beyond dispute in the diary of His Excellency Ching Shan, and unmistakably confirmed by other independent witnesses, were not then available in the Chancelleries. Accordingly, when Jung Lu first paid his formal official calls upon the Foreign Ministers, he was anything but gratified at the reception accorded to him. In vain it was that he assured one member of the Diplomatic body, with whom he had formerly been on fairly good terms, that as Heaven was his witness he had done nothing in 1900 except his utmost to defend and save the Legations; his statements were entirely disbelieved, and so greatly was he chagrined at the injustice done him, that he begged the Empress Dowager in all seriousness to allow him to retire from the Grand Council. But Tzǔ Hsi, fully realising the situation, assured him of her complete confidence, and in a highly laudatory decree refused his request:—

"The Grand Secretary, Jung Lu," she said, "is a most patriotic and loyal servant of the Throne, upon whose services we have long and confidently relied. During the whole of the Boxer Rebellion crisis it was he, and he alone, who calmly and fearlessly held to the path of firmness, whilst all around him was confusion and shouting, so that without doubt, he was the means of saving the Empire. Most glorious indeed is his merit. Although it may be said that the situation has now been practically saved, we have by no means recovered from the effects of this grievous national disaster, and there is urgent necessity for the abolition of countless abuses and the introduction of a programme of Reform. It is fitting that all should assist us to this end. Whilst we ourselves, in the seclusion of the Palace, labour unceasingly, how is it possible that the Grand Secretary, who has received such high favour at our hands, should even think of withdrawing from the stress of public life, leaving to us incessant and harassing labour? Would not his conscience drive him to remorse when reflecting on the self-denying duties of every loyal Statesman in the service of his Sovereign? His prayer is refused."

On two subsequent occasions before her death, the populace and the foreign community in Peking were afforded opportunities of witnessing the Empress Dowager's return to the city from short excursions by railway, and on each of these her affable, almost familiar, attitude was a subject of general comment. The first occasion was in the following spring, when she visited the Eastern Tombs, and upon her return, sacrificing as usual before the shrine of the God of War in the *enceinte* of the Ch'ienmen, she talked volubly with several of the ladies whom she had met at Court. After emerging from the Temple, she called upon one of the eunuchs to bring her opera glasses, with which she eagerly scanned the crowd looking down from the wall of the city, waving her handkerchief whenever she perceived a familiar face. On one occasion she even shouted up an inquiry asking after the health of the daughter of one of the Foreign Ministers. The Manchu Princes and Chamberlains of the Court were unable to conceal their indignation and wrath at such condescension on the part of the Empress Dowager towards those whom, in spite of 1900, they still regarded (and regard to this day) as outer barbarians. So much incensed were they that they even urged Chi Lu to beg Her Majesty to desist, and to re-enter her chair, an invitation to which she paid not the slightest attention, being evidently well pleased at the violation of ceremonial etiquette which she was committing. It was noticed that the Emperor, on the other hand, took no notice whatsoever of the foreigners, and seemed to be sunk in a deep, listless melancholy.

The second occasion was after the Empress Dowager's visit to the Western Tombs in April, 1903, four days after the death of her faithful friend and adviser, Jung Lu. On this occasion Her Majesty appeared to be in very low spirits, descending from the train slowly, and with none of her wonted vivacity. She greeted Kuei Hsiang, her brother, who was kneeling on the platform to receive her, with one curt sentence, "You have killed Jung Lu by recommending that useless doctor," and passed on to her chair without another word. It was on this occasion, receiving certain foreign ladies in the travelling Palace erected for her at Pao-ting fu, that the Old Buddha alluded directly to the massacres of foreign missionaries which had taken place in that city, "with which she had, of course, nothing to do." No doubt by this time, and by force of repetition, Tzŭ Hsi had persuaded herself of her complete innocence; but however this may be, she undoubtedly won over most of the foreigners with whom she came in contact, by the charm and apparent sincerity of her manner.

Before settling down to the accustomed routine of life in the Palace, the Empress Dowager, whose *penchant* for personal explanation in Imperial Edicts seemed to be growing upon her, issued a

Decree which gained for her renewed sympathy from all classes of Chinese officials. After the usual exhortations to her faithful subjects to co-operate loyally in her schemes for Reform, to put off the old bad ways and to persist energetically in well-doing, she gives a graphic description of the hardships which she and the Emperor endured during her compulsory "tour to the West." After referring to the unforgettable shocks and sorrows of that journey, the Edict says: —

"I have now returned once more to my Palace and find the ancestral Temples reposing as of old in dignified and unbroken serenity. Beneath the deep awe which overcomes me in the presence of my glorious ancestors my soul feels an added weight of grief and remorse, and I only hope that by Heaven's continued favour I may yet live to accomplish some meritorious work."

And again, in a later passage, after referring to the drought which had brought Shensi and Shansi to the verge of famine, she says: —

"The Empire has come upon days of dire financial distress, and my people have been compelled to find funds for me from their very life blood; ill would it be for me to requite their loyalty by further levies of taxation, and the Throne is therefore bound to curtail its ordinary expenditure and to make strict economy its guiding rule for the future. With the exception of such repairs as are necessary to the Temples and ancestral shrines, I hereby command that no expenditure be incurred for repairs or decoration of the Palaces, except in cases of absolute necessity."

XXIV

HER MAJESTY'S NEW POLICY

THE crisis of 1900, all the horror of that abomination of desolation in her Capital and the hardships of her wandering in the wilderness, had brought home to the Empress the inherent weakness of her country and the stern necessity for remedial measures. Already, before the issue of the penitential Decree, quoted in an earlier chapter, she had announced to the world, with characteristic decision, her intention to adopt new measures and to break with those hoary traditions of the past which, as she had learned, were the first cause of the rottenness of the State. Her subsequent policy became in fact (though she was careful never to admit it) a justification of those very measures which the Emperor had so enthusiastically inaugurated in 1898, but her methods differed from his in that she omitted no precaution for conciliating the conflicting interests about the Throne and for disarming the opposition of the *intransigeants* of the provinces.

The first intimation of Her Majesty's conversion to new ideals of Government was given to the world in an Edict issued at Hsi-an on the 28th January, 1901, in the name of the Emperor. This document, drafted with the assistance of Jung Lu, is a remarkable example of Tzŭ Hsi's masculine intelligence and statecraft, though somewhat marred by those long-winded repetitions in which Chinese Edicts abound. It was received with enthusiastic delight by the *literati* throughout the Empire, even in Canton and the southern provinces, where, at the moment, Her Majesty was not personally popular. The vernacular Press claimed it as the most striking Edict in Chinese history. It combined an eloquent appeal to the people to accept the principle of reform together with a masterful justification of China and her people *vis-à-vis* the outside world. It was most skilfully worded so as to placate all parties in the State and thus to enhance the reputation of the Old Buddha. The "Young China" party was particularly enthusiastic, for by this Decree Her Majesty definitely abandoned the principle of absolute autocracy which had been for centuries the corner-stone of the Chinese system of government. It was realised that so complete a departure from the traditions of the Manchu Dynasty, of the Imperial Clan and of all her previous convictions, could not have been attained but for the bitter lessons of 1900, and, admiration was therefore the more keen for the skill and courage with which, on the verge of old age, she resumed the burden of government in her ravaged capital. It was the ruling passion bravely asserted, and the sympathy of the nation could hardly be withheld from a ruler who thus bore her share in the national humiliation, who so frankly accepted responsibility for past errors and promised new and better methods for the future.

It was, of course, inevitable, in the light of all experience, that many of her subjects, as well as most foreigners, should doubt her sincerity, and should regard this Edict, like many others, as a case of "when the devil was sick." But gradually, after the return of the Court, as it became clear to her immediate retainers and high officials that this self-confident woman was really in earnest, and as she continued steadily to impress her new policy upon the reluctant Clansmen, her popularity with the people at large, and especially in the south (where it had been much damaged by her fierce suppression of the Cantonese reformers of 1898), was gradually restored. From this time forward to the end of her life, whatever may have been the good or bad-faith of her advisers and chief officials, every act of her career is stamped with unmistakable signs of her sincerity in the cause of reform, borne out by her recorded words and deeds.

From the Boxer movement she had learned at a bitter cost the lesson she was now putting into practice, but for all that she remained to the end faithful in her affection for the memory of the Boxer leaders; to the last she never failed to praise their loyalty to her person and the patriotic bravery of their attempt to expel the foreigner. But she had been compelled to learn in the hard school of experience the utter hopelessness of that attempt, and she was forced to the conclusion that, for the future, and until China should be strong enough, all anti-foreign proceedings must be suppressed.

Unflinchingly, therefore, she announced to her people a change of front unparalleled in the history of China. Certain it is (as was fully proved in the case of the Emperor in 1898) that no other ruler of the Dynasty could have proclaimed such drastic changes without causing serious dissensions and possibly civil war. But so masterly were her methods of dealing with the necessities of the situation, and so forcibly did the style and arguments of her Decrees appeal to the *literati*, that they carried very general conviction. Even the most bigoted Confucianists were won by her subtle suggestions as to what would have been the attitude of the Sage himself if confronted by such problems as the nation had now to face.

The text of the Decree recording her conversion is interesting: —

"Throughout the entire universe there exist certain fixed principles which govern the conduct of men, but nowhere do we find any finally fixed form of government. It is written in the *Book of Changes*[1] that when any given condition of affairs has run its natural course, and has been succeeded by another, there is no saying how long this new state may

---

1. Precisely the same quotation was used by Ch'ung Hou in a despatch to the British Minister (Mr. Wade) in 1861, under somewhat similar circumstances. Since that date the most frequent criticism of foreign observers on the subject has been *"plus ça change, plus c'est la même chose."*

last; also in the Dialogues of Confucius it is written, that there is no difficulty in tracing the changes and reforms which each Dynasty has made
in regard to the methods of its predecessors. Certain things remain ever
unchanged, namely, the three fundamental bonds, between Sovereign
and subject, father and son, husband and wife; also the five great moral
obligations. These vary not, but are all as the sun and moon, enlighten-
ing the world. But in other matters there should be no fixed objection
to change, no hide-bound finality of ideas; to obtain music from a lute
or guitar one must touch all the strings. Each Dynasty in turn, since the
beginning of time, has seen fit to introduce changes and has abolished
certain customs of its predecessors; our own ancestors have set us many
an example in modifying their conduct to meet the exigencies of their
day. The system which prevailed at the date when first the Manchus
captured Peking was very different from that in vogue when Moukden
was the capital of our Empire.

"Looking at the matter broadly, we may observe that any system
which has lasted too long is in danger of becoming stereotyped, and
things that are obsolete should be modified. The essential need which
confronts us is at all costs to strengthen our Empire and to improve the
condition of our subjects. Ever since our journey to the West the Empress Dowager has been over-burdened with the labours and cares of
the State.[1]

"Bitterly have we reproached ourselves with the thought that for the
past twenty years abuses have steadily been increasing, while means of
suppressing them have been continually put off until, at last, the state
of our country has become parlous indeed. At this moment, when peace
negotiations are proceeding, it is a matter of urgent necessity that steps
be taken to reorganise our system of government so that hereafter our
Celestial Empire may recover its ancient place of wealth and power. The
Empress Dowager has now decided that we should correct our shortcomings by adopting the best methods and systems which obtain in
foreign countries, basing our future conduct upon a wise recognition
of past errors.

---

1. The literal translation of the Chinese is, "She has eaten her meal at sunset, and worn her
clothes throughout the night."

"Ever since the 23rd and 24th years of Kuang Hsü (1897 and 1898) there has been no lack of plans for reform, and suggestions of administrative change, but they have all been marked by vagueness and foolish looseness of thought. The crisis which was brought about in 1898 by the arch-traitor K'ang Yu-wei was in its possible consequences even more dangerous than the evil which has since been brought about by the unholy arts of the Boxers. To this day K'ang and his associates continue to preach treason and to disturb the public mind by means of their writings from overseas. The object of their writings is simply anarchy, nor do they scruple to use catchwords which, while apparently appealing to the patriotism of our people, are really intended to create dissension. Thus they talk of the "defence of the Empire" and the "protection of the Chinese race," and many of their dupes fail to realise that their main object is not reform, but a revolution against the Manchu Dynasty, and that they hope to create ill-feeling between the Empress Dowager and the Emperor. With treacherous cunning those conspirators took advantage of our weak state of health, and we were therefore glad when at our urgent request Her Majesty the Empress Dowager resumed the Regency. With amazing rapidity she grasped all the needs of the situation and delivered us from imminent peril, visiting swift punishment upon those traitors. But, whilst ridding the State of these evil-doers it was never Her Majesty's wish or intention to block reform measures, whilst we, on our side, though recognising the necessity for change in certain directions, were never guilty of any desire to abolish all the ancient ways of our ancestors. Our loyal subjects must recognise that it has been Her Majesty's invariable wish, and our own, to follow the happy mean, we, as mother and son, being in complete accord, to steer a wise middle course between conflicting policies.

"We have to-day received Her Majesty's orders, and learn that she is now thoroughly bent on radical reform. Nevertheless, whilst we are convinced of the necessity of blending in one harmonious form of administration the best customs and traditions of Chinese and European Governments, there is to be no talk of reaction or revolution. The chief defect in our system of administration is undoubtedly too close an adherence to obsolete methods, a too slavish devotion to the written word;

the result is a surfeit of commonplace and inefficient officials, and a deplorable lack of men of real talent. The average commonplace man makes a god of the written word, whilst every bureaucrat in the land regards it as a talisman wherewith to fill his purse, so that we have huge mountains of correspondence eternally growing up between one government office and another, the value of which is absolutely *nil* so far as any good to the country is concerned. On the other hand men of real ability lose heart and give up the public service in disgust, prevented from coming to the front by the mass of inefficiency that blocks the way. Our whole system of government has come to grief through corruption, and the first steps of progress in our Empire are clogged by the fatal word 'Precedent.'

"Up to the present the study of European methods has gone no further than a superficial knowledge of the languages, literature and mechanical arts of the West, but it must be evident that these things are not the essentials upon which European civilisation has been founded. The essential spirit of that civilisation is to be looked for in the fact that real sympathy and understanding exists between rulers and people, that officials are required to be truthful in word and courageous in action. The teachings handed down to us by our sacred ancestors are really the same as those upon which the wealth and power of European countries have been based, but China has hitherto failed to realise this and has been content to acquire the rudiments of European languages or technicalities, while changing nothing of her ancient habits of inefficiency and deep-rooted corruption. Ignoring our real needs we have so far taken from Europe nothing but externals; how can we possibly hope to advance on such lines? Any reforms to be effective and permanent must be made with a real desire for efficiency and honesty.

"We therefore hereby decree and command that the officials concerned shall now make close enquiry and comparison as to the various systems of government in force in European countries with special reference to those which obtain in China to-day, not only as regards the constitution of the Court and central government, but also concerning those things which make for the prosperity of our subjects, such as the system of examinations and education, the administration of the army and the regulation of finance. They will be required to report as to what changes are advisable and what institutions should be abolished; what methods we should adopt from abroad and what existing Chinese institutions should be retained. The things we chiefly need are a constant supply of men of talent, a sound basis of national finance, and an efficient army. Reports on these matters must be forwarded within two months, and upon them we shall humbly address Her Majesty, and ask for her decision before we take any definite action.

"Whilst the Court was in residence at T'ai-yüan we urgently called upon our subjects to assist us, and many Memorials were received, but as a general rule the advice they tendered was either stupid plagiarism taken from newspaper articles or else the narrow and bigoted views of untravelled scholars. They frequently sounded quite reasonable, but were in reality sheer nonsense, their principal characteristic being overweening conceit, which effectively prevented any breadth of argument. Very few of the suggestions advanced were practicable, for the reason that in recommending any course of action writers laid stress upon its alleged advantages without realising its drawbacks. There are many who talk glibly of reform and the wealth and power of foreign States, but deceive themselves as to the real origin of all knowledge; on the other hand your bigoted Confucianist will discourse endlessly upon the doctrines of the Sages, without in the least realising the needs of the present day. It is now for you, our officials, to steer a reasonable midway course, avoiding both these defects in submitting your proposals. We desire that your views shall be elaborated in the fullest detail for our consideration in determining upon a course of action.

"The first essential, however, more important even than the devising of new systems, is to secure men of administrative ability. Without talent no system can be made to succeed. If the letter of our projected reforms be not illuminated and guided by this spirit of efficiency in our officials then must all our hopes of reforming the State disappear into the limbo of lost ideals. We fully recognise that foolish adherence to the system of promotion by seniority has been one of the main factors in bringing about a condition of affairs that is almost incurable. If we would now be rid of it, our first step evidently is to think no more of selfish interests, but to consider the common-wealth only and to secure efficiency by some new and definite method, so that competent persons only may be in charge of public affairs. But if you, our officials, continue to cling to your ancient ways, following the ruts of procrastination and slothful ease; should you persist in evading responsibility, serving the State with empty catch-words while you batten on the fruits of your misdeeds, assuredly the punishment which the law provides stands ready, and no mercy will be shown you! Let this Decree be promulgated throughout the land."

It will be observed that in this Decree the Emperor is made to renounce and condemn the Reformers of 1898 and all their works. This, however sincerely convinced Her Majesty might be of the necessity for remedial measures, was only natural. For it was never one of the weaknesses of this masterful woman to make direct confession of error for the benefit of her own immediate entourage; not thus is prestige maintained in the atmosphere of an Oriental Court. She was now prepared to adopt many of the reforms which K'ang Yu-wei and his friends had advocated, but for all-important purposes of "face" it must be made quite clear that, in her hands, they were something radically different and superior. In promulgating her new opinions she could not afford to say anything which might be construed as direct justification of that reform movement which she herself had so ruthlessly suppressed. And so the "stupid people" must clearly understand that her present programme was by no means "revolutionary" like that of K'ang Yu-wei and his fellow-"conspirators." Nevertheless, her proposals for reform went as far as theirs, and, in some cases, even further, the only real difference being that in this case she, the Old Buddha, was a prime mover, where before she had been an opponent.

Looking back on the six years of her life and rule which followed the return from exile, there can be but little doubt of the sincerity of her conversion to reform, although there is no reason to believe that her sentiments towards foreigners had undergone any change for the better. The lesson which had been brought home to her with crushing force in the rise and fall of the Boxer movement and in the capture of Peking, was that national inefficiency means national extinction, a lesson which not all the statesmen of western lands have fully learned. She had realised that the material forces of the western world were not to be met and overthrown by quotations from the classics, and that, if China was to continue to exist as an independent State she must follow the example of Japan and put her house in order with equipment and defences adapted from western models. And with Tzŭ Hsi to realise was to act, a quality which, more than all others, distinguished her from the ruck of her Manchu kinsmen and officials, sunk in their lethargic fatalism and helplessness.

The situation which confronted her at the outset was anything but simple. Apart from the time-honoured privileges of the Imperial clans, whose arrogant ignorance she had come to appreciate at its proper value, she must needs be cautious in handling the susceptibilities of the provincial gentry and *literati*, the backbone of China's collective intelligence. At the same time, as far as the foreign Powers were concerned, she must be careful to preserve to the full that dignity on which her prestige with her own people depended, that *"l'empire c'est moi"* attitude which had been rudely shaken by the events of 1900. Not as the chastened penitent would she appear in their eyes, but as the innocent and injured victim of circumstances beyond her control. There were, in fact, several distinct *rôles* to be played, and none of them were easy.

The Edict issued from Hsi-an in February 1901 had been warmly applauded by scholars throughout the Empire as a literary feat of the first order, but most of the provincial officials (justified by all tradition and experience) regarded it as merely a classical "obiter dictum," and proceeded, therefore, in their old way, certain in their minds that the Old Buddha was only amusing herself, as was her wont, by throwing dust in the eyes of the barbarian, and that she would not be displeased if her lieutenants were to proceed slowly in carrying them into effect. Unto the end, even in the face of the earnest exhortations of her valedictory Decree, there were many provincial officials who, for reasons of personal prejudice and self-interest, professed to believe that the Old Buddha had been merely playing a part, but we can find nothing in her official or private record during these six years to justify that belief. Just before her return to Peking she issued an Edict in which her own convictions were very clearly indicated: —

"Ever since my sudden departure from the capital a year ago," she declared, "I have not ceased for a moment to brood over the causes of our national misfortunes and to feel deep remorse. Now, thanks to the protection of our tutelary deities, I am about to return to the capital. Whenever I think of the reasons for our undoing and the causes of our collective weakness I sincerely deplore the fact that I have not long ago introduced the necessary reforms, but I am now fully determined to put in force all possible measures for the reform of the State. Abandoning our former prejudices, we must proceed to adopt the best European methods of government. I am firmly determined to work henceforward on practical lines, so as to deliver the Empire from its present rotten state. Some of the necessary measures will naturally require longer periods of preparation than others, but after my return to Peking they must one and all gradually be introduced.

"In view of the urgent importance of this matter, Jung Lu and his colleagues have urged me to make a clear statement of my intentions and to declare without possibility of hesitation or doubt the irrevocable decision of the Throne, so that every official in the land may be stimulated to sincere and unremitting co-operation. For this reason I issue the present Decree solemnly recording my opinion that the condition of the Empire permits of no further evasion or delay in the matter of reform. Therein lies our only hope for the future. Myself and the Emperor, in the interests of all that we hold dear, have no alternative but to face, and steadily to pursue, this new policy; we must make up our minds what are the things to strive for, and employ the right men to help us to attain them. We are, as mother and son, of one mind, endeavouring only to restore our fallen fortunes. You, our people, can best serve by united efforts to this end."

Tzŭ Hsi had not only realised the immense superiority of the material forces of the western world, but she had also been convinced of the immense intellectual and political forces which education and increased means of communication were steadily creating amongst her own subjects, forces with which, as she perceived, the effete and ignorant Manchus would have to reckon sooner or later. It is quite plain from her Edicts on this delicate subject that she realised clearly the dangers which threatened the Manchu rule. She saw that their class privileges, the right to tribute, and all the other benefits of sovereignty which the founders of the Dynasty had won by force of arms and opportunity, had now become an anachronism, and must in the near future involve the Manchus themselves in serious dangers and difficulties, unless, by fusion, means could be found to avert them. Among the rules laid down by the founders of the Dynasty for the maintenance of the pure Manchu stock, was that which forbade intermarriage with Chinese. This law, though frequently violated in the garrisons of the south, had remained generally effective within the Metropolitan province, where it had served its purpose of maintaining the ruling class and its caste. But the Empress had now come to understand that if China was to be preserved as a sovereign State, it must be rather by means of Chinese energy and intelligence grafted on to the Manchu stock, than by the latter's separate initiative. In January 1902, immediately after her return to Peking, she gave effect to her convictions on this subject in a remarkable Decree whereby she recommended that, for the future, Manchus and Chinese should intermarry. "At the time of the founding of our Dynasty," she says, "the customs and languages of the two races were greatly different, and this was in itself reason sufficient for prohibiting intermarriage. But at the present day, little or no difference exists between them, and the time has come, therefore, to relax this law for the benefit of the Empire as a whole, and in accordance with the wishes of our people." In the same Edict Her Majesty deprecated the Chinese custom, which the Manchus had never adopted, of foot-binding, and urged that the educated classes should unite to oppose a custom so injurious to health and inhuman in practice. There was, however, to be no compulsion in this matter. In one respect only did she desire to adhere to the exclusive Manchu traditions, namely, as regards the selection of secondary wives for the Imperial harem, who must continue to be chosen exclusively from Manchu families; she did not desire "to incur any risk of confusion or dissension in the Palace, nor to fall into the error committed by the Ming Dynasty, in the indiscriminate selection of concubines, a matter affecting the direct and legitimate succession to the Throne." Nor would she expose her kinsmen to the risk of conspiracy against the Dynasty which would certainly occur if the daughters of the great Chinese houses were admitted to the Palace. The law had been laid down once and for all by Nurhachu, and it was binding on every occupant of the Dragon Throne, namely, "no Manchu eunuchs, no Chinese concubines."

Her next step, in a decree which frankly deplored the hopeless ignorance of her kinsmen, was to authorise the Imperial clansmen and nobles to send their sons to be educated abroad, so that perchance the lump of their inefficiency might yet be leavened. Eligible youths, between the ages of fifteen and twenty-five, and of good physique, were to be selected and their expenses would be defrayed by the Government.

This much for the Manchus; but in regard to the whole question of education, which she declared to be the very root of all China's difficulties, she perceived, after prolonged consultations with Yüan Shih-k'ai and Chang Chih-tung, that so long as the classical system continued, with its strong hold of tradition upon the masses, it must constitute the chief obstacle to any effective reform of the body politic. After much careful deliberation she decided that unless the whole system of classical examinations were abolished, root and branch, no tinkering with western learning could be of any practical use. The ancient system of arguing in a circle, which for over two centuries had characterised the ideal essay and hypnotised the ideal official, must undoubtedly triumph over all other educational methods, so long as it remained part of the official curriculum. Her Majesty took pains to point out by Edict that colleges had undoubtedly existed in the days of that model ruler, the Regent Duke Chou, more than two thousand five hundred years ago, on lines not greatly different from those of the foreign Universities of the present day; she proved also that the classical essay system was, so to speak, quite a recent innovation, having been introduced for the first time under the Ming Dynasty, about A.D. 1390. Eventually, in 1904, upon the advice of Yüan Shih-k'ai, approved by Chang Chih-tung, a Decree was issued finally abolishing the old system of examinations and making graduation at one of the modern colleges the only recognised path to official employment. At the same time, realising that the training of students in Japan, which had been proceeding on a very large scale, had produced a body of revolutionary scholars most undesirable in the eyes of the Government, she gave orders that arrangements should be made for sending more students in future to Europe and America.

This epoch-making announcement was followed by several other important Decrees, notably that which ordered the complete abolition of the opium traffic within a period of ten years, a Decree, which, embodying a sincere and powerful consensus of public opinion, has produced most unexpected results, marvellously creditable to the moral sense and recuperative energies of the Chinese race. The contrast is most striking between the widespread reform effected under this Edict, and the almost complete failure of those which set forth to reform the Metropolitan administration; these, thanks to the steady passive resistance of the mandarin in possession, resulted merely in perpetuating the old abuses under new names. The one new Ministry created at that time, and saluted by foreigners as a sign of genuine progress, was that of Posts and Communications (Yu-Ch'uan pu), which has been a byword for corrupt practices since its establishment, and a laughing stock among the Chinese themselves for inefficiency and extravagance.

After dealing with education, the Old Buddha turned her attention to a question which had frequently figured in recent Memorials of progressive officials, namely, the abolition of torture and other abuses prevalent in the so-called judicial system of the Empire. She realised that if China were ever to obtain the consent of the western Powers to the abolition of the foreigner's rights of extraterritoriality, she must devise and enforce civil and criminal codes similar to those of civilised countries. Her Edict on this subject, though in form excellent, seems to lack something of the conviction which marks her other Decrees of this period; it is very different, for instance, from those dealing with the abolition of opium and the reform of education. Its principles were obviously contrary to all her previous ideas and practice, and it is only fair to say that its result, in spite of much drafting of codes, has been little or none, as far as the barbarous practices of the provincial Yamêns are concerned. She decreed that, pending the introduction of the criminal code, decapitation should be the extreme penalty of the law; dismemberment and mutilation were to be abolished as barbarous; branding, flogging, and the vicarious punishment of relatives were to cease. These savage penalties, she observed, were originally introduced into China under the Ming Dynasty, and had only been adopted by the Manchus, with other Chinese customs, against their own more merciful instincts.

Finally, in deference to the unmistakable and growing tendencies of public opinion in the south, Tzŭ Hsi took the first steps towards the introduction of constitutional government by sending an Imperial Commission (under Duke Tsai Tse) to study the various systems in force in foreign countries, and their results. The return of this Mission was followed in the autumn of 1905 by the issue of the famous Decree in which she definitely announced her intention to grant a constitution, which should come into effect sooner or later, according to circumstances and the amount of energy or procrastination displayed by the officials and people in preparing themselves for the change. As an example of subtle argument calculated to appeal to the Chinese mind, the document is a masterpiece in its way. It says: —

"Ever since the foundation of the Dynasty one wise sovereign after another has handed down sage counsels to posterity; it has always been their guiding principle that methods of Government should be modified and adapted to meet the exigencies of the moment and changing conditions. China's great and increasing danger to-day is largely due to her unwise adherence to antiquated methods; if we do not amend our educational and political systems, we shall be violating the spirit which animated our Imperial ancestors, and shall disappoint the best hopes of our people. Our Imperial Commissioners have reported to us that the prosperity and power of foreign nations are largely due to principles of constitutional government based on the will of the people, which assures bonds of union and sympathy between the Sovereign and his subjects. It is therefore our duty to consider by what means such a Constitution may be granted as shall retain the sovereign power in the hands of the Throne, and at the same time give effect to the wishes of the people in matters of administration. Our State being at present unprepared, and our people uneducated, any undue haste is inadvisable, and would lead to no practical results. We must first reform the official system, following this by the introduction of new laws, new methods of education, finance and military organisations, together with a police system, so that officials and people may come to realise what executive government means as a foundation and preparation for the granting of a Constitution."

It was not to be expected that even Tzŭ Hsi could frame so radical and comprehensive a programme of change without incurring the strongest opposition and criticism of those to whom the established order meant loaves and fishes: at Peking, however, owing to the absence of an outspoken press, the opposition ran beneath the surface, exercised in the time-honoured form of dogged adherence to the ancient methods by the officials and bureaucrats on whose goodwill all reform ultimately depends. Against anyone less masterful and less popular than Tzŭ Hsi the Clansmen would undoubtedly have concerted other and more forcible measures, but they knew their Old Buddha and went in wholesome fear of her wrath. It was only her exceptional position and authority that enabled her to introduce the machinery for the establishment of constitutional government, based on the Japanese model, and there is reason to believe that even at this moment many conservative Manchus do not regard that measure seriously.

But despite the promise of constitutional government, public opinion in the south, never restrained in its utterances by the free-lances of the vernacular press of Hongkong and Shanghai, was outspoken in condemnation of Her Majesty's new policy, criticising her policy in general on the ground of her undignified truckling to Europeans. Lacking alike her masculine intelligence and courageous recognition of hard facts, making no allowance for the difficulties with which she was encompassed, and animated in many instances by a very real hatred of the Manchu rule, they attacked her in unmeasured terms of abuse; while the foreign press of the Treaty Ports, naturally suspicious of her motives and mindful of her share in the anti-foreign rising, was also generally unsympathetic, if not hostile. In both cases knowledge of the woman's virility and vitality was lacking. Her critics failed to realise that, like most mortals, the Empress was a mixture of good and bad, of wisdom and error, largely swayed by circumstances and the human equations around her, as well as by an essentially feminine quality of mutability; but withal, and above all, a born leader of men and a politician of the very first order.

The following extracts from articles published in the Shanghai press at that time, throw an instructive light on the spirit of Young China (like that of the Babu of India) as displayed in its anti-Manchu proclivities and bigoted chauvinism. One critic, taking for his text the entertainments given by Her Majesty to the Foreign Legations, wrote:—

"There can be no objection to giving a banquet to anyone who is likely to be grateful and show some return for hospitality, but what possible good purpose can be served by feasting those who treat you with suspicion? We Chinese are wont to despise our ignorant rustics when they display servility to foreigners, but what is to be said when one in the exalted position of the Empress Dowager demeans herself by being on terms of affectionate intimacy with the wives of Foreign Ministers, and even with women belonging to the commercial and lower classes? Nowadays foreign food is served at the Palace in a dining-room decked out in European style: the guests at these entertainments thank their Imperial hostess on taking leave, and the very next day their Legations will furiously rage against China at our Foreign Office. Therefore, as for moderating their barbarous ways, her food and her wines are simply wasted. As a matter of fact, these guests of hers do not scruple to compare her banquets of to-day with the melons and vegetables which she sent to the Legations during the siege, a comparison by no means flattering to Her Majesty. The thing is becoming a scandal. When Russia poured out entertainments in honour of Li Hung-chang she got something for her money; can it be that Her Majesty is looking to similar results in the present case for herself?"

Another critic, nearer the truth as we know, doubted whether the Empress Dowager was in reality enamoured of foreign ways, and whether she was not simulating good relations, while preparing some deep-laid scheme of future revenge.

"It is scarcely credible," he observed, "that, at her time of life, she should be able to change all her habits and form ties so completely alien to her education and nature. Would not the foreigners naturally ask themselves whether she was likely to cherish any real affection for people who had plundered her palace and had forced her to hand over to the executioners her most faithful and trusted officials?"

This writer had difficulty, however, in believing that she contemplated another Boxer movement and frankly confessed himself perplexed.

"As Her Majesty's chief occupation at the present time would appear to be to accumulate money at all costs rather than to reorganise and strengthen the resources of the Empire, her ultimate object may well be to secure that whatever happens, her old age shall be comfortably provided for."

Nevertheless, unheeding of criticism and strong in the wisdom of her own convictions, Tzŭ Hsi continued steadily on the lines which she had laid down as necessary for the future safety of the Empire. It was not to be expected that even her strong personality could overcome in a day the entrenched forces of native prejudice and conservatism within and without the palace. At the time of her death many of the chief strongholds of the ancient system (*e.g.*, the power of the eunuchs and the organised corruption of officials) remained practically uncriticised and untouched; but at her passing she had marked out a rough course by which, if faithfully followed, the ship of State might yet be safely steered through the rocks and shallows of the dangerous seas ahead.

XXV

THE VALEDICTORY MEMORIAL
OF JUNG LU

THE death of Jung Lu was a great grief to the Empress Dowager. In the course of her long life there was hardly any crisis or important event of her reign wherein she had not been greatly assisted by this devoted follower. Upon hearing of his death she issued a Decree from the Travelling Palace at Pao-ting-fu, praising the patriotism and clear-sighted intelligence of the deceased, who, since the beginning of his career as an honorary licentiate had risen to be Controller of the Imperial Household, Tartar General and Viceroy, in all of which capacities he had rendered signal service. At the time of his death he had attained to the highest honours open to a subject in China, namely, the position of Grand Secretary and Grand Councillor. In this Decree Her Majesty laid particular stress on his endeavours to promote a good understanding with the foreign Powers in 1900. Further, in token of her affectionate regard, she bestowed upon him a coverlet with charms worked thereon from the Dharani Sutra in Sanscrit and Thibetan, to be used as a pall for his burial, and she commanded Prince Kung to proceed to the residence of the deceased, with ten officers of the Imperial Guard, to perform a sacrifice on her behalf to the soul of the departed statesman. She granted him the posthumous designation of "learned and loyal," together with the highest hereditary rank open to one who had not been a victorious military commander or a member of the Imperial Clan. His ancestral tablet was given a place at the Shrine of Good and Virtuous Officials, and three thousand taels (£350) were issued from the privy purse towards his funeral expenses.

Jung Lu's valedictory Memorial has never been published in China, but those in attendance on Her Majesty reported that it affected her very deeply. On the day after it reached her, she issued the following Decree:—

"The deceased Grand Secretary, Jung Lu, was our senior Grand Councillor at a time of critical danger to the State, and his sage counsel and eminent services to the Throne have never been sufficiently appreciated either in China or abroad. He was absolutely indispensable to us, and we depended entirely upon his advice. Two months ago, owing to his ill-health, we were compelled to grant him leave of absence, but, unfortunately, all remedies have proved unavailing, and he has passed away. We have perused his valedictory Memorial, full of a deep and touching earnestness in regard to the future of our Empire and the condition of the Chinese people; and in recalling all the incidents of his distinguished career the violence of our grief can only find expression in tears. Following upon the posthumous honours already conferred upon him, we hereby decree that a second Imperial sacrifice shall be offered to his spirit on the day before his remains are removed for burial, and, furthermore, that the record of his life be transmitted to the Historiographers' Department for inclusion in the annals of our Dynasty. All faults that may have been recorded against him shall be expunged, so that the depth of our sincere affection for this faithful servant may be made manifest."

Jung Lu was sixty-seven years of age at the date of his death (April 11th, 1903), and it is probable that had it not been for the severe hardships and mental strain which he endured during the Boxer crisis, he would have lived much longer to serve his

Imperial mistress. By his death Prince Ch'ing and his corrupt following rose to increased power (Prince Ch'ing being the only available Manchu of rank sufficient to succeed Jung Lu as head of the Grand Council), and they have retained it, in the subterranean labyrinths of Palace intrigues, ever since.

Jung Lu was essentially a middle-course man, striving earnestly for that "happy mean" which the Empress Dowager professed to desire. Had he lived, it is safe to say that he would not have approved of the haste with which she proceeded to sanction the undigested programme for constitutional government, and with his advice against it the Old Buddha would probably not have persisted in the idea. He had repeatedly urged her, before the return of the Court, to make it quite clear in her Edicts that a reform policy was necessary for the preservation of the Empire, but, like the late Prince Ito, he was all for a slow and cautious procedure, and present-day observers of events connected with the constitutional government programme can hardly doubt the wisdom of his advice.

The following is a translation of his, hitherto unpublished, valedictory Memorial, a document which throws valuable light on the *coup d'état* and the relations between Tzŭ Hsi and the Emperor at that time. In other respects it confirms many conclusions wherein Jung Lu's authoritative testimony was lacking to complete an otherwise satisfactory chain of evidence.

"I, your slave, Jung Lu, a Grand Councillor and Grand Secretary of the Wen Hua Throne Hall, having grievously failed to requite the favours of your Majesties, now that my breath is almost spent, respectfully upon my knees do present this my valedictory Memorial, and beg that your Majesties may be pleased to cast your divine glance upon it.

"I, all unworthy, have received no small bounty at the hands of your Majesty the Empress Dowager, and had hoped that Heaven might grant me length of days, wherein to display my utmost endeavour in your Majesty's service. Respectfully I recall the fact that I began my career of service as an Imperial guardsman, and was on duty with H.M.

Hsien-Feng in his excursion to the hunting park at Mulan (Jehol) in the tenth year of his reign. At that time the situation of the Empire was one of great danger; within there was the grave peril of the rebellion, while from without the English and French barbarians had captured our sacred capital. We witnessed the violation of the Imperial shrines and saw the sacred chariot of His Majesty leave Peking, in accordance with the principle laid down by Mencius that a sovereign should leave his capital when it is threatened by invasion of barbarians.

"After the Court's arrival at Jehol, I had the honour of attending on your Majesty the Empress Dowager as Chamberlain, and when His Majesty Hsien-Feng lay on his deathbed, I had the honour to warn your Majesty and the Empress Consort that the Princes Cheng and Yi were conspiring against the State. After the death of His Majesty, those wicked Princes usurped the Regency and for many days your Majesty was in danger so great that it may not be spoken of by any loyal subject. Happily, your Majesty, acting on your own firm initiative and by the favour of Heaven, dealt with those abominable traitors in the twinkling of an eye and rescued the State from its dire peril. For years thereafter you carried on the Regency, rebellions were suppressed and peace reigned within the four seas.

"Your slave received many marks of the Imperial favour and rose to be Minister of the Household; I was thus constantly in attendance on your Majesty. When the late Emperor T'ung-Chih mounted the dragon and ascended on high, it was to me that your Majesty confided the duty of bringing the present Emperor Kuang-Hsü to the Palace. Favours vast as the universe have I received, and for these I have made no return.

"While acting as Captain General of the Peking Gendarmerie, I incurred your Majesty's displeasure; thereafter for seven years I awaited, without incurring, the fitting penalty for my offence. Later, when His Majesty came to his majority and you were pleased to hand over to him the reins of government, you conferred on me the post of Tartar General at Hsi-an. Subsequently I was recalled to my former position at the capital. In the 24th year of Kuang-Hsü (1898) your Majesties determined on the introduction of European methods of government and the Emperor summoned me to audience and conferred on me the post of Viceroy of

Chihli at Tientsin where I was ordered to select and introduce reforms based on foreign methods in order to remedy the weakness of China's administration. But who could then have believed that the damnable treasons of K'ang Yu-wei should be the means of thwarting your Majesties' great plans? His Majesty the Emperor, by giving ear to the lying inventions of that traitor and his associates, if only for a little while, undoubtedly allowed his filial piety to suffer temporary decline. This was particularly the case when he wrote with his own Imperial hand a Decree stating that his reform proposals were being blocked by your Majesty and that, as you were opposed to the spirit of progress, your interference in State affairs was a danger to the nation. Towards me also His Majesty displayed his divine wrath, so that once more had your slave deserved the penalty of 'axes and halberds.' But when I sought your Majesty in secret audience and laid before you the details of the plot, once more did your Majesty, without a moment's hesitation respond to our prayer and resume the control of affairs, swiftly visiting upon evildoers of that treacherous crew the might of your august displeasure.

"In the 26th year of Kuang-Hsü, certain Princes and Ministers, statesmen deficient in virtue, gained your Majesty's ear, and even your divine wisdom was misled to believe in the unholy arts and magic of the Boxers until the ancestral shrines were the centre of cataclysmic disaster and the destinies of the Empire trembled in the balance. Again and again I besought your Majesty to put an end to these traitors, but could not gain your consent. I incurred at that time your censure on more than one occasion, and for forty days waited in my house fully expectant of doom. But even so your Majesty repeatedly sought my advice, and though it was not always followed, I was able to avert the crowning misfortune which would have resulted from the killing of the foreign Ministers. For this service your Majesty has since deigned frequently to express gratitude.

"When your Majesties left the city on your tour of inspection to Hsi-an, you decided upon punishing those evil-minded Princes and Ministers, and thereafter to introduce a policy of gradual and effective reform in every branch of the administration. Already, during the past two years, considerable progress has been made. By your return to the capital the sun has been restored to our firmament, and even the barbarians of the east and west have acclaimed your Majesty's benevolence and impartial solicitude for all, Chinese and foreigners alike.

"For the past year I have been continually ill, but until two months ago was able to continue in the performance of my arduous duties. Since then I have been compelled to apply for sick-leave and have sought permission to resign my offices, but your Majesty sent eunuchs to me with gracious messages and presents of ginseng[1] and commanded that I should make all haste to recover and resume my duties.

"But even the beneficent protection of your Majesty has failed to avert from me the last ravages of illness. Repeated attacks of asthma, with increasing difficulty in breathing, have now brought me to the last stage of weakness and the very point of death. With my last breath I now entreat your Majesty vigorously to continue in the introduction of reforms, so that gradually our Middle Kingdom may attain to a condition as prosperous as that of the great States of Europe and Japan. During my tenure of the office of Grand Councillor I have seen many men appointed to offices for which they were by no means fitted; herein lies a source of weakness, but above all it is necessary that a radical change should be made in the selection of District Magistrates and in the methods by which taxation is levied and collected. It were well if the good example of economy which your Majesty is setting were more generally followed. In the seclusion of the Palace it is impossible for your Majesty to know the truth as to the condition of your subjects, and were it not for the prohibitive cost of transporting your enormous retinues, I should advise that the Throne should make regular tours of inspection in various parts of the Empire. His Majesty Ch'ien-Lung made several such tours, and among the wise sovereigns of ancient times the custom was regularly observed. At this moment my mind is becoming confused; I can say no more. Humbly do I pray that your Majesty's fame may continue to grow, and that all my good wishes on your Majesty's behalf may be fulfilled. Then, even though I die, yet shall I live.

---

1. Ginseng, the specific remedy of the Chinese pharmacopœia for debility, supposed to possess certain magical qualities when grown in shapes resembling the human form or parts thereof. The best kind, supplied as tribute to the Throne, grows wild in Manchuria and Corea.

"I have dictated this, my valedictory Memorial, to my adopted son, Liang Ku'ei, for transmission to your Majesty, in temporary residence at Pao-ting fu. Though conscious of its numerous shortcomings, for which I beg forgiveness, I reverently entreat your Majesty to peruse it. Prostrate before the Throne, with my dying breath, I, Jung Lu, now conclude my Memorial.

"(Dated the 10th April, 1903.)"

XXVI

HER MAJESTY'S LAST DAYS

IN the summer of 1908 Tzŭ Hsi's generally robust health showed signs of failing, a fact which is recorded in her valedictory Decree, and one of no small importance in considering the coincident fact of the illness of the Emperor. Of the causes and manner of the latter 's death, nothing will ever be definitely known; they lie buried with many another secret of the Forbidden City, in the hearts of Li Lien-ying and his immediate satellites. Even among the higher officials, Manchu and Chinese, of the capital, opinions differ, and many conflicting theories are current to account for the remarkable coincidence of the death of Tzŭ Hsi and her unhappy nephew on successive days. For those who seek it there is no lack of circumstantial evidence to justify the conclusion that the long-threatened Emperor was "removed" by the reactionaries, headed by the chief eunuch, who had only too good cause to fear his unfettered authority on the Throne. At the same time it is conceivably possible that many of the plots and proceedings of the Summer Palace at that time might have been unknown to Tzŭ Hsi, and that she was purposely kept in ignorance by those who foresaw the possibility of her early death and took their precautions accordingly, after the Oriental manner. Indeed, in the light of much trustworthy evidence of eye-witnesses, this seems

a rational explanation of events to which any solution by theories of coincidence is evidently difficult. Most of the following
account of Her Majesty's last days is derived from the statements
of two high officials, one Manchu and the other Chinese, who
were at that time on duty with the Court. Their testimony and
their conclusions coincide, on the whole, with those of the best-
informed and most reliable Chinese newspapers, whose news
from the capital is also generally from official sources. We accept them, naturally, with all reserve, yet with an inclination to
give the Empress Dowager, on this occasion, the benefit of their
good opinions and our own doubts. The simultaneous deaths
may possibly have been due to natural causes, but it is to be observed by the most sympathetic critic, that the account given by
Her Majesty's loyal servants of her behaviour immediately after
the Emperor's death, is by no means suggestive of sorrow, but
rather of relief.

It was in the previous autumn that the Emperor became very
ill, so much so that he was gradually compelled during the last
year of his life to desist from performance of the usual sacrifices,
which entail no small expenditure of physical energy through
their genuflections and continual prostrations. The impression
gradually gained ground that His Majesty was not likely to live
much longer, and it was remarked, and remembered as a significant fact, that the Old Buddha had some time before given orders for the engagement of special wet-nurses for the infant son
of Prince Ch'un, born in February, 1906. It was understood that
these orders implied the selection of this infant Prince to succeed
Kuang-Hsü, but although many attempts were made to induce
her to declare herself on this subject, she declined to do so on the
ground that her previous experience had been unlucky, that her
selections had been the cause of much misunderstanding, and
that, moreover, it was a house-law of the Dynasty that the heir
to the throne could only be lawfully selected when the sovereign
was *in extremis* a rule which she had completely disregarded in

View, from the K'un Ming Lake, of the Summer Palace.

the nomination of Prince Tuan's son in 1900.[1]

In this connection, there is every reason to believe that Tzŭ Hsi's superstitious nature, and the memory of the prophecies of woe uttered by the Censor Wu K'o-tu at the time of his protesting suicide, had undoubtedly led her to regret the violation of the sacred laws of succession which she committed in selecting Kuang-Hsü for the Throne. On more than one occasion in recent years she had endeavoured to propitiate the shade of the departed Censor, and public opinion, by conferring upon him posthumous honours. Towards the end of her reign, after the humiliations inflicted on China in successive wars by France, Japan and the coalition of the Allies, she was frequently heard to express remorse at having been led into courses of error which had brought down upon her the wrath of Heaven. In 1888, when the Temple of Heaven was struck by lightning, and again, when the chief gate of the Forbidden City took fire and was destroyed, she interpreted these events as marks of the Supreme Being's disapproval of her actions. The Emperor's subsequent conspiracy with K'ang Yu-wei and his associates of 1898, became in her eyes another judgment and visitation of Heaven. It may therefore reasonably be assumed that when the Boxer Princes persuaded her of the efficacy of their magic arts and of their ability to drive the foreigner into the sea, she seized upon the hope thus offered as a means of regaining the favour of the gods and atoning for past errors. Although in selecting the son of Prince Tuan to be heir to her son, the Emperor T'ung-Chih (thus passing over Kuang-Hsü), she had once more violated the house-laws of the Dynasty, there is no doubt that she took her risks in the certain hope that further prestige must accrue to her house and to herself, by the fact that the boy Emperor's father, next to herself in power, would be hailed by the Chinese people as the Heaven-sent deliverer, the conqueror of the hated barbarian, and the saviour of his country. In other words, recognising that the mistakes she had

---

1. This house-law was made by the Emperor Ch'ien Lung to prevent his Court officials from intriguing for the favour of the Heir Apparent.

committed had seriously injured her in the eyes of the nation, she determined to endeavour to retrieve them by one last desperate throw. Later, after the return from exile, when she realised that this heroic venture had been as misguided in its inception as any of her former misdeeds, she showed her splendid courage and resource by a swift *volte-face* in the adoption of those very reform measures which she had formerly opposed, and by annulling the appointment of Prince Tuan's son as Heir to the Throne. She thus cut herself adrift from all connection with the Boxer leaders as completely and unhesitatingly as she wiped out from the annals of her reign all reference to the Edicts which she had issued in their favour. The present-day result brought about by this change of policy, and of the succession of Prince Ch'un's infant son to the Throne, has been to establish more firmly than ever that junior branch of the Imperial family. It is now believed, if not accepted, at Court, that the first Prince Ch'un, the father of Kuang-Hsü and grandfather of the present sovereign, will eventually be canonised with the title of "Ti" or Emperor, which would practically make him, by posthumous right, the founder of a new Dynastic branch. The problem of the direct succession, even in Chinese eyes, is not simple, and it was generally supposed (*e.g.* by the *Times* correspondent at Peking in October 1908) that the Empress Dowager would nominate Prince P'u Lun to succeed Kuang-Hsü, thus restoring the succession to the senior branch of the family. This would certainly have appealed to orthodox and literary officials throughout the Empire, and, as a means of appeasing the distressed ghost of the protesting Censor, would have been more effective than the course she actually adopted. Doctor morrison, discussing this question of the succession before the event, expressed the general opinion that the appointment of another infant to succeed the Emperor Kuang-Hsü (involving another long Regency) would be fraught with great danger to the Dynasty. There is no doubt that the present situation, lacking that strong hand which for half a century has held together the chaotic fabric of China's Government, suffers from the fact that for many years to come the supreme authority must remain in the hands of a Regent, and a Regent whose position is *ab initio* undermined by the powerful influences brought to bear by the senior branch of the Imperial Clan. Tzŭ Hsi was fully aware of the position which would be created, or rather prolonged, by the selection of Prince Ch'un's son, and for this reason, no doubt, the selection of Kuang-Hsü's successor was postponed until the very day of her death. When, at last, confronted by the imperative necessity for action, she had to make up her mind, there were two things that chiefly weighed with her. These were, firstly, the promise that she had made to Jung Lu, and, secondly, her un-concealed dislike for Prince Ch'ing, who had made himself the chief spokesman for the claims of Prince P'u Lun. It was also only natural that she should wish to leave to her favourite niece (the Consort of Kuang-Hsü) the title and power of Empress Dowager, if only in reward for years of faithful and loyal service to herself. In other words, the claims of the human equation and her own inclinations outweighed, unto the end, the claims of orthodox tradition and the qualms of her conscience.

Throughout the winter of 1907 and the following spring, the Empress enjoyed her usual vigorous health. In April she went, as usual, to the Summer Palace, where she remained all through the hot season. With the heat, however, came a recurrence of her dysenteric trouble and in August she had a slight stroke of paral-ysis, as the result of which her face, hitherto remarkably youth-ful for a woman of seventy, took on a drawn and tired appear-ance. In other respects her health seemed fairly good; certainly her vigour of speech remained unimpaired, and she continued to devote unremitting attention to affairs of State. She was wont frequently to declare her ambition of attaining to the same age as Queen Victoria, a ruler for whom she professed the greatest admiration; she would say that she could trace, in the features of the English Queen, lines of longevity similar to those in her own. The Taoist Abbot, Kao, whom she used to receive in frequent au-diences, and who possessed considerable influence over her, had prophesied that she would live longer than any former Empress of the Dynasty; but his prophecy was not fulfilled, for she died younger than three of her predecessors.

In the summer of 1908 the Old Buddha took a keen interest in the impending visit of the Dalai Lama, which had been arranged for the autumn. The chief eunuch, Li, begged her to cancel this visitation on the ground that it was notoriously unlucky for the "Living Buddha" and the Son of Heaven to be resident in one city at the same time. Either the priest or the sovereign would surely die, he said.[1] To this Tzŭ Hsi replied that she had long since decided in her mind that the Emperor's illness was incurable, and she saw no reason, therefore, to stop the coming of the Dalai Lama. Nevertheless, in July, she summoned certain Chinese physicians, educated abroad, to attend His Majesty, who had become greatly emaciated and very weak. They reported that he was suffering from Bright's disease. Their examination of the august patient and their diagnosis of his symptoms were necessarily perfunctory, inasmuch as etiquette prevented the application of the proper tests, but they professed to have verified the fact that the action of the heart was very weak. On the other hand, writers in the newspapers of the south did not hesitate to assert that the whole medical performance was a farce and that the death of the Emperor would undoubtedly take place so soon as the powers about the Throne had made up their minds that the Empress Dowager was not likely to live much longer.

According to the general consensus of opinion in the capital, the relations between the Old Buddha and His Majesty were not unfriendly at this period. It was said that shortly before his illness became acute the Empress Dowager had encouraged him to take a more active part in affairs of State, and to select candidates for certain high offices: she certainly renewed the practice of showing him Decrees for the formality of his concurrence. When the reformer Wang Chao returned from flight, and gave himself up

---

1. The chief eunuch in reality objected to the Buddhist pontiff on his own account, for the Lama's exactions from the superstitious would naturally diminish his own opportunities.

to the police, she, who had vowed the death of this man in 1898, invited His Majesty to decide what punishment should now be inflicted upon him. The Emperor, after long reflection, suggested that his life be spared. "By all means," replied the Old Buddha, "I had fully intended to forgive him, but desired to hear your opinion. Full well I know your sincere hatred of fellows like K'ang Yu-wei and his associates, and I was afraid, therefore, that you might insist on the immediate decapitation of Wang Chao." She evidently believed that she had completely eradicated from His Majesty's mind all opposition to her wishes.

As the Emperor's health grew worse, the eunuchs were instructed not to keep him waiting when calling upon the Empress Dowager and he was also excused at the meetings of the Grand Council from awaiting her arrival and departure on his knees. A Manchu holding a high position at Court testifies to the truth of the following incident. One morning, after perusal of a Censor's Memorial, which contained several inaccurate statements, His Majesty observed to the Grand Council, "How little of truth there is in common rumour. For instance, I know myself to be really ill, yet here it is denied that there is anything the matter with me." The Empress Dowager here broke in:—"Who has dared to utter such falsehoods? If caught, he will certainly be beheaded." Kuang-Hsü then proceeded to say:—"I am really getting weaker every day, and do not see my way to performing the necessary ceremonies on the occasion of Your Majesty's approaching birthday." Compassionately the Old Buddha replied:—"It is more important to me that you should recover your health than that you should knock your head on the ground in my honour." The Emperor fell on his knees to thank her for these gracious words, but collapsed in a fainting fit. Prince Ch'ing thereupon advised that a certain doctor, Chü Yung-chiu, trained in Europe, should be called in, but his advice was not followed till later. On the following day His Majesty enquired of the Court physicians in attendance, whose medical training is the same as that which has been handed down since the days of the T'ang Dynasty, whether

THE EMPRESS DOWAGER, WITH THE CHIEF EUNUCH, LI LIEN-YING.

his disease was likely to be fatal. "The heart of your Emperor is greatly disturbed," said he. Dr. Lu Yung-pin replied:—"There is nothing in Your Majesty's present condition to indicate any mortal disease. We beseech Your Majesty to be calm: it is for us, your servants, to be perturbed in spirit."

After Tzŭ Hsi's stroke of paralysis, the wildest rumours were circulated as to her condition, so much so that, realising the excited state of provincial opinion, and its relation to the question of the Constitution which was to have been granted, Her Majesty decided to carry out without further delay the promise she made in 1906. On the 1st of the 8th Moon, she therefore promulgated a Decree, showing signs of the same spirit of lofty statesmanship as was displayed by the rulers of Japan, and evidently based on their example, whereby it was promised that a constitutional form of government would be completely established within a period of nine years. At the same time it was decreed that every branch of the government should institute the changes necessary to facilitate the introduction of the new dispensation. On issuing this Decree she expressed her hope of living to witness the convening of the first Chinese Parliament, and added that if Prince Tuan's son had proved himself worthy, and had remained Heir Apparent, he would by now have been of age to carry on the government after the Emperor's death. Age was creeping upon her, and she would be glad to retire to the Summer Palace for her declining years. As long as matters remained in their present state, it would be necessary to refer important questions for her decision, but she greatly wished that the period of her Regency should not be indefinitely prolonged.

In September occurred the fiftieth birthday of the ex-Viceroy of Chihli Yüan Shih-k'ai, while the Court was still in residence at the Summer Palace. The Old Buddha showered costly gifts upon her trusted Minister, and almost every high official in Peking attended the birthday ceremonies to present congratulations and gifts. Conspicuous by his absence, however, was the Emperor's brother, Prince Ch'un (the present Regent), who had applied for short leave in order to avoid being present, and who offered no presents.

A significant incident occurred in connection with the birthday ceremonies. Among the many complimentary scrolls, presented by friends and hanging on the walls, were a pair which attracted much attention, until they were hurriedly removed. One contained the following inscription: — "5th day of the 8th Moon of the Wu Shen year" (this was the date of the crisis of the *coup d'état* when Yüan Shih-k'ai warned Jung Lu of the plot, and thus brought about the practical dethronement of the Emperor), and on the other were the words: — "May the Emperor live ten thousand years! May Your Excellency live ten thousand years."

The words *"wan sui"* meaning "ten thousand years," are not applicable to any subject of the Throne, and the inner meaning of these words was, therefore, interpreted to be a charge against Yüan of conspiring for the Throne. It was clear that some enemy had sent the scrolls as a reminder of Yüan's betrayal of his Sovereign ten years before, and that they had been hung up either as the result of connivance or carelessness on the part of Yüan's people. Four months later, when the great ex-Viceroy fell, this incident was remembered and inevitably connected with Prince Ch'un's non-appearance at the birthday ceremonies.

In September, the Dalai Lama reached Peking, but owing to a dispute on certain details of ceremonial, his audience was postponed. It was finally arranged that the Pontiff should kowtow to the Throne, and that the Emperor should then rise from his seat and invite the Lama to sit beside him on a cane couch. This ceremonial was most reluctantly accepted, and only after much discussion, by the Dalai Lama, who considered his dignity seriously injured by having to kowtow. He had brought with him much tribute, and was therefore the more disappointed at the Old Buddha's failure to show him the marks of respect which he had expected. His audience was held early in October, when Her Majesty requested him to offer up prayers regularly for her long life and prosperity.

In October, the foreign Ministers were also received at the Summer Palace, and on the 20th of that month the Court returned to the Lake Palace for the winter. On this, her last State progress, the Empress Dowager approached the city as usual in her State barge, by the canal which joins the Summer Palace Lake with the waters of the Winter Palace, proceeding in it as far as the Temple of Imperial Longevity, which is situated on the banks of this canal. It was observed that as she left the precincts of the Summer Palace she gazed longingly towards the lofty walls that rise from the banks of the lake, and from thence to the hills receding into the far distance. Turning to the "Lustrous" concubine who sat at her feet, she expressed her fears that the critical condition of the Emperor would prevent her from visiting her favourite residence for a long time to come.

The Old Buddha sat in a cane chair on the raised deck of her magnificent barge adorned with carved dragons and phœnixes; she was surrounded by her favourite eunuchs, and half a dozen of the chief ladies of the Court. As she descended from the barge, supported by two eunuchs, and entered the sedan chair which bore her to within the temple precincts, her vivacity and good spirits formed a subject of general comment. She performed the usual sacrifices at the Temple of Imperial Longevity, a shrine which she had liberally endowed; but it was remembered after her death, as an unfortunate omen, that the last stick of incense failed to ignite. Upon leaving the temple she begged the priests to chant daily liturgies and to pray for her longevity, in view of her approaching birthday.

After leaving the temple precincts she proceeded with her ladies-in-waiting to the Botanical and Zoological Gardens, which lie just outside the "West-Straight gate" of the city. On arrival at the gates, she insisted upon descending from her sedan chair, and made the entire round of the gardens on foot. She expressed interest and much pleasure at the sight of animals which she had never seen before, and announced her intention of frequently visiting the place. She asked numerous questions of the keepers, being especially interested in the lions, and created much amusement amongst her immediate entourage by asking the director of the gardens (a Manchu official of the Household) for information as to where the animals came from, a subject on which he was naturally quite uninformed. "You don't seem to know much about zoology," she observed, and turned from the crestfallen official to address one of the keepers in a most informal manner. The chief eunuch, Li Lien-ying, wearied by such unwonted exercise, implored Her Majesty not to tire herself, but the Old Buddha took pleasure, clearly malicious, in hurrying him round the grounds. The occasion was unusual and remarkably informal, and the picture brings irresistibly to the English mind memories of another strong-minded Queen and her inspection of another garden, where heads were insecure for gardeners and Cheshire cats. Eye-witnesses of that day's outing commented freely on their Imperial Mistress's extraordinary spirits and vitality, predicting for her many years of life.

Her Majesty, whose memory on unexpected subjects was always remarkable, referred on this occasion to the elephant which had been presented to her by Tuan Fang upon his return from Europe, and which, together with several other animals for which she had no fitting accommodation in the Palace grounds, was the first cause and first inmate of the Zoological Gardens. The elephant in question had originally been in charge of the two German keepers who had accompanied it from Hagenbeck's establishment; these men had frequently but unsuccessfully protested at the insufficient rations provided for the beast by the Mandarin in charge. Eventually the elephant had died of slow starvation, and the keepers had returned to Europe, after obtaining payment of their unexpired contracts, a result which brought down upon the offending official Her Majesty's severe displeasure. She referred now to this incident, and expressed satisfaction that most of the animals appeared to be well cared for, though the tigers' attendant received a sharp rebuke.

After Her Majesty's return to the Winter Palace, everything

was given over to preparations for the celebration of her seventy-third birthday on the 3rd of November. The main streets of the city were decorated, and in the Palace itself arrangements were made for a special theatrical performance to last for five days. A special ceremony, quite distinct from the ordinary birthday congratulations of the Court, was arranged for the Dalai Lama, who was to make obeisance before Her Majesty at the head of his following of priests. The health of His Majesty did not permit of his carrying out the prescribed ceremony of prostration before Her Majesty's Throne in the main Palace of Ceremonial Phœnixes; he therefore deputed a Prince of the Blood to represent him in the performance of this duty, and those who knew its deep significance on such an occasion realised that the condition of his health must indeed be desperate. This impression was confirmed by the fact that he was similarly compelled to abandon his intention of being present at a special banquet to be given to the Dalai Lama in the Palace of Tributary Envoys. The high priest, who had been compelled to kneel outside the banquet hall to await the arrival of His Majesty, was greatly incensed at this occurrence.

At eight in the morning of the birthday His Majesty left his Palace in the "Ocean Terrace" and proceeded to the Throne Hall. His emaciated and woe-begone appearance was such, however, that the Old Buddha took compassion upon him, and bade his attendant eunuchs support him to his palanquin, excusing him from further attendance. Later in the day she issued a special Decree praising the loyalty of the Dalai Lama, and ordering him to return promptly to Thibet, "there to extol the generosity of the Throne of China, and faithfully to obey the commands of the Sovereign power." The Empress Dowager spent the afternoon of her birthday in the congenial amusement of a masquerade, appearing in the costume of the Goddess of Mercy, attended by a numerous suite of concubines, Imperial Princesses, and eunuchs, all in fancy dress. They picnicked on the lake, and Her Majesty appeared to be in the very highest spirits. Unfortunately, towards evening, she caught a chill, and thereafter, partaking too freely of a mixture of clotted cream and crab apples, she had a return of the dysenteric complaint from which she had suffered all through the summer. On the following day she attended to affairs of State as usual, reading a vast number of Memorials and recording her decision thereon, but on the 5th of November neither she nor the Emperor were sufficiently well to receive the Grand Council, so that all business of government was suspended for two days. Upon hearing of Her Majesty's illness, the Dalai Lama hastened to present her with an image of Buddha, which, he said, should be despatched forthwith to her mausoleum at the hills, the building of which had just been completed under the supervision of Prince Ch'ing.[1] The high priest urged all haste in transmitting this miracle-working image to her future burial-place; if it were done quickly, he said, her life would be prolonged by many years, because the unlucky conjunction of the stars now affecting her adversely would avail nothing against the magic power of this image. The Old Buddha was greatly reassured by the Dalai Lama's cheerful prognostications, and next morning held audience as usual. She commanded Prince Ch'ing to proceed without delay to the tombs, and there to deposit the miraculous image on the altar.[2] She ordered him to pay particular attention to the work done at the mausoleum, and to make certain that her detailed instructions had been faithfully carried out. Prince Ch'ing demurred somewhat at these instructions, inquiring whether she really wished him to leave Peking at a time when she herself and the Emperor were both ill. But the Old Buddha would brook no argument, and peremptorily ordered him to proceed as instructed. "I am not likely to die," she said, "during the next few days; already I am feeling much better. In any case you will do as you are told." On Monday, November 9th, both the Empress Dowager and the Emperor were present at a meeting of the Grand

---

1. He had succeeded Jung Lu as custodian of the mausolea.
2. The Imperial Mausoleum lies about ninety miles to the east of Peking, covering a vast enclosure of magnificent approach and decorated with splendid specimens of the best style of Chinese architecture. It consists of four palaces, rising one behind the other, and at the back of the fourth and highest stands the huge mound classically termed the "Jewelled Citadel," under which lies the spacious grave chamber.

Council, and a special audience was given to the Educational Commissioner of Chihli province, about to leave for his post. At this audience the Old Buddha spoke with some bitterness of the increasing tendency of the student class to give vent to revolutionary ideas, and she commanded the Commissioner of Education to do all in his power to check their political activities.

Shortly afterwards four more physicians, who had come up from the provinces, were admitted to see His Majesty. That same afternoon he had a serious relapse, and from that day forward never left his palace. On the following morning he sent a dutiful message (or it was sent for him) enquiring after the Empress Dowager's health, she being also confined to her room and holding no audiences. The Court physicians reported badly of both their Imperial patients: being fearful as to the outcome, they begged the Comptroller-General of the Household to engage other physicians in their place. The Grand Council sent a message to Prince Ch'ing, directing him to return to Peking with all haste, his presence being required forthwith on matters of the highest importance. Travelling night and day, he reached the capital at about eight o'clock in the morning of the 13th, and hastened to the palace. He found the Old Buddha cheerful and confident of ultimate recovery, but the Emperor was visibly sinking, his condition being comatose, with short lucid intervals. His last conscious act had been to direct his Consort to inform the Empress Dowager that he regretted being unable to attend her, and that he hoped that she would appoint an Heir Apparent without further delay. Whether these dutiful messages were spontaneous or inspired, and indeed, whether they were ever sent by the Emperor, is a matter upon which doubt has been freely expressed.

Immediately after the arrival of Prince Ch'ing, an important audience was held in the Hall of Ceremonial Phœnixes. Her Majesty was able to mount the Throne, and, although obviously weak, her unconquerable courage enabled her to master her physical ailments, and she spoke with all her wonted vehemence and lucidity. A well-informed member of the Grand Council, full of wonder at such an exhibition of strength of will, has recorded the fact that she completely led and dominated the Council. There were present Prince Ch'ing, Prince Ch'un, the Grand Councillor Yüan Shih-k'ai, and the Grand Secretaries Chang Chih-tung, Lu Ch'uan-lin and Shih Hsü.

Her Majesty announced that the time had come to nominate an Heir to the Emperor T'ung-Chih, in accordance with that Decree of the first day of the reign of Kuang-Hsü, wherein it was provided that the deceased Sovereign's ancestral rites should be safeguarded by allowing him precedence over his successor of the same generation. Her choice, she said, was already made, but she desired to take the opinion of the Grand Councillors in the first instance. Prince Ch'ing and Yüan Shih-k'ai then recommended the appointment of Prince P'u Lun, or, failing him, Prince Kung. They thought the former, as senior great-grandson of Tao-Kuang, was the more eligible candidate, and with this view Prince Ch'un seemed disposed to agree. The remaining Grand Councillors, however, advised the selection of Prince Ch'un's infant son.

After hearing the views of her Councillors, the Old Buddha announced that long ago, at the time when she had betrothed the daughter of Jung Lu to Prince Ch'un, she had decided that the eldest son of this marriage should become Heir to the Throne, in recognition and reward of Jung Lu's lifelong devotion to her person, and his paramount services to the Dynasty at the time of the Boxer rising. She placed on record her opinion that he had saved the Manchus by refusing to assist in the attack upon the Legations. In the 3rd Moon of this year she had renewed her pledge to Jung Lu's widow, her oldest friend, just before she died. She would, therefore, now bestow upon Prince Ch'un as Regent, the title of "Prince co-operating in the Government," a title one degree higher than that which had been given to Prince Kung in 1861, who was made "Adviser to the Government" by herself and her co-Regent.

THE SON OF HEAVEN.
Hsuan-T'ung, Emperor of China.

Upon hearing this decision, Prince Ch'un arose from his seat and repeatedly kowtowed before Her Majesty, expressing a deep sense of his own unworthiness. Once more Yüan Shih-k'ai courageously advanced the superior claims of Prince P'u Lun: he was sincerely of opinion that the time had come for the succession to be continued along the original lines of primogeniture; it was clear also that he fully realised that Prince Ch'un was his bitter enemy. The Old Buddha turned upon him with an angry reprimand. "You think," she said, "that I am old, and in my dotage, but you should have learned by now that when I make up my mind nothing stops me from acting upon it. At a critical time in a nation's affairs a youthful Sovereign is no doubt a source of danger to the State, but do not forget that I shall be here to direct and assist Prince Ch'un." Then, turning to the other Councillors, she continued:—"Draft two Decrees at once, in my name, the first, appointing Tsai-feng, Prince Ch'un, to be 'Prince co-operating in the Government' and the second commanding that P'u Yi, son of Prince Ch'un, should enter the palace forthwith, to be brought up within the precincts." She ordered Prince Ch'ing to inform the Emperor of these Decrees.

Kuang-Hsü was still conscious, and understood what Prince Ch'ing said to him. "Would it not have been better," he said, "to nominate an adult? No doubt, however, the Empress Dowager knows best." Upon hearing of the appointment of Prince Ch'un to the Regency, he expressed his gratification. This was at 3 P.M.; two hours later the infant Prince had been brought into the Palace, and was taken by his father to be shown both to the Empress Dowager and the Emperor. At seven o'clock on the following morning the physicians in attendance reported that His Majesty's "nose was twitching and his stomach rising," from which signs they knew that his end was at hand. During the night, feeling that death was near, he had written out his last testament, in a hand almost illegible, prefacing the same with these significant words:—

"We were the second son of Prince Ch'un when the Empress Dowager selected Us for the Throne. She has always hated Us, but for Our misery of the past ten years Yüan Shih-k'ai is responsible, and one other" (the second name is said to have been illegible). "When the time comes I desire that Yüan be summarily beheaded."

The Emperor's consort took possession of this document, which, however, was seen by independent witnesses. Its wording goes to show that any conciliatory attitude on the part of the Emperor during the last year must have been inspired by fear and not by any revival of affection.

Later in the day a Decree was promulgated, announcing to the inhabitants of Peking and the Empire that their sovereign's condition was desperate, and calling on the provinces to send their most skilful physicians post-haste to the capital so that, perchance, His Majesty's life might yet be saved. The Decree described in detail the symptoms, real or alleged, of Kuang-Hsü's malady. It was generally regarded as a perfunctory announcement of an unimportant event, long expected.

At 3 P.M. the Empress Dowager came to the "Ocean Terrace" to visit the Emperor, but he was unconscious, and did not know her. Later, when a short return of consciousness occurred, his attendants endeavoured to persuade him to put on the Ceremonial Robes of Longevity, in which etiquette prescribes that sovereigns should die. It is the universal custom that, if possible, the patient should don these robes in his last moments, for it is considered unlucky if they are put on after death. His Majesty, however, obstinately declined, and at five o'clock he died, in the presence of the Empress Dowager, his consort, the two secondary consorts, and a few eunuchs. The Empress Dowager did not remain to witness the ceremony of clothing the body in the Dragon Robes, but returned forthwith to her own palace, where she gave orders for the issue of his valedictory Decree and for the proclamation of the new Emperor.

The most interesting passage of the Emperor's valedictory Decree was the following:—"Reflecting on the critical condition of our Empire, we have been led to combine the Chinese system with certain innovations from foreign countries. We have endeavoured to establish harmony between the common people and converts to Christianity. We have reorganised the army and founded colleges. We have fostered trade and industries and have made provision for a new judicial system, paving also the way for a Constitutional form of government, so that all our subjects may enjoy the continued blessings of peace." After referring to the appointment of the Regent and the nomination of a successor to the Dragon Throne, he concludes (or rather the Empress concluded for him) with a further reference to the Constitution, and an appeal to his Ministers to purify their hearts and prepare themselves, so that, after nine years, the new order may be accomplished, and the Imperial purposes successfully achieved.

The Old Buddha appeared at this juncture to be in particularly good spirits, astonishing all about her by her vivacity and keenness. She gave orders that a further Decree be published, in the name of the new Emperor, containing the usual laudation of the deceased monarch and an expression of the infant Emperor's gratitude to the Empress Dowager for her benevolence in placing him on the Throne.

It will be remembered that the Censor Wu K'o-tu committed suicide at the beginning of Kuang-Hsü's reign, as an act of protest at the irregularity in the succession, which left no heir to the Emperor T'ung-Chih, that monarch's spirit being left desolate and without a successor to perform on his behalf the ancestral sacrifices. The child, P'u Yi, having now been made heir by adoption to T'ung-Chih, in fulfilment of the promise made by Tzŭ Hsi at the time of this sensational suicide, it appeared as if the irregularity were about to be repeated, and the soul of Kuang-Hsü to be left in a similar orbate condition in the Halls of Hades, unless some means could be found to solve the difficulty and meet the claims of both the deceased Emperors. In the event of Kuang-Hsü being left without heir or descendant to perform the all-important worship at his shrine, there could be but little doubt that the feelings of the orthodox would again be outraged, and the example of Wu K'o-tu might have been followed by other Censors. The Empress Dowager, realising the importance of the question, solved it in her own masterful way by a stroke of policy which, although without precisely applicable precedent in history, nevertheless appeared to satisfy all parties, and to placate all prejudices, if only by reason of its simplicity and originality. Her Decree on the subject was as follows:—

"The Emperor T'ung-Chih, having left no heir, was compelled to issue a Decree to the effect that so soon as a child should be born to His Majesty Kuang-Hsü, that child would be adopted as Heir to the Emperor T'ung-Chih. But now His Majesty Kuang-Hsü has ascended on high, dragon-borne, and he also has left no heir. I am, therefore, now obliged to decree that P'u Yi, son of Tsai Feng, the 'Prince co-operating in the Government,' should become heir by adoption to the Emperor T'ung-Chih, and that, at the same time, he should perform joint sacrifices at the shrine of His Majesty Kuang-Hsü."

To those who are acquainted with the tangled web of Chinese Court ceremonial and the laws of succession, it would seem that so simple (and so new) an expedient might suitably have been adopted on previous similar occasions, since all that was required was to make the individual living Emperor assume a dual personality towards the dead, and one cannot help wondering whether the classical priestcraft which controls these things would have accepted the solution so readily at the hands of anyone less masterful and determined than Tzŭ Hsi.

In a subsequent Decree the Empress Dowager handed over to the Regent full control in all routine business, reserving only to herself the last word in all important matters of State. The effect of this arrangement was to place Prince Ch'un in much the same position of nominal sovereignty as that held by Kuang-Hsü himself, until such time as the young Emperor should come of age, or until the death of the Empress Dowager. In other words, Tzŭ Hsi had once more put in operation the machinery by which she had acquired and held the supreme power since the death of her husband, the Emperor Hsien-Feng. There is little doubt that at this moment she fully expected to live for many years more, and that she made her plans so as to enjoy to the end uninterrupted and undiminished authority. In her Decree on this subject, wherein, as usual, she justifies her proceedings by reference to the critical condition of affairs, she states that the Regent is to carry on the Government "subject always to the instructions of the Empress Dowager," and there can be no doubt that had she lived the Emperor's brother would no more have been permitted any independent initiative or authority than the unfortunate Kuang-Hsü himself.

XXVII

TZŬ HSI'S DEATH AND BURIAL

AT the close of a long and exciting day, Her Majesty retired to rest on the 14th of November, weary with her labours but apparently much improved in health. Next morning she arose at her usual hour, 6 A.M., gave audience to the Grand Council and talked for some time with the late Emperor's widow, with the Regent and with his wife, the daughter of Jung Lu. By a Decree issued in the name of the infant Emperor, she assumed the title of Empress Grand Dowager, making Kuang-Hsü's widow Empress Dowager. Elaborate ceremonies were planned to celebrate the bestowal of these new titles, and to proclaim the installation of the Regent. Suddenly, at noon, while sitting at her meal, the Old Buddha was seized with a fainting fit, long and severe. When at last she recovered consciousness, it was clear to all that the stress and excitement of the past few days had brought on a relapse, her strength having been undermined by the long attack of dysentery. Realising that her end was near, she hurriedly summoned the new Empress Dowager, the Regent and the Grand Council to the Palace, where, upon their coming together, she dictated the following Decree, speaking in the same calm tones which she habitually used in transacting the daily routine of Government work: —

"By command of the Empress Grand Dowager: Yesterday I issued an Edict whereby Prince Ch'un was made Regent, and I commanded that the whole business of Government should be in his hands, subject only to my instructions. Being seized of a mortal sickness, and being without hope of recovery, I now order that henceforward the government of the Empire shall be entirely in the hands of the Regent. Nevertheless, should there arise any question of vital importance, in regard to which an expression of the Empress Dowager's opinion is desirable, the Regent shall apply in person to her for instructions, and act accordingly."

The significance of the conclusion of this Decree is apparent to anyone familiar with Chinese Court procedure and with the life history of the Empress herself. Its ingenious wording was expressly intended to afford to the new Empress Dowager and the Yehonala Clan an opportunity for intervention at any special crisis, thus maintaining the Clan's final authority and safeguarding its position in the event of any hostile move by the Regent or his adherents. And the result of this precaution has already been shown on the occasion of the recent dismissal of Tuan Fang[1] from the Viceroyalty of Chihli for alleged want of respect in connection with the funeral ceremonies of the Empress Dowager, an episode which showed clearly that the Regent has no easy game to play, and that the new Empress Dowager, Lung Yu, has every intention to defend the position of the Clan and to take advantage thereof along lines very similar to those followed by her august predecessor.

After issuing the Decree above quoted, the Empress Dowager, rapidly sinking, commanded that her valedictory Decree be drafted and submitted to her for approval. This was done quickly. After perusing the document, she proceeded to correct it in several places, notably by the addition of the sentence, "It became my inevitable and bounden duty to assume the Regency." Commenting on this addition, she volunteered the explanation that she wished it inserted because on more than one occasion

---

1. *Vide* Biographical Note in the Appendix.

her assumption of the supreme power had been wrongfully attributed to personal ambition, whereas, as a matter of fact, the
welfare of the State had always weighed with her as much as
her own inclinations, and she had been forced into this position.
From her own pen also came the touching conclusion of the Decree, that sentence which begins: "Looking back over the memories of these fifty years," etc. She observed, in writing this, that
she had nothing to regret in her life, and could only wish that it
might have lasted for many years more. She then proceeded to
bid an affectionate farewell to her numerous personal attendants
and the waiting maids around her, all of whom were overcome
by very real and deep grief. To the end her mind remained quite
clear, and, at the very point of death, she continued to speak as
calmly as if she were just about to set out on one of her progress-
es to the Summer Palace. Again and again, when all thought the
end had come, she recovered consciousness, and up to the end
the watchers at her bedside could not help hoping (or fearing, as
the case might be with them) that she would yet get the better of
Death. At the last, *in articulo mortis*, they asked her, in accordance
with the Chinese custom, to pronounce her last words. Strangely
significant was the answer of the extraordinary woman who had
moulded and guided the destinies of the Chinese people for half
a century: "Never again," she said, "allow any woman to hold the
supreme power in the State. It is against the house-law of our Dynasty and should be strictly forbidden. Be careful not to permit
eunuchs to meddle in Government matters. The Ming Dynasty
was brought to ruin by eunuchs, and its fate should be a warning
to my people." Tzŭ Hsi died, as she had lived, above the law, yet
jealous of its fulfilment by others. Only a few hours before she
had provided for the transmission of authority to a woman of
her own clan: now, confronting the dark Beyond, she hesitated
to perpetuate a system which, in any but the strongest hands,
could not fail to throw the empire into confusion. She died, as
she had lived, a creature of impulse and swiftly changing moods,
a woman of infinite variety.

At 3 P.M., straightening her limbs, she expired with her face
to the south, which is the correct position, according to Chinese
ideas, for a dying sovereign. It was reported by those who saw
her die that her mouth remained fixedly open, which the Chinese interpret as a sign that the spirit of the deceased is unwilling
to leave the body and to take its departure for the place of the
Nine Springs.

Thus died Tzŭ Hsi; and when her ladies and handmaidens
had dressed the body in its Robes of State, embroidered with the
Imperial Dragon, her remains and those of the Emperor were
borne from the Lake Palace to the Forbidden City, through long
lines of their kneeling subjects, and were reverently laid in separate Halls of the Palace, with all due state and ceremony.

The valedictory Decree of Tzŭ Hsi, the last words from that
pen which had indeed been mightier than many swords, was for
the most part a faithful reproduction of the classical models, the
orthodox swan song of the ruler of a people which makes of its
writings a religion. Its text is as follows:—

The Valedictory Mandate of Her Majesty Tz'ŭ-Hsi-Tuan-Yu-
K'ang-I-Chao-Yü-Chuang-Cheng-Shou-Kung-Ch'in-Hsien-Ch'ung-
Hsi, the Empress Grand Dowager, declareth as follows:—

"I, of humble virtue, did reverently receive the appointment
of the late Emperor Hsien-Feng, which prepared for me a place
amongst his Consorts. When the late Emperor T'ung-Chih succeeded in early childhood to the Throne, there was rebellion still
raging in the land, which was being vigorously suppressed. Not
only did the Taiping and turbaned rebels engage in successive
outbreaks, but disorder was spread by the Kuei-chou aborigines
and by Mahomedan bandits. The provinces of the coast were in
great distress, the people on the verge of ruin, widespread distress confronting us on all sides.

"Co-operating then with the senior Consort of Hsien-Feng,
the Empress Dowager of the Eastern Palace, I undertook the

heavy duties of Government, toiling ever, day and night. Obeying the behests of His late Majesty, my husband, I urged on the
Metropolitan and provincial officials, as well as the military commanders, directing their policies and striving for the restoration
of peace. I employed virtuous officials and was ever ready to
listen to wise counsel. I relieved my people's distress in time
of flood and famine. By the goodwill and bounty of Heaven, I
suppressed the rebellions and out of dire peril restored peace.
Later, when the Emperor T'ung-Chih passed away and the Emperor Kuang-Hsü, now just deceased, entered by adoption upon
the great heritage, the crisis was even more dangerous and the
condition of the people even more pitiable. Within the Empire
calamities were rife, while from abroad we were confronted by
repeated and increasing acts of aggression.

"Once again it became my inevitable and bounden duty to
assume the Regency. Two years ago I issued a Decree announcing the Throne's intention to grant a Constitution, and this present year I have promulgated the date at which it is to come into
effect. Innumerable affairs of State have required direction at
my hands and I have laboured without ceasing and with all my
might. Fortunately, my constitution was naturally strong, and
I have been able to face my duties with undiminished vigour.
During the summer and autumn of this year, however, I have
frequently been in bad health, at a time when pressing affairs
of State allowed me no repose. I lost my sleep and appetite, and
gradually my strength failed me. Yet even then I took no rest,
not for a single day. And yesterday saw the death of His Majesty
Kuang-Hsü; whereat my grief overwhelmed me. I can bear no
more, and so am I come to the pass where no possible hope of
recovery remains.

"Looking back upon the memories of these last fifty years, I
perceive how calamities from within and aggression from without have come upon us in relentless succession, and that my life
has never enjoyed a moment's respite from anxiety. But to-day
definite progress has been made towards necessary reforms. The

new Emperor is but an infant, just reaching the age when wise instruction is of the highest importance. The Prince Regent and all our officials must henceforth work loyally together to strengthen the foundations of our Empire. His Majesty must devote himself to studying the interests of the country and so refrain from giving way to personal grief. That he may diligently pursue his studies, and hereafter add fresh lustre to the glorious achievements of his ancestors, is now my most earnest prayer.

"Mourning to be worn for only twenty-seven days.

"Cause this to be everywhere known!

"Tenth Moon, 23rd day (November the 15th)."

The title by which Her Majesty was canonised contains no less than twenty-two characters, sixteen of which were hers at the day of her death, the other six having been added in the Imperial Decrees which recorded her decease and praised her glorious achievements. The first character "Dutiful" — *i.e.* to her husband — is always accorded to a deceased Empress. It is significant of the unpractical nature of the *literati*, or of their cynicism, that the second of her latest titles signifies "reverend," implying punctilious adherence to ancestral traditions! The third and fourth mean "Equal of Heaven," which places her on a footing of equality with Confucius, while the fifth and sixth raise her even higher than the Sage in the national Pantheon, for it means "Increase in Sanctity," of which Confucius was only a "Manifestor." In the records of the Dynasty she will henceforth be known as the Empress "Dutiful, Reverend and Glorious," a title, according to the laws of Chinese honorifics, higher than any woman ruler has hitherto received since the beginning of history.

Since her death the prestige of the Empress Dowager, and her hold on the imagination of the people, have grown rather than decreased. Around her coffin, while it lay first in her Palace of Peaceful Longevity and later in a hall at the foot of the Coal Hill, north of the Forbidden City, awaiting the appointed day propitious for burial, there gathered something more than the conventional regrets and honours which fall usually to the lot of China's rulers. Officials as well as people felt that with her they had lost the strong hand of guidance, and a personality which appealed to most of them as much from the human as from the official point of view. Their affectionate recollections of the Old Buddha were clearly shown by the elaborate sacrifices paid to her *manes* at various periods from the day of her death to that day, a year later, when her ancestral tablet was brought home to the Forbidden City from the Imperial tombs with all pomp and circumstance.

On the All Souls' day of the Buddhists, celebrated in the 7th Moon, and which fell in the September following her death, a magnificent barge made of paper and over a hundred and fifty feet long was set up outside the Forbidden City on a large empty space adjoining the Coal Hill. It was crowded with figures of attendant eunuchs and handmaidens, and contained furniture and viands for the use of the illustrious dead in the lower regions. A throne was placed in the bows, and around it were kneeling effigies of attendant officials all wearing their Robes of State as if the shade of Tzŭ Hsi were holding an audience.

On the morning of the All Souls' festival the Regent, in the name of the Emperor, performed sacrifice before the barge, which was then set alight and burnt, in order that the Old Buddha might enjoy the use of it at the "yellow springs." A day or two before her funeral, hundreds of paper effigies of attendants, cavalry, camels and other pack animals, were similarly burnt so that her spirit might enjoy all the pomp to which she had been accustomed in life.

The following account of her funeral is reproduced from *The Times* of 27th November, 1909: —

"The 9th of November at 5 A.M. was the hour of good omen originally chosen by the Astrologers for the departure of the remains of Her late Majesty the Empress Dowager from their temporary resting place in the Forbidden City to the mausoleum prepared for her at the Eastern Hills. To meet the convenience of the foreign representatives, the hour was subsequently changed to 7 A.M.

"The arrangements for the procession and the part taken therein by the Diplomatic Body, were generally similar to those of the funeral of His Majesty Kuang-Hsü, but the mounted troops were more numerous and better turned out, the police were noticeably smarter and well-dressed, and the pageant as a whole was in many respects more imposing. But for those who, in May last, witnessed the late Emperor's funeral, the scene lacked one element of its brilliantly picturesque effect, namely, the bright sunshine which on that occasion threw every detail and distinctive note of the *cortège* into clear relief against the grey background of the Palace walls. The day was cold, with lowering clouds, and the long delay which preceded the appearance of the catafalque at the point where the Diplomatic Body was stationed had an inevitably depressing effect on the spectators.

"The catafalque was borne by eighty-four bearers, the largest number which can carry this unwieldy burden through the City gates; but beyond the walls the coffin was transferred to a larger bier borne by one hundred and twenty men. In front walked the Prince Regent, the bodyguard of Manchu Princes and the members of the Grand Council, attended by the Secretariat staff. Behind rode first a smart body of troops, followed by a large number of camels whose Mongol attendants carried tentpoles and other articles for use in the erection of the 'matshed palaces,' wherein the coffin rests at night at the different stages of the four days' journey to the tombs. Behind the Mongols were borne in procession the gaudy honorific umbrellas presented to the Old Buddha on the occasion of her return from exile at Hsi-an fu in 1901: all these were burnt on the 16th instant when the body was finally entombed. Following the waving umbrellas came a body of Lama dignitaries, and after them a contingent from the Imperial Equipage Department bearing Manchu sacrificial vessels, Buddhist symbols and embroidered banners. Conspicuous in the *cortège* were three splendid chariots with trappings and curtains of Imperial yellow silk, emblazoned with dragons and phœnixes, and two palanquins similar to those used by the Empress Dowager on her journeys in State; these also were burned at the mausoleum. Noticeable figures in the procession were the six chief eunuchs, including the notorious Li Lien-ying and the short handsome attendant who usually accompanied the Empress's sedan chair. The spectacle, as a whole, was most impressive; no such pomp and circumstance, say the Chinese, has marked the obsequies of any Empress of China since the funeral of the Empress Wu (*circa* A.D. 700) of whom the annals record that hundreds of attendants were buried alive in her mausoleum.

"The police arrangements attracted general attention by their remarkable efficiency, which many Chinese attribute to the present Empress Dowager's constant fear of assassination. Every closed door along the route of the procession was closely guarded by soldiers and special precautions taken against bomb-throwing. The street guards were numerous and alert, and the arrangements generally were characterised by discipline and decorum. There was little confusion in the *cortège*, and none of the unseemly shouting usual on such occasions.

"Ninety miles away, in a silent spot surrounded by virgin pine forest and backed by protecting hills, are the Eastern Tombs, towards which, for four days, the great catafalque made its way along the yellow-sanded road. There stands the mausoleum, originally built by the faithful Jung Lu for his Imperial Mistress at a cost which stands in the government records at eight millions of taels. It is close to the 'Ting Ling,' the burial-place of her husband, the Emperor Hsien-Feng. To the west of it stands the tomb of her colleague and co-Regent (the Empress Tzǔ An), and on the east that of the first Consort of Hsien-Feng, who died before his accession to the Throne, and was subsequently canonised as Empress. Throughout her lifetime, and particularly of late years, Yehonala took great interest and pride in her last resting-place, visiting it at intervals and exacting the most scrupulous attention from those entrusted with its building and adornment. On one occasion, in 1897, when practically completed, she had it rebuilt because the teak pillars were not sufficiently massive. After the death of Jung Lu, Prince Ch'ing became responsible for the custody of the tomb and its precious contents — the sacrificial vessels of carved jade, the massive vases and incense burners of gold and silver, which adorn the mortuary chamber; the richly-jewelled couch to receive the coffin, and the carved figures of serving maids and eunuchs who stand for ever in attendance. After the last ceremony at the tomb, when the Princes, Chamberlains and high officials had taken their final farewell of the illustrious dead, while the present Empress Dowager, with her attendants and the surviving consorts of the Emperors Hsien-Feng and T'ung-Chih, offered the last rites in the mortuary chamber, the massive stone door of the tomb was let down and the resting-place of Tzŭ Hsi closed for ever.

"The cost of the late Emperor's funeral has been officially recorded, with the nice accuracy which characterises Chinese finance, at 459,940 taels, 2 mace, 3 candareens and 6 *li*. As the cost of a funeral in China closely reflects the dignity of the deceased and the "face" of his or her immediate survivors, these figures become particularly interesting when compared with the cost of the Empress Dowager's funeral, which is placed at one and a-quarter to one and a-half million taels. Rumour credited the Regent with an attempt to cut down this expenditure, which attempt he abandoned at the last moment in the face of the displeasure of the powerful Yehonala Clan. That the Old Buddha's magnificent funeral was appreciated by the populace of Peking is certain, for to them she was for fifty years a sympathetic personality and a great ruler.

"The conveyance of Her Majesty's ancestral tablet from the tombs of the Eastern Hills to its resting-place in the Temple of Ancestors in the Forbidden City was a ceremony in the highest degree impressive and indicative of the vitality of those feelings which make ancestor-worship the most important factor in the life of the Chinese. The tablet, a simple strip of carved and

MARBLE BRIDGE OVER THE LAKE IN THE WESTERN PARK WHICH SURROUNDS THE LAKE PALACE.

"TI WANG MIAO" OR TEMPLE TO THE MEMORY OF VIRTUOUS EMPERORS OF PREVIOUS DYNASTIES.

lacquered wood, bearing the name of the deceased in Manchu and Chinese characters, had been officially present at the burial. With the closing of the great door of the tomb the spirit of the departed ruler is supposed to be translated to the tablet, and to the latter is therefore given honour equal to that which was accorded to the sovereign during her lifetime. Borne aloft in a gorgeous chariot draped with Imperial yellow silk and attended by a large mounted escort, Tzŭ Hsi's tablet journeyed slowly and solemnly, in three days' stages, from the Eastern Hills to Peking. At each stage it rested for the night in a specially constructed pavilion, being 'invited' by the Master of the Ceremonies, on his knees and with all solemnity, to be pleased to leave its chariot and rest. For the passage of this habitation of the spirit of the mighty dead the Imperial road had been specially prepared and swept by an army of men; it had become a *via sacra* on which no profane feet might come or go. As the procession bearing the sacred tablet drew near to the gates of the capital, the Prince Regent and all the high officers of the Court knelt reverently to receive it. All traffic was stopped; every sound stilled in the streets, where the people knelt to do homage to the memory of the Old Buddha. Slowly and solemnly the chariot was borne through the main gate of the Forbidden City to the Temple of the Dynasty's ancestors, the most sacred spot in the Empire, where it was 'invited' to take its appointed place among the nine Ancestors and their thirty-five Imperial Consorts. Before this could be done, however, it was necessary that the tablets of Tzŭ Hsi's son, T'ung-Chih, and of her daughter-in-law, should first be removed from that august assembly, because due ceremony required that the arriving tablet should perform obeisance to those of its ancestors, and it would not be fitting for the tablet of a parent to perform this ceremony in the presence of that of a son or daughter-in-law. The act of obeisance was performed by deputy, in the person of the Regent acting for the child Emperor, and consisted of nine kowtows before each tablet in the Temple, or about 400 prostrations in all. When these had been completed, with due regard to the order of seniority of the deceased, the tablets of the Emperor T'ung-Chih and his wife were formally 'invited' to return to the Temple, where obeisance was made on their behalf to the shade of Tzǔ Hsi which had been placed in the shrine beside that of her former colleague and co–Regent, the Empress Tzǔ An. Thus ended the last ceremonial act of the life and death of this remarkable woman; but her spirit still watches over the Forbidden City and the affairs of her people, who firmly believe that it will in due time guide the nation to a happy issue out of all their afflictions. As time goes on, the weaknesses of her character and the errors of her career are forgotten, and her greatness only remembered. And no better epitaph could be written for this great Manchu than that of her own valedictory Decree which, rising above all the pettiness and humiliations of her reign, looking death and change steadfastly in the face, raises her in our eyes (to quote a writer in the *Spectator*)[1] 'to that vague ideal state of human governance imagined by the Greek, when the Kings should be philosophers and the philosophers Kings.' "

---

1. 2nd January, 1909.

XXVIII

CONCLUSION

"ALL sweeping judgments," says Coleridge, "are unjust." "*Comprendre*" says the French philosopher, "*c'est tout pardonner.*" To understand the life and personality of the Empress Dowager, it is before everything essential to divest our minds of racial prejudice and to endeavour to appreciate something of the environment and traditions to which she was born. In the words of the thoughtful article in the *Spectator*, already quoted, "she lived and worked and ruled in a setting which is apart from all western modes of thought and standards of action, and the first step in the historian's task is to see that she is judged by her own standards and not wholly by ours." Judged by the rough test of public opinion and accumulating evidence in her own country, Tzŭ Hsi's name will go down to history in China as that of a genius in statecraft and a born ruler, a woman "with all the courage of a man, and more than the ordinary man's intelligence."[1]

Pending that reform and liberty of the press which is still the distant dream of "Young China," no useful record of the life and times of the Empress Dowager is to be expected from any Chinese writer. Despite the mass of information which exists in the diaries and archives of metropolitan officials and the

---

1. *Vide* the Diary of Ching Shan, page 262-3.

personal reminiscences of those who knew her well, nothing of any human interest or value has been published on the subject in China. From the official and orthodox point of view, a truthful biography of the Empress would be sacrilege. It is true that in the vernacular newspapers under European protection at the Treaty Ports, as well as in Hongkong and Singapore, Cantonese writers have given impressions of Her Majesty's personality and brief accounts of her life, but these are so hopelessly biassed and distorted by hatred of the Manchus as to be almost worthless for historical purposes, as worthless as the dry chronicles of the Dynastic annals. Reference has already been made to the best known of these publications, a series of letters originally published in a Singapore newspaper and republished under the title of "The Chinese Crisis from within,"[1] by a writer who, under the *nom-de-plume* of "Wen Ching," concealed the identity of one of K'ang Yu-wei's most ardent disciples. His work is remarkable for sustained invective and reckless inaccuracy, clearly intended to create an atmosphere of hatred against the Manchus (for the ultimate benefit of the Cantonese) in the minds of his countrymen, and to dissuade the foreign Powers from allowing the Empress to return to Peking. Drawing on a typically Babu store of "western learning," this writer compares the Empress to Circe, Semiramis, Catherine de Medici, Messalina, Fulvia, and Julia Agrippina; quoting Dante and Rossetti to enforce his arguments, and leavening his vituperation with a modicum of verifiable facts sufficient to give to his narrative something of *vraisemblance*. But his judgment is emphatically sweeping. He ignores alike Tzŭ Hsi's undeniable good qualities and her extenuating circumstances, the defects of her education and the difficulties of her position, so that his work is almost valueless.

Equally valueless, for purposes of historical accuracy, are most of the accounts and impressions of the Empress recorded by those Europeans (especially the ladies of the Diplomatic Body and their friends) who saw her personality and purposes

---

1. Grant Richards, 1901.

reflected in the false light which beats upon the Dragon Throne on ceremonial occasions, or who came under the influence of the deliberate artifices and charm of manner which she assumed so well. Had the etiquette of her Court and people permitted intercourse with European diplomats and distinguished visitors of the male sex, she would certainly have acquired, and exercised over them also, that direct personal influence which emanated from her extraordinary vitality and will-power, influence such as the western world has learned to associate with the names of the Emperor William of Germany and Mr. Roosevelt. Restricted as she was to social relations with her own sex amongst foreigners, she exerted herself, and never failed, to produce on them an impression of womanly grace and gentleness of disposition, which qualities we find accordingly praised by nearly all who came in contact with her after the return of the Court, aye, even by those who had undergone the horrors of the siege under the very walls of her Palace. The glamour of her mysterious Court, the rarity of the visions vouchsafed, the real charm of her manner, and the apparently artless *bonhomie* of her bearing, all combined to create in the minds of the European ladies who saw her an impression as favourable as it was opposed to every dictate of common sense and experience. In certain notable instances, the effect of this impression reacted visibly on the course of the Peace Protocol negotiations.

From the diary of Ching Shan we obtain an estimate of Tzŭ Hsi's character, formed by one who had enjoyed for years continual opportunities of studying her at close quarters — an estimate which was, and is, confirmed by the popular verdict, the common report of the tea-houses and market places of the capital. Despite her swiftly changing and uncontrolled moods, her childish lack of moral sense, her unscrupulous love of power, her fierce passions and revenges, Tzŭ Hsi was no more the savage monster described by "Wen Ching," than she was the benevolent, fashion-plate Lady Bountiful of the American magazines. She was simply a woman of unusual courage and vitality, of strong will and unbounded ambition, a woman and an Oriental, living out her life by such lights as she knew, and in accordance with the traditions of her race and caste. Says Ching Shan in the Diary: "*The nature of the Empress is peace-loving: she has seen many springs and autumns. I myself know well her refined and gentle tastes, her love of painting, poetry and the theatre. When in a good mood she is the most amiable and tractable of women, but at times her rage is awful to witness.*" Here we have the woman drawn from life, without *arrière pensée*, by a just but sympathetic observer, the woman who could win, and hold, the affectionate loyalty of the greatest men of her time, not to speak of that of her retainers and serving maids; the woman whose human interest and sympathy in everything around her, were not withered by age nor staled by custom; yet who, at a word, could send the fierce leaders of the Boxers cowering from her presence. *Souvent femme varie.* Tzŭ Hsi, her own mistress and virtual ruler of the Empire at the age of twenty-four, had not had much occasion to learn to control either her moods or her passions. Hers, from the first, was the trick and temper of autocracy. Trained in the traditions of a Court where human lives count for little, where power maintains itself by pitiless and brutal methods, where treason and foul deeds lie in waiting for the first signs of the ruler's weakness, how should she learn to put away from the Forbidden City the hideous barbarities of its ways?

Let us remember her time and place. Consider the woman's environment and training, her marriage to a dissolute puppet, her subsequent life in that gilded prison of the Imperial City, with its endless formalities, base intrigues and artificial sins. Prior to the establishment of China's first diplomatic relations with European nations, the Court of Peking and its ways bore a strong resemblance to those of Medieval Europe; nor have successive routs and invasions since that date changed any of its cherished traditions and methods. In the words of a recent writer on medieval history, the life of the Peking Palace, like that of our fourteenth century, "was one of profound learning and crass stupidity, of infantile gaiety and sudden tragedy, of flashing fortunes and swift dooms. There is a certain innocence about the very sinners of the thirteenth and fourteenth centuries. Many of their problems, indeed, arose from the fact that this same childlike candour was allied to the unworn forces of full manhood." Whatever crimes of cruelty and vengeance Tzŭ Hsi committed — and they were many — be it said to her credit that she had, as a rule, the courage of her convictions and position, and sinned *coram publico*. Beneath the fierceness without which an Oriental ruler cannot hope to remain effective, there certainly beat a heart which could be kind, if the conditions were propitious, and a rough sense of humour, which is a common and pleasing trait of the Manchus.

Let us also remember that in the East to-day (as it was with us of Europe before the growth of that humanitarianism which now shows signs of unhealthy exaggeration) pain and death are part of the common, every-day risks of life, risks lightly incurred by the average Oriental in the great game of ambitions, loves and hates that is for ever played around the Throne. Tzŭ Hsi played her royal part in the great game, but it is not recorded of her that she ever took life from sheer cruelty or love of killing. When she sent a man to death, it was because he stood between her and the full and safe gratification of her love of power. When her fierce rage was turned against the insolence of the foreigner, she had no scruple in consigning every European in China to the executioner; when the Emperor's favourite concubine disputed her Imperial authority, she had no hesitation in ordering her to immediate death; but in every recorded instance, except one, her methods were swift, clean, and, from the Oriental point of view, not unmerciful. She had no liking for tortures, or the lingering death. In all her Decrees of vengeance, we find the same unhesitating firmness in removing human obstacles from her path, combined with a complete absence of that unnecessary cruelty which is so frequently associated with despotism. Her methods, in fact, were Elizabethan rather than Florentine.

If Tzŭ Hsi developed self-reliance early in life, the fact is not to be wondered at, for it was little help that she had to look for in her entourage of Court officials. Amongst the effete classical scholars, the fat-paunched Falstaffs, the opium sots, doddering fatalists and corrupt parasites of the Imperial Clans, she seems, indeed, to have been an anachronism, a "cast-back" to the virility and energy that won China for her sturdy ancestors. She appeared to be the born and inevitable ruler of the degenerate Dynasty, and if she became a law unto herself, it was largely because there were few about her fit to lead or to command.

Imbued with a very feminine love of luxury, addicted to pleasure, and at one period of her life undoubtedly licentious after the manner of her Court's traditions, she combined these qualities with a shrewd common sense and a marked *penchant* for acquiring and amassing personal property. To use her own phrase, she endeavoured in all things to observe the principle of the "happy mean," and seldom allowed her love of pleasure to obscure her vision or to hinder her purposes in the serious businesses of life.

Like many great rulers of the imperious and militant type, she was remarkably superstitious, a punctilious observer of the rites prescribed for averting omens and conciliating the myriad gods and demons of the several religions of China, a liberal supporter of priests and soothsayers. Nevertheless, as with Elizabeth of England, her secular instincts were *au fond* stronger than all her superstitions. That sturdy common sense, which played so successfully upon the weaknesses and the passions of her corrupt entourage, never allowed any consideration for the powers unseen to interfere seriously with her masterful handling of things visible, or to curb her ruling passion for unquestioned authority.

The qualities which made up the remarkable personality of the Empress were many and complex, but of those which chiefly contributed to her popularity and power we would place, first, her courage, and next, a certain simplicity and directness—both qualities that stand out in strong relief against the timorous and tortuous tendencies of the average Manchu. Of her courage there could be no doubt; even amidst the chaos of the days of the Boxer terror it never failed her, and Ching Shan is only one of many who bear witness to her unconquerable spirit and *sang froid*. Amidst scenes of desolation and destruction that might well shake the courage of the bravest men, we see her calmly painting bamboos on silk, or giving orders to stop the bombardment of the Legations to allow of her excursion on the Lake. How powerful is the dramatic quality of that scene where she attacks and dominates the truculent Boxer leaders at her very doors; or again when, on the morning of the flight, she alone preserves presence of mind, and gives her orders as coolly as if starting on a picnic! At such moments all the defects of her training and temperament are forgotten in the irresistible appeal of her nobler qualities.

Of those qualities, and of her divine right to rule, Tzŭ Hsi herself was fully convinced, and no less determined than His Majesty of Germany, to insist upon proper recognition and respect for herself and her commanding place in the scheme of the universe. Her belief in her own supreme importance, and her superstitious habit of thought were both strikingly displayed on the occasion when her portrait, painted by Miss Carl for the St. Louis Exposition, was taken from the Waiwpu on its departure to the United States. She regarded this presentment of her august person as entitled, in all seriousness of ceremonial, to the same reverence as herself and gave orders for the construction of a miniature railway, to be built through the streets of the capital for its special benefit. By this means the "sacred countenance" was carried upright, under its canopy of yellow silk, and Her Majesty was spared the thought of being borne in effigy on the shoulders of coolies — a form of progress too suggestively ill-omened to be endured. Before the portrait left the Palace, the Emperor was summoned to prostrate himself before it, and at its passing through the city, and along the railway line, the people humbly knelt, as if it had been the Old Buddha of flesh and blood. Incidents of this kind emphasise the impossibility of fairly judging the Empress by European standards of conduct and ideas. To get something of the proper atmosphere and perspective, we must go back to the early days of the Tudors.

Blunt of speech herself, she was quick to detect and resent flattery. Those who rose highest in her affection and regard were essentially strong men, blunt outspoken officials of the type of Jung Lu, Tseng Kuo-fan, and Tso Tsung-t'ang; for those who would win her favour by sycophancy she had a profound contempt, which she was at no pains to conceal, though in certain instances (*e.g.*, Chang Chih-tung) she overlooked the offence because of ripe scholarship or courage. An amusing example of this trait in her character occurred on one occasion when, after perusing the examination papers for the selection of successful candidates for the Hanlin Literary degrees, she expressed herself in the following trenchant Decree:—

"A certain candidate in the Hanlin examination, named Yen Chen, has handed in some verses, the style of which is excellent, but their subject matter contains a number of allusions laudatory of the present Dynasty. This person has evidently gone out of his way to refer to the present rulers of the Empire, and has even seen fit to display gross flattery, for his essay contains, amongst others, a sentence to the effect that 'we have now upon the Throne a female embodiment of Yao and Shun.'[1] Now, the Throne defines merit in candidates to-day on the same principles as those which were in force under former Dynasties, its object being to form a correct idea of the moral standards of candidates by perusal of their essays and lyrical compositions. But this effort of Yen Chen is nothing more than a laudatory ode, entirely lacking in high seriousness. This is a grave matter: the question involved is one closely affecting character and moral training; such conduct cannot possibly be permitted to continue. The examiners have placed Yen Chen at the top of the list in the First Class; he is hereby relegated to the last place in that class. Let our examiners for the future take more care in scrutinising the papers submitted."

---

1. Two patriarchial rulers of China (B.C. *circa* 2300) whose wise principles of government were immortalised by Confucius.

As was only natural, Tzŭ Hsi was not above favouring her own people, the Manchus, but one great secret of the solidity of her rule undoubtedly lay in her broad impartiality and the nice balance which she maintained between Chinese and Manchus in all departments of the Government. She had realised that the brains and energy of the country must come from the Chinese, and that if the Manchus were to retain their power and sinecure positions, it must be with the good will of the Chinese and the loyalty of the Mandarin class in the provinces. From the commencement of her rule, down to the day when she handed over her Boxer kinsmen to the executioner, she never hesitated to inflict impartial punishment on Manchus, when public opinion was against them. A case in point occurred in 1863, in connection with one of her favourite generals, named Sheng Pao, who had gained her sincere gratitude by his share in the war against the British and French invaders in 1860, and who, by luck and the ignorance of the Court, had been credited with having stopped the advance of the Allies to Jehol. For these alleged services she had awarded him special thanks and high honour. In 1863, however, he was engaged in Shensi, fighting the Taipings, and, following a custom not unusual amongst Chinese military commanders, had asked leave to win over one of the rebel leaders by giving him an important official position. Tzŭ Hsi, who had had ample opportunities to learn something of the danger of this procedure, declined to sanction his request, pointing out the objections thereto. Sheng Pao ventured to suppress her Decree, and gave the rebel the position in question. Success might have justified him, but the ex-bandit justified Tzŭ Hsi by going back on his word. Awaiting a good opportunity, he raised once more the standard of revolt, massacred a number of officials, and captured several important towns. General Sheng Pao was arrested and brought in custody to Peking; under cross-examination he confessed, amongst other misdemeanours, that he had permitted women to accompany the troops during this campaign, which, by Chinese military law, is a capital offence. Other charges against him, however, he denied, and, preserving an insolent attitude, demanded to be confronted with his accusers. Tzŭ Hsi issued a characteristically vigorous Decree in which she declared that the proper punishment for his offence was decapitation, but inasmuch as he had acquired merit by good work against the Taipings, as well as against the British and French invaders, she graciously granted him the privilege of committing suicide, of which he promptly availed himself.

Tzŭ Hsi, as we have said, was extremely superstitious; nor is this matter for wonder when we bear in mind the medieval atmosphere of wizardous necromancy and familiar spirits which she had perforce absorbed with her earliest education. Following the precepts of Confucius, she preserved always a broad and tolerant attitude on all questions of religion, but, while reluctant to discuss things appertaining to the unknown gods, she was always prepared to conciliate them, and to allow her actions in everyday affairs to be guided by the words of her wise men and astrologers—"by dreams, and by Urim and by prophets." Thus we find her in the first year of the Regency of her son's minority (1861) issuing, in his name, a Decree, which carries back the mind irresistibly to Babylon and those days when the magicians and soothsayers were high personages in the State.

"During the night of the 15th of the 7th Moon," it begins, "there occurred a flight of shooting stars in the southern hemisphere; ten days later, a comet appeared twice in the sky to the north-west. Heaven sends not these warnings in vain. For the last month Peking has been visited by a grievous epidemic, whereof the continued severity fills us with sore dismay. The Empresses Dowager have now warned us that these portents of Heaven are sent because of serious wrong in our system of government, of errors unreformed and grievances unredressed," and the Decree ends by exhorting all concerned "to put away frivolous things, so that Heaven, perceiving our reverend attitude, may relent."

In previous chapters we have shown with what punctilious attention she consulted her astrologers in regard to the propitious

PORTRAIT OF THE EMPRESS DOWAGER.
Painted from life by Miss Catharine A. Carl for the St. Louis Exposition
and now the property of the American Nation.

day for re-entering her capital on the Court's return from exile, her anxiety for scrupulous observance of their advice being manifestly sincere. In her concern for omens and portents she seemed, like Napoleon, to obey instincts external and superior to another and very practical side of her nature, which, however, asserted itself unmistakably whenever vital issues were at stake and her supreme authority threatened. She was at all times anxious to secure the goodwill of the ancestral spirits, whose presence she apprehended as a living reality, but even with these, when it came to a direct issue between her own despotic authority and their claims to consideration, she never hesitated to relegate the mighty dead to the background, content to appease them in due season by suitable expressions of reverence and regret. The most notable instance of this kind occurred when, disregarding the Dynastic laws of succession, she deprived her son, the Emperor Tung-Chih, of the rites of ancestral worship, committing thus a crime which, as she well knew, was heinous in the eyes of the Chinese people.

Her superstitious tendencies were most remarkably displayed in the matter of the selection of the site of her tomb, and its building, an occasion of which the Court geomancers took full advantage. When T'ung-Chih reached his majority in 1873, his first duty was to escort the Empresses Dowager to the Eastern Mausolea, where, with much solemnity, two auspicious sites, encircled by hills and watered by streams, were selected and exorcised of all evil influences. Further ceremonies and mystic calculations were required to determine the auspicious dates for the commencement of building operations; in these, and the adornment of the tomb, Tzǔ Hsi continued to take the keenest interest until the day of her death. In order to secure scrupulous regard for its construction in accordance with the requirements of her horoscope, and to make her sepulchre a fitting and all-hallowed resting-place, she entrusted its chief supervision to Jung Lu, who thus secured a permanent post highly coveted by Manchu officials, in which huge "squeezes" were a matter of precedent. The geomantic conditions of these burial places gave unusual trouble, the tomb of the Empress Tzŭ An having eventually to be shifted fifteen feet two inches northwards, and four feet seven and a half inches westwards, before the spirits of her ancestors were perfectly satisfied, while that of Tzŭ Hsi was removed seven feet four inches to the north and eight inches to the eastward.

Tzŭ Hsi feared no man. From the first moment of her power, secure in the sense of divine right and firmly believing in her "star," she savoured her authority like a rich wine. The pleasure she derived from delivering homilies to the highest officials in the Empire may be read between the lines of her Decrees. Already in 1862, that is to say, before she was twenty-seven years of age, we find her solemnly admonishing the Grand Council on their duties, urging them to adopt stricter standards of conduct, and to put a check on their corrupt tendencies. "They are, of course, not debarred from seeking advice from persons below them in society, but let them be careful to avoid any attempt at forming cabals or attracting to themselves troops of followers." And on another occasion, when she specially invited the Censors to impeach Prince Kung, she observed: "In discussing the principles of just government you should remember the precept of the Confucian school, which is, 'Be not weary in well-doing: strict rectitude of conduct is the road royal to good government. Face and overcome your difficulties, and thus eventually earn the right to ease.'" Tzŭ Hsi could turn out this sort of thing, which appeals to every Chinese scholar, in good style and large quantities. She took pride in the manufacture of maxims for the guidance of the Mandarins, but there was always a suspicion that her tongue was in her cheek while she carefully penned these copybook platitudes, just as we know there was when she set herself to display what *The Times* correspondent at Peking called her "girlish abandon," in order to regain the affection of Mrs. Conger and the ladies of the Diplomatic Body.

Of the Empress Dowager's popularity and prestige with all classes of her subjects, there is no doubt. At Peking especially, and throughout the Metropolitan Province, she was the object of a very general and very sincere affection; seldom is her name spoken except with expressions of admiration and regard, very similar in effect to the feelings of the British people for Her Majesty Queen Victoria. Although her share of responsibility for the Boxer rising and for the consequent sufferings inflicted on the people was matter of common knowledge, little or no blame was ever imputed to the Old Buddha. Her subjects loved her for her very defects, for the foolhardy courage that had staked the Empire on a throw. Amongst the lower classes it was the general opinion that she had done her best, and with the best intentions. The scheme itself was magnificent—to drive the foreigner into the sea—and it appealed to her people as worthy of their ruler and of a better fate. If it had failed for this time, it was the will of Heaven, and no doubt at some future date success would justify her wisdom. If they blamed her at all, it was for condescending to intimate relations with the hated foreigner after the Court's return to Peking; but even in this, she had the sympathy rather than the censure of her subjects.

To the great mass of her people, who had never seen her, but knew her only by cumulative weight of common report, the Old Buddha stood for the embodiment of courage, liberality and kindness of heart. If, as they knew, she were subject to fierce outbursts of sudden rage, the fact did her no injury in the eyes of a race which believes that wrath-matter undischarged is a virulent poison in the system. The simple Chihli folk made allowance, not without its sense of humour, for their august sovereign's capacity to generate wrath-matter, as for her feminine mutability: To them she was a great ruler and a *bon enfant*. In a country where merciless officials and torture are part of the long-accepted order of things, no more stress was laid on her numerous acts of cold blooded tyranny than, shall we say, was laid on the beheading of Earls at the close of the fifteenth century in England.

One of the writers had the good fortune once to see the Empress when proceeding in her palanquin to the Eastern tombs.

She had breakfasted early at the Tung Yueh temple outside the Ch'i Hua gate, and was on her way to T'ung chou. As her chair passed along a line of kneeling peasantry, the curtains were open and it was seen that the Old Buddha was asleep. The good country people were delighted. "Look," they cried, "the Old Buddha is sleeping. Really, she has far too much work to do! A rare woman—what a pleasure to see her thus!"

Tzŭ Hsi was recognised to be above criticism and above the laws which she rigorously enforced on others. For instance, when, a few weeks after the issue of a Decree prohibiting corporal punishment and torture in prisons, she caused the Reformer Shen Chin to be flogged to death (July, 1904), public opinion saw nothing extraordinary in the event. A few days later, when preparations were being made for the celebration of her seventieth birthday, she issued another Decree, declining the honorific title dutifully proffered by the Emperor, together with its emoluments, on the ground that she had no heart for festivities, "being profoundly distressed at the thought of the sufferings of my subjects in Manchuria, owing to the destruction wrought there by the Russian and Japanese armies. My one desire," she added, "is that my officials may co-operate to introduce more humane methods of Government, so that my people may live to enjoy good old age, resting on couches of comfortable ease. This is the best way to honour the seventieth anniversary of my birth." No doubt the shade of Shen Chin was duly appeased.

Of her vindictive ferocity on occasions there can be no question. As Ching Shan admits, even her most faithful admirers and servants were aware that at moments of her wrath it was prudent to be out of her reach, or, if unavoidably present, to abstain from thwarting her. They knew that those who dared to question her absolute authority or to criticise the means by which she gained and retained it, need look for no mercy. But they knew also that for faithful service and loyalty she had a royal memory and, like Catherine of Russia, she never forgot her friends.

Her unpopularity in central and southern China, which

became marked after the war with Japan and violent at the time of the *coup d'état*, was in its origin anti-dynastic and political. It was particularly strong in Kuangtung, where for years Her Majesty was denounced by agitators as a monster of unparalleled depravity. The political opinions of the turbulent and quick-witted Cantonese have generally been expressed in a lively and somewhat ribald form, and when we bear in mind the popular tendency (not confined to the Far East) of ascribing gross immorality to crowned heads, we are justified in refusing to attach undue importance to the wild accusations levelled against the Empress Dowager in this quarter. The utterances of the hotspurs and lampooners of southern China are chiefly interesting in that they reveal something of the vast possibilities of cleavage inherent in the Chinese Government system, and prove the Manchu rule to have fallen into something like contempt in that region where the new forces of education and political activity are most conspicuous.

One of the doggerel verses current in 1898 fairly describes the attitude of the Cantonese man in the street towards the Dynasty. Freely translated, it runs thus:—

> *"There are three questions which men must not ask about our Great Manchu Dynasty:*
> *"At what ancestral grave does His Majesty make filial obeisance?*
> *"To what deity does the Empress Dowager sacrifice?*
> *"To what husbands are the Imperial Princesses married?*

The first question is in allusion to the Emperor's alleged doubtful parentage, while the second refers to a mythical New Year sacrifice, akin to those of Moloch, which the scurrilous Cantonese attributed to Tzŭ Hsi and the ladies of her Court. The last refers to the Manchu clan's custom of intermarriage which, in the eyes of the Chinese (who disapprove even of marriage between persons of the same surname), is illegal and immoral.

These, however, are but local manifestations, and they lost

much of their inspiration after the *coup d'état*. The anti-dynastic tendencies noticeable in the vernacular press of Shanghai, many of which assumed the form of personal hostility to the Empress, were also little more than the local result of Young China's vague aspirations and desire for change, and reflected little weight of serious opinion. The official class and the *literati* as a whole were loyal to Her Majesty and regarded her with respect. They do not fail to express admiration of her wisdom and statecraft, which kept the Empire together under circumstances of great difficulty. To her selection and support of Tseng Kuo-fan they generally attribute China's recovery from the disasters of the Taiping rebellion, and to her sagacity in 1898 they ascribe the country's escape from dangers of sudden revolution. They admit that had it not been for her masterly handling of the Tsai Yüan conspiracy (1860-61), it is doubtful whether the Dynasty could have held together for a decade, and they realise, now that her strong hand no longer grasps the helm, that the ship of State is likely to drift into dangerous waters.

The everyday routine of Tzŭ Hsi's life has been well described in Miss Carl's accurate and picturesque account of the Palace ceremonial and amusements,[1] the first authoritative picture of *la vie intime* of the Chinese Court. Apart from a keen natural aptitude for State affairs (similar to that of Queen Victoria, whom she greatly admired from afar), Tzŭ Hsi maintained to the end of her days a lively interest in literature and art, together with a healthy and catholic appetite for amusement. She had an inveterate love for the theatre, for masques and pageants, which she indulged at all times and places, taking a professional interest in the players and giving much advice about the performances, which she selected daily from a list submitted to her. It was a matter of comment, and some hostile criticism by Censors, that even during the sojourn of the Court in the provincial wilderness at Hsi-an, she summoned actors to follow the Court and perform as usual.

Her private life had, no doubt, its phases. Of its details we

---

1. *With the Empress Dowager of China* (Eveleigh Nash, 1906).

know but little prior to the period of the restoration of the Summer Palace in the early nineties. In middle age, however, when she had assimilated the philosophy and practice of the "happy mean," her tastes became simple and her habits regular. She was passionately fond of the Summer Palace, of its gardens and the lake amongst the hills, and towards the end of her life went as seldom as possible into the city. She loved the freedom of the I-ho Yüan, its absence of formal etiquette, her water-picnics and the familiar intercourse of her favourite ladies, with whom she would discuss the day's news and the gossip of the Imperial Clans. With these, especially with the wife of Jung Lu and the Princess Imperial, she would talk endlessly of old times and make plans for the future.

Her love of literature and profound knowledge of history did much to win for her the respect of the Mandarin class, with whom the classics are a religion. In her reading she was, however, broad-minded, not to say omnivorous; it was her custom to spend a certain time daily in having ancient and modern authors read aloud by eunuchs specially trained in elocution. She believed thoroughly in education, though realising clearly the danger of putting new wine into old skins; and she perceived towards the end of her life that the rapidly changing conditions of the Empire had rendered the wisdom of China's Sages of little practical value as a basis of administration. Her clearness of perception on this point, contrasted with her action in 1898, is indeed remarkable, but it should be remembered that much of her opposition to the Emperor's policy of reform was the result of personal pique and outraged dignity, as in the case of her decision to become a Boxer leader in 1900. As far back as 1876, at the time of the establishment of the Tung Wen College at Peking for the teaching of languages and science, we find her publicly rebuking a Censor who had declared that mathematics was a subject suitable only for the Court of Astronomers.

"The Throne has established this College," she observed, "because it is incumbent on our scholars to learn the rudiments of mathematics and astronomy. These are not to be regarded, as the Memorialist suggests, as cunning and mechanical branches of knowledge. Let our officials study them earnestly, and they will soon acquire proficiency; at the same time let them avoid that undesirable specialisation which comes from concentrated study of the classics. We are now borrowing educational methods from foreign countries with a view to broadening our own and increasing its accuracy, but we have no intention of abandoning the teachings of the Sages. How, then, can our action prove detrimental to the minds of scholars?"

Frequent reference has been made in previous chapters to the extravagance and licentious display of Tzŭ Hsi's Court during the years of the first Regency. The remonstrances of the Censors on the subject were so numerous and outspoken, so circumstantial in their charges, as to leave little room for doubt that the Empress deserved their indignant condemnation. All the records of that period, and particularly from 1862 to 1869, point to the evil and steadily-increasing influence of the eunuchs, whose corruption and encouragement of lavish expenditure resulted in continual demands on the provincial exchequers. But even at the height of what may fairly be called her riotous living, Tzŭ Hsi always had the good grace to concur publicly in the virtuous suggestions of her monitors, and to conciliate public opinion by professions of a strong desire for economy. She would have her Imperial way, her splendid pageants and garnered wealth of tribute, but the Censors should have their "face." On the occasion of the Emperor T'ung-Chih's wedding in 1869, when the Grand Council had solemnly deprecated any increase in her Palace expenditure because of the impoverished state of the people brought about by the Taiping rebellion, she issued a Decree stating that, "so great was her perturbation of mind at the prevalent sufferings of her people, that she grudged even the money spent on the inferior raiment she was wearing, and the humble fare that was served at her Palace table." She was, in fact, as lavish of good principles as of the public funds. But it is to be remembered that a large proportion of the vast sums spent on her Palaces, on the building of her tomb, and on her Court festivities, represents the squeezes of officials and eunuchs, which, however solemnly the Grand Council might denounce extravagance, are in practice universally recognised as inseparable from the Celestial system of government. Tzŭ Hsi was fully aware that much of the enormous expenditure charged to her Privy Purse went in "squeeze," but she good-humouredly acquiesced in a custom as deeply ingrained in the Chinese as ancestral worship, and from which she herself derived no small profit. At her receptions to the ladies of the Diplomatic Body she would frequently enquire as to the market prices of household commodities, in order, as she cheerfully explained, to be able to show her Chief Eunuch that she was aware of his monstrous over-charges.

Combined, however, with her love of sumptuous display and occasional fits of Imperial munificence, Tzŭ Hsi possessed a certain housewifely instinct of thrift which, with advancing age, verged on parsimony. The Privy Purse of China's ruler is not dependent upon any well-defined civil list, but rather upon the exigencies of the day, upon the harvests and trade of the Empire, whence, through percentages of squeezes levied by the provincial authorities, come the funds required to defray the expenses of the Court.[1] The uncertainty of these remittances partly explains the Empress Dowager's hoarding tendencies, that squirrel instinct which impelled her to bury large sums in the vaults of the Palace, and to accumulate a vast store of silks, medicines, clocks, and all manner of valuables in the Forbidden City. At the time of her death her private fortune, including a large number of gold Buddhas and sacrificial vessels stored in the Palace vaults, was estimated by a high official of the Court at about sixteen millions sterling. The estimate is necessarily a loose one, being Chinese, but it was known with tolerable certainty that the hoard of

---

1. Since the days of the Emperor Ch'ien-Lung, these expenses have averaged some forty millions of taels per annum, *vide "The Times,"* special article, 7th Dec., 1909.

gold[1] buried in the Ning-Shou Palace at the time of the Court's flight in 1900, amounted to sixty millions of taels (say, eight millions sterling), and the "tribute" paid by the provinces to the Court at T'ai-yüan and Hsi-an would amount to as much more.

Tzŭ Hsi was proud of her personal appearance, and justly so, for she retained until advanced old age a clear complexion and youthful features. (To an artist who painted her portrait not long before her death she expressed a wish that her wrinkles should be left out.) By no means free from feminine vanity, she devoted a considerable amount of time each day to her toilet, and was particularly careful about the dressing of her hair. At the supreme moment of the Court's flight from the Palace, in 1900, she was heard to complain bitterly at being compelled to adopt the Chinese fashion of head-dress.

Her good health and vitality were always extraordinary. She herself attributed them chiefly to early rising, regular habits, and the frequent consumption of milk, which she usually took curdled, in the form of a kind of rennet. She ate frugally but well, being an epicure at heart and delighting in dainty and *recherché* menus. Opium, like other luxuries, she took in strict moderation, but greatly enjoyed her pipe after the business of the day was done. It was her practice then to rest for an hour, smoking at intervals, a *siesta* which the Court knew better than to disturb. She fully realised the evils wrought by abuse of the insidious drug, and approved of the laws, introduced by the initiative of T'ang Shao-yi and other high officials, for its abolition. But her fellow-feeling for those who, like herself, could use it in moderation, and her experience of its soothing and stimulating effect on the mind, led her to insist that the Abolition Decree (November 22nd, 1906) should not deprive persons over sixty years of age of their accustomed solace. She was, in fact, willing to decree prohibition for the masses, but lenient to herself and to those who had sufficiently proved their capacity to follow the path of the

---

1. The nucleus of this hoard was the money confiscated from the usurping Regent Su Shun in 1861.

happy mean.

Such was Tzǔ Hsi, a woman whose wonderful personality and career cannot fail to secure for her a place amongst the rulers who have become the standards and pivots of greatness in the world's history. The marvellous success of her career and the passionate devotion of her partisans are not to be easily explained by any ordinary process of analysis or comparison; but there is no doubt that they were chiefly due to that mysterious and indefinable quality which is called charm, a quality apparently independent alike of morals, ethics, education, and what we call civilisation; universal in its appeal, irresistible in its effect upon the great majority of mankind. It was this personal charm of the woman, combined with her intense vitality and accessibility, that won for her respect, and often affection, even from those who had good reason to deplore her methods and deny her principles. This personal charm, this subtle and magnetic emanation, was undoubtedly the secret of that stupendous power with which, for good or evil, she ruled for half a century a third of the population of the earth; that charm it was that won to her side the bravest and best of China's picked men, and it is the lingering memory and tradition of that charm which already invest the name of the Old Buddha with attributes of legendary virtue and superhuman wisdom.

Europeans, studying the many complex and unexpected phases of her extraordinary personality from the point of view of western moralities, have usually emphasised and denounced her cold-blooded ferocity and homicidal rage. Without denying the facts, or extenuating her guilt, it must, nevertheless, be admitted that it would be unjust to expect from her compliance with standards of morals and conduct of which she was perforce ignorant, and that, judged by the standards of her own predecessors and contemporaries, and by the verdict of her subjects, she is not to be reckoned a wicked woman. Let it be remembered also that within comparatively recent periods of English history, death was dealt out with no niggard or gentle hand to further

The Imperial Dais in the Ch'ien Ch'ing Hall.†

the alleged interests of the State; men were hanged, drawn and quartered in the days of Elizabeth and Mary Stuart, gentle ladies both, and averse to the spilling of blood, for the greater glory of Thrones, and in defence of the Christian religion.

Tzŭ Hsi died as she had lived, keen to the last, impatient of the bonds of sickness that kept her from the new day's work, hopeful ever for the future. Unto the last her thoughts were of the Empire, of that new plan of Constitutional Government wherein she had come to see visions of a new and glorious era for China and for herself. And when the end came, she faced it, as she had faced life, with a stout heart and brave words, going out to meet the Unknown as if she were but starting for a summer picnic. Reluctantly she bade farewell to the world of men, to the life she had lived with so keen a zest; but, unlike England's Tudor Queen, she bowed gracefully to the inevitable, leaving the scene with steadfast and Imperial dignity, confident in her high destinies to come.

FINIS.

APPENDIX

BIOGRAPHICAL NOTES ON CHANG CHIH-TUNG, TSO TSUNG-T'ANG, SUN CHIA-NAI, AND TUAN FANG

CHANG CHIH-TUNG

HER Majesty was never on terms of any great intimacy with Chang Chih-tung, but she respected him on account of his brilliant literary style and profound knowledge of the classics. The career of this official strikingly illustrates the power of the pen in China. He first came to be known by a critical Memorial in reference to the funeral ceremonies of the Emperor Tung-Chih, in 1879; his subsequent rapid advancement was due to the Memorial in which he denounced the cession of Ili to Russia by the Manchu Ambassador, Ch'ung Hou, in 1880. At this time Chang was still a poor scholar, earning a precarious livelihood by composing Memorials for certain wealthy Censors. He spoke the Mandarin dialect badly, having been brought up by his father (a Taotai) in the province of Kueichou. By patient study, a splendid memory and a natural talent for historical research and criticism, he became at an early age a recognised authority on all questions of State precedents and historical records, so that his pen found no lack of work in the drafting of official patents of rank, Imperial inscriptions and similar documents. Nevertheless, Tzŭ Hsi never cared for the man, realising that this brilliant scholar was by nature an opportunist, and that his opinion was rarely based on sincere conviction. Her estimate of him was amply justified on more than one occasion, for he frequently changed his views to meet the exigencies of party politics at the capital; it is indeed somewhat remarkable, since this estimate of his character was shared by most of his colleagues, that he should have retained her good will and risen to the highest position in the Government. His successful career[1] is explained by the fact that even men like Jung Lu and Li Hung-chang, who disliked him thoroughly, were unable to deny his claims as an unrivalled scholar.

As an illustration of his historical knowledge and methods, it is interesting to recall the main features of his Memorial against the Treaty of Livadia with Russia. By this Treaty, negotiated by Ch'ung Hou under the direct instructions of the Empress Dowager, Ili was to be retroceded to China upon payment of five million roubles, Russia securing Kuldja in exchange, with the right to open Consulates at certain places in the New Territory and on the Kansu frontier. Russian goods were also to be free of duty in Chinese Turkestan, and a new trade route was to be opened up through Central China, viâ Hsi-an in Shensi. When the terms of the Treaty became known, a storm of angry criticism was directed against the Manchu Ambassador: Tzŭ Hsi promptly ordered him to be cashiered and arrested for disregard of her instructions. The whole matter was referred to the Grand Council, who were directed to consult with Prince Ch'un and the various Government Boards. Chang Chih-tung, who was at this time a junior official in the Department of Public Instruction, drew attention to himself and practically decided the course of events by the advice given in his lengthy Memorial on the subject. The result of the advice therein submitted was, that a son of Tseng Kuo-fan was sent to Russia to negotiate a new Treaty, in which the objectionable clauses were eventually abandoned. Ch'ung

---

1. An account of his life was given in a memoir published by *The Times* on the 6th October, 1909.

Hou considered himself lucky that, as the result of Russia's diplomatic intervention on his behalf, he escaped with his life.

Chang's famous Memorial is typical of the mental processes and puerile *naïveté* of the *literati*. It began by showing that if the Treaty of Livadia were ratified, the whole of China would be open to Russian troops, who would enter the country as merchants accompanying caravans (since the Treaty expressly provided for merchants carrying fire-arms), and that the retrocession of Ili would prove valueless to China in course of time, inasmuch as Russia would remain in command of all strategic points. Chang urged that China could repudiate the Treaty without danger to herself, for several good reasons; the first being the Imperial prerogative and the unpopularity of the Treaty, whereby the martial spirit of the Chinese people would be aroused, and the second, that the future security of the Empire justified the adoption of right and reasonable precautions. He recommended that, in order to show that the displeasure of the Sovereign was sincere, Ch'ung Hou should be decapitated forthwith; this would be a clear intimation that his negotiations were disavowed; an excellent precedent existed in the case of Ch'i Ying,[1] who had been permitted to commit suicide under similar circumstances by the Emperor Hsien Feng.

As regards Russia's position in the matter, he was of opinion that China had earned the contempt of the whole world by allowing herself to be so easily intimidated. The Russian Minister at Peking might talk as loudly as he liked about hauling down his flag, but this was only bluff, and if he really desired to take his departure he should be allowed to do so. China should then address an identical Note to all the Powers protesting against Russia's action, which Note would be published throughout the civilised world. Russia had been weakened by her war with Turkey, and the life of her Sovereign was daily threatened by Nihilists. He was therefore of opinion that she could by no means fight a successful war against China.

---

1. *Vide supra*, Chapter I., page 13.

Russia's position in the neighbourhood of Ili by this Treaty would eventually involve China in the loss of the New Territory. Now China had not yet taken over Ili, and the Treaty had not been ratified by the Sovereign, so that Russia could have no good ground for insisting upon its terms; if, however, Russia were intent on compelling China to yield or fight, it would be necessary to look to the defences of the Empire in three directions, namely Turkestan, Kirin and Tientsin. As regards Turkestan, Tso Tsung-t'ang's victorious armies, which had just succeeded in suppressing the Mahomedan rebellion after a campaign of several years, would be quite capable of dealing with Russia's forces were she to attempt an invasion. As for Manchuria, it was too far from Russia's base of operations to render success even possible, while the stalwart natives of the Eastern Provinces might be relied upon to dislodge her should she eventually succeed in establishing a foothold. A few months would certainly witness her irrevocable defeat. As to invading China by sea, Russia's Navy was not to be compared to that of other Powers, and if the huge amount which had been spent by Li Hung-chang on armaments for the Army and Navy were ever to be turned to any good account, now was the time to do it. If at this juncture Li Hung-chang proved incapable of dealing with the situation, he was for ever useless. The Throne should direct him to prepare for war, and he should equip his troops with the latest pattern of French artillery. If victorious, a Dukedom should be his reward, and if defeated, his head should pay the penalty. The money which would be saved by not carrying out the Treaty, might very well be devoted to the equipment of the military forces.

Russia's designs in Turkestan, he continued, threatened England no less than China. If Li Hung-chang could persuade the British Minister that England's interests were identical with those of China, surely the British Government's assistance might be forthcoming? China possessed, moreover, several distinguished generals, who should forthwith be summoned to the capital, and given command of troops at different points between Peking and Manchuria. It was high time that China's prestige should be made manifest and re-established. And in his peroration he says: —

"I am not indulging in empty resounding phrases, or asking Your Majesties to risk the Empire upon a single throw of the dice, but the crisis daily increases in seriousness: Europe is interfering in our sovereign rights, while even Japan threatens to take territory from us. If now we submit to the arbitrary proceedings of Russia, all the other Powers will imitate her action, and we shall be compelled sooner or later to take up arms in self-defence. The present, therefore, is the moment for a decisive campaign; we have good chances of victory, and even should we meet with defeat in the New Territory it would not serve Russia greatly, for she could scarcely hope to penetrate beyond the Great Wall, or to cross the border into Kansu, so that, even if victorious, she would be severely embarrassed. If we postpone action for a few years Tso Tsung-t'ang will be too old to conduct military operations, and Li Hung-chang will be also advancing in years. Russia will hem us in on all sides, and our courage will suffer from our very inaction. It is better to fight Russia to-day on our furthermost frontier, than to wait until we have to give battle at the gates of Peking: it will then be too late for repentance. We must fight sooner or later, and in any case, we cannot consent to the retrocession of Ili. Come what may, Ch'ung Hou must be beheaded. This is not merely my private opinion, but the unanimous decision of all your leading Statesmen. The provinces may work together to prepare for war, all your servants may set an example of courage. Our Foreign Office may clearly express and insist upon our rights, but in the last instance the decision of affairs rests with Your Majesty the Empress Dowager, to whom we must needs look for a firm and consistent policy."

In spite of its childish arguments and colossal ignorance of foreign affairs, and in spite of the absurdity of allowing the nation's military operations to be criticised and dictated by a theoretical scholar, this Memorial had a most remarkable effect on the opinion of the Court, and Tzŭ Hsi commanded that its author should be consulted by the Foreign Office on all important questions of State—a striking case of *parmi les aveugles*. Chang was promoted to be Vice-President of a Board, and within a year was made Governor of Shansi, where he further increased his reputation by his entirely sincere attack upon opium smoking and poppy cultivation. Throughout his career, safe in the comfortable seclusion of his Yamên, and judging every question of foreign policy by the light of the history of previous Dynasties, Chang Chih-tung was always of a bellicose disposition on paper. He displayed it again in 1884, when he advocated the war with France, and became acting Viceroy at Canton. (He was a firm believer in the military genius of the swash-buckling Li Ping-heng, even to the day when this notorious reactionary met his death with the forlorn hope of the Boxers.) When the French troops were defeated by the Chinese forces at Langshan, Chang claimed and received no small credit for an event so unusual in Chinese modern history, and became so elated thereby that he sent in a Memorial strongly recommending that the victory should be followed up by an invasion of all French territory between the Chinese frontier and Hanoi. When this advice was rejected, he put in another bitter Memorial of remonstrance which created an immense impression on public opinion. He denounced the peace which was subsequently signed and by which China lost Annam, and he never forgave his rival and opponent, Li Hung-chang, for his share in this result.

Chang's share in the *coup d'état* of 1898 aptly illustrates his opportunism. It was he who from Wuch'ang originally recommended some thirty "progressives" to the notice of the Emperor at the beginning of that fateful year, and amongst these was Liang Ch'i-ch'ao, the chief colleague and henchman of K'ang Yu-wei. Rejoiced at the great Viceroy's support, the Emperor summoned him to Peking to assume direction of the new movement, hoping the more from his assistance as Chang's views always carried weight with the Empress Dowager. It is impossible to say what course Chang would have followed had he come to Peking, or what effect his presence might have had in preventing the collapse of the Emperor's plans, but as luck would have it, he had only proceeded as far as Shanghai, when he was ordered back to his post in Hupei by an Imperial Decree, which directed him first to settle a troublesome missionary case that had just arisen. Immediately after this, the dismissal of Weng Tung-ho, and the appointment of Jung Lu to Tientsin, showed him that a crisis was impending and that the reactionary party held the better cards; he played therefore for his own hand, anticipating that the Empress Dowager would speedily come to the front as leader of the Manchu Conservatives. It was at this particular juncture that he wrote and published his famous treatise on education, intended to refute the arguments of a revolutionary pamphlet that was then being widely circulated in the provinces of his jurisdiction. His treatise, by its brilliant style rather than by its arguments, created a great impression; its effect on the Chinese reader's mind was to emphasise the wisdom of learning everything possible of the material arts and forces of Europe, while keeping the foreigner himself at arm's length.

In 1900, at the urgent request of the Viceroy of Nanking (Lui K'un-yi)and of Li Hung-chang, he agreed to join in a Memorial impeaching Prince Tuan, and telegrams were exchanged between these high officials to discuss the form which this document should take. In the first instance, Chang had declined to protest against the Emperor's deposition for the reason, which he justified by historical precedent, that the suicide of the Censor Wu K'o-tu, twelve years before, had justified Her Majesty in placing a new Emperor on the Throne. He concurred in the decision of the Nanking Viceroy to head off any Boxer rising in the Yangtsze Provinces, but he was obviously uneasy at his own position in having to disobey the Empress Dowager's anti-foreign Decrees, and he hedged to the best of his ability by beheading two prominent reformers at Wuch'ang. No sooner had the form of the document impeaching Prince Tuan been practically decided, than he took fright at the thought that the Prince might eventually triumph and, as father of the Emperor-elect, wreak vengeance on his enemies; he therefore telegraphed to Li Hung-chang at Shanghai, begging that his signature be withheld from the Memorial. Li Hung-chang, who dearly loved his joke, promptly sent off the Memorial with Chang Chih-tung's signature attached thereto, and then telegraphed informing him that he had done so, and asking whether he desired that a second telegram be sent to Her Majesty cancelling his signature? Chang was for several days in a state of the greatest distress (which was only relieved when the Boxers were finally routed), and his mood was not improved when a pair of scrolls were sent to him anonymously, with inscriptions which may be roughly translated as follows: —

"Full of patriotism, but quite devoid of any real ability or intelligence."

"As an administrator a bungler, but remarkable for originating magnificent schemes."

Before his death, Chang had achieved a curiously mixed reputation, revered as he was by all scholars throughout the Empire, yet denounced on all sides for administrative incapacity. As an instance of the childish self-sufficiency which characterised him to the end, nothing is more remarkable than the suggestion which he solemnly submitted to the Throne, during the course of the peace negotiations for the Portsmouth Treaty after the conclusion of the war between Russia and Japan. At this juncture, the Empress Dowager had telegraphed inviting suggestions for China's future policy from all the high provincial authorities. Chang telegraphed five suggestions in reply, one of which was that China should come to an agreement with Japan to send two hundred thousand Japanese troops to Manchuria, and in the event of Russia proceeding to attack Chinese territory, that Japan should be requested to garrison Urga. This was the idea of China's foremost literary statesman in July, 1905, but there were not lacking enemies of his who avowed that his political views were considerably affected by the fact that he had contracted loans from Japanese financiers. Whatever the cause of his views, he had reason to change them completely before he died.

TSO TSUNG-T'ANG

The Chinese look upon Tseng Kuo-fan, the conqueror of the Taiping rebels, as the greatest military commander in modern history; but they regard Tso Tsung-t'ang, the hero of the long Mahomedan campaign, as very near to him in glory. Both Generals were natives of Hunan (a fact which seems to entitle the people of that province to assume something of a truculent attitude to the rest of the Empire), and both were possessed of indisputable qualities of leadership and organisation, remarkable enough in men trained to literary pursuits. Both were beloved of the people for their personal integrity, courage and justice.

Tso was born, one of nine sons in a poor family, in 1812. He took his provincial graduate degree at the age of twenty; thereafter, he seems to have abandoned literary work, for he never passed the Metropolitan examination. This did not prevent the Empress Dowager from appointing him, after his victorious campaign, to the Grand Secretariat, the only instance of a provincial graduate attaining to that high honour. For three years he was Tseng Kuo-fan's ablest lieutenant against the Taipings, and became Governor of Fukhien in 1863. In 1868 he was appointed Commander-in-Chief of the Imperial forces against the Mahomedan rebels, and began a campaign which lasted, with breathing spaces, until the beginning of 1878. His victorious progress through the western and north-western provinces began at Hsiang-Yang, on the Han river, in Hupei. Thence, after driving the rebels from Hsi-an, through Shansi and Kansu, he came to a halt before the strong city of Su-chou fu, on the north-west frontier of Kansu. The siege of this place lasted nearly three years, for his force was badly off for ordnance, and he was compelled to wait until his deputies purchased artillery for him from a German firm at Shanghai.

The guns were sent up in the leisurely manner affected by the Mandarins, and Tso was obliged to put his troops to agricultural work in order to provide himself with commissariat.

Su-chou had been for ten years in the hands of the rebels. It fell to the Imperialists in October, 1873, some say by treachery, according to others by assault. Be this as it may, Tso, whose method of dealing with rebels was absolutely pitiless, reduced the place to a heap of ruins, killing men, women and children indiscriminately, throughout large tracts of country. So fearful were the wholesale massacres and treacherous atrocities committed by his Hunanese troops, that General Kauffmann, commanding the Russian forces on the frontier, considered it his duty to address him on the subject, and to protest indignantly at the indiscriminate killing of non-combatants. General Kauffmann alluded chiefly to the massacre which had followed the taking of the town of Manas (November, 1876), but similar atrocities had been perpetrated at Su-chou, Hami, and many other important places. At Hami the entire population was put to the sword. Eyewitnesses of the scene of desolation, which stretched from Hsi-an in Shensi to Kashgar, have recorded that scarcely a woman was left alive in all those ruined cities — one might ride for days and not see one — a fact which accounts for the failure of the country unto this day to recover from the passing of that scourge. In more than one instance, Tso said with pride that he had left no living thing to sow new seeds of rebellion.[1]

Nor do the Chinese find anything reprehensible in his action. Instinctively a peace-loving people, they have learned through centuries of dreadful experience that there can be no humanitarianism in these ever-recurring rebellions, which are but one phase of the deadly struggle for life in China, and that the survival of the fittest implies the extermination of the unfit. Tso had first learned this lesson in the fierce warfare of the Taiping rebellion,

---

1. It has remained thus in many districts until now, vast solitudes of ruins being the chief characteristic of a region that, before the rebellion, supported some thirty million inhabitants.

where there was no question of quarter, asked or given, on either side. "If I destroy them not," he would say with simple grimness, "if I leave root or branch, they may destroy me."

In private life the man was genial and kindly, of a rugged simplicity; short of stature, and in later years stout, with a twinkling eye and hearty laugh; sober and frugal in his habits, practising the classical virtues of the ancients in all sincerity: a strict disciplinarian, and much beloved of his soldiers. He delighted in gardening and the planting of trees. Along the entire length of the Imperial highway that runs from Hsi-an to Chia-Yü Kuan beyond the Great Wall, thirty-six days' journey, he planted an avenue of trees, a stately monument of green to mark the red route of his devastating armies. One of the few Europeans who saw him at Kami records that it was his habit to walk in the Vice-regal gardens every afternoon, accompanied by a large suite of officials and Generals, when he would count his melons and expatiate on the beauty of his favourite flowers. With him, ready for duty at a word, walked his Chief Executioner.

He was as careful for the welfare of his people as for the extermination of rebels, and erected a large woollen factory at Lan-chou fu, whereby he hoped to establish a flourishing industry throughout the north-western provinces. He was fiercely opposed to opium cultivation, and completely suppressed it along the valley of the Yellow River for several years. The penalty for opium-smoking in his army was the loss of one ear for a first offence, and death for the second.

Yakoub Beg, the last leader and forlorn hope of the rebellion, died in May, 1877. Tso, following up his successes, captured in turn Yarkand, Kashgar and Khotan (January, 1878), and thus ended the insurrection. At the conclusion of the campaign he had some forty thousand Hunanese troops at Hami, and twenty thousand more under General Liu[1] at Kashgar. One of his Generals was that Tung Fu-hsiang who subsequently became known to the world as the leader of the bloodthirsty Kansuh soldiery at

---

1. Subsequently Governor of Formosa.

Peking in 1900; at the taking of Khotan he laid the foundations of his reputation for truculent ferocity. Tso firmly believed that his Hunanese were the finest fighting men in the world, and was most anxious to use them, in 1879, in trying conclusions with the Russians, boasting that with two hundred thousand of them he would easily march to St. Petersburg and there dictate a peace which should wipe out the humiliating concessions negotiated by Ch'ung Hou in the Treaty of Livadia. Fortunately for him, his patriotic ambitions came to the ears of the Empress Dowager, who, desiring no more complications, recalled him in hot haste to Peking, where she loaded him with honours and rewards.

His was the simple nature of the elementary fighter, inured to the hard life of camps. He knew little of other lands, but professed the greatest admiration for Bismarck, chiefly because of the enormous indemnity which the German conqueror had exacted as the price of victory, Tso's own troops being accustomed to live almost exclusively on the spoils of war. He despised wealth for himself, but loved plunder for his men.

Upon his triumphant return to Peking he was informed that the Palace authorities expected him to pay forty thousand taels as "gate-money" before entering the capital. Tso flatly refused. "The Emperor has sent for me," he said, "and I have come, but I will not pay a cash. If he wishes to see me, he must either obtain for me free entry or pay the gate-money himself." He waited stolidly five days and then had his way, entering scot-free. Later, when the Empress Dowager made him a present of ten thousand taels, he divided the money between his soldiers and the poor.

SUN CHIA-NAI

This official, chiefly known to fame among his countrymen as one of the tutors of His Majesty Kuang-Hsü, was a sturdy Conservative of the orthodox type, but an honest and kindly man. His character and opinions may be gauged from a well-known saying of his: "One Chinese character is better than ten thousand words of the barbarians. By knowing Chinese a man may rise to

CEILING AND PILLARS OF THE TAI HO TIEN.

become a Grand Secretary; by knowing the tongues of the barbarians, he can at best aspire to become the mouth-piece of other
men."

In his later years he felt and expressed great grief at the condition of his country, and particularly in regard to the strained
relations between the Empress Dowager and the Emperor. He
traced the first causes of these misfortunes to the war with Japan, and never ceased to blame his colleague, the Imperial Tutor
Weng T'ung-ho, for persuading the Emperor to sign the Decree
whereby that war was declared, which he described as the act
of a madman. Weng, however, was by no means alone in holding the opinion that China could easily dispose of the Japanese
forces by land and by sea. It was well-known at Court, and the
Emperor must have learned it from more than one quarter, that
several foreigners holding high positions under the Chinese Government, including the Inspector-General of Customs (Sir Robert
Hart), concurred in the view that China had practically no alternative but to declare war in view of Japan's high-handed proceedings and insulting attitude. Prestige apart, it was probable
that the Emperor was by no means averse to taking this step on
his own authority, even though he knew that the Empress Dowager was opposed to the idea of war, because of its inevitable interference with the preparations for her sixtieth birthday; at that
moment, Tzǔ Hsi was living in quasi-retirement at the Summer
Palace. After war had been declared and China's reverses began,
she complained to the Emperor and to others, that the fatal step
had been taken without her knowledge and consent, but this was
onlv "making face," for it is certain that she had been kept fully
informed of all that was done and that, had she so desired, she
could easily have presented the issue of the Decree, and the despatch of the Chinese troops to Asan. Sun Chia-nai's reputation
for sagacity was increased after the event, and upon the subsequent disgrace and dismissal of Weng Tung-ho he stood high in
Her Majesty's favour. Nevertheless his loyalty to the unfortunate
Emperor remained unshaken.

In 1898, his tendencies were theoretically on the side of reform, but he thoroughly disapproved of the methods and self-
seeking personality of K'ang Yu-wei, advising the Emperor
that, while possibly fit for an Under-Secretaryship, he was quite
unfitted for any high post of responsibility. When matters first
approached a crisis, it was by his advice that the Emperor directed K'ang to proceed to Shanghai for the organisation of the
Press Bureau scheme. Sun, peace-loving and prudent, hoped
thereby to find an outlet for K'ang Yu-wei's patriotic activities
while leaving the Manchu dovecots unfluttered. Later, after the
coup d'état, being above all things orthodox and a stickler for
harmonious observance of precedents, he deplored the harsh
treatment and humiliation inflicted upon the Emperor. It is reported of him that on one occasion at audience he broke down
completely, and with tears implored the Empress Dowager not
to allow her mind to be poisoned against His Majesty, but without effect.

Upon the nomination of the Heir Apparent, in 1900, which he,
like many others, regarded as the Emperor's death sentence, he
sent in a strongly worded Memorial against this step, and subsequently denounced it at a meeting of the Grand Council. Thereafter, his protests proving ineffective, he resigned all his offices,
but remained at the capital in retirement, watching events. At the
commencement of the Boxer crisis, unable to contain his feelings,
he sent in a Memorial through the Censorate denouncing the
rabid reactionary Hsü Tung, whom he described as "the friend
of traitors, who would bring the State to ruin if further confidence were placed in him." Throughout his career he displayed
the courage of his convictions, which, judged by the common
standard of Chinese officialdom, were conspicuously honest. He
was a man of that Spartan type of private life which one finds
not infrequently associated with the higher branches of Chinese
scholarship and Confucian philosophy; it was his boast that he
never employed a secretary, but wrote out all his correspondence
and Memorials with his own hand.

A pleasing illustration of his character is the following: He was seated one day in his shabby old cart, and driving down the main street to his home, when his driver collided with the vehicle of a well-known Censor, named Chao. The police came up to make enquiries and administer street-justice, but learning that one cart belonged to the Grand Secretary Sun, they told his driver to proceed. The Censor, justly indignant at such servility, wrote a note to Sun in which he said: "The Grand Secretary enjoys, no doubt, great prestige, but even he cannot lightly disregard the power of the Censorate." Sun, on receiving this note, proceeded at once on foot in full official dress to the Censor's house, and upon being informed that he was not at home, prostrated himself before the servant, saying: "The nation is indeed to be congratulated upon possessing a virtuous Censor." Chao, not to be outdone in generosity, proceeded in his turn to the residence of the Grand Secretary, intending to return the compliment, but Sun declined to allow him to apologise in any way.

TUAN FANG

In 1898, Tuan Fang was a Secretary of the Board of Works; his rapid promotion after that date was chiefly due to the patronage of his friend Jung Lu. For a Manchu, he is remarkably progressive and liberal in his views.

In 1900, he was Acting-Governor of Shensi. As the Boxer movement spread and increased in violence, and as the fears of Jung Lu led him to take an increasingly decided line of action against them, Tuan Fang, acting upon his advice, followed suit. In spite of the fact that at the time of the *coup d'état* he had adroitly saved himself from clear identification with the reformers and had penned a classical composition in praise of filial piety, which was commonly regarded as a veiled reproof to the Emperor for not yielding implicit obedience to the Old Buddha, he had never enjoyed any special marks of favour at the latter's hands, nor been received into that confidential friendliness with which she frequently honoured her favourites.

In his private life, as in his administration, Tuan Fang has always recognised the changing conditions of his country and endeavoured to adapt himself to the needs of the time; he was one of the first among the Manchus to send his sons abroad for their education. His sympathies were at first unmistakably with Kang Yu-wei and his fellow reformers, but he withdrew from them because of the anti-dynastic nature of their movement, of which he naturally disapproved.

As Acting-Governor of Shensi, in July, 1900, he clearly realised the serious nature of the situation and the dangers that must arise from the success of the Boxer movement, and he therefore issued two Proclamations to the province, in which he earnestly warned the people to abstain from acts of violence. These documents were undoubtedly the means of saving the lives of many missionaries and other foreigners isolated in the interior. In the first a curious passage occurs, wherein, after denouncing the Boxers, he said:

"The creed of the Boxers is no new thing: in the reign of Chia-Ch'ing, followers of the same cult were beheaded in droves. But the present-day Boxer has taken the field ostensibly for the defence of his country against the foreigner, so that we need not refer to the past. While accepting their good intentions, I would merely ask, is it reasonable for us to credit these men with supernatural powers or invulnerability? Are we to believe that all the corpses which now strew the country between Peking and the sea are those of spurious Boxers and that the survivors alone represent the true faith?"

After prophesying for them the same fate which overtook the Mahomedan rebels and those of the Taiping insurrection, he delivered himself of advice to the people which, while calculated to prevent the slaughter of foreigners, would preserve his reputation for patriotism. It is well, now that Tuan Fang has fallen upon evil days, to remember the good work he did in a very difficult position. His Proclamation ran as follows:—

"I have never for a moment doubted that you men of Shensi are brave and patriotic and that, should occasion offer, you would fight nobly for your country. I know that if you joined these Boxers, it would be from patriotic motives. I would have you observe, however, that our enemies are the foreign troops who have invaded the Metropolitan province and not the foreign missionaries who reside in the interior. If the Throne orders you to take up arms in the defence of your country, then I, as Governor of this province, will surely share in that glory. But if, on your own account, you set forth to slay a handful of harmless and defenceless missionaries, you will undoubtedly be actuated by a desire for plunder, there will be nothing noble in your deed, and your neighbours will despise you as surely as the law will punish you.

"At this very moment our troops are pouring in upon the capital from every province in the Empire. Heaven's avenging sword is pointed against the invader. This being so, it is absurd to suppose that there can be any need for such services as you people could render at such a time. Your obvious and simple duty is to remain quietly in your homes, pursuing your usual avocations. It is the business of the official to protect the people, and you may rely upon me to do so. As to that Edict of Their Majesties which, last year, ordered the organisation of trained bands, the idea was merely to encourage self-defence for local purposes, on the principle laid down by Mencius of watch and ward being kept by each district."

A little later the Governor referred to that Decree of the Empress Dowager (her first attempt at hedging) which began by quoting the "Spring and Autumn Classic" in reference to the sacred nature of foreign Envoys, and used it as a text for emphasising the fact that the members of the several missionary societies in Shensi had always been on the best of terms with the people. He referred to the further fact that many refugees from the famine-stricken districts of Shansi, and numbers of disbanded soldiers, had crossed the borders of the province, and fearing lest these lawless folk should organise an attack upon the foreigners, he once more urged his people to permit no violation of the sacred laws of hospitality. The province had already commenced to feel the effects of the long drought which had caused such suffering in Shansi, and the superstitious lower classes were disposed to attribute this calamity to the wrath of Heaven, brought upon them by reason of their failure to join the Boxers. Tuan Fang proceeded to disabuse their minds of this idea.

"If the rain has not fallen upon your barren fields," he said, "if the demon of drought threatens to harass you, be sure that it is because you have gone astray, led by false rumours, and have committed deeds of violence. Repent now and return to your peaceful ways, and the rains will assuredly fall. Behold the ruin which has come upon the provinces of Chihli and Shantung; it is to save you from their fate that I now warn you. Are we not all alike subjects of the great Manchu Dynasty, and shall we not acquit ourselves like men in the service of the State? If there were any chance of this province being invaded by the enemy, you would naturally sacrifice your lives and property to repel him, as a matter of simple patriotism. But if, in a sudden access of madness, you set forth to butcher a few helpless foreigners, you will in no wise benefit the Empire, but will merely be raising fresh difficulties for the Throne. For the time being, your own consciences will accuse you of ignoble deeds, and later you will surely pay the penalty with your lives and the ruin of your families. Surely, you men of Shensi, enlightened and high-principled, will not fall so low as this? There are, I know, among you some evil men who, professing patriotic enmity to foreigners and Christians, wax fat on foreign plunder, but the few missionary Chapels in this province offer but meagre booty, and it is safe to predict that those who begin by sacking them will certainly proceed next to loot the houses of your wealthier citizens. From the burning of foreigners' homes, the conflagration will spread to your own, and many innocent persons will share the fate of the slaughtered Christians. The plunderers will escape with their booty, and the foolish onlookers will pay the penalty of these crimes. Is it not a well-known fact that every anti-Christian outbreak invariably brings misery to the stupid innocent people of the district concerned?

Is not this a lamentable thing? As for me, I care neither for praise nor blame; my only object in preaching peace in Shensi is to save you, my people, from dire ruin and destruction."

Tuan Fang was a member of the Mission to foreign countries in 1905 and has received decorations and honours at the hands of several European sovereigns. In private life he is distinguished by his complete absence of formality; a genial, hospitable man, given to good living, delighting in new mechanical inventions and fond of his joke. It is he who, as Viceroy of Nanking, organised the International Exhibition now being held in that city. As Viceroy of Chihli, he was in charge of the arrangements for the funeral of the Empress Dowager in November of last year, and a week after that impressive ceremony was denounced for alleged want of respect and decorum. It was charged against him that he had permitted subordinate officials to take photographs of the *cortège* and that he had even dared to use certain trees in the sacred enclosure of the Mausolea as telegraph poles, for which offences he was summarily cashiered; since then he has lived in retirement. The charges were possibly true, but it is matter of common knowledge that the real reason for his disgrace was a matter of Palace politics rather than funereal etiquette, for he was a protégé of the Regent and his removal was a triumph for the Yehonala clan, at a time when its prestige called for a demonstration of some sort against the growing power and influence of the Emperor Kuang-Hsü's brothers.

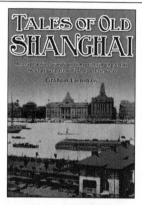

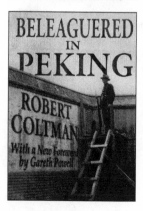
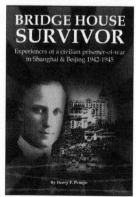
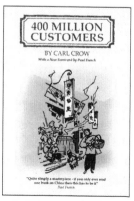